Unknown Soldiers

Unknown Soldiers

How terrorism transformed the modern world

Matthew Carr

PROFILE BOOKS

976,300 | 363.325

First published in Great Britain in 2006 by
PROFILE BOOKS LTD
3A Exmouth House
Pine Street
Exmouth Market
London
EC1R 0JH
www.profilebooks.com

1 3 5 7 9 10 8 6 4 2

Typeset in Palatino by MacGuru Ltd
info@macguru.org.uk
Printed and bound in Great Britain by
Clays, Bungay, Suffolk

A CIP catalogue record for this book is available from the British Library.

ISBN-10: 1 86197 730 1
ISBN-13: 978 1 86197 730 4

Contents

What vileness should you not suffer to
Annihilate vileness?
If at last you could change the world, what
Could make you too good to do so?
Who are you?
Sink in filth
Embrace the butcher, but
Change the world: It needs it!

Bertolt Brecht, The Measures Taken

The Bomb in the Baby Carriage

Terror: Extreme fear; ~ *stricken,* ~ *struck* ...
Terrorist: One who favours or uses terror-inspiring methods of governing or coercing government or community.

Oxford Concise Dictionary

In November 2002, the daughter of the notorious German terrorist, Ulrike Meinhof, filed a lawsuit in Stuttgart demanding the recovery of her mother's brain for formal burial. The missing organ had been removed from Meinhof's body by the German authorities after she was found hanging in her cell in Stannheim prison in 1976. The brains of two other members of the so-called Baader Meinhof Gang who committed suicide in the same prison had also been removed. The authorities initially denied that the brains were in their possession, but it subsequently emerged that they had been used for neurological research into the origins of their terrorist behaviour. A German psychiatrist who worked on Meinhof's brain concluded that it showed signs of 'pathological modifications' resulting from an earlier operation, which may have accounted for her subsequent evolution into a terrorist.[1]

The authorities did not announce what irregularities, if any, were found in the brains of the other two. But the bizarre post-mortem tells us more about the investigators than their subjects. Official representations of 'terrorism' have often depicted its protagonists as a uniquely alien breed of humanity, driven by bloodlust, insane hatred or pure evil. From the point of view of mainstream society, even the most violent criminality seems more comprehensible than politically motivated homicide. Yet in 1911 the libertarian activist Emma Goldman took a very different view of the anarchist assassins who were sowing bombs and bullets across Europe and America:

Compared with the wholesale violence of capital and government, political acts of violence are but a drop in the ocean. That so few resist is the strongest proof how terrible must be the conflict between their souls and unbearable social iniquities. High strung, like a violin string, they weep and moan for life, so relentless, so cruel, so terribly inhuman. In a desperate moment the string breaks. Untuned ears hear nothing but discord. But those who feel the agonized cry understand its harmony; they hear in it the fulfillment of the most compelling moment of human nature. Such is the psychology of political violence.[2]

This is not a perspective we are used to hearing in an era in which terrorists have been responsible for suicide attacks on urban commuters and the casual mass slaughter of civilians in various countries. But even though Goldman was writing at an earlier period, when 'political violence' was more discriminating in its targets, the attitude of mainstream society towards these events was not very different from our own era. In the early years of the twentieth century the Catalan capital of Barcelona was the scene of thousands of bombings that were generally attributed to anarchists. Writing in response to a particularly intense wave of bombings in 1906, the conservative newspaper *La Vanguardia* asked:

What do these people want? To produce a state of terror and alarm, to remove from life its attractive or at least tolerable normality, to sow the seeds of panic, perhaps in the belief that by acting in this way on an isolated society ... they will force the world to surrender and change the universal conditions of life.[3]

La Vanguardia was essentially responding to its own question with a hypothesis, which it presented as an established fact. Today, at the start of the new century, a consensus of politicians, media commentators and Western security analysts have engaged in a similar process. As a result of the September 11 attacks, the United States has declared a global war against an enemy that supposedly threatens the very existence of civilisation, whose malignant intentions are matched by an endless array of destructive methods, from radioactive 'dirty bombs' in suitcases to poisons smeared on car door handles. On 5 October 2005, authorities in New York announced news of a 'specific threat' to the city's subway system in which an al-Qaeda terrorist cell planned to explode up to nineteen remotely controlled or timed bombs concealed in baby carriages or suitcases within the next four days.

The alleged plot had supposedly been uncovered following the arrests of three Iraqi insurgents near Baghdad connected to al-Qaeda in Iraq. Though an official at the US Department of Homeland Security described the threat as 'specific but not credible', the New York authorities deployed thousands of uniformed and plainclothes police on the subway system. The city's police commissioner warned that baby carriages and suitcases would be regarded with particular suspicion and advised the public to avoid using these items whenever possible. In the event, no attack took place and the authorities announced that a 'series of arrests' had thwarted the plot, though no details were given as to who had been arrested or whether the arrests had been made in Iraq or the United States.

Such phantasmal plots and rumours have become a routine feature of the early twenty-first century, in a world that has become haunted by the spectre of terrorist atrocities, both real and imagined. The current 'state of terror and alarm' cannot entirely be attributed to nineteen hijackers armed with pocket knives and boxcutters. Like *La Vanguardia*, governments have tended to present their own particular interpretation of terrorism as the 'true' version, regardless of whether there is any evidence to sustain it. Thus, George Bush has repeatedly declared that the September 11 attacks represented an attack on American 'freedom', even though this motivation has been explicitly rejected by Osama bin Laden on various occasions. In the wake of the suicide bombings in London in July 2005, Tony Blair repeatedly called the attacks an assault on 'democracy' and civilised 'values', despite clear evidence that their protagonists regarded them as a response to specific Western policies in the Muslim world, and the Iraq war in particular.

The idea that 'terrorism' represents an attack on 'democracy' is part of a ritualised official response to terrorist events, which is often accompanied by the narcissistic invocation of the superior moral qualities of the civilisation supposedly under attack. This 'closed' interpretation is frequently ring-fenced by a praetorian guard of outraged moralists and media pundits, who dismiss any attempt to establish a political context for even the most horrific acts of violence as a form of moral collusion with their perpetrators. Such a response may be driven by various motives, from the requirements of propaganda to genuine outrage at terrorist atrocities, but it tends to be intellectually shallow, manipulative and even blatantly dishonest. Not only does the official representation of 'terrorism' obscure and distort the meaning of the violence it purports to condemn, often deliberately, but it may even serve to perpetuate such violence by reducing complex political conflicts to a struggle between absolute good and absolute evil, in which, as George Bush told Congress in 2002, 'Every nation, in every region, now has a decision to make – either you are with us or you are with the terrorists.'

These are not parameters that this book accepts. As a result of the September 11 attacks the world has been sucked with frightening speed into a vicious downward spiral of war and atrocity, in which elementary notions of legality, morality and human dignity are being trampled on by both sides.

Faced with an apparently limitless and frequently duplicitous 'War on Terror' supposedly aimed at protecting freedom and democracy, I believe that those of us who are being terrorised have the right and even the obligation to re-examine how terrorism came to acquire such fearsome ascendancy over our era. This book is intended to be a contribution to that re-examination. Such an investigation cannot be achieved by retreating into sanctimonious cant or the banal contemplation of our own virtues, nor can it be limited to the immediate crisis itself. For as unprecedented as the current terrorist threat appears to be, much of the rhetoric that sustains the 'War on Terror' stems from official narratives about terrorism that have been repeated so often that their assumptions are now taken for granted. It is my aim to challenge some of those assumptions and trace the major historical episodes that have helped shape our understanding of terrorism in the modern world.

The indefinable evil

'Terror' is not a specifically modern phenomenon. Throughout history armies have engaged in extreme acts of violence in order to instil 'extreme fear' in their military opponents and the civilian populations that support them. Terror has also been used as a tool of governance and repression, from the tyrants of the ancient world and the Holy Inquisition to the police states and dictatorships of the twentieth century. But 'terrorism' is a more recent concept, which initially emerged in reference to the period of the French Revolution known as 'the Terror' between 1793 and 1794. In 1798 the fifth edition of the Academie Française Dictionary refers for the first time to the *'systeme, regime de la terreur'* introduced by the Jacobins. To European governments, the public execution of aristocrats by revolutionary zealots using the macabre innovation of the guillotine was an unprecedented and alarming spectacle whose architects became known as 'Terrorists', a pejorative term most famously used by Edmund Burke in his condemnation of the Jacobin 'Hell-hounds called Terrorists'.

The association between terror and revolutionary violence is still reflected in the Oxford dictionary reference to terror as *'Reign of T~ , the T~ ,* period of French Revolution, 1793–4 (& of similar periods marked by sanguinary excesses of revolutionaries, also *Red T~*, or reactionaries, also *White T~)'*. In contemporary usage, however, terrorism has generally come to refer to acts of violence carried out by unofficial groups or individuals, rather than revolutionary regimes. For all the condemnation such violence has tended to attract, the concept of terrorism has always been notoriously elusive and difficult to define. The US Department of Defense defines it as 'the unlawful use of, or threatened use of violence to inculcate fear, intended to coerce or intimidate governments or societies as to the pursuit of goals that are generally political, religious or ideological'. On the surface this definition could incorporate a potentially limitless range of violent acts, from riots and demonstrations to bombings and assassinations. It could also refer to acts of violence carried out by governments in order to 'coerce or intimidate', from conventional and unconventional wars to the new forms of tyranny that emerged in the twentieth century. The inclusion of the adjective 'unlawful', however, shifts the emphasis to acts of violence *against* governments.

There are dozens of variants, but the majority share the same emphasis.[4] Other definitions are even more tendentious. The former Israeli prime minister Benjamin Netanyahu once defined terrorism as 'the deliberate and systematic murder, maiming, and menacing of the innocent to inspire fear for political ends'.[5] The wording is carefully framed to preclude any possibility that the acts it describes could ever be morally acceptable. Yet if Netanyahu's definition were rigorously applied, many of the groups described as terrorists by Israel and the United States would be excluded from this category. In practice the exact meaning of terrorism is often irrelevant, since the term is frequently used by governments to describe any unofficial group or organisation using violence against them, regardless of their targets or the methods they use. As leader of the armed wing of the African National Congress in the early 1960s, Nelson Mandela was imprisoned for organising a limited campaign of economic sabotage against the apartheid regime that specifically avoided civilian targets, but he was nevertheless depicted as a terrorist both by the apartheid regime and by pro-South African politicians such as Margaret Thatcher.

All states seek to monopolise both the means of violence and the moral and legal right to engage in it when necessary. From the point of view of established authority, any violence directed against the state is unlawful and the concept of terrorism provides a convenient category of unacceptable violence through which its unconstitutional opponents can be stripped of political and moral legitimacy. The fact that some of these opponents have engaged in savage acts of violence makes the process of delegitimisation easier. Not surprisingly, the organisations and individuals to whom the label has been attached have tended to reject it, preferring to use other terms such as 'freedom fighter', 'guerrilla', 'revolutionary', or even 'soldier' to justify their activities.

As a result the vexed question of the definition of terrorism is frequently made irrelevant by the often selective way in which the label is applied and by the irreconcilable interpretations that can be placed on the same acts of violence. Most Western governments regard Hamas as a Palestinian 'terrorist organisation' responsible for suicide attacks on Israeli civilians. In the eyes of Israel, the United States and the EU, the 'terrorist' label effectively disqualified the stunning Hamas victory in the January 2006 Palestinian elections, in which the organisation won a large majority. Yet the election result merely confirmed a widely-held view in the Middle East which regards Hamas as a resistance organisation fighting Israeli occupation and see Israel as a primary practitioner of 'state terrorism'. These conflicting interpretations are partly responsible for the fact that the United Nations has still not agreed on a common definition of terrorism in more than half a century. At the UN's 60th anniversary in September 2005, the General Assembly failed once again to agree on a shared definition during the latest of many fractious debates on the subject.

It is not my intention here to offer an overarching definition of terrorism to replace those that have already been put forward. Nor do I wish to enter the largely futile discussion over who constitutes the 'real' terrorists. Both states and revolutionary organisations have carried out atrocities, crimes and acts of terror, even if the former have done so on a far greater scale. This book is largely concerned with a particular 'technique' of revolutionary violence that first emerged in Russia and Europe in the late nineteenth century. The essence of this technique is the use of violence against symbolic targets in order to achieve a political rather than a military victory over a particular government or regime. Such violence may be used to draw attention to a cause, to broaden a political confrontation, or draw a more powerful enemy into a debilitating showdown. The methods used to achieve these ends may vary, but the overall technique tends to be an expression of military weakness which allows its protagonists to 'punch above their weight'.

Not all the organisations mentioned in this book have gone to the same extremes to realise their objectives, but virtually all of them have borrowed to some extent from this nineteenth-century tradition. Despite their varied ideologies and political aims, many of them share a similar inner culture in which the use of violence is validated and legitimised by a cult of heroism and self-sacrifice that often seems bizarre and improbable to outsiders. Their inclusion in this book does not mean that I regard them as 'terrorist' in the sense that George Bush or Netanyahu have used the term, nor does it mean that I share their conception of themselves as heroes. There is nothing heroic or noble about killing Israeli teenagers in a pizzeria or Russian schoolchildren at Beslan. But even the vilest such actions occur for reasons that are rarely explained in official representations of 'terrorism'. In his 1977 Edinburgh lectures on *Custom, Law, and Terrorist Violence*, the anthropologist Edmund Leach reminded his audience that 'However incomprehensible the acts of the terrorists appear to be, our judges, our policemen, and our politicians must never be allowed to forget that terrorism is an activity of fellow human beings.' Such advice should not be controversial, but such is the peculiar horror that terrorism inspires that it has often been ignored or forgotten.[6]

Monsters

Whereas the noun 'criminal' may simply be a statement of fact, 'terrorist' is always a pejorative expression of an attitude rather than the depiction of an objective phenomenon. A sense of its wider cultural meaning can be gleaned from the following list of synonyms for terrorist in the 1952 *Roget's Thesaurus*:

Maleficent being. Evildoer, wrong doer, mischief-maker, marplot, anarchist, nihilist, … firebrand, incendiary, evil genius. Frankenstein's monster. Savage, brute, ruffian, blackguard … a snake in the grass … a scourge of the human race … a fiend in human shape; worker of iniquity …

New terms have been accumulated over the years. Terrorists have been described as vermin, insects, creatures from the lower reaches of the animal kingdom. In 1986 Netanyahu attributed what he saw as a new international response to terrorism to 'the realisation that wild beasts prowl our airways and waterways',[7] while the British tabloid the *Sun* used the same bestial imagery in 1988 in an article on the shooting of three unarmed IRA members by the SAS in Gibraltar with the headline 'Why the Dogs Had to Die'. One of the slain 'dogs', killed in what the coroner described as a 'frenzied assault', was Mairead Farrell, a militant republican and feminist who joined the IRA at the age of 18. Farrell's partner, Seamus Finucane, later remembered her as 'a strong woman. She wanted children, she was like any other girl, she liked socialising, dancing, music, fashion, and loved meeting people.'

Though initial reports that Farrell and her comrades were about to set off a bomb turned out to be fabrications, it was clear that the IRA team was planning an attack on a military band in which both soldiers and civilian bystanders would almost certainly have been killed. But Farrell's short life and violent death encapsulates the jarring contradictions of unofficial terrorism, between the 'normality' of its protagonists and the savagery of their methods. Margarita Cagol, one of the founders of the Italian Red Brigades, was a gifted classical guitarist known for her concern for the sick and the elderly in her teenage years, whose social conscience eventually led her into one of the most violent left-wing organisations in Italy. Mohammed Siddique Khan, one of the suicide bombers who blew himself up in London on 7 July 2005, was a school mentor who worked in primary schools for children with learning difficulties.

The willingness of such disparate individuals to embrace the most atrocious acts of violence as a political necessity suggests a more complex human reality than the establishment depiction of terrorism reveals. Farrell's involvement in the IRA appears to have emanated from political conviction, rather than the depiction of the IRA by Britain's then Lord Chancellor, Lord Hailsham, as 'servants of the devil' who had 'taken evil into their souls'. Such language is a recurring feature of official anti-terrorist discourse, where the label 'terrorist' tends to invoke absolute moral repudiation. Often the term has functioned as a contemporary version of the malediction, or anathema, that the church once pronounced on witches and heretics. Where witches were once perceived by the church as an invisible and all-powerful conspiracy, terrorists are often depicted by the state not just as the enemies of a specific regime or social and political order but as a destructive force intent on toppling civilisation into the void.

This presentation is rarely accurate. In the majority of cases revolutionary terrorism is entirely coherent and directed towards achieving specific objectives, and although its history has largely been one of tragic failure, in some cases it has been at least partially successful in achieving its political aims, such as the IRA's first campaign against British rule between 1919 and 1921, the EOKA campaign against British rule in Cyprus in the 1950s and the campaign by Hezbollah and other armed organisations that eventually led to the Israeli withdrawal from Lebanon in 2000.

In all these cases violence was used in order to achieve very specific political goals that were widely shared, yet their protagonists were variously described as murderers, thugs and fanatical killers driven by their enemies. At times this demonisation of the terrorist has become a justification for a violent 'counter-terrorist' response. In the name of counter-terrorism terrorists have been hunted down in jungles, mountains and swamps, in the hills of South Armagh or the Rhodesian bush that harbour 'terrorist nests' or 'breeding grounds' from which terrorists must be 'cleansed', 'drained' or 'flushed out'. In 1978 South African paratroopers massacred more than 700 Namibian refugees at the Kassinga refugee camp in Angola, many of them women and children. The South African press nevertheless hailed a great victory over SWAPO 'terrorists', while lamenting the fact that impressionable young paratroopers were obliged to shoot 'women in terrorist uniforms' who were hiding 'in the trenches alongside the guerrillas'.

Even in liberal democracies the peculiar dread that surrounds terrorism can be invoked to justify brutal acts of violence against real or suspected terrorists, such as the killing of a Brazilian commuter by British police following the July 2005 London Underground bombings. Such is the power of the malediction that the state can claim impunity for its own acts of violence, even when those acts blatantly contradict the rule of law and the 'values' that it claims to embody. Yet if the malediction can become a licence for extermination, it can also be revoked, sometimes with startling alacrity, so that former terrorist monsters find themselves seamlessly transformed into statesmen and peacemakers. Thus the imprisoned terrorist Nelson Mandela became president of post-apartheid South Africa, while the Israeli prime minister and former bête noir of the British in Palestine Menachem Begin received the Nobel Prize for Peace for signing the Camp David agreement, sharing it with his co-signatory, the Egyptian president Anwar Sadat, who had himself carried out the assassination of a pro-British Egyptian official. In 1998 the Kosovo Liberation Army (KLA) was described by US officials as a 'terrorist organisation', yet the following year the KLA was an ally of NATO, fighting heroically against the Serbs.

The history of terrorism is filled with similar anomalies, in which governments condemn terrorism as an absolute moral evil, for reasons that owe more to statecraft and realpolitik than morality. Though terrorist violence has often been depicted as antithetical to Western democratic norms, democratic governments have at times colluded with 'terrorist organisations' or engaged in the same acts that they so vociferously condemn. All these contradictions are part of the dark phenomenon of violence that we call terrorism. I do not claim to be able to weld these contradictions into an overall explanation of what constitutes terrorism and what does not. On the contrary, I believe that the phenomenon of terrorism is in many ways the sum of its contradictions. For this reason this book is not only concerned with the 'terrorists' themselves. The irreconcilable opposites between the terrorist as demon and the terrorist as hero require not just an examination of the terrorist 'Other' but of the different ways in which terrorist events have been perceived and interpreted by their different audiences. For our understanding of terrorism derives not merely from the accumulation of specific historical episodes, but from the ways in which these episodes have been represented, not only by their protagonists, but by soldiers, politicians and terrorism 'experts', by novelists, film-makers and journalists. These are the various tributaries I propose to explore, and even if they fail to reveal the 'truth' about terrorism, they are likely to tell us more than Ulrike Meinhof's brain was ever going to reveal.

PART I

BEGINNINGS

1

The Hero Takes the Stage

Upon the horizon there appeared a gloomy form, illuminated by a light as of hell, who with lofty bearing, and a look breathing forth hatred and defiance, made his way through the terrified crowd to enter with a firm step upon the scene of history. It was the Terrorist.

Sergei 'Stepniak' Kravchinsky, *Underground Russia*, 1888

On Sunday 1 March 1881 Tsar Alexander II was returning to the Winter Palace from his weekly inspection of the Cossack military parade at the Hippodrome in St Petersburg, in a bomb-proof carriage given to him by Napoleon III. The tsar was wearing his ceremonial uniform with a blue cloak and plumed helmet and accompanied by a small detachment of mounted Cossacks. The decision to attend the parade had been taken against the wishes of his interior minister, General Loris-Melikov, and his young wife, the Princess Yurevskaya. Only the previous day the Russian police had arrested Andrei Zhelyabov, a member of a revolutionary organisation called the Narodnaya Volya, or People's Will, which had tried on seven previous occasions to kill the tsar. Zhelyabov warned that another attempt would soon be made, but Alexander refused to change his official schedule, though he did accede to his wife's request to change his route, stopping on the way to visit a cousin, the Grand Duchess Catherine, at the nearby Mikhailovsky Palace.

The princess's fears were more prescient than she realised. Had her husband followed his usual route he would have passed by a newly opened cheese shop on Malaya Sadovaya Street, where a member of the People's Will had been waiting all morning to ignite a tunnel that was primed with dynamite. In the wake of Zhelyabov's arrest, the operation was now led by his lover, Sofia Perovskaya. Early that morning Perovskaya met the other members of the group in a café and distributed a number of grapefruit-sized bombs, prepared during a night of intense activity for use as a contingency plan should their target fail to pass by the mined cheese shop.

When Perovskaya saw Alexander's carriage pass alongside the narrow

Catherine Canal on its way to the barracks, she assumed that he would return by the same route and hurriedly deployed the throwers at intervals along the canalside railings. She then stationed herself on the opposite bank, from which she would be able to monitor the tsar's approach. At 2.15 the cortège approached Nikolai Rysakov, the first thrower. When Perovskaya raised a white handkerchief in the agreed signal Rysakov threw his five-pound bomb. The explosion caught the back of Alexander's carriage, seriously wounding a number of Cossacks and pedestrians.

Rysakov made no attempt to escape and was immediately apprehended by some of the Cossacks as the procession ground to a halt. Shaken but uninjured, the tsar alighted to inspect the wounded and spoke briefly to his attacker. He was just about to return to his carriage when a Polish revolutionary, Ignatei Grinevitsky, stepped forward and threw his bomb at the emperor's feet from no more than a pace away, setting off another shattering explosion. When the smoke cleared, both Grinevitsky and the tsar were lying together in the blood- and sulphur-stained snow. Grinevitsky was dying and the tsar was so badly injured that one of his legs had been nearly severed at the thigh. The wounded emperor was carried back to the Winter Palace, where he died that same night, watched over by his family and his distraught wife. Three other people were also killed in the two explosions and another twenty seriously wounded. At the eighth attempt, the world's first self-styled terrorist organisation had finally succeeded in killing the most powerful ruler on earth.

Alchemists of the revolution

The assassination of Alexander was the most significant act of regicide since the execution of Louis XIV during the French Revolution. It heralded the advent of the new kind of violence that the modern world has come to associate with terrorism. Throughout history conspirators have murdered rulers and kings who have abused their power, but the novelty of Alexander's assassination lay not so much in the act itself but in the reasons for which it was carried out and the strategic concept of violence that it embodied. Unlike previous tyrannicides, Alexander was killed not because of his personal despotism but because of the system of power that he embodied. In attacking the supreme representative of tsarism, Alexander's assassins hoped to inspire their supporters and undermine the confidence of the regime itself.

The People's Will called these tactics terrorism, in a direct reference to the French revolutionary Terror. To Maximilien Robespierre, the principal architect of the Jacobin purges, the Terror was both a righteous instrument of revolutionary justice and a means of defending the revolutionary regime from its internal enemies. The People's Will shared the same perspective on the use of terror.[1] Its members saw themselves as the heirs of the French revolutionary tradition, engaged in a people's war against Russian autocracy. For them, terrorism was both a means of defending the revolution and an instrument of revolutionary justice. But whereas the French Terror had been a means of *defending* a successful revolution, Alexander's assassins saw terrorism as a means of instigating one. Though they claimed to express the will of the population as a whole, their use of violence was a form of political warfare by a minority acting *on behalf of* an absent revolutionary majority; a minority whose aim was to provoke a wider confrontation by deliberately reconfiguring and polarising Russian society.

The organisation came into existence following an increasingly bitter political struggle between the tsarist regime and a small revolutionary vanguard to which the majority of the Russian population had remained indifferent. Through the selective assassination of high state officials the People's Will hoped to compensate for its political weakness and strike what it called a 'blow at the centre', thereby drawing the regime into a prolonged and debilitating conflict with an invisible clandestine organisation in which, as the People's Will propagandist Sergei 'Stepniak' Kravchinsky predicted, 'the strong is vanquished, not by the arms of his adversary, but by the continuous tension of his own strength, which exhausts him, at last, more than he would be exhausted by defeats.'[2]

Both the tactics and the ethical conception of violence that supported them were products of a new era in human history, in which governments could no longer take their monopoly of violence for granted and the morality of political homicide was increasingly decided not by established laws, customs and authority, but by its political objectives. In the aftermath of the French Revolution, political ideas regarding individual and collective freedom and popular sovereignty carried greater weight than at any other time in human history. The terrorists who killed Alexander were the sons and daughters of the Enlightenment, socialists, anarchists and believers in human progress, whose members came mostly from the middle and upper classes. The majority of them belonged to that peculiarly Russian variant of socialism known as populism, which believed that the salvation of Russia lay in an agrarian revolution based round the traditional peasant commune.

Alexander's assassins were not oblivious to the brutality of political murder, but they did not regard their tactics as especially cruel or immoral. On the contrary, the People's Will theorist Nikolai Morozov described terrorism as a selective form of violence, since it 'replaces by a series of individual political assassinations, which always hit their target, the massive revolutionary movements, where people often rise against each other because of misunderstanding and where a nation kills off its own children'.[3] For Sergei Kravchinsky, the terrorist was a new historical figure, one that was 'noble, terrible, irresistibly fascinating, for he combines in himself the two sublimities of human grandeur: the martyr and the hero'.[4]

To the regime they were 'evil-doers' and 'ill-disposed elements'. In the outside world they were known as 'nihilists' – a word that has often been attached to terrorist violence, with a meaning very different from its original use in the Russian context. This essential dichotomy has remained with us ever since. Almost every organisation that has ever been called 'terrorist' has retained elements from the Russian tradition, in terms of their tactics, organisation and morality, regardless of their aims or ideology. Almost every terrorist organisation has been viewed from a similar perspective to that of the tsarist regime. For this reason it is worth taking a closer look at Kravchinsky's hero and the historical circumstances that brought him into the world.

'The intensification of calamities'

The majority of Alexander's assassins had barely learned to walk when the new emperor ascended to the throne in 1855. His coronation was greeted by expectations of reform from Russian liberals and gradualist radicals such as Alexander Herzen, following the unrelieved despotism of Alexander's father, Nicholas I. Initially, the new tsar seemed disposed to fulfil the great hopes thrust upon him, promoting a spate of reforms including the historic emancipation of the serfs. But the liberal instincts of the 'Tsar Liberator' were tentative and lukewarm and his reforms were always intended to perpetuate autocracy rather than pave the way for genuine popular representation. Within a few years the bright hopes of Russian liberalism had largely faded and a new and more militant challenge to tsarism was beginning to emerge.

The early 1860s also coincided with the broader youthful revolt that Turgenev depicted in his 1862 novel, *Fathers and Sons*. It was Turgenev who coined the term 'nihilist' to describe his disaffected anti-hero, Bazarov. At first, nihilism was used to describe the intellectual and philosophical revolt articulated by literary critics such as Dimitri Pisarev, with his aggressive calls for a new spirit of materialist scientific inquiry to replace the obscurantism and superstition that dominated Russian intellectual life, but the word soon began to acquire a sinister aura beyond its original meaning and was used as a generic term to describe the disaffected youth subculture that emerged during Alexander's reign. The nihilists opposed what they regarded as the hypocritical social mores of middle-class Russian society with a cult of 'sincerity', which expressed itself in various ways, from the sulky long-haired male students to the feminist women who wore tinted glasses and cut their hair short and smoked cigarettes.

To many of these youthful rebels, the ultimate confirmation of Russian bourgeois hypocrisy was the continued poverty of the peasant population on which their parents' wealth depended. This guilty sense of class privilege increasingly found an outlet in the radical ideas that were beginning to permeate the Russian educated classes in the 1860s, such as socialism, Marxism and anarchism. Initially, the more politicised members of the nihilist subculture concentrated on educating the workers and peasants, but other tendencies were also beginning to emerge from the margins, such as the revolutionary commune Hell, whose existence first came to light in 1866 following a failed assassination attempt on the tsar. The members of Hell lived in accordance with the stringent asceticism decreed by its founder, Nikolai Ishutin. The Ishutin circle had begun to consider suicidal political assassinations, including one particularly macabre fantasy to kill landlords and public officials in which the assassins would disfigure themselves before carrying out their attacks so that they could not be identified afterwards. Though Hell was not directly involved in the attempt on the tsar's life, Ishutin and his closest followers were sentenced to hard labour in Siberia and the case focused official attention on the potentially subversive tendencies within the nihilist milieu.

One of the most notorious figures to emerge from the Russian revolutionary fringe was Sergei Nechaev. Born in 1847, the son of a house painter, Nechaev has a reputation in the history of terrorism that is hardly warranted by his actual achievements. A host of revolutionaries from Lenin to the Black Panthers have paid tribute to him while anti-Soviet historians have vilified him as the precursor of Bolshevik fanatics such as 'Iron Felix' Dzershinsky, the chief of the first Soviet secret police organisation, the Cheka. The earliest extant photograph of Nechaev shows a young man, hair parted in the middle and combed back over his abnormally large ears. The face seems slightly askew, the position of the eyes and neck out of kilter. The expression is cold, detached and sulky, the image of what Turgenev called in *Virgin Soil* 'a particular class of unfortunate beings, very plentiful in Russia, whom justice satisfies, but does not rejoice, whilst injustice, against which they are very sensitive, revolts them to their innermost being'.

The photograph gives no indication of the charisma and restless energy that fascinated many of his contemporaries, including the exiled anarchist Mikhail Bakunin, who became besotted with him. Nechaev's brief trajectory through Russian revolutionary politics began in 1866, when he went to St Petersburg to become a schoolmaster. Having spent most of his life in the mediocrity of a small provincial town, Nechaev immersed himself in radical student politics, where he rapidly distinguished himself by his impatience with any form of theoretical discussion, describing his student companions as 'a corrupt and inane herd of babbling doctrinaires'.

In a document entitled 'A Programme of Revolutionary Action', Nechaev wrote, 'If we think of our surroundings, we must inevitably conclude that we are living in the kingdom of the mad – so terrible and unnatural are people's relations to each other; so strange and unbelievable their attitude towards the mass of injustices, vileness and baseness that constitutes our social regime'.[5] From Nechaev's perspective such a society could be transformed only by violent revolutionary action. For reasons known only to himself Nechaev decided that a nationwide insurrection would break out in 1870 on the ninth anniversary of the emancipation of serfdom. To prepare for the conflagration he created his own revolutionary society, the Narodnaya Rasprava, or People's Vengeance. The exact size of the society is not known, and Nechaev always exaggerated it. Nevertheless, it probably never amounted to more than a few hundred and its political impact was negligible. The man of action who once proposed cutting out the tongues of writers owes his lasting reputation to his words rather than his deeds, in particular the notorious 'Catechism of the Revolutionist', in which he outlined the aims and methods of his society.

The document begins by describing the structure of the organisation, with its hierarchical division into cells of five members, whose activities are to be kept secret from everybody except its members and the central cell. In a section entitled 'Principles by which the Revolutionary Must be Guided', Nechaev then defines the type of revolutionary personality that will make up the organisation:

1. The revolutionary is a doomed man. He has no interests of his own, no affairs, no feelings, no belongings, not even a name. Everything in him is absorbed by a single exclusive interest, a single thought, a single passion – the revolution.

2. In the very depths of his being, not only in words but also in deeds, he has broken every tie with the civil order and the entire cultured world, with

all its laws, proprieties, social conventions, and its ethical rules. He is an implacable enemy of this world, and if he continues to live in it, that is only to destroy it more effectively.[6] 976, 300 | 363·325

For Nechaev, the revolutionary was a tragic hero who suppresses his own humanity for the greater good:

> Hard toward himself, he must be hard toward others also. All the tender and effeminate emotions of kinship, friendship, love, gratitude, and even honor must be stifled in him by a cold and single-minded passion for the revolutionary cause … Night and day he must have one thought, one aim – merciless destruction.[7]

Nechaev's vision of a secret terrorist organisation made up of ruthless amoral Jacobins was both a philosophical and a tactical innovation, in which the relationship between the ends and means posed no moral problems, since 'everything is moral which assists the triumph of revolution. Immoral and criminal is everything which stands in its way.' What kind of society would these grim prototypes deliver if they ever came to power? Could a revolutionary behave in an inhuman and immoral way without being morally corrupted and even despotic in the process? Such questions were not on his agenda. In Nechaev's apocalyptic imagination the energies of his revolutionary generation were to be entirely devoted to that 'intensification and an increase in those calamities and evils which must finally exhaust the patience of the people and drive it to a popular uprising'.

Here Nechaev anticipates what would later become one of the essential strategies of twentieth-century revolutionary terrorism. Although the efforts of his society are all supposedly devoted to 'the happiness of the people', the people need to be roused from their passivity in order to reach the critical mass in which revolution becomes possible. If this outcome is to be achieved, their situation must become intolerable and their rulers must be provoked into greater and more indiscriminate acts of repression. Nechaev wrote this hair-raising document at the age of 22 and it has been alternately condemned and celebrated ever since. In effect the 'Catechism' anticipated a key concept of twentieth-century communism that would subsequently be given artistic expression in Bertolt Brecht's *The Measures Taken* and Jean-Paul Sartre's play *Dirty Hands*: the revolutionary anti-hero who performs the vilest but necessary acts as a willing instrument of history.

There was always something more to Nechaev's amorality than an altruistic desire to subjugate his better instincts on behalf of the revolution. On

21 November 1869 he and four members of the People's Vengeance brutally murdered a student, Ivan Ivanov, in St Petersburg. Though Nechaev was accused of being a police agent provocateur, Ivanov's real crime seems to have been that he questioned Nechaev's own authority. The squalid affair received widespread publicity in Russia. Dostoevsky first read about it in a Dresden library and later used Nechaev in *The Devils* as a model for Peter Verkoevensky, who brings murder, suicide and madness to a Russian provincial town. Verkoevensky was the first of Nechaev's many fictional incarnations, from the crazed Russian anarchist Souvarine in Emile Zola's *Germinal*, who argues that 'all reasoning about the future is a crime because it prevents pure destruction and halts the march of the revolution', to the Chinese terrorist Chen in André Malraux's *Man's Fate*.

To some extent these fictional extrapolations were based on the revolutionary template in the 'Catechism' rather than Nechaev himself, whose own motivation was never entirely clear even to his contemporaries. Some of the most revealing glimpses of his manipulative character are contained in Michael Confino's collection, published in 1974, of the letters between Nechaev, Bakunin and Natalie Herzen: *Daughter of a Revolutionary*. The correspondence took place during Nechaev's second visit to Switzerland, where he fled after the murder of Ivanov and resumed his plotting with Bakunin. In January 1870 Alexander Herzen died and Nechaev and Bakunin embarked on a sordid attempt to manipulate Herzen's daughter Natalie and his old comrade Nikolai Ogarev. The unmarried Natalie had recently recovered from a nervous breakdown and Nechaev seems to have exercised the same fascination over her as he did for so many of his contemporaries.

Nechaev appears to have regarded Herzen's daughter as an aristocratic ingénue from whom he could extract money, and he almost succeeded in drawing her into his nebulous revolutionary conspiracies through a combination of seduction and appeals to her social conscience. When Nechaev professed his love for her, Natalie was not fooled and expressed her incredulous amazement in her diary that 'this crude, half-savage ruffian could ever have uttered a single word about love'. Eventually she managed to break off the relationship and in 1872 Nechaev was arrested by the Swiss authorities and extradited back to Russia. The following year he stood trial for the murder of Ivanov. During the trial the 'Catechism' made a sensational public appearance when the prosecution produced it as evidence. By this time Nechaev was considered so dangerous that the tsar himself took a personal interest in the trial. Nechaev treated the proceedings with studied contempt, drumming his fingers on the ledge and calling out periodically:

'I do not recognise the Court! I do not recognise the tsar! I do not recognise the laws!'

The judges sentenced him to twenty years in Siberia but Alexander recommended that Nechaev be imprisoned 'for ever' in the SS Peter and Paul fortress. In 1881 he managed to involve his guard at the fortress in a plot to help him escape. Using his contacts he also managed to smuggle coded messages to the People's Will, to the amazement of its members, who believed him dead. The plot was discovered and Nechaev's privileges were withdrawn. On 21 November 1882 he died of scurvy at the age of 35, leaving nothing behind him but a handful of novels written in prison which have since been lost, and the grim template of the revolutionary destroyer.

The reluctant assassins

Nechaev's peculiar combination of fanaticism and cynicism was not typical of his revolutionary generation. Most of the revolutionary groups that sprang up in the early 1870s preferred to concentrate their efforts on political agitation and propaganda rather than on merciless destruction, in the belief that a long period of ideological gestation was necessary before the people were ready for revolution. But in a closed despotism, such activity could not be carried on openly and even the simple process of gaining access to peasant villages and urban factories was fraught with difficulty. These difficulties were glaringly revealed in the summer of 1874, when thousands of young men and women flocked to the countryside in response to the populist ideologue Peter Lavrov's exhortations to 'go to the people.'

In the backroads of rural Russia an extraordinary spectacle unfolded as the sons and daughters of wealthy families went out like secular apostles, shoeless or dressed in rags, to preach socialism to what they believed would be a receptive audience. The members of this movement became known as 'narodniks'– from the Russian word *narod*, meaning 'people'. The majority of these outsiders were regarded with suspicion or outright hostility and in some cases they were denounced by the very people they wanted to reach. In certain villages they were regarded as witches and burned at the stake; in others they were turned over to the authorities. By the end of the summer some 4,000 narodniks had been arrested and hundreds were held in administrative detention as the police cracked down on 'the unhappy political fanatics ... who carried their impractical fantasies into the villages'.

The repression also spread to the cities, where the revolutionary circles were broken up and dozens more arrests made. One of those arrested was Sofia Perovskaya, a member of the Chaikovsky revolutionary circle in St Petersburg and the daughter of one of the country's most prominent families. Strong willed and intellectually curious, with a highly developed social conscience, Perovskaya had fought a bitter battle with her despotic father to educate herself and live independently in an urban commune, where she worked long hours in one of the city's barrack-like factory compounds in order to disseminate socialist propaganda. The privileged background shared by so many populist revolutionaries has led some historians to attribute their involvement in terrorism to an unhappy childhood or class guilt.

While such cases undoubtedly existed, we should be wary of reductionist and politically convenient explanations for revolutionary violence which seek its causes in the individual neuroses of its protagonists. The populist ranks also included men such as Andrei Zhelyabov, the son of a serf, and Alexander Mikhailov, the main strategist and organiser of the People's Will, who later wrote in prison that, 'My childhood was one of the happiest that a man can have. I can only compare it to a bright spring dawn, untouched by storms or bad weather, or by cloudy days.'[8]

Another upper-class revolutionary was Vera Figner, the child of a patriarchal family who dreamed of becoming tsarina as a child. A striking beauty, she seemed destined to take up a glittering place in high society, but chose instead to train to be a doctor and was one of the first Russian women to study abroad, in Zurich, where she became involved in the 'Frichi' society of revolutionary women students. In her memoirs she referred in passing to a 'severe but Spartan childhood' and attributed her decision to study medicine to a desire 'to give thanks to someone for the blessings of the world, the blessings of life. I wanted to do something good ... so good that it would benefit both myself and someone else.'[9]

These are not the voices of Nechaev's amoral nihilist destroyers. For Figner, Mikhailov and many others, it was the collision between their youthful idealism and the harsh world of Russian autocracy that eventually turned them towards revolutionary violence. In 1876 Figner returned to Russia without finishing her training and followed the narodnik pilgrimage to the people, working for ten months as a physician with her youngest sister Evgenia in a Russian peasant village that had never seen a doctor:

> Till evening I patiently distributed powders and salves, explaining three or four times how to use the medicine, and at the end of the work I would drop on the heap of straw prepared on the ground for my bed. Despair would seize me. Was there an end to this truly terrifying poverty? Were not all these prescrip-

tions a hypocrisy amidst the surrounding squalor? Could there be any thought of protest under such conditions? Would it not be irony to speak of resistance, of struggle, to people completely crushed by their physical privations?[10]

After ten months the Figner sisters were forced to leave the village by the police, when the village priest denounced them for spreading atheism. The same experience was repeated in villages across Russia as the narodniks found themselves expelled from the countryside or driven underground. Isolated from the peasant constituency they wanted to serve, with hundreds of their comrades in jail, the survivors of the crackdown formed a new revolutionary organisation called Zemlya y Volya (Land and Freedom), which was increasingly divided between the populist traditionalists who wanted to continue with political agitation and a new faction that favoured violent resistance.

Between 1877 and 1878 the debate sharpened as the two big trials of the 'mad summer' finally took place in St Petersburg. Of the hundreds of prisoners originally charged, seventy-five had either gone insane, killed themselves or died of illness after spending more than four years in prison. Nevertheless, dozens of defendants were given eight to ten years' hard labour for the most minor offences. The severity of the sentences and the dignified behaviour of the principal defendants aroused widespread sympathy in liberal and radical circles. In January 1878 a female populist named Vera Zasulich shot and wounded General von Trepov, a widely loathed official, for ordering the flogging of an imprisoned revolutionary who later went insane as a result. To the consternation of the regime Zasulich was acquitted in a jury trial, even after she had pleaded guilty, and acclaimed as a heroine outside the courtroom by an enthusiastic crowd.[11]

The Zasulich episode strengthened the militant faction within Land and Freedom, who argued that only revolutionary terrorism could advance their cause. In the summer of 1879 the debates between the 'propagandists' and the advocates of terrorism resulted in the formal division of Land and Freedom and the formation of the People's Will. In the bourgeois spa town of Lipetsk, the newly formed 'Executive Committee' formally sentenced the tsar to death while pretending to be on a picnicking and boating excursion in the countryside. For all its political justifications, the decision to kill Alexander was born of desperation, after a painful political journey in which the People's Will had seen the best hopes of its generation wrecked. In these circumstances, even those who had previously been opposed to terrorism such as Perovskaya, Zhelyabov and Figner came to accept the death of Alexander as a political necessity and they set out to implement the death sentence with the same disciplined tenacity that they had shown in their previous revolutionary activities.

The duel

The chosen instrument of execution was a new explosive invented by a Swedish scientist called Alfred Nobel. In 1866 Nobel finally managed to discover a safe way of transporting nitroglycerine following years of hazardous research, in which his laboratories had blown up in several accidents and his younger brother Emil had been killed. The result of these investigations was a malleable paste which Nobel patented in 1867 together with a detonating cap under the trade name dynamite. The People's Will now began to put Nobel's invention at the service of the revolution, using mines and explosive charges devised by their principal bomb-maker, the engineer and inventor Nikolai Kibalchich.

An extraordinary and unprecedented spectacle now unfolded, in which the Executive Committee relentlessly pursued the tsar back and forth across Russia in an increasingly desperate attempt to kill him before the police could uncover their organisation. Various complicated plots were hatched and subsequently abandoned as the 'crowned game' changed his schedule or narrowly escaped by sheer good fortune, including an audacious attempt on the Winter Palace itself, when a carpenter called Stepan Khalturin smuggled a huge quantity of dynamite into the cellar and ignited it to coincide with the royal lunch. Though Alexander escaped unharmed, dozens of soldiers were killed or injured in what an awestruck Sergei Kravchinsky later described as 'the frightful explosion at the Winter Palace, the infernal character of which seemed to surpass everything the imagination could conceive.'[12]

Even allowing for Kravchinsky's characteristic hyperbole, the penetration of the tsar's own palace by a humble workman armed with the new revolutionary superweapon was a powerful symbolic message, imbuing the Executive Committee with what Vera Figner called an 'implacable quality' in the eyes of the public and the regime. At the same time Figner observed what would later become a recurring feature of terrorist violence, in which the contest between the state and the People's Will increasingly resembled a private duel and where the latter 'created a cult of dynamite and the revolver, and crowned the terrorist with a halo; murder and the scaffold acquired a magnetic charm and attraction for the youth of the land, and the weaker their nervous system, and the more oppressive the life around them, the greater was their exaltation at the thought of revolutionary terror'.[13]

In a phenomenon that would later be repeated in other terrorist episodes, the populist intellectuals who had once sought a spiritual bonding with the people now found that sense of belonging in a shared culture of self-sacrifice that characterised the group itself. They devised new plots. They dug tunnels that had to be mined and then abandoned, at times with their bare hands. They searched for new safe houses and assumed new identities. They evaded spies and constructed bombs. They pursued the tsar across the country on bumpy roads with a horse and cart loaded with nitroglycerine, while all the time the political police known as the Third Section continued to pursue the pursuers.

By the beginning of 1881 the contest was taking its toll. Zhelyabov was prone to fainting fits and Perovskaya herself was in a state of nervous exhaustion. In the months leading up to the assassination the two of them became lovers and lived together in what the Russian revolutionaries called a 'civic marriage'. On a snowy night in February history records that the group took a rare night off and danced and sang in one of their safe houses, where any discussion about their 'work' was forbidden. Such moments of gaiety were rare in the atmosphere of asceticism and high moral purpose that infused the group. In another society men and women with their talent, intelligence and commitment might have found more creative outlets for their aspirations. Even as he worked in his clandestine explosives laboratories Kibalchich found time to devise a blueprint for a rocket-propelled flying machine that Soviet scientists would later claim as a precursor of Sputnik. On 1 March the goal that had absorbed them for so long was finally realised. Vera Figner recalled afterwards how the streets

> hummed with talk, and there was evident excitement. People were speaking of the tsar, of his wounds, of blood and death. When I entered my own dwelling and saw my friends who as yet suspected nothing, I was so agitated that I could hardly utter the words announcing the death of the tsar. I wept and many of us wept: that heavy nightmare, which for ten years had strangled young Russia before our very eyes, had been brought to an end; the horrors of prison and exile, the violence, executions and atrocities inflicted on hundreds and thousands of our adherents, the blood of our martyrs, all were atoned for by this blood of the tsar, shed by our hands. A heavy burden was lifted from our shoulders: reaction must come to an end and give place to a new Russia.[14]

These predictions did not materialise. On 10 March Perovskaya herself was arrested. Her father refused to see his daughter but her mother visited her in prison. The matrons later told Figner how Perovskaya would lie with her head on her mother's lap 'Like a sick, tired child, motionless and speechless'. At the trial Prosecutor Muraviev, a former childhood playmate of Perovskaya's, denounced the conspirators as 'the enemies of justice, of order, of morality, of family life'. The defendants denied these accusations. Zhelyabov claimed to have taken moral inspiration from the teachings of Jesus Christ, while Kibalchich claimed that there would have been no need for violence if the tsar had acted more 'patriarchally' and answered the demand for reform. The night before his death Kibalchich was still working on sketches for his flying machine and pleading with the Russian military to examine his designs. On Friday 3 April the five terrorists were led to their execution, facing backwards on horses, bearing placards inscribed with the single word 'Tsaricide' and hanged before a crowd of some 100,000.

The giant killers

Though Vera Figner tried for a while to reconstitute the Executive Committee, the People's Will effectively came to an end when she too was arrested in 1883 and sentenced to death the following year. Conscious of the international criticism that the execution of Perovskaya had generated, Tsar Alexander III chose not to execute another woman terrorist and Figner's sentence was commuted to life imprisonment in the fearsome Schlusselburg island fortress. As Figner later recalled, 'the Clock of Life stopped' in October 1884 and it would not start again until her release twenty years later. By the time her imprisonment began, virtually everyone associated with the assassination had been executed or imprisoned. In the aftermath of the assassination the People's Will sent a courteous letter to the new tsar listing its political demands and urging the regime to 'realise the will of the people'. The letter was another demonstration of their political naivety.[15] The new tsar was in no mood to make concessions to his father's assassins. Urged on by his reactionary advisor Pobedonostsev, Alexander reversed most of his father's reforms and tightened the machinery of the police state. Though some members of the liberal intelligentsia were privately sympathetic to the People's Will, the main public reaction to Alexander's assassination was grief, anger and incomprehension.

To all intents and purposes the 'blow at the centre' had been a tragic political failure and yet the tactical model introduced by the People's Will would prove astonishingly durable. Much of the credit for this belongs to Sergei

Kravchinsky, the organisation's most talented propagandist, who did more than anyone else to propagate a sympathetic view of his comrades' struggle to the outside world. The son of an artillery officer, known as 'Bluebird' to his comrades, Kravchinsky was an indefatigable narodnik 'revolutionary general'. In 1876, at the age of 24, he fought a guerrilla campaign against the Ottomans in Bosnia. The following year he tried to incite an anarchist revolt in southern Italy, posing as an English tourist. In August 1878, as a member of Land and Freedom, he stabbed to death General Mezentzov, the head of the Third Section.

As a result of this assassination Kravchinsky was obliged to flee the country and he settled in London, where his friends included William Morris, George Bernard Shaw and the children's writer E. H. Nesbitt, who used him as the inspiration for 'the Russian gentleman' in *The Railway Children*, sent to Siberia by the tsar for writing 'a beautiful book about poor people and how to help them'. Kravchinsky also appears in the Rosetti sisters' youthful roman à clef *A Girl Amongst the Anarchists* as Nekrovitch, 'a huge powerful man, so massive and striking in appearance that he suggested comparison rather with some fact of nature – a rock, a vigorous forest tree – than with another man'. Unlike so many of his contemporaries Kravchinsky evaded the prison and the scaffold, and was killed by a passing train at a level crossing near his home in Bedford Park in 1895 at the age of 43. It was during his long exile in Europe that Kravchinsky became the foremost interpreter of Russian terrorism to the outside world, through his best-selling *Underground Russia*, a sensationalist but compelling account of the terrorist struggle, first published in Italian in 1880 and subsequently translated into most European languages.

By this time Russian nihilism was a source of much fascination in the outside world, reflected in both newspaper articles and popular novels, from G. A. Henty's *Condemned as a Nihilist: A Story of Escape from Siberia* to American writer Kathleen O'Meara's *Narka the Nihilist* to Oscar Wilde's *Vera; or, The Nihilist*. Kravchinsky was well aware of the exotic aura of mystery surrounding nihilism and his book skilfully plays to the expectations of his audience, alternating dramatic descriptions of escapes and bomb plots with eulogistic portraits of former comrades such as Vladimir Ossinsky ('... as beautiful as the sun. Lithe, well-proportioned, strong and flexible as a blade of steel') and Perovskaya ('A small, slender and very graceful figure, and a voice as charming, silvery, and sympathetic as could be').

While these handsome heroes and freedom-loving heroines might have sprung from the pages of Johann Schiller or Victor Hugo, they inhabit a hidden urban subculture of clandestine printing presses, secret meetings, safe houses and spies that would later become part of the terrorist underground in cities across the world from Algiers, Berlin or Rio de Janeiro. In Kravchinsky's melodramatic and hyperbolic prose, the terrorist is a titan, a modern-day William Tell who boldly steps into the arena to confront the tyrant when all other forces have been vanquished:

> Proud as Satan rebelling against God, he opposed his own will to that of the man who alone, amid a nation of slaves, claimed the right of having a will. But how different is this terrestrial god from the old Jehovah of Moses! How he hides his trembling head under the daring blows of the Terrorist! True, he still stands erect, and the thunderbolts launched by his trembling hand often fail; but when they strike, they kill. But the terrorist is immortal. His limbs may fail him, but as if by magic, they regain their vigour, and he stands erect, ready for battle after battle until he has laid low his enemy and liberated the country.[16]

What qualities does this hero possess? Unlike the dreamy populist intellectuals, he is first of all a man of action, 'a wrestler, all bone and muscle' for whom 'daring acts' and 'sanguinary projects' have replaced the 'power of words'. He is the people's champion, with 'the force of mind, the indomitable energy, and the spirit of sacrifice' that stems from 'the grandeur of his mission, in the strong passions which this marvellous, intoxicating, vertiginous struggle arouses in his heart'. Naturally, he is willing to die. From the moment he takes up the people's cause he is 'consecrated to Death'.

This heady vision of the martyr/warrior has remained an intrinsic element of vanguard terrorism ever since, including groups that have engaged in far bloodier actions than the People's Will was willing to contemplate. Stripped of his urban habitat, the dagger and dynamite, Kravchinsky's terrorist echoes a concept of martial heroism that was already becoming obsolete even in the nineteenth century, as the practice of warfare became increasingly dependent on tactics, organisation and technology. For Kravchinsky, the former army officer, political murder was able to retain overtones of chivalrous combat by presenting violence as a clash of symbolic abstractions. Thus his own stabbing of the unsuspecting General Mezentzov represents not so much the death of a human being but an honourable challenge in which 'the Terrorism … boldly threw down its glove in the face of autocracy. From that day forth it advanced with giant strides, acquiring strength and position, and culminating in the tremendous duel with the man who was the personification of despotism.'[17]

Kravchinsky does not mention the less glorious aspects of the terrorist struggle, such as the savage punishment meted out to a suspected informer named Gorinovich in 1878 by two future members of Land and Freedom, who beat him with an iron ball attached to a chain and then poured sulphuric acid on his face, blinding and hideously disfiguring him. By leaving out the concrete details of pain and death and presenting the targets of terrorist violence in terms of their political significance, his modern-day knight preserves his heroic David versus Goliath status. If the moral grandeur that Kravchinsky conferred on his warrior/hero was exaggerated, it was no less so than the official anathema pronounced on the Russian terrorists by Prosecutor Muraviev. The anathema also reached the outside world. On 28 December 1878 Pope Leo XIII promulgated the encyclical *Quod apostolici muneris*, condemning 'the sect of those who, with diverse and barbarous names, call themselves socialists, communists and nihilists', whom he defined as a 'deadly pestilence that winds through the innermost recesses of society and brings it to the extreme danger of ruin'.

In 1880, the president of the Alliance Literary and Debating Society in London, Edward Lawrence Levy, delivered a lecture tracing the historical background of the nihilist movement in which he compared the new methods used in Russia against tsarist autocracy to the more 'open' revolutionary struggle conducted in Italy by patriotic freedom fighters such as Giuseppe Garibaldi. In Levy's view, 'The struggle must take place in the fierce light of open, public opinion; it must be a struggle shoulder to shoulder, with the whole world as spectators. Contrast the glorious battle the Italian patriot, the hero of Aspromonte fought, the Polish patriot encountered or the Hungarian general led, with the assassination and dynamite of your Russian nihilist!'[18]

If this critique tended to romanticise the movements it applauded, it also ignored the fact that revolutionary armies were not available to the Russian nihilists. Marxists were also critical of heroic terrorism, on political rather than ethical grounds, arguing that its methods tended towards elitism and revolutionary 'voluntarism'. While Marx respected the courage of the People's Will he was opposed to secret revolutionary conspiracies as a principle, dismissing their perpetrators as 'alchemists of the revolution' who 'throw themselves on inventions that should work revolutionary miracles: incendiary devices, destructive devices of magical impact'.[19] For Marx and his successors individual heroism was not relevant in a protracted political struggle against capitalism that could only be won by a popular revolutionary movement fighting on a variety of fronts.

Nevertheless, the heroic image of the People's Will continued to percolate out into the wider world though newspapers and the influential pamphlets of ex-People's Will members such as Nikolai Morozov and 'Tarnovski' (Gerasim Romanenko), and books such as Lev Tikhomirov's *La Russie politique et sociale*, published in France in 1886. Solzhenitsyn devoted a long and heavily ironic section of *August 1914* to the People's Will, in which two populist aunts celebrate the memory of Perovskaya and the other 'Queens of Terror' like secular saints.

The aura of romantic martyrdom that surrounded the People's Will was also preserved and diffused in photographs. One of the bomb-maker Kibalchich's descendants was the revolutionary Victor Kibalchich, better known as Victor Serge, who later recalled his drifting childhood in Belgium and France in which 'On the walls of our humble and makeshift lodgings there were always the portraits of men who had been hanged. The conversations of grown-ups dealt with trials, executions, escapes, and Siberian highways.'[20] In an era when portrait photographs were nearly always taken in a studio even the photographs of executed revolutionaries have an air of distinguished formality about them. The few photographs of Mikhailov and his comrades bear no resemblance to the murderous 'evil doers' described by the prosecution. In their oval portraits their faces appear as Kravchinsky described them, youthful, attractive, serious, exuding intelligence and high moral purpose, the doomed founders of a violent tradition.

The second wave

For more than twenty years after the death of Alexander II terrorism disappeared as a significant political phenomenon in Russia. But the heroic example of the People's Will remained part of the populist tradition and was resurrected by their political descendants, the Socialist Revolutionaries (SRs), who in 1902 established a specialist terrorist organisation to carry out 'unavoidable and expedient' assassinations of state officials, police spies and informers, arguing that such actions could speed up the revolutionary process and compel people 'to think politically, even against their will'. Whereas the People's Will had combined terrorism with other tasks such as the publication of its underground newspaper and propaganda abroad, the SRs established a clear separation between the party and its terrorist wing. Membership of the Combat Organisation or Terrorist Brigade was kept secret even from the party leadership. Removed from direct political control, this terrorist elite was expected to act on its own initiative, thus allowing the party to continue its work of political agitation while simultaneously claiming credit for the acts of violence carried out in its name, such as the sensational killing of Nicholas II's reactionary minister of the interior Wenzel von Plehve, whose entourage was attacked with a bomb in 1904 while it was passing the Warsaw hotel in St Petersburg.

By chance the *Daily Telegraph*'s correspondent in Russia was standing near the hotel:

> Suddenly the ground before me quivered, a tremendous sound as of thunder deafened me, the windows of the houses on both sides of the broad streets rattled, and the glass of the panes was hurled onto the stone pavements. A dead horse, a pool of blood, fragments of a carriage, and a hole in the ground were part of my rapid impressions. My driver was on his knees devoutly praying and saying that the end of the world had come ...[21]

It was a sign of the changed political climate in Russia that the correspondent was able to report how 'von Plehve's end was received with semi-public rejoicings. I met nobody who regretted his assassination or condemned the authors.' For the SRs the killing of such a high-ranking official was an honour and a privilege, so much so that one of von Plehve's assassins who was wounded in the attack later wrote to his comrades to thank them for the 'incomparable ... moral satisfaction' that his membership of the Combat Organisation's 'knightly order' had brought him. Isolated from society and even from their own party, the members of the Combat Organisation regarded themselves as a spiritual elite, united 'by love for the organisa-tion and devotion to terror', as the Combat Squad leader Boris Savinkov described it.[22] The SRs were generally circumspect about taking unnecessary casualties, so much so that Ivan Kaliayev, the assassin of Archduke Sergei in 1905, refused to throw his bomb on an earlier occasion because the target was accompanied by his wife and children.

This incident later formed the basis for Albert Camus's play *Les Justes*, in which Kaliayev appears as the noble terrorist who refuses to take innocent life in the name of an abstract notion of revolutionary justice. While some SR terrorists embraced terrorism as a noble revolutionary calling, there were others for whom it was a painful but necessary duty, such as the bomb-maker Dora Brilliant, of whom Savinkov observed 'she could not compromise with the spilling of blood. It was easier for her to die than to kill. And yet her constant request was to be given a bomb.'[23] For Savinkov it was precisely the willingness of SR terrorists to suppress their instinctive aversion to violence that elevated their actions to a higher moral plane. A gambler, womaniser and morphine addict, Savinkov was also the author of two novels, including one about terrorism called *The Pale Horse* which scandalised the SR leadership when it was published in 1909.

This self-consciously decadent tale was written in diary form by a terrorist organiser called 'George' and describes the assassination of an unnamed provincial governor. While the events themselves could easily have come from Savinkov's memoirs, the prevailing mood of the novel is one of ennui and cynicism rather than revolutionary fervour. Not only are the political objectives of the assassination secondary to the narrator's personal longing for death, but 'George' portrays himself and his own comrades as hollow, dispirited killing machines, observing how, 'We have become harsh, we are like beasts.'[24] Whether this bleak tale reflected the inner reality of terrorism, as Savinkov saw it, or whether it was merely a modish literary experiment, such a depiction was not what the SR leadership wanted to see from the leader of the Combat Organisation and Savinkov's novel was roundly condemned by the party for its 'counter-revolutionary content'.

As Russia lurched towards revolution and civil war other organisations and political parties began to emulate the SRs' tactics, both within Russia and on the fringes of the Russian empire. The expansion of the railway system facilitated the transportation of explosives and weapons from bomb factories in Russia and western Europe. It also made it possible for potential bombers and assassins to travel from neighbouring countries to carry out attacks and retreat afterwards. In addition, the rise of mass-circulation newspapers increased the potential audience for terrorist events. Not only were there more newspaper correspondents and reporters available to provide eyewitness reports, but the stylised and often melodramatic artists' impressions and engravings of the past had been replaced by documentary photographs of anarchist bomb laboratories and crime scenes: von Plehve's shattered armoured carriage, the corpses of terrorists shot dead in a gunfights and exhibited like trophies, the scorched remains of a group of 'Revolutionary Avengers' burned alive during a police raid.

Photography was also used by the police for identification purposes and many of Russia's most prominent terrorists are captured in tsarist police mugshots, handcuffed, in suits or prison clothes, in profile and looking at their captors with expressions of anger, indifference or contemptuous defiance. Some of these were the 'terrorists of a new type' described by the historian Anna Geifman in her remorseless 1993 demystification of pre-revolutionary Russian terrorism *Thou Shalt Kill*. According to Geifman's statistics terrorist violence claimed some 9,000 lives between 1905 and 1907, when soldiers, policemen, factory owners and suspected spies were shot, stabbed or blown up in all corners of the empire.

The variegated terrorist fauna that flourished in the pre-revolutionary era included criminals, suicides, fanatics and mentally unbalanced individuals such as the tormented Tatiana Leonteva, who took part in an aborted SR plot to kill Tsar Nicholas in 1904 and was sent by her parents to a psychiatric clinic in Europe, where she eventually shot and killed a 70-year-old French businessman in a Swiss hotel in the mistaken belief that he was the Russian minister of the interior. Taking her cue from Dostoevsky, Geifman tends to attribute the explosion of violence to the fanaticism of its perpetrators, but fanaticism and violence were not restricted to the opponents of the regime. As the Russian empire teetered towards revolution, the tsarist state lashed out at its enemies with equal ferocity. The result was the pitiless struggle that Leo Tolstoy denounced in his pamphlet 'I Cannot Be Silent' and which also became the subject of Leonid Andreyev's powerful 1908 novella *The Seven Who Were Hanged*, based on the executions of seven members of the SR Northern Flying Combat Detachment, whose calm serenity during their trial led the state procurator to describe them as 'real heroes'.

At a time when even the Bolsheviks were prepared to engage in revolutionary terrorism in order to weaken and destabilise a tottering regime, there was no shortage of volunteers willing to carry out heroic assassinations even at the cost of their own lives. At the same time the pre-revolutionary period saw the emergence of another recurring figure in terrorist history, the informer/terrorist with ambiguous motivation, such as the extraordinary Yevno Asev, a Russian police agent who rose to become the head of the SR Combat Organisation. For more than a decade Asev informed on his comrades in return for a salary from the Ochrana, the successor to the Third Section, while simultaneously carrying out his responsibilities as an SR terrorist conspirator. Not only did Asev fail to inform his superiors about coming attacks but he planned many of them himself and worked closely with Savinkov in organising the assassination of von Plehve. Asev became the inspiration for Pavel Yakovlevich in Andrei Biely's hallucinatory masterpiece *St Petersburg*, set against the events of 1905, the police agent and revolutionary who orders the dilettante revolutionary Nikolai Appollonovich to blow up his father, the Senator Ableukkhov, with a bomb concealed in a sardine can.

Savinkov's real-life plots were becoming progressively wilder and less feasible. In 1907 he and Asev tried to raise money to build a 'flying machine' designed by an anarchist called S. I. Bukalo, which they planned to load with explosives and crash into one of the tsar's palaces. The plan never materialised. Even as the 'SR Maximalists' and other fringe splinter groups continued to pursue terrorist tactics, including an attempted suicide bomb attack on Prime Minister Stolypin's house which killed its protagonists but not the Prime Minister, the violence was beginning to subside. By 1909 the high-water mark of Russian terrorism had passed and the heroic aura of SR terrorism was irrevocably tarnished when Asev was exposed by one of his own comrades. Though he managed to disappear before punishment could be administered, the revelation that the Combat Organisation had been directed by a tsarist police agent was a fatal blow to the notion of exemplary heroism that lay at the heart of the SR's terrorist tactics.

The Bolsheviks were quick to take advantage of the SRs' embarrassment, with a broadside by Trotsky in 1909 in which he reiterated the Marxist critique of 'heroic' individual terrorism where 'the revolvers of solitary heroes replace the people's cudgels and pitchforks; bombs replace barricades'.[25] The Social Revolutionaries were also turning away from terrorism, though a trickle of assassinations continued, culminating in the shooting of Stolypin in 1911 by Dmitri Bogrov, another SR terrorist of dubious motivation.

The 'Russian method' spreads

By this time what one of Kravchinsky's genteel English reviewers called 'the frightful struggle taking place in Russia' had spilled out beyond the borders of the empire. Across Europe the Russian revolutionary upheaval revealed itself in eruptions of desperate violence. In 1906 a Russian anarchist blew himself up in the Bois de Boulogne while testing a bomb. Another Russian opened fire on the Gardes Républicains in the Place de la République on May Day 1907. In 1909 a suspected police informer was killed and mutilated by Polish revolutionaries in a hotel in Rome. These incidents were regarded by western European governments with alarm. But even democratic socialists who did not approve of such methods in their own countries regarded assassinations and bombings inside Russia as a legitimate response to the 'empire of the night'. In other countries the heroic image of Russian terrorism exercised a peculiar magnetism. In Japan the fascination with Russian nihilism was reflected in the publication of some sixty-three books on the subject between 1881 and 1883 alone, in which aristocratic female revolutionaries such as Sofia Perovskaya and Vera Zasulich were a particular source of inspiration for titles such as *Stories from Europe about Women with a Purpose in Life* and *Strange News from Russia about the Criminal Case of a Heroine*.[26]

In China, the lives and achievements of Russian terrorists were celebrated in romanticised books and magazine stories. The 'Russian method' of political combat also reached India, particularly Bengal, where the British authorities became increasingly concerned about the influence of the Russian SRs on local nationalists, some of whom received instruction on bomb-making from exiled SRs in Paris. As late as 1931, two teenage Indian girls killed a British magistrate in East Bengal, in what one police officer described as an attempt 'to set up an Indian record of female heroism to emulate that of the tsar'. The Russian terrorist influence was most strongly felt in the Balkans, in the various nationalist struggles against Turkish rule. Between 1900 and 1913 the Balkans was second only to Russia in the number of political murders and assassination attempts, as a generation of young nationalists in different countries became enraptured by nihilist and anarchist writings and the heroic image of terrorism proselytised by Kravchinsky and others. In Macedonia the Internal Macedonian Revolutionary Organisation (IMRO), one of the most violent and long-lasting revolutionary nationalist organisations in the region, was strongly influenced by the Russian terrorist model.[27]

Before its collapse into gangsterism and its suppression in the 1930s, the IMRO and its offshoots were responsible for a string of political murders across the Balkans. But the single most catastrophic act of Balkan terrorism occurred in 1914, when a frail, ascetic Serbian student called Gavrilo Princip assassinated Archduke Ferdinand and his wife in Sarajevo. Princip and his five teenage co-conspirators shared many of the characteristics of Tsar Alexander's assassins: the same bookish background, the same eagerness to sacrifice themselves, the same emotional empathy with the peasantry and the same blinkered faith in assassination as a political tool. Though they had tenuous links to a Serbian secret society called the Black Hand, the decision to assassinate the archduke was taken on their own initiative. Not for the first time this exemplary terrorist assassination had catastrophic consequences that the self-sacrificing assassins had not predicted, ushering in a chain of events that brought about the virtual destruction of Serbia and led ultimately to the collapse of the tsarist regime itself. Indirectly, therefore, the adoption of the 'Russian method' by Serbian nationalists helped realise the aims of its original founders. And in revolutionary Russia in 1917 the French ambassador Maurice Paléologue witnessed an unusual spectacle in the imperial box of the Moscow Opera House, where the tsar himself had once sat:

It was occupied by some thirty persons, old gentlemen and several old ladies, with grave, worn, curiously expressive and unforgettable faces, who turned wondering eyes on the assembly. These were the heroes and heroines of terrorism who, scarcely three weeks ago, were living in exile in Siberia, or in the cells of Schlusselburg and the Fortress of SS. Peter and Paul. Morozov, Lopatin, Vera Figner, Catherine Ismailovitch, etc., were there. I shivered to think of all that the little party stood for in the way of physical suffering and moral torment, borne in silence and buried in oblivion. What an epilogue for Kropotkin's *Memoirs*, or Dostoevsky's *Memories of the House of the Dead*![28]

The audience listened to a rendition of the 'La Marseillaise' and a speech by the revolutionary Alexander Kerensky, before Vera Figner herself took to the stage and made a brief speech. She had spent twenty-two years entombed in the Schlusselburg island fortress until her release in 1906. In all that time she had never wavered in her revolutionary faith. Now the grande dame of Russian terrorism spoke to an enraptured audience in the hall where the tsars had once sat, grey-haired and severe in a black woollen gown and shawl, and recalled 'the countless army of obscure victims who have bought the present triumph of the revolution with their lives, all those nameless ones who have succumbed in state prisons or the penal settlements of Siberia. The list of martyrs came forth like a litany or a piece of recitative.'[29] It had been thirty-five years since Figner and her comrades killed Alexander II in the streets of St Petersburg. The former terrorist who had once dreamt of becoming tsarina survived the civil war and Stalin's purges, concentrating on charity work for the poor. In 1942 she died at the age of 90, as the German army closed in on the capital, and the last surviving member of the world's first terrorist organisation passed into history.

Anarchists and Dynamitards

Ever reviled, accursed, ne'er understood
Thou art the grisly terror of our age

John Henry Mackay, 'Anarchy', 1900

The fear of terrorism is often greatest in times of relative peace and stability, when violence appears to be a social anomaly. One of the clearest demonstrations of this process was the so-called 'anarchist terror' that preoccupied Europe and America in the last two decades of the nineteenth century, when ministers, presidents, rulers and royalty were assassinated on both sides of the Atlantic and the impact of the smallest bombing incident was often magnified by melodramatic and sensational press coverage. In 1894 a series of explosions occurred in Paris, where Emile Zola's English translator, Ernest Vizetelly, observed how the city's inhabitants

> lived in daily dread of some fresh eruption, which might occur at any moment, and in any part of the city. If a trifling mishap occurred to a tram car, through an electric wire getting out of order, people imagined that an explosive had been deposited on the line, and a panic ensued. When an accident happened to the scenery of a naval piece performed at the Galté Theatre, and a few ballet girls, acting as sailors, dropped on to the stage shaken, no doubt, but by no means seriously hurt, half the ladies in the audience screamed hysterically, and many people rushed away fearing lest they might be blown to pieces. 'Les Anarchistes! Une bombe!' were the exclamations heard at the least untoward incident which occurred in any place of public resort.[1]

The same pattern occurred elsewhere in Europe, where magazines and newspapers routinely carried stories on anarchist bombers with their 'infernal machines' and reported the discovery of the most terrifying and destructive plots. Anarchist violence was frightening not just because of its methods but because of its perceived aims. The People's Will could still be seen even by liberal European observers as a recognisably political response to the particular conditions of tsarist despotism, however much they frowned on assassination as a tactic. But anarchism was a philosophy supposedly aimed at the overthrow of everything – an aspiration that transcended politics altogether and opened up the possibility of the downfall of authority and civilisation itself. From this point of view anarchist violence was not only morally abhorrent, it was insane. It was in this period that the image of the mad anarchist bomber, with a smoking bomb beneath his black cloak, was first disseminated into the wider world through cartoons and engravings and also through popular fiction, in penny dreadfuls and lurid potboilers such as the exceptionally ludicrous *The Anarchist – a Story of Today* by a forgotten American writer named Colonel Richard Henry Savage.

This dim period piece describes a foreign anarchist plot to deprive the beautiful American heiress Evelyn Hartley of her inheritance in order to finance a subversive takeover of the United States by the anarchist Mikhail Bakunin. Despite its lack of any literary merit, Savage's hysterical denunciation of anarchism contains all the ingredients of the malignant terrorist conspiracy that would later be repeated in depictions of 'international communism' and contemporary images of al-Qaeda. There is the sinister central committee co-ordinating violent events across the world, which meets in a remote Alpine eyrie, the 'wild-eyed' foreign nihilists intent on the destruction of society, impervious to law and rationality. There is the confrontation between good and evil, civilisation and barbarism, described by Savage's mouthpiece, the reactionary Judge Wilkinson Fox, who is prone to anti-anarchist diatribes such as the following:

> *We have had about enough of this anarchistic bullying.* We will stand, under the law, and absolutely crush the terrorists! They shall be stoned at the gates like the outcasts of Israel! There is a time when mercy is mad folly. Nothing contents these modern lunatics ... in America, their bodies shall perish ... and our principles shall survive! The governments of the civilized world will be forced to join hands in systematic repression! These deserters, spies, and marauders in the campaign of human progress, seek a doom which is forced on organized society as the only remedy![2]

The anarchist beast
For Wilkinson Fox, the only response to this affront to human decency was to 'furnish rope to grip the necks of the men of the torch and bomb'. In Savage's portrayal of terrorism as the work of 'modern lunatics' beyond the reach of law and civilisation we can already glimpse the essential contours that

have endured for more than a century. In fact the actual number of anarchist attacks and the casualties incurred during the period known as the 'anarchist terror' was relatively small. Between 1880 and 1912, anarchists killed six heads of state, while some historians have calculated the total number of deaths caused by anarchist attacks in the same period at little more than 100.[3] Nevertheless, the spectre of anarchist violence continued to haunt Europe. In an era marked by ostentatious social privilege and enormous disparities of wealth, with an emergent urban working class largely excluded from political power and the massacres of the Paris Commune still a recent memory, violent protest was frequently indistinguishable from perceived apocalyptic intent.

Such was the level of bourgeois anxiety, that even an apolitical novelist such as Henry James felt moved to write about anarchist violence in his 1886 novel *The Princess Casamassima*. 'Are we on the eve of great changes or are not?' James's aristocratic heroine anxiously asks the hapless anarchist conspirator Hyacinth Robinson. 'Is everything that is gathering force, underground, in the dark, in the night, in little hidden rooms, out of sight of governments and policemen and idiotic "statesmen" – heaven save them! – is all this going to burst forth some fine morning and set the world on fire?'

Novelists were not the only ones asking such questions. Policemen and governments were also wondering what forces were incubating beneath what James called 'the vast smug surface' – the better to combat and suppress them. For their part, the bloody suppression of the Paris Communards and the continent-wide repression of the left that followed led a growing number of anarchists to regard heroic individual acts of 'propaganda by deed' as the only way to reinvigorate the revolutionary movement in a period of political dormancy. Over the coming decade the strategy of propaganda by deed was propagated much more often than it was practised, in increasingly incendiary speeches by influential anarchists and publications such as the Italian terrorist journals *Pensiero e Dinamite* and *Il Pitroleo*. One French anarchist journal in the 1880s offered a dagger and a pistol as competition prizes, while *La Droit Sociale* in 1883 recommended the destruction of a theatre in Lyons whose clientele supposedly consisted of 'the fine flower of the bourgeoisie' – a recommendation that was acted upon later that year when a bomb was thrown at the theatre restaurant, killing one of its employees. Other anarchist publications offered detailed instruction on the use of explosives and dynamite, such as the French *L'Anarchiste Indicateur* which was translated into Spanish and Italian.

Even more than the Russian populists, the anarchists greeted Alfred Nobel's invention with rapturous acclaim and revelled in its destructive power. In the post-Paris Commune era, dynamite was seen as 'the great emancipator', a revolutionary superweapon that could compensate for the absence of a mass movement and provide the humblest revolutionary with the means of violence to rival the rifles and cannons of the state. 'It is essential that the conflict in which we are engaged should, to some extent, be waged in the future with chemicals,' proclaimed the anarchist paper *Struggle* in 1890, in a regular column on the manufacture of 'Anti-Capitalist Products'.[4]

In some anarchist publications the virtues of dynamite were celebrated with gleeful relish, such as the fringe Italian journal *Il Ciclone*, which offered instructions on the manufacture of dynamite under the title 'Anarchist Cuisine: Meatballs for the Bourgeoisie'. There were also do-it-yourself terrorism manuals dispensing technical advice in a flippant style that was often as alarming as the content itself, such as Johan Most's *Science of Revolutionary Warfare* ('a manual for the use and preparation of Nitro-glycerine, Dynamite, Guncotton, Fulminating Mercury, Bombs, Fuses, Poisons etc.'), which cheerfully informed its readers:

> Some bombs have also been tried with satisfactory results, and create great destruction if thrown between a crowd of social reptiles. It must, however, not be reckoned upon to do much damage inside of a building if the persons to be injured are not in the same room where the missile is thrown into, or near by where the bomb falls.[5]

Such language was intended to shock and it generally succeeded, though some of the most violent and provocative anarchist journals were actually financed by the police or written by police provocateurs in an attempt to flush out potential conspiracies, such as the French journal *La Révolution Sociale*, founded in 1881 by an informer working for the Paris police chief Louis Andrieux.[6]

One French provocateur, Auguste Coulon, who infiltrated anarchist circles in London on behalf of Scotland Yard, was known for his frivolously violent 'International Notes' in the pages of *Commonweal*. Coulon played an instrumental role in indicting the so-called Walsall anarchists in 1892, six supposed conspirators in a bomb plot involving an English anarchist in Walsall and French and Italian anarchists in London. The main evidence against them consisted of a bomb cast, a sketch of a bomb found in the house of one of the accused and some incendiary publications, including the notorious *Anarchist Feast at the Opera*, a cheerfully rabid document of the period purportedly translated from French, which explained how to inflict maximum carnage at an opera house by cutting its gas pipes and planting slow-burning incendiary devices in the seat covers: eventually the gas would explode and roast the pampered bourgeois. Even though many anarchists believed the *Feast* to be a fake, the mere fact that the Walsall defendants had it in their possession was used as circumstantial evidence against them and resulted in the conviction of four of the accused for conspiracy to manufacture a bomb.[7] Though the purpose of this unconstructed bomb was never revealed, three of the accused were given ten-year sentences and the other received five years. This was one of several similar miscarriages of justice during this period involving hypothetical anarchist conspiracies. Nor was this the only case in which conspiracies were imagined or conjured up.[8]

The search for the 'Black International'

The similarity in the language of many anarchist publications, and the fact that anarchist assassinations were often carried out in response to state executions and acts of repression, fuelled the belief that these actions were being co-ordinated by a clandestine international organisation. The only serious attempt to create such an organisation took place in July 1881, when forty-five anarchist delegates from around the world met in a London tavern to discuss the formation of an international anarchist body, but these attempts soon foundered and the congress did not reconvene until 1907.

Nevertheless the belief in a sinister 'Black International', orchestrating acts of anarchist violence, persisted. The mystique of secret societies, revolutionary brotherhoods with vast powers, esoteric blood oaths and arcane initiation ceremonies, had always exercised a powerful fascination over the nineteenth-century imagination, and the perception of the 'anarchist terror' borrowed from the same tradition. The spectre of a vast conspiracy of destruction was partly a fantasy, but it was also politically convenient. Then, as now, the exaggeration or invention of such conspiracies had obvious advantages for reactionary governments. In 1878 two separate assassination attempts on Kaiser Wilhelm I gave the German chancellor, Otto von Bismarck, a pretext to push through the repressive Anti-Socialist Laws, which resulted in a wave of arrests and deportations of anarchists and socialists, often on the flimsiest pretexts.

Similar episodes occurred in Italy and France. In Spain in 1883 a supposed anarchist conspiracy was uncovered in the south of the country called La

Mano Negra (Black Hand), that was reputed to be planning the murder of all the landowners in Andalusía. Although no convincing evidence of the conspiracy was ever produced, some 300 anarchists were imprisoned and eight others publicly garrotted, in what some historians believe was simply a pretext to destroy the powerful anarchist movement in the region.

The apparent similarity in the methods and targets of anarchist violence was misleading. The anarchist propagandists of the deed were linked by a shared philosophy rather than a shared organisation. In France during the 1880s there were dozens of anarchist groups, mostly based in Paris and Lyons, with fearsome-sounding names like La Panthére de Batignolles, La Dynamite de Lyons, Les Vengeurs, La Revolté and Les Affames. Similar groups existed in Italy and Spain, many of which were little more than discussion forums rather than revolutionary cells engaged in subversive activity or bomb-making.

As in our own era, the belief in an orchestrated international conspiracy intent on chaos and destruction was always crucial to the fear and revulsion that anarchism aroused. But violent anarchism was only one manifestation of a political philosophy which regarded itself as the highest expression of the rationalist spirit of the age and which often combined an almost millenarian conviction in the coming anarchist utopia with an equally fervent belief that a rotten bourgeois order was on the point of collapse. Even Peter Kropotkin, the anti-Darwinian theorist of mutual aid and co-operation, subscribed for a time to the cult of propaganda by deed. While the great anarchist intellectuals such as Kropotkin, Jean Grave and the French geographer Elisée Reclus achieved a degree of bourgeois respectability even as they elaborated their critiques of capitalist society and extolled anarchist ideas in books, lectures and articles, there were more marginal figures, such as the paranoid Italian 'Giannoli' in Isabel Meredith's *A Girl amongst the Anarchists*, who were committed 'to destroy utterly the fabric of existing society by all possible means, by acts of violence and terrorism, by expropriation, by undermining the prevailing ideas of morality'.

'Isabel Meredith' was the nom de plume of Helen and Olivia Rosetti, the precocious nieces of Christina and Dante Gabriel Rosetti, who founded an anarchist magazine *The Torch* in their teens. Despite its ironic attitude to what the sisters clearly regarded as youthful folly, *A Girl amongst the Anarchists* offers many thinly fictionalised portraits of the foreign anarchist refugees who fled to London in the late nineteenth century to escape from anti-anarchist repression on the continent. Throughout the period of the 'anarchist terror' anarchists were hounded by the police and authorities in various countries. In Italy during the 1890s thousands were routinely subjected to indefinite detention without trial in island penal colonies known as *domicilio coatto* (forced domicile), regardless of whether they had committed any offence. In France anarchists were similarly subjected to special legislation and mass arrests on suspicion of involvement in chimerical conspiracies.

To politicians and the press, anarchists were variously described as beasts, criminals, degenerates and 'odious fanatics prompted by perverted intellect and morbid frenzy'. According to the highbrow British monthly *Blackwood's* 'The mad dog is the closest parallel in nature to the Anarchist', while one political scientist in *Harper's Weekly* referred to 'the king of all Anarchists, the arch-rebel satan'. In these depictions of the anarchist we can already glimpse the subsequent portrayal of 'the terrorist' as wild man, immune to civilisation and worthy only of exemplary punishment and extermination. On the other side the language was equally extreme. Anarchist publications such as the scurrilous French journal *Le Père Peinard* were aware of the fear and dread that anarchism aroused and often responded to it with equally ferocious and contemptuous language that was calculated to offend bourgeois sensibilities. And in 1886, the inflammatory language of violent anarchism rebounded with devastating impact, in one of the defining political tragedies of the era.

Haymarket

The setting was Chicago, which by the mid-1880s had become the second largest city in the United States. A booming, polyglot metropolis which embodied many of the worst features of the robber-baron capitalism of the era, Chicago's economic growth was built on the ruthless industrial exploitation of a largely immigrant workforce, imported mostly from Germany and eastern Europe. Attempts to improve labour conditions or unionise the workforce were met with implacable hostility by the city's employers, who responded to strikes with lockouts, police assaults and the use of hired gunmen. Chicago was one of the most important centres of anarchist and socialist activity and the home of influential anarchists such as Albert Parsons, the editor of *The Alarm*, and August Spies, who edited the German-language *Arbeiter Zeitung*.

Chicago's anarchist papers were as mesmerised by the possibilities of dynamite as their European counterparts and both *The Alarm* and the *Arbeiter Zeitung* lyrically sang the praises of 'Giant Powder' and carried articles on how to use it. In May 1886 the fractious labour relations in the city erupted in violence once again, when police opened fire on striking workers outside the McCormick Reaper plant, killing two strikers and wounding many more. At the end of a public protest meeting called by a group of anarchist leaders in the city's Haymarket square, the thuggish police chief Captain John Bonfield ordered his men to charge the crowd. In the ensuing mêlée, a bomb was thrown into the police ranks by an unknown assailant, killing one police officer and wounding several more. The remaining police began firing wildly in all directions and later claimed that they had been fired on. What is certain is that by the end of the night, seven police officers were dead and sixty-odd were wounded, and that the carnage owed as much to their own panic-stricken shooting as it did to bomb fragments. Though an unknown number of crowd members were also killed and wounded, the public image of the 'Haymarket Riot' was epitomised by the engraver Thomas Nast's sensationalised *Harper's Weekly* front cover, showing a mob of wild-eyed foreigners shooting at the police or running away, urged on by a bearded speaker, while another foreign-looking anarchist prepares to throw a bomb. Though the bomber was not identified, eight anarchists were eventually indicted for conspiracy and incitement to murder, including Parsons and Spies.

At the trial, the prosecution evoked the anarchist bomber in all his demonic proportions, unveiling bloodstained police uniforms in court, together with a full array of 'infernal machines' supposedly used by the anarchists, including a range of fuses, dynamite caps and explosives that had no direct bearing on the case. But the crucial evidence consisted of the defendants' own words or words published in their journals. Out of 133 pieces of state evidence produced in court, 114 consisted of articles from anarchist publications, in an attempt to prove that the Haymarket bomb was the result of a premeditated anarchist conspiracy to murder.

The trial took place against a background of anti-anarchist hysteria, in which the prosecution's depiction of the accused was echoed in cartoons and engravings in the popular press and in lurid dimestore novels, such as *The Red Flag, or the Anarchists of Chicago*.[9] Both the press and the public wanted vengeance and readily accepted the caricature monsters supplied by men such as Art Young, illustrator for the *Chicago Daily News*, who later came to regret his contribution to a book entitled *Anarchists and Bomb-Throwers* which depicted 'Law and Order, personified by an Amazonian woman, throttling a bunch of dangerous-looking men.'[10]

This was the framework through which many Americans viewed the Haymarket events, in what the liberal novelist and critic William Howells described as 'a trial by passion, by terror, by prejudice, by hate, by newspaper'. Howell was one of the few prominent Americans willing to question the prosecution's presentation of the Haymarket bombing as the tip of a vast subversive conspiracy, as the white-collar jury predictably delivered a unanimous guilty verdict and the judge sentenced seven of the anarchists to death.

In their closing speeches the defendants denied any involvement in the Haymarket bombing. Albert Parsons, the only native-born defendant, spoke for eight hours in a lucid exposition of anarchism and political economy that aroused the grudging admiration of his tormentors in the *Chicago Tribune*. Only Louis Lingg, the youngest of the eight defendants, made no attempt to appeal to the moral conscience of the nation, contemptuously inviting the court to hang him. In his 1909 novelistic account of the Haymarket episode, *The Bomb*, Frank Harris presents Lingg as a beguiling philosopher-terrorist who persuades the fledgling anarchist reporter Rudolf Schnaubelt to throw the bomb. Harris describes these events with an odd mixture of social protest and erotic fervour that nevertheless contains one of the few sympathetic fictional portrayals of anarchist violence of the era.

After a lengthy appeals process, supported by an international campaign for clemency, the governor of Illinois commuted the death sentences for three of the defendants to life imprisonment and upheld the remaining four. Five days before the day of execution, Lingg blew himself up in his cell with smuggled dynamite, causing *The Times* to lament 'the lax discipline which allowed Lingg to cheat the hangman'. On 11 November 1887 the remaining four anarchists were hanged without incident, despite the presence of thousands of police and soldiers in expectation of an anarchist rebellion.

In 1893 the Haymarket affair became front-page news again, when the new governor of Illinois, John Peter Altgeld, pardoned the three imprisoned defendants and issued a report condemning virtually every aspect of the trial, from the selection of the jury to the conduct of the police and the judge. Altgeld's report not only dismissed the anarchist conspiracy theory out of hand but he accused the police of fabricating it. Altgeld also addressed the question of police behaviour before the Haymarket affray and included various eyewitness descriptions of police brutality, before concluding with this devastating indictment of the Chicago police chief John Bonfield:

> While some men may tamely submit to being clubbed and seeing their brothers shot down, there are some who will resent it and will nurture a spirit of hatred and seek revenge for themselves, and the occurrences that preceded the Haymarket tragedy indicate that the bomb was thrown by some one who, instead

of acting on the evidence of anybody, was simply seeking personal revenge for having been clubbed, and that Captain Bonfield is the man who is really responsible for the death of the police officers. [11]

Few establishment politicians have ever responded to an act of 'terrorist' violence with this kind of honesty and Altgeld's moral and political courage unleashed a ferocious campaign of threats, innuendoes and insults that wrecked his career. Even at this early stage in the history of terrorism, the essential parameters of the establishment anathema were already beginning to emerge, and Altgeld's suggestion that society bore some of the responsibility for the Haymarket bombing was politically unacceptable. It would be another century before Chicago was ready to accept some official responsibility, when the city's first black mayor, Harold Washington, opened 'Labor History Month in Chicago' with a proclamation commemorating 'the tragic miscarriage of justice which claimed the lives of four labor activists.'

'The harmony between deeds and words'

The majority of the anarchist propagandists of the deed were poorly educated young men from the lower strata of society whose understanding of anarchism was gleaned from limited reading of fringe anarchist publications. In his haunting 1976 sequence of paintings *The Art of Anarchy* the Italian painter Flavio Costantini portrayed the nineteenth-century anarchist assassins as doomed rebels against a far more powerful enemy. Victor Serge described himself and his French anarchist comrades of the turn of the century as desperate men, for whom anarchism represented a search for 'the harmony between deeds and words'.[12] Some of these solitaires were on the fringes of derangement, such as Léon Léauthier, a French shoemaker, who went to dine in a plush Paris restaurant in 1893 and then knifed the nearest customer (who turned out to be the Serbian ambassador) before informing a passing policeman that he had just 'stabbed a bourgeois and eaten a fine meal'.

The annals of anarchist terrorism are filled with similar examples of marginalised loners motivated by visceral class hatred or suicidal idealism. In 1898 Luigi Lucheni, an illegitimate Italian drifter with vague anarchist ideas, stabbed the Empress Elizabeth of Austria with a sharpened file in Lake Geneva. Lucheni had considered various other aristocratic targets before settling for the neuralgic and inoffensive empress with a tragic personal life who despised the Hapsburg court. Sentenced to solitary imprisonment for life, Lucheni was led from the court shouting, 'If there were only two hundred brave men like myself all the thrones would soon be vacant!'

Such men were not lacking. In 1878 a 29-year-old Italian cook named Giovanni Passanante wounded King Umberto I during a state visit to Naples. Passanante was so poor that he could not afford a gun and had to bargain for the price of a knife. He was given a death sentence, which King Umberto subsequently commuted to life imprisonment. This act of royal largesse was less generous than it seemed, because Passanante was systematically beaten by his warders for years before being transferred to an insane asylum, physically and mentally broken, where he died in 1914. Nevertheless, he outlived Umberto, who was shot dead by an Italian-American anarchist named Giovanni Bresci from New Jersey in retaliation for royal support of the vicious repression during the 1898 Milan bread riots, in which dozens of protesters were killed by the army.

Other acts of anarchist violence were directed at symbols of bourgeois society rather than specific individuals, such as the dynamite bomb tossed into the Liceo Opera House in Barcelona in 1893, which killed twenty-two members of the audience. The most notorious French dynamitard of the 1890s was François Ravachol, another marginal figure from the anarchist fringe who emerged from an impoverished rural background to embark on a precocious criminal career as a forger before graduating to robbery and murder. In one of his most scandalous crimes, Ravachol disinterred the corpse of the Contesse de Rochetaillée in the mistaken belief that aristocratic women were always buried with their jewellery. In 1892 Ravachol first emerged as a propagandist of the deed, when he was arrested for trying to blow up the judge and public prosecutor responsible for the harsh verdicts handed out after an anarchist disturbance in Clichy. Elegantly dressed in a frock coat and silk hat and armed with two revolvers, Ravachol carried his home-made bombs in a leather case and deposited them in the buildings where his chosen targets lived. Though no one was killed, the buildings were severely damaged and Ravachol's trial generated enormous publicity both nationally and abroad.

In court Ravachol was cheerfully unrepentant, declaring that his bombs had been intended as a warning to future administrators of justice 'to be more clement if they want better treatment themselves'. The dapper accordion-playing sociopath proved surprisingly popular with some of the French middle-class intellectuals who gravitated towards anarchism in the Belle Epoque, who variously compared him to Socrates and Jesus Christ. The novelist and anarchist fellow-traveller Octave Mirbeau described Ravachol, rather portentously in the anarchist review *L'Endehors*, as 'the thunder clap that is followed by the glory of the sun and the calm sky' whose bombs heralded the collapse of a violent and unjust social order. The establishment view of Ravachol was summed up by the Paris correspondent of *The Times*, who described his actions as 'the war of disorder and chaos against order and law … It is murder and havoc acting in the service of covetousness, hatred and all evil.'[13]

This combination of hysteria and hyperbole epitomised the establishment view of anarchism. In retrospect it is difficult to see why Ravachol should have assumed either the demonic or the saintly status assigned to him. But the greater the horror he aroused on one side, the more fringe anarchist publications like *Le Père Peinard* sung his praises. In a second trial Ravachol was sentenced to death for his earlier criminal murders rather than his bombings and he was led to the guillotine defiantly singing a popular anti-clerical song. Afterwards his canonisation continued in idealised portraits of his moustachioed face with the guillotine in the background, in popular novels such as *L'Exploits Du Ravachol* and *Les Amours de Ravachol* and songs by anarchist *chansoniers*, such as the following:

> Dansons la Ravachole
> Vive le son, vive le son
> Dansons la Ravachole
> Vive le son de l'explosion!

Avengers

The Ravachol trial represented the beginning of the French 'anarchist terror' which reached a new pitch of hysteria in December 1893, when August Vaillant, another lone anarchist, threw a bomb at the French Chamber of Deputies. Vaillant was a particularly tragic figure. Born in the Ardennes in 1861, he was turned out into the street by his father at the age of 10 and left to fend for himself on the street. In the course of an unbelievably bleak and harsh existence on the margins of French society, Vaillant somehow taught himself to read and became converted to anarchism. A thinly disguised Vaillant appears in Zola's bitter indictment of the corrupt Third Republic, *Paris*, as Salvat, the lone anarchist *justicier* roaming the fringes of the Belle Epoque with a bomb in his pocket '… tall, thin and ravaged, with dreamy yet flaming eyes, which set his pale starveling's face aglow'. In the novel Salvat throws a bomb at a corrupt aristocratic financier, killing an errand girl by mistake. The real-life Vaillant attempted a more spectacular statement, in order to articulate what he called 'the cry of a whole class which demands its rights and will soon join acts to words'.

After painstakingly constructing a bomb by putting aside a tiny portion of his meagre income each week to buy metals and sulphuric acid and cobblers' nails for shrapnel, he gained entrance to the Chamber of Deputies while parliament was in session. It was characteristic of Vaillant's wretched life that his arm accidentally caught a woman who was standing beside him as he was throwing the bomb, which exploded above the heads of the deputies, killing no one and causing only minor injuries. Vaillant was immediately arrested and a mass roundup of anarchists was followed by the enactment of the *lois scélérates* – the 'scoundrelly laws' which proscribed any publications engaging in direct or 'indirect' incitement to terrorist acts – an offence that anticipated later terrorist episodes. Though Vaillant's 'statement' caused no fatalities he was nevertheless sentenced to death, after a government ballistics expert blew up ten dogs in a wood using a similar bomb in order to show what would have happened had Vaillant's aim not been deflected. Despite appeals for clemency, the political climate was not conducive to acts of mercy and President Marie Carnot refused to commute the sentence. Vaillant was guillotined, after refusing the offer of the chaplain on the grounds that 'religion is a grotesque and useless thing'. A few days after the execution a palm wreath was laid on his grave accompanied by a mourning card containing the lines: 'You can sleep your calm slumber/ O martyr … *you will be avenged.'*

The vengeance was not long in coming. A week after the execution, on 12 February 1894, a young anarchist named Emile Henry threw a bomb at the customers of the popular Café Terminus and was arrested running away from the scene, as he tried to shoot at the policemen chasing him. The child of a middle-class former Paris Communard who died in exile when his son was eight years old, Henry demonstrated an icy hatred and contempt towards the proceedings at his trial, cooly informing the court that his bomb at the Terminus had been intended to kill as many people as possible. When the prosecutor asked him what sort of man could contemplate killing so many innocent people, Henry contemptuously replied, 'No bourgeois can possibly be an innocent person.'

Henry's closing statement was one of the most coldly lucid and unrepentant defences of terrorism ever made, in which he listed the crimes of the bourgeois order he had come to loathe, from the Haymarket executions to the bloody suppression of a May Day march at the town of Fourmies. In explaining his early attempt to blow up a mining company involved in a bitter industrial dispute, Henry told the court:

I wanted to demonstrate to the bourgeoisie that from now on it would no longer enjoy the delights of a bliss too perfect, that its arrogant triumphs would be troubled, that its golden calf would be violently shaken on its pedestal until the final push would topple it into the mud and blood.[14]

On 21 May Henry was guillotined, watched by some 100 spectators. A *Figaro* reporter described him, 'pale and trembling all over', as he was led out, covered with an overcoat, to become another of the executioner Deibler's 'patients'. There was still one last act in the grim saga of violence and revenge that had followed Vaillant's failed bomb. On 24 June 1894 a 21-year-old Italian baker named Caserio made his way to Lyons and plunged a knife into the French president's chest while he was riding in his carriage. At his trial Caserio insisted that he had acted alone and that he had decided to kill Carnot in retaliation for Vaillant's execution. The former altar boy was good humoured, relaxed and generally indifferent to the proceedings. The trial was over within two weeks and the verdict was inevitable. On 16 August Caserio was led out to face Deibler's machine and the trail of violence that had begun at the Chamber of Deputies the previous year was closed.

The same deadly cycle was repeated elsewhere in Europe. In 1896 a bomb was thrown at the Corpus Christi procession in Barcelona, killing twelve people and wounding many others. Some 400 suspects were arrested, many of whom had no connection with anarchism at all, and taken to the notorious Montjuich fortress, where they were tortured with such savagery that several of them died before eighty-seven were finally indicted. The 'Montjuich tortures' were widely condemned across Europe, so that only twenty-six prisoners were eventually sentenced, five of whom were executed. Even those who had not been indicted were transported to a penal colony by the government. The following year an Italian anarchist called Michele Angiolillo shot dead the prime minister, Antonio Cánovas, outside a health spa in northern Spain in retaliation for his approval of the sentences. Angiolillo was garrotted in turn.

The arena

Angiolillo could easily have escaped, but the willingness of the anarchist propagandists of the deed to sacrifice themselves was an essential element in the inspirational message their assassinations were intended to convey. The whole strategy of propaganda by deed was based on the assumption that anarchist 'statements' would be transmitted to the widest possible audience. In a world that was becoming increasingly interconnected by modern transportation systems, by the spread of railways and shipping networks, by telephone and telegraph, by the rise of literacy and the spread of mass-circulation newspapers, propaganda by deed was a product of the same bourgeois world it aspired to overthrow. The very fact that Haymarket received such attention, and the outrage that greeted the Opera House bombing in Barcelona, reflected the new availability of information, which increasingly transmitted the most distant events to an international audience. Even Luigi Lucheni, the wretched assassin of the Empress Elizabeth, expressed a very modern aspiration when he reportedly told a friend beforehand of his desire 'to kill somebody. But it must be someone important so it gets into the papers.'

In the same way Leon Czolgosz, the assassin of William McKinley, initially became obsessed with the idea of killing the American president after reading a newspaper account of Bresci's assassination of King Umberto. Through further research he was able to find out the president's schedule and track him down. The expansion of transportation networks, of shipping routes and trains, made even more remote targets potentially accessible, so that Bresci could journey by ship from New Jersey to assassinate King Umberto in Milan, and Angiolillo could travel to Spain from London to kill the Spanish prime minister. At a time when even the highest state officials regarded security and bodyguard protection as beneath their dignity, access to potential targets was also far easier than it would subsequently become.

The sense of a common threat from violent anarchism increasingly preoccupied governments and legal and criminal experts, prompting suggestions that anarchists should be interned in mental hospitals or imprisoned in an international penal colony. Some French criminologists argued that anarchism was a contagious disease of the brain, while the influential Italian criminologist, Cesare Lombroso, believed that men like Ravachol were an evolutionary throwback who possessed 'the degenerative characters common to criminals and the insane, being anomalies and possessing these traits by heredity'.[15]

In Lombroso's analysis these degenerative features included large ears and simian jaws. Lombroso drew his conclusions from samples of anarchist prisoners in Italian prisons and attempted to match them with the Haymarket anarchists, pointing out the 'moral insensibility' of Albert Parsons and especially Lingg, in whom the criminologist detected 'a truly ungovernable epileptoid idea' that drove him towards anarchism. In the last years of the nineteenth century some legal theorists attempted to elaborate a new category of 'social crime' that would incorporate not only violent anarchist acts but the ideas that supported them. One proposal in the United States suggested that anarchism should be regarded as an international offence akin to piracy. There were also attempts by European governments to find a common international response to the menace, such as the 1898 'International Anti-Anarchist Conference' of police and home office officials convened by the Italian premier Luigi Pelloux in Rome, which failed to agree on any significant points, largely due to the reluctance of Britain, Switzerland and Belgium to change their liberal asylum laws.[16]

By this time violent anarchism was on the decline in many countries and a number of prominent voices from within the libertarian left had begun to question the whole strategy of propaganda by deed, after more than two decades of sporadic bombings and assassinations that had generated a great deal of repression and very little revolutionary momentum. In the coming decade the notion of heroic and exemplary assassinations would be gradually displaced by more collectivist forms of political struggle. In a new period in which the working classes were beginning to form their own political organisations and trade unions, anarchists began to overcome their traditional aversion to formal organisation and adopt a new strategy of revolutionary syndicalism in the workplace, which made propaganda by deed increasingly anachronistic. Isolated bombings and acts of violent anarchism spluttered on, from the followers of the Italian anarchist Luigi Galeani in the United States to the anarcho-bank robbers the Bonnot Gang in France, known as *la bande tragique*.[17] In December 1910 the spectre of violent anarchism emerged in Britain once again in the so-called siege of Sydney Street, in east London, when two anarchist burglars fought a gun battle with 700 police and a unit of military marksmen, watched by the home secretary, Winston Churchill. By the end of the Great War, however, the anarchist terror was a distant episode of history, but the image of the mad anarchist bomber with his infernal machines, intent on the destruction of everything, has never entirely disappeared, and its traces can still be detected even in the depiction of terrorists with a very different ideology.

The catastrophic imagination

Part of the explanation for this longevity lies in the literary fascination with violent anarchism that began at the end of the nineteenth century and continued well beyond it. In fin-de-siècle France, anarchism became fashionable in literary and artistic circles and a number of literary fellow-travellers took a vicarious satisfaction from the more extreme expressions of anarchist revolt, such as the poet Laurent Tailharde, who famously asked at a literary supper, in reference to Vaillant's attack on the French parliament, 'What do the victims matter, as long as the gesture is beautiful?' Tailharde was less appreciative of the beauty of the gesture when a bomb exploded in a restaurant where he was eating shortly afterwards and blinded him in one eye, but his frivolous statement was characteristic of a certain breed of intellectual, who saw the actions of primitive rebels such as Ravachol and Vaillant as a counterpoint to their own intellectual revolt.

Others, like Emile Zola, saw in violent anarchism a confirmation of their own gloomy premonitions of imminent social collapse and upheaval. Apocalyptic anarchist violence was a recurring theme in Zola's novels, from the nihilist Souvarine's destruction of the mine in *Germinal* to the sprawling *Paris*, in which a brilliant chemist invents an explosive powder and attempts to blow up the Basilica in Paris with 10,000 pilgrims inside it, in order to demonstrate the follies of militarism and promote world peace. Zola's fictional portrayal of anarchist violence indirectly influenced the most literary of anarchist bombers, Emile Henry, who paid tribute to the master himself at his trial, declaring that, 'At this moment of embittered struggle between the middle class and its enemies, I am almost tempted to say, with Souvarine in *Germinal*: "All discussions about the future are criminal, since they hinder pure and simple destruction and slow down the march of the revolution."'[18]

Henry could have found virtually identical words in more authentic texts by Nechaev or Bakunin and there is some irony in the fact that he referred to a fictional character created by a middle-class novelist in order to explain his actions. In his pre-World War I pamphlet 'Bourgeois Influences on Anarchism', the anarchist Luigi Fabri argued that men like Henry were attracted to anarchism precisely because of the distorted views of it put forward in the popular press and by bourgeois writers with no sympathy or connection with the anarchist movement. In Fabri's view, 'The desire to satisfy the public appetite for new and strange things brings novelists, journalists, and pseudo-scientists to invent a whirlwind of a thousand demons'.[19] Novelists, according to Fabri, were particularly inspired to write about anarchist violence, which 'even in its most tragic manifestations ... presents undeniable characteristics of originality and attractiveness.'[20]

These observations could have been applied to Joseph Conrad, Henry James or G. K. Chesterton. Conrad, the Edwardian gentleman and social pessimist, was not remotely sympathetic to anarchism and regarded both its utopian aspirations and its violence as equally absurd. At the same time he was fascinated by the subworld of police, informers and anarchists and wrote about anarchism on various occasions, not only in his masterpiece *The Secret Agent*, but in short stories. Conrad's material drew on real characters and events, from the French anarchist Martial Bourdin who blew himself up in Greenwich Park to the Johann Most-like anarchist in *The Informer*, and the appearance of Ravachol's accomplice 'Simon the Biscuit' in *The Anarchist – a Desperate Tale*.[21] Chesterton also wrote an anarchist novel, in his baroque fantasy *The Man who Was Thursday*, in which both the anarchist conspiracy directed by 'President Sunday' and the police chasing them turn out to be the same personnel.

For the bourgeois novelist, living an ordered and sedentary life in a writer's study, the possibility of chaos and disorder is always faintly intriguing and exciting. All these writers approached the subject of anarchist violence in different ways, but they shared a common recognition of a new historical phenomenon. Few of them had any real contact with anarchist circles and tended to focus on the bizarre and freakish figure of the anarchist bomber, whom they depicted in varying degrees of madness or tragic absurdity. The fascination with violent anarchism was also reflected in penny dreadfuls, popular novels and science fiction, such as E. Douglass Fawcett's *Hartmann the Anarchist*, subtitled *the Doom of a Great City* (1893), in which a band of anarchists assault London in an airship loaded with 'infernal machines', which they fly into Big Ben, bringing the tower toppling down and wreaking havoc on the city. In H. G. Wells's *The War in the Air* (1908) urban catastrophe is visited on New York, not by anarchists, but by an attack from the German Zeppelin fleet, whose airships 'smashed up the city as a child will shatter its cities of brick and mud. Below they left ruins and blazing conflagrations and heaped and scattered dead.'

These fantasies of universal destruction emerged at a period when these imaginary conflagrations were becoming real scientific possibilities, as a result of the development of modern weapons. Even the term 'infernal machine' suggested a combination of diabolical intent and scientific possibility in which, as one British police officer warned in 1898 'the world is nowadays threatened by new forces, which if recklessly unchained, may some day wreak universal destruction'.[22] The catastrophic scenarios in popular fiction reflected these fears and also enhanced them. Then, as now, industrial civilisation was felt by its inhabitants to be a fragile and vulnerable construction, and the putative figure of the terrorist madman acted as a distorting mirror in which societies could glimpse the awful possibility of their own violent collapse. Not for the last time, this fearful gaze tended to overlook the destructive forces that bourgeois civilisation already contained within itself. In 1914 these forces were finally unleashed, and the result was a conflagration that proved to be infinitely more destructive than anarchist dynamite.

'Bold fenian men'

The new tactics of revolutionary combat were not restricted to the left. In the same period the methods of 'uncivilised warfare' were adopted for the first time as a weapon of Irish republicanism, when the Irish Revolutionary Brotherhood, more commonly known as the Fenians or the Fenian Brotherhood, began to carry out attacks on the British mainland, following a failed attempt to promote insurrection in Ireland in 1867. In December that year, a group of Fenians attempted to rescue a Fenian prisoner from Clerkenwell prison by placing a gunpowder charge outside the prison wall, but the explosion blew apart a row of adjoining tenements, killing twelve people and injuring another 120. The devastation caused by this explosion of 'Fenian fire' was the result of a miscalculated charge rather than the onset of a terrorist bombing campaign, but it nevertheless caused considerable alarm in Britain and fuelled an upsurge in anti-Irish sentiment. Even Karl Marx, despite his sympathy for the Irish cause, condemned the bombing in a letter to Engels in which he predicted that 'The London masses, who have shown great sympathy for Ireland, will be made wild by it and driven into the arms of the government party. One cannot expect the London proletarians to allow themselves to be blown up in honour of the Fenian emissaries.'[23]

Despite the general outrage, the execution the following year of Michael Barrett, one of the men responsible, brought unexpected propaganda benefits to the Fenians. The execution was the last public hanging in the United Kingdom and the London *Daily News* lamented the fact that the crowd's 'bastard pride in his animal courage and the brutal delight that he died game made the law and its ministers seem to them to be the real murderers, and Barrett to be a martyred man'. Though the bombing was criticised by sections of the Fenian movement, a number of US-based Fenian organisations advocated further attacks on the British mainland, against a background of growing anti-landlord unrest in rural Ireland itself. The most prominent advocates of such tactics were the Chicago-based secret society the Clan na Gael – the family of the Gaels and the fiery exiled Fenian leader Jeremiah O'Donovan Rossa, who advocated the formation of a group of 'Skirmishers' that would 'strike England year after year'. Like the anarchists, the Fenian factions saw Alfred Nobel's invention as a substitute for their political and military weakness in Ireland itself.

In 1881, Rossa's 'United Irishmen' began their skirmishing campaign with a dynamite explosion outside Salford infantry barracks that killed a seven-year-old boy and wounded three passers by. The Clan na Gael followed suit with dynamite bombings of their own, in a campaign that became known as the Dynamite War. These bombings were mostly aimed at symbolic targets, such as prominent buildings, statues and monuments, and claimed few casualties, but they nevertheless came as a shock to Victorian Britain. In addition to the bombing of Scotland Yard and the empty House of Commons chamber, the Fenians also carried out dynamite attacks on the London Underground. On 30 October 1883, two attacks took place in a single night, including a bomb attack on a third-class carriage near Edgware Road station, where a far more lethal suicide bombing would take place more than a century later.

No one was killed in these attacks, but several passengers were injured and *The Times* observed that the new underground tunnels offered 'vast possibilities of destruction'.[24] The British government had previously regarded bombings and assassinations as continental diseases born of bad government and resolutely opposed pressure from European governments to change Britain's asylum laws and deport suspected anarchists. Now Britain found itself facing a bombing campaign organised from the United States, by groups that the home secretary, William Harcourt, denounced as the 'enemies of the human race' comparable to the Russian nihilists. In addition, these activities were carried on with open support from the Irish 'dynamite press', such as O'Donovan Rossa's *United Irishmen*, which carried an advertisement on 11 February 1885 offering a reward for the body of the Prince of Wales, dead or alive. British intelligence sources in the United States began to send increasingly alarming reports back to England regarding forthcoming deliveries of dynamite and assassination plots against the royal family, including a plan to blow up Queen Victoria using battery-operated dynamite bombs concealed in coffins at Windsor Chapel.

Much of this was rumour and fantasy, but some stories were deliberate fabrications from within the British political establishment, which sought to use the Fenian bombing campaign to undermine Charles Parnell, the most formidable constitutional nationalist politician of his era.[25] In 1881 Parnell and some 800-odd members of the tenant farmers Land League were arrested and imprisoned on the orders of the Irish Secretary, W. E. Forster. And in May 1882 a previously unknown secret society called the Invincibles carried out one of the most shocking acts of Fenian terrorism, when five of their members stabbed to death Forster's successor as Chief Secretary for Ireland, Lord Frederick Cavendish, and his under-secretary, T. H. Burke, in Phoenix Park, Dublin.

The Invincibles consisted of no more than forty members led by a central committee of four, none of whom fitted the English magazine caricatures

of the ape-like Fenian, armed with bomb and knife. All four were patriotic Dublin citizens of impeccable reputation, members of the urban lower
middle classes from which the Fenian movement drew much of its support.
The British public reaction to these brutal killings was one of outrage and
revulsion, but when five members of the group were hung in Dublin, crowds
gathered outside the prison gates and acclaimed them as martyrs, who had
killed and died in the name of Irish freedom

In 1887 *The Times* published a series of letters purporting to have been
written by Parnell known as the 'Pigott letters', which appeared to endorse
the killings. Parnell was eventually exonerated when a parliamentary commission revealed them to be forgeries. In the short term the murders were
overshadowed by the intensification of the Fenian dynamite campaign on
the mainland which targeted *The Times*, the London Underground and the
empty House of Commons chamber. Though Henry James saw these events
as another sign of the British empire's approaching doom, the dynamite
war was minimal in comparison with subsequent IRA bombings, and its
impact on British public opinion was negligible, causing Sir Algernon West
to observe, 'It is very curious how calmly people take these outrages as
matters of course.'[26]

One of its long-term consequences was the formation of a new detective
section in 1883 called the Special Irish Branch, which later became the Special
Branch. But the only legislative response to the dynamite war was the 1883
Explosives Act, which obliged those in possession of dynamite to prove that
they were using it for a legitimate purpose. By 1885 the dynamite war had
petered out, as Parnell's constitutional nationalism became the dominant
force in Irish republican politics. Though sporadic Fenian bombing campaigns on the British mainland continued into the next century, it was not
until after 1916, in the aftermath of another failed Irish uprising, that their
heirs would unleash a campaign of revolutionary terrorism inside Ireland
itself, with a ferocity and intensity that would finally go some way to realising the seventeenth-century Irish revolutionary Wolfe Tone's exhortation
to 'break the connection' with Britain. Their tactics would change the way
revolutions were fought and establish a new method of political warfare that
would prove itself increasingly ubiquitous in the coming century.

Terror and Resistance

> He who fires in ambush on German soldiers, who are only doing their duty here, and who are safeguarding the maintenance of a normal life, is not a patriot but a cowardly assassin and the enemy of all decent people.
>
> Nazi proclamation, France, September 1941[1]

By the end of World War I the bombs of Ravachol and Emile Henry had largely faded into historical memory, so much so that in 1933 the *Encyclopedia of the Social Sciences* published an article by Jacob Hardman which argued that terrorism, in the sense that the nineteenth-century Russians had envisioned it, had become 'outmoded as a revolutionary method' in the twentieth century. According to Hardman, terrorism had been overtaken by new political developments, such as 'the rising mass movement and the spread of nation-wide economic and political strikes'. These predictions turned out to be premature. It was true that in the inter-war period, terrorism as a tactic of revolutionary violence was largely overshadowed by the re-emergence of the original French revolutionary concept of terror, in describing the actions of the twentieth-century dictatorships and police states in Russia and Germany. The Bolsheviks described their counter-revolutionary purges during the Russian Civil War as the 'Red Terror' in an explicit reference to the Jacobin Terror. Like the Jacobins, the Bolsheviks regarded the methods of the Cheka as a means of defending the revolution from its enemies. Under Stalin, the use of terror was taken to unprecedented extremes for very different reasons. In 1937 the assassination of the Bolshevik leader Sergei Kirov, almost certainly carried out on Stalin's orders, prompted one of the most horrific episodes of state terrorism in history, in which millions of Russians were killed or imprisoned. In Germany in 1933 an arson attack on the Reichstag by a mentally unbalanced Dutch Marxist was similarly used by the Nazis as a pretext for the introduction of emergency powers for 'the protection of the State and its citizens' which effectively eliminated the last vestiges of Weimar democracy.

Acts of unofficial terrorism also preoccupied European governments, particularly in the Balkans, where right-wing nationalist groups were responsible for a series of high-profile assassinations, including the shooting of King Alexander of Yugoslavia by Croat and Macedonian nationalists in Marseilles in 1934. In 1937 the League of Nations attempted to draw up a 'Convention for the Prevention and Punishment of Terrorism'. This was the first international attempt to elaborate a common response to terrorism, which the convention defined as 'criminal facts directed against a State and of which the goal or nature is to cause terror towards determined personalities, groups of people or the population'.

These 'criminal facts' included sabotage, assassination, the manufacture and use of explosives and the procurement of weapons. In its attempts to define terrorism as a new form of supra-national crime the convention was in effect reiterating what were already illegal acts in virtually every country in the world and it was never ratified. Attempts to achieve an international legal and moral consensus on what constitutes terrorism have often foundered on the same reefs that undermined the League of Nations convention. In societies enjoying a modicum of social and political harmony, murder, sabotage and arson are universally regarded as 'criminal facts'. But most groups who carry out such acts for political purposes do so because they believe themselves to be acting in a context in which the law is either illegitimate, irrelevant or an instrument of domination. In these circumstances even the most brutal 'criminal facts' may be regarded by their protagonists as legitimate acts of resistance or war. This was the case in Russia during the nineteenth century and afterwards, where the People's Will and their descendants regarded the criminality of the regime they wished to overthrow as justification for their own actions. The Irish Fenians also claimed legitimacy for similar reasons. In both cases, revolutionary terrorism was a form of political combat employed by a small minority in periods when the revolutionary movements they wished to represent were weak. Had terrorism consisted only of heroic acts of propaganda by deed carried out by isolated groups or individuals, Hardman's predictions might well have been borne out. But the category of violence that we call terrorism has not always failed, nor has it always been restricted to spectacular exemplary assassinations. At certain times in modern history, the 'technique' of terrorism has been used not by an isolated or marginal minority, but by a wider and more representative movement. If this technique was not able to inspire social revolution, as the nineteenth-century anarchists once hoped, it could, in certain circumstances, obtain more limited political objectives. One of the first examples of such success occurred in Ireland, where revolutionary terrorism contributed for the first time to the creation of a new state. In doing so it set an example of revolutionary violence that would inspire numerous other anti-colonial movements across the world, and ensure the continuation of nineteenth-century revolutionary terrorism into the twentieth century, and beyond.

The irish model

In 1916 a former Fenian and a member of the Irish Volunteers named Michael Collins narrowly escaped execution for his part in the failed Easter Rising in Dublin. From the British point of view this proved to be a costly oversight. Collins was determined to break the republican tradition of glorious defeat and used his considerable organisational talents to construct a fighting force that would avoid open military confrontations with the imperial enemy and use guerrilla tactics, cunning and subterfuge. Spurred by the electoral victory of Sinn Fein in December 1918 and the proclamation of Irish independence by the illegally constituted Dublin Parliament, the Daíl Eireann, Collins organised a new clandestine fighting force called the Irish Republican Army (IRA) and set out to make 'regular government impossible, and the cost of holding the country so great that the British would be compelled to withdraw'.

An IRA unit carried out its first operation in January 1919, ambushing a convoy taking gelignite to a quarry and killing two of its police escorts. Over the next twelve months IRA 'flying columns' of between fifteen and thirty volunteers attacked Royal Irish Constabulary barracks, burned down court houses, tax offices, and coastguard stations and ambushed policemen and soldiers. By the end of the year the IRA had carried out nearly 3,000 raids on police and army barracks, and killed 200 policemen and soldiers, in a vicious hit-and-run campaign in which policemen were ambushed on country roads or shot and stabbed in the back in city streets by assassins who melted into the surrounding population or rode away on bicycles.

These tactics became known as 'ditch murder' in British military circles and they shocked both British politicians and the public. Faced with what prime minister David Lloyd George called 'a real murder gang, dominating the country and terrorising it', the British government took the fateful decision to counter the IRA's tactics by creating a special paramilitary constabulary made up of demobilised soldiers, which became known in Ireland by the derisory nickname of the Black and Tans, after the pack of hounds used in the Limerick hunt and its special uniform of khaki tunic, tam-o'-shanter berets and black leather belts and holsters. Together the Black and Tans and an auxiliary unit of the Royal Irish Constabulary known as the

'Auxies' set out to 'terrorise the terrorists' and make Ireland 'a hell for rebels to live in'. The two units soon acquired an unrivalled reputation for violence and thuggery, as they rampaged through towns and villages burning shops and creameries and houses and carrying out beatings and summary executions in response to actions by the IRA.

To much of the British public and press, the methods used to suppress the IRA were as disturbing as the methods used by the IRA themselves. Though the British government tried to present such actions as unauthorised excesses or lapses of discipline, the policy of reprisals received tacit and even direct official approval. These tactics played into Collins's hands, drawing new recruits to the ranks of the IRA and tarnishing Britain's image abroad, to the point when even the jingoist *Daily Mail* worried that 'half the world is coming to feel that our Government is condoning vendetta and turning a blind eye upon the execution of lawless reprisals'. Unlike the People's Will, neither Collins nor Sinn Fein needed to instigate a social revolution in order to win an outright victory, but merely to sustain the level of mayhem and disorder until the price of suppressing it became more than Britain was willing to pay.

What successes the British did enjoy against the IRA were mainly derived from accurate intelligence information gathered through its undercover agents. But on 21 November 1920, the IRA counter-intelligence assassination team known as the 'the Squad' dealt a shattering blow to the British intelligence network when its members killed eleven British agents in Dublin within a half-hour period. The killings were carefully planned and clinically executed, as the agents were picked off one by one in their rooms and lodging houses. One was killed climbing out of a window; others were shot in their pyjamas even as their wives pleaded for mercy. Privately the British government recognised the annihilation of its Dublin intelligence network as a major victory for the IRA, but the actual role of the dead soldiers was concealed from the British public, who were led to believe that they were regular officers murdered off the battlefield.

As a result, the killings were presented as further evidence of the IRA's murderous gangsterism. The soldiers were given a state funeral at Westminster Cathedral, where a furious reporter from the *Evening News* imagined one of their assassins 'with the blood reeking on his hands and stench of foul murder rising from his heart. I wonder if this man trembles and grows faint as he knows secretly that the furies, the dark maidens with serpents twining in their hair, and black blood dripping from their eyes, are following him and hunting him, hounding him on to an awful bloody end'.[2] The gothic imagery reflected the novelty of Collins's form of warfare. The *Manchester Guardian* took a similar view, concluding that the IRA killers of an elderly informer had 'debauched their minds with base casuistry of a "state of war" which makes them a curse to any cause they pretend to honour'. But the vilification of the IRA and its methods was not universal. When Terence MacSwiney, the Lord Mayor of Cork and an IRA member, went on hunger strike following his imprisonment, there were demonstrations of support across the world. MacSwiney died on 25 October 1920 but not before observing that, 'It is not those who can inflict the most, but those who endure the most who will conquer.'

This was the essence of the IRA's campaign. As brutal and unorthodox as their methods were, Collins and his men nevertheless regarded themselves as a clandestine army fighting a different kind of war. Using a rationale that has been invoked on many subsequent occasions, one former member of Collins's Squad described himself and his colleagues as 'soldiers doing our duty', adding how, 'I often went in and said a little prayer for the people that we'd shot'. Even after the mechanised mass slaughter of World War I, wars fought between armies in uniform on a battlefield were still considered a more inherently ethical and acceptable form of violence than the shooting of an 'off-duty' soldier in his pyjamas. Collins was unrepentant about having 'put out the eyes of the British' intelligence network, but nevertheless insisted that, 'we conducted the conflict, difficult as it was, with the unequal terms imposed on us by the enemy, as far as possible, according to the rules of war'.[3]

The former postman was a sensitive and even sentimental man, described by one married woman to whom he was romantically linked as 'a man with a great and tender heart, who loved the beautiful in nature and in art as far as he had time or opportunity to find it'.[4] As a military leader, however, he was implacable and ruthless, conducting the IRA's campaign like a general on a battlefield. But even though the British government portrayed both Collins and his organisation as brutes and criminals, its officials knew better. As Lieutenant-General Sir Henry Lawson observed:

> The Irish Republican Army seems to be particularly free from ruffians of the professional type, and the killings of police and others, sometimes under circumstances which evoke horror, were almost certainly done by members of the IRA acting under military orders – young men imbued with no personal feeling against their victims, with no crimes to their record, and probably then shedding blood for the first time in their lives … Behind their organisation is

the spirit of a nation – of a nation which is certainly not in favour of murder, but which, on the whole, sympathises with them and believes that the IRA are fighting for the cause of the Irish people.[5]

By the end of 1920 the British government had begun to recognise that the IRA was supported by a broad sector of the Irish population and in June 1921 Lloyd George agreed to 'shake hands with murder' and enter into negotiations with Sinn Fein as an alternative to a massive further deployment of troops. At the negotiating table Collins was out-manoeuvred and forced to accept the partition of Ireland, a settlement which provoked a civil war within the IRA itself and paved the way for further violence to come. In 1922 Collins was killed by his former IRA comrades in the same kind of ambush that his men had used so successfully against the British. Nevertheless, his achievement did not go unnoticed. Despite the huge military disparity between the opposing forces, an organisation of 'ruffians' had fought the most powerful empire in the history of the world to a stalemate and obtained at least some of its political objectives, by waging a campaign of assassination, sabotage and guerrilla warfare that defied conventional definitions of warfare. It was an example that was to produce numerous imitators, perhaps the most surprising of whom was Her Majesty's Government itself.

Resistance

Even the most powerful nations will observe the rules of conventional war only as long as they have some chance of winning through conventional means. For all the moral opprobrium heaped on Collins and his 'murder gang' by the British government, the IRA's method of warfare had a decisive influence on the British involvement with the European resistance organisations during World War II. As early as 1938–9 the British General Staff had commissioned pamphlets such as 'The Art of Guerrilla Warfare', 'The Partisan Leader's Handbook' and 'The Housewife's Guide to High Explosives' in anticipation of rearguard operations in Europe. The rapid German victories in the first months of the war placed Britain in a situation unprecedented in its history, in which conventional military options in Europe were impossible. In July 1940, the new Labour minister of economic warfare Hugh Dalton wrote to Prime Minister Churchill calling for the formation of a 'democratic international' in Europe that would 'organise movements in enemy occupied territory comparable to the Sinn Fein movement in Ireland, to the Chinese guerrillas now operating against Japan, to the Spanish irregulars

... We must use many different methods, including industrial and military sabotage, labour agitation and strikes, continuous propaganda, terrorist acts against traitors and German leaders, boycotts and strikes.'[6]

Churchill gave his consent, telling Dalton to 'set Europe ablaze'. The result was the creation of the Special Operations Executive (SOE), two of whose leading officers, J. C. F. Holland and Lieutenant-Colonel Collin Gubbins, had served in Ireland during the Troubles and observed the tactics of the IRA at first hand. The decision by Her Majesty's Government to adopt the techniques of Collins's 'murder gang' met with some opposition in more orthodox military circles, whose leaders, as Gubbins later recalled, were 'still fighting the last war but one, and dreamed of the Charge of the Light Brigade'.[7] Such reservations were soon ignored, however, as SOE provided bombs and explosives training to the European resistance and parachuted agents into Europe to carry out ambushes, acts of sabotage and assassinations alongside partisan groups and resistance organisations, in what would later be described in other contexts as 'state-sponsored terrorism'. The Nazi response to this unprecedented explosion of irregular warfare was an equally unprecedented policy of massive reprisals against the civilian population. To the German occupation forces in France resistance groups were 'terrorists' and *'francs-tireurs'* rather than legitimate combatants, who would therefore be liable to the death penalty when captured.

In September 1941 the German military command in France went further with the introduction of the notorious Hostages Code, which stipulated the mass execution of civilian hostages in response to any act of violence from 'communist or anarchist terror gangs'. Similar principles were enacted throughout the countries under Nazi occupation. In Czechoslovakia the villages of Lidice and Lazarky were razed to the ground and their inhabitants killed or deported in response to the assassination of the Protector of Bohemia and Moravia, Reinhard Heydrich, by resistance fighters.[8]

After the war such actions were rightly regarded as war crimes by the victorious allies, yet there was no doubt that the actions carried out by the resistance did not conform to the rules of land war adopted by the 1907 Hague Peace Conference. Across Europe the resistance killed German soldiers, informers or collaborators with whatever weapons were available, from bombs in restaurants and cinemas frequented by German soldiers, to individual assassinations with the gun, the knife or wires strung across roads to decapitate motorcycle riders. In German military propaganda, all these actions were the work of criminals, terrorists and unlawful combatants, who were not subject to the rules of war. 'Liberation by the army of crime!' proclaimed anti-resistance posters showing pictures of Jewish or foreign maquisards with photographs of civilian victims and derailed trains. Even Klaus Barbie, the 'butcher of Lyons', justified the random murder of French civilians in reprisal for the shooting of two German soldiers at Lyons railway station on the grounds that 'they shouldn't have shot our soldiers in the back. It was against all the laws.'[9]

Coming from a notorious Nazi torturer and member of an occupying army which killed some 29,000 French hostages during the course of the war, it is difficult to feel much sympathy with Barbie's indignation. By the end of the war the concept of 'resistance' was regarded both in Europe and beyond as a morally unassailable right and an admirable manifestation of patriotic heroism. Within a few years, however, many former resistance fighters would find the roles reversed, as they found themselves fighting insurgencies in the European colonies. In some cases these rebellions were led by men and women who hailed the resistance as a tactical model and a moral inspiration. To the armies engaged in fighting them, however, the members of these organisations were always terrorists. And it is here, in the chain of battlefields that stretched from Jerusalem to Nicosia, from the jungles of Malaya to the slopes of Mount Kenya and the South African townships, that these different terrorisms first began to merge into a single recognisable phenomenon.

Propaganda

At the beginning of Ian Fleming's *From Russia With Love*, the Russian counterespionage officer General G. presents his colleagues with a triumphant summary of recent Soviet achievements against the Western democracies. All this is received with satisfaction by the SMERSH 'moguls of death':

> There were smiles of pleasure and pride round the table. What a brilliant policy! What fools we are making of them in the West!
>
> 'At the same time,' continued General G., himself smiling thinly at the pleasure he had caused, 'we continue to forge everywhere stealthily ahead – revolution in Morocco, arms to Egypt, friendship with Yugoslavia, trouble in Cyprus, riots in Turkey, strikes in England, great political gains in France – there is no front in the world on which we are not advancing.'

Fleming's cartoonish depiction of Soviet methods and intentions was a fairly exact reflection of the way the world looked to Western policymakers when the novel was published in 1956. From the earliest days of the Cold War 'terrorism' was frequently depicted in the Western world as an instrument of 'international communism'. In his 1947 speech which articulated the Truman Doctrine for the first time, US president Harry S. Truman appealed to Congress for economic and military aid to the Greek government in order to help it defend itself against 'the terrorist activities of several thousand armed men, led by communists'. At the time the Greek government was widely reported to be engaged in the systematic torture, murder and imprisonment not only of communists but of liberal and republican opponents. But the notion that 'terrorism' was a specifically communist phenomenon was reproduced in numerous conflicts during the Cold War, particularly in the colonial world, where 'terrorist' became the standard label for any anti-colonial revolutionary movement. In Malaya in the 1950s the British combined both concepts in their designation of Malayan Races Liberation Army (MRLA) as communist terrorists or 'CTs'. In the early period of the conflict posters of dead guerrillas were placed around the country which were virtually identical to those used by the Nazi occupation forces in Europe:

THESE MEN WERE COMMUNIST TERRORISTS

THEY CHOSE TO LIVE BY VIOLENCE, EXTORTION, MURDER

THEY MET THE FATE OF ALL THAT DO LIKEWISE

The link between terrorism and communism was often made even when communist involvement in terrorist events was conspicuously absent. Visiting Saigon during the French Indochina war in 1951 Graham Greene found a siege-like atmosphere, where elegant French cafés were fronted with metal grilles to protect their clients from grenade attacks and where bombs concealed in bicycles exploded at random in the streets. The majority of these bombings were the work of a renegade Catholic general, General Thé, whom the CIA considered to be a potential alternative to communist and French rule in Vietnam. Greene was in Saigon in January 1952, when a massive bomb exploded in the main square of the city, killing dozens of people. Even after General Thé claimed responsibility for the bombing, the *New York Times* accused the Vietminh of responsibility, and *Life* magazine published a famous photograph of a mutilated rickshaw driver as an example of the barbarity of Ho Chi Minh and the communists. Greene later recalled the same incident in his 1955 indictment of American foreign policy in Vietnam *The Quiet American*, where he controversially suggested that

General Thé had received the material for the bomb from American intelligence operatives.

Greene's parable about the naivety and cynicism of American foreign policy was a rare departure from what was already becoming an established consensus. In rebellions where evidence of communist manipulation was unconvincing or non-existent, counter-insurgency propaganda tended to concentrate on the methods of its opponents rather than their objectives. Thus in 1956 the British Colonial Office took the unusual step of publishing extracts from the captured diaries of the insurgent EOKA (National Organisation of Cypriot Fighters) leader Colonel Georgios Grivas, together with an appendix listing 'the brutal and cowardly crimes that have been committed in Cyprus ... in order to show to what ugly and bestial reality fine words and exhortations have been translated.'

A similar booklet was published by the French administration in Algeria in 1957 entitled *Aspects véritables de la rébellion algérienne,* known as 'the Green Book', containing photographs of victims of nationalist violence. As in Cyprus the booklet was intended to refute the claims made by the Front de Liberation National (FLN) that it was fighting 'a just cause, a humanitarian cause' with graphic images from the full panoply of Algerian horror, showing children with their vocal cords ripped out, castrations, mutilations and throat-cuttings. In white settler societies that already saw themselves as the torchbearers of civilised values, such violence was often presented as a reversion to native savagery. The notion that anti-colonial 'terrorism' represented an atavistic withdrawal from civilisation was not entirely removed from the nineteenth-century perception of anarchist violence as a harbinger of social implosion and collapse, but it was also a reflection of already existing racial attitudes. In 1954 a Kenyan Special Branch report described the Mau Mau as 'a terrorist organisation composed not of ordinary humans fighting for a cause, but of primitive beasts who have forsaken all moral codes'. The same language was echoed decades later by the white regime in Rhodesia during its long war with black insurgents, when a 1978 Rhodesian radio broadcast declared:

> It is doubtful if the terrorist, or his leader, has any political objective worthy of the name, outside the exercise of raw, naked power. They want power, and they will do anything to win power. These men are armed thugs, criminals bent on taking Africa back to another dark age, when it was known as the Dark Continent. To dignify them with names like 'freedom fighters' and 'guerrillas' is to afford them a status they do not and will never deserve.[10]

The chief of the Rhodesian armed forces was General Peter Wall, a former SAS officer during the Malayan emergency. Under Wall's leadership the Rhodesian military applied many of the techniques used by the British in Malaya, creating its own psychological operations unit and employing advertising agencies to churn out leaflets, comics and radio broadcasts aimed at the civilian population and the guerrillas themselves. In Rhodesian army jargon black guerrillas were always terrorists, or 'terrs', and killing them was described as 'slotting terrs' or 'slotting gooks'. Like the British, the Rhodesian army showered leaflets on insurgent areas showing photographs of guerrilla corpses, or 'floppies', to demoralise the enemy. Other leaflets were aimed at the guerrillas' civilian supporters, with crude comic-book drawings of smiling terrorists standing over their bleeding victims, bearing messages such as, 'Terror and death is the way of the communist terrorists in Rhodesia'. The Smith regime also employed a mobile cinema unit which broadcast propaganda films in villages, including one film entitled *War on Terror*.

Similar techniques were employed in other colonial conflicts, as propaganda leaflets alternated with bombs, helicopter assaults and search-and-destroy operations. Whatever their particular racial or cultural characteristics, the propaganda image of the terrorist tended to exhibit the same universal characteristics. He is sadistic, ruthless, cowardly and deluded. He is a false prophet, promising freedom and liberation when his ultimate goal is tyranny. He is often against Christianity and always against civilisation. He is an agent of chaos, a gangster and a criminal, an alien presence from outside the community. Whereas colonial governments always rule by democratic consensus, the terrorist relies on intimidation and fear to compensate for the fact that he represents only a tiny minority.

The overall effect of this propaganda was to present 'the terrorist' as a subhuman creature worthy only of extermination. Propaganda has many different audiences and through endless repetition can sometimes achieve the status of accepted fact. If the identikit portrait of the 'universal terrorist' was aimed at the potential supporters of the insurgent cause within the country where the conflict was taking place, it also aimed to win over public opinion in the wider world. And as the methods of revolutionary violence continued to reproduce themselves, it often appeared to the metropolitan public in Europe as though a new fanaticism had mysteriously entered the world, in which the most brutal acts were carried out in pursuit of the noblest objectives.

The new barbarians

One of the earliest and most dramatic manifestations of the new violence occurred on 22 July 1946, when the Zionist underground organisation the Irgun Zvai Leumi (National Military Organisation) blew up the King David Hotel in Jerusalem, which housed the British military HQ in Palestine as well as the civilian government known as the Secretariat. The explosion reduced six storeys of the building and twenty-eight offices to rubble. Ninety-one people were killed, forty-one of them Arabs, and scores more seriously wounded. More than half the dead were low-ranking clerical workers, secretarial staff and hotel employees. At that time it was the most devastating single terrorist atrocity in history, and it was greeted with universal condemnation, even from prominent Zionist leaders and publications.

The Irgun insisted that the hotel was a legitimate political and military target and that the British had deliberately ignored a telephone warning to evacuate the building – a claim that the British denied. The debates about who was responsible and whether casualties were intended would go on for years. But for all the moral condemnation it aroused, the destruction of the hotel was a huge blow to British prestige in Palestine, which offered no comparable target in return. In effect, the bombing was an early example of what would later be called 'asymmetric warfare'. The following year the Irgun provided what seemed to be further evidence of its barbarous cruelty in retaliation for the death sentences given to three of their members, kidnapping two British sergeants whom they threatened to hang if the sentences were not rescinded. When the Irgun members were executed, the drama reached a predictably macabre conclusion, as the Irgun hanged both sergeants from an olive tree and booby-trapped the corpses, seriously injuring some of the soldiers who came to take them down.

The Irgun claimed that its executions were no worse than those carried out by the British, but few members of the British public were prepared to recognise such symmetry when confronted with the photographs of the two hooded soldiers hanging from the olive tree which appeared on the front pages of British newspapers. 'I always felt it was somehow not fair on the British that so few "terrorists" had horns, wild unruly hair and gleaming fanatical eyes,' recalled the South African-born Irgun fundraiser Doris Katz, who described her first meeting with Menachem Begin, the Irgun's military commander and the British Public Enemy Number 1, washing nappies in his underground hideout.

In Katz's opinion, Begin 'made war ... not for the sake of violence, but in the same way as a surgeon, with ruthless kindness, cauterises a festering growth, or amputates a rotting limb in order to save a precious life'.[11] Colonel Grivas, the scourge of the British in Cyprus, similarly rejected suggestions that EOKA had been guilty of 'unnecessary cruelty', insisting in his memoirs that:

> The truth is that our form of war, in which a few hundred fell in four years, was far more selective than most, and I speak as one who has seen battlefields covered with dead. We did not strike, like the bomber, at random. We shot only British servicemen who would have killed us if they could have fired first, and civilians who were traitors or intelligence agents. To shoot down your enemies in the street may be unprecedented, but I was looking for results, not precedents … All war is cruel and the only way to win against superior forces is by ruse and trickery; you can no more afford to make a difference between striking in front or behind than you can between employing rifles and howitzers.[12]

The idea that terrorism is a form of warfare, brutal in the short term but less costly in terms of overall casualties than conventional war, is one of the most common arguments offered in its defence. Grivas was a particularly skilled and ruthless exponent of the new methods, evading thousands of British troops for three years in a small island that offered little natural protection, while continuing to direct a campaign of guerrilla ambushes, bombings and assassinations that the British were never able to suppress. Though the majority of EOKA attacks were directed against soldiers or police, a number of its actions strained any accepted definition of a 'military' target, such as the shooting of two British servicemen's wives while they were shopping with their children in a supermarket near Famagusta, one of whom was killed and the other seriously wounded. Following the attack, hundreds of outraged British troops left their barracks and rampaged through Famagusta, assaulting any Greeks they could find, thereby alienating the population still further.

The shootings were almost certainly intended to provoke precisely this reaction. The individuals who were prepared to carry out such acts were certainly ruthless, and some of them may well have been cruel. But their actions were carried out in accordance with a clear political strategy that was shared by many other organisations of their era. Both Begin and Grivas were products of an era of unprecedented international savagery, in which the rules that supposedly governed conventional warfare were routinely disregarded through new military innovations such as the introduction of strategic bombing.

During World War II both sides accepted that civilian population centres could be targeted in order to destroy the morale of the enemy. Whereas in World War I the majority of casualties were soldiers killed on the battlefield, more than half the casualties in World War II were non-combatants. The transformation was not simply the result of the increased destructive power of military technology. The decision to bomb civilian population centres such as London, Tokyo or Dresden was a strategic *choice*, whose proponents argued that maximum violence in the short term would 'save lives' in the long term. This was the rationale used by President Truman to justify the use of the atom bomb at Hiroshima, when he told the American people on 12 August 1945 that the bombing had been carried out 'in order to shorten the agony of war'. The other justification for strategic bombing stemmed from the belief in the essential rightness of the Allied cause itself. As Michael Walzer has argued in *Just and Unjust Wars*, the moral evaluation of these tactics was often determined by a 'sliding scale – the more justice, the more right' according to which 'The greater the justice of my cause, the more rules I can violate for the sake of the cause.'[13]

Many, perhaps the majority of 'terrorist' organisations have made exactly the same defence of their own actions. But if the broader moral justifications were often similar to those of the governments they were fighting, the strategic conception of violence drew heavily on the nineteenth-century revolutionary tradition. As Begin wrote in *The Revolt*, in language strikingly reminiscent of Kravchinsky:

> The very existence of an underground, which oppression, hangings, torture and deportations, fail to crush or to weaken must, in the end, undermine the prestige of the colonial regime that lives by the legend of its omnipotence. Every attack which it fails to prevent is a blow to its standing. Even if the attack does not succeed, it makes a dent in that prestige, and that dent widens into a crack which is extended with every succeeding attack.[14]

Like Michael Collins before him, Begin saw that Britain could not be defeated militarily. But he also recognised the political weakness of the colonial government at a time when crisis in Palestine had become the subject of international attention and Israel resembled 'a glass house' into which 'the World was looking with ever-increasing interest and could see most of what was happening inside'. In this context, according to Begin, 'arms were our means of attack; the transparency of the "glass" was our shield of defence.'[15] Though Begin does not say so, the same transparency also magnified the rebels' achievements, since Britain could not use all-out military force against the Irgun without undermining its political position still further.

In this context even actions with no obvious military significance, such as the tit-for-tat flogging of British soldiers, made the colonial administration seem powerless and ineffective, while any overreaction by the security forces played into the hands of the Zionist propaganda machine. The Irgun's campaign was not the only reason for the British withdrawal from Palestine in 1948, but it was certainly a significant factor. Similar methods were used in Cyprus, where between 200 and 300 EOKA fighters eventually sucked in some 40,000 British troops, who responded to EOKA provocations with the usual range of searches, roadblocks, floggings, curfews, internment and executions, all of which, as Grivas later noted with satisfaction, 'might have been deliberately designed to drive the population into our arms'.

As in other colonial conflicts, such as Vietnam and Algeria, EOKA carried out exemplary killings of informers and pro-British officials amongst the Greek Cypriot population in order to establish itself as a 'parallel hierarchy' to rival the colonial administration. All these actions enhanced the aura of power and implacability that surrounded Grivas and his organisation. But revolutionary movements that rely solely on terror rarely succeed. For all its brutality, EOKA would not have brought about a British withdrawal from Cyprus had its objectives not coincided with those of a substantial majority of the Greek Cypriot population, who supported the organisation and engaged in strikes and demonstrations of their own against British rule.

To men like Begin, their methods were justified by their military weakness and by the transcendental nature of the cause itself. The same man who later routinely referred to the PLO as 'terrorists' and 'two-legged beasts' was sensitive to accusations of terrorism himself and frequently uses the word with indignation or heavy-handed irony, asking 'what has a struggle for the dignity of man, against oppression and subjugation, to do with the word "terrorism"?' In 1974 Yasser Arafat subjected the term to the same scrutiny in his historic address to the United Nations, claiming:

> The difference between the revolutionary and the terrorist lies in the reason for which each fights. For whoever stands by a just cause and fights for the freedom and liberation of his land from the invaders, the settlers and the colonialists, cannot possibly be called terrorist; otherwise the American people in their struggle for liberation from the British colonialists would have been called terrorists, the European resistance against the Nazis would be terrorism, the struggle of the Asian, African and Latin American peoples would also be

terrorism, and many of you who are in this Assembly Hall were considered terrorists.[16]

Arafat was certainly correct in his assessment of his audience. But in rejecting the label of terrorist, both the PLO leader and Begin were essentially aiming their arguments at a propaganda caricature that was as removed from reality as their own invocation of the heroic freedom fighter. For the cliché that 'one man's terrorist is another man's freedom fighter' is not the contradiction it seems to be. The apparent dichotomy depends on the retrospective tendency to mythologise the former, while passing over the more squalid means through which freedom is sometimes achieved.

Those who regard men like Begin, Grivas and Arafat as terrorists tend to emphasise the means, while those who see them as freedom fighters emphasise the cause they fought for. Both presentations drift easily into propaganda on the one hand and self-deception on the other. To the 'terrorist' all forms of violence are equally forbidden, while to the 'freedom fighter' any violence that contributes to victory is permitted. In the conflicts that marked the end of European colonial rule, the morality of violence tended to be dictated by political and military considerations on both sides, in which the only objective was winning. And today, when the threat of terrorism has been invoked to justify a supposedly benign imperialism for the twenty-first century, it is worth remembering the way that some of the empires of the twentieth came to an end.

PART II

Freedom Fighters

4

Savages

I will go to the forest for justice.
The people will flock to me.
I right their wrongs from the green shade,
And kill the rulers with arrows.
The horsemen stumble with fear.

Han Suyin, And the Rain My Drink, 1956

The wars of decolonisation that shaped post-war perceptions of terrorism were rarely called wars by the colonial regimes engaged in fighting them. Even after France had poured more than half a million troops into Algeria the insurgency was described as 'the war without a name' or 'the events'. Britain called its colonial conflicts of the 1950s 'emergencies', an elastic concept capable of justifying military intervention in a variety of contexts. To the metropolitan public in Europe these conflicts did not look like previous wars. For the most part there were no fixed front lines and few decisive military engagements. Instead they were fought largely through small-scale encounters, urban bombs and isolated skirmishes in forests and jungles, and a steady drip-drip of murders and atrocities that often seemed as meaningless as they were horrific. As the colonial armies elaborated and homogenised their responses to insurgency, the wars of decolonisation began to exhibit the same features: sandbags outside public buildings, barbed wire, checkpoints, curfews, searches and internment camps.

The similarity between these colonial battlefields was matched by the similarity in the methods used by the insurgent enemy, all of which added to the impression that a new kind of barbarism had mysteriously entered the world. 'In the face of terrorism and counter-terrorism as employed in the contemporary world, the would-be humane and impartial onlooker feels a sense of moral helplessness', declared the liberal Oxford historian Margery Perham in 1963.[1] In 1959 Lawrence Durrell described his beloved Cyprus 'slowly erupting in little spots of hate like the spark of single matches struck here and there in the darkness of a field' as EOKA bombs exploded in cinemas, car parks and graveyards and civilians and soldiers were shot down in cafés or in the street.[2] To Camus's friend, the liberal writer Jules Roy, terrorism in Algeria was 'abomination considered as a normal mode of combat'.[3]

These gloomy ruminations from the liberal end of the European political spectrum are a testament to the apparently irreversible phenomenon that terrorism had already become in the revolutionary era that followed World War II. To the metropolitan public in Europe, such violence often appeared as an expression of the same native barbarism that colonialism was supposedly intended to suppress, particularly when the violence of the colonial regimes themselves tended to receive a more muted or positive coverage. Tactically, revolutionary terrorism followed the broad contours established by Collins and the IRA in Ireland, but in the post-war era a range of new constituencies now existed that anti-colonial or national liberation movements could appeal to, from the United Nations, to the decolonised Third World countries and the communist bloc. All these audiences could potentially bring political pressure to bear on the colonial powers. To reach these constituencies, revolutionary organisations were often prepared to go to extreme lengths in a world that was becoming increasingly inured to extreme violence. The more extreme the violence, the more the colonial regimes presented themselves as the natural arbiters of legitimate authority, defending outposts of Western civilisation against a combination of international communism and indigenous native savagery.

Small wars on terror

The laboratory

Revolutionary terrorism was a major ingredient of the longest-running British colonial insurgency, which began in Malaya in June 1948 when the colonial government declared a state of emergency in response to a wave of violent disorder in rural areas of the country. The unrest was assumed by the authorities to be the work of the Chinese-dominated Malayan Communist Party (MCP) as part of a plan to destabilise the country and install itself in power, following orders from the Soviet Union. Evidence to support this thesis has never been produced, but there was no need to search for external factors to explain the unrest in the colony, much of which stemmed from post-war economic distress.

Though the communists and the British had formed an unlikely alliance during the Japanese occupation, the wartime marriage of convenience quickly unravelled as the British attempted to reassert control over Malaya and re-establish their traditional alliance with the Malay sultans, culminating in the definitive rupture of the emergency. With the colony officially on a war footing, the MCP Central Committee ordered its members to return to the jungle and launch an all-out rebellion against a government which it claimed was about to wage 'a colonial war aimed at slaughtering the people'. The 6,000 guerrillas who made up the Malayan Races Liberation Army (MRLA) faced a serious political disadvantage, in that their support was drawn almost entirely from the Chinese community. In addition, the guerrillas faced some 40,000 British soldiers and colonial troops, backed up by more than 200,000 Malay police, Special Branch and home guards.

In their favour the communists had years of combat experience in Malaya's vast jungles and an extensive civilian support network, the Min Yuen, estimated at 70,000. From their jungle bases they set about disrupting the colony, attacking isolated police stations, ambushing trains and buses and slashing rubber trees and plantations in an attempt to wreck the economy. The guerrillas also carried out exemplary punishments of civilian 'running dogs' perceived to be disloyal or insufficiently co-operative. Often the brutality was part of the message. In one incident, a Chinese squatter was shot dead and his wife hacked to death in a district of Johore. In another, MRLA guerrillas hammered a nail through the head of a young Chinese girl. In October 1951 the MCP Central Committee sought to reduce attacks that caused 'unpleasantness for the general public'. Nevertheless the throat cuttings and atrocities continued.

Few testimonies exist to explain the exceptional cruelty that the communists often displayed, beyond the statements of captured guerrillas, which were frequently tailored for propaganda effect. According to the historian Noel Barber, the author of a hagiographic account of the British conduct of the emergency, the guerrillas 'were mesmerised by Communist lectures which left a deep, inexplicable impression that somehow they had been given a privileged glimpse of a mystic source of power.'[4] But this image of brainwashed killers does not match the impressions of the communists given by more neutral observers, such as the British 'stay behind' officer, Colonel F. Spencer Chapman, who spent two and a half years fighting with the Chinese guerrillas during World War II. In *The Jungle Is Neutral* Chapman describes their highly disciplined camps in engaging terms, with their pedantic Stalinist politics, their self-criticism sessions, communal singing and earnest discussions of the virtues of smoking and life in the Soviet Union. Though resolutely unsympathetic to their politics, Chapman wrote of the guerrillas themselves that 'The rank and file were absolutely magnificent. I can hardly find words to express my admiration for their courage, fortitude and consistent fearlessness in adversity'.[5]

One of the finest fictional portrayals of the emergency was Han Suyin's remarkable *And the Rain My Drink* (1956). A Dutch-Chinese doctor working in Malaya, Suyin's broad canvas depicted the emergency as a tragic and complex confrontation in which neither side had a monopoly of good or evil. Though she recognised the brutality of the communists, she also understood the alienation of the Chinese community that fuelled the revolt against the British 'pig-faces'. To the British public and national servicemen in Malaya, however, the Communist Terrrorists were bandits and killers, their aura of exotic oriental evil enhanced by externally imposed nicknames such as the Raven, the Fat One and the Bearded Terror of Kanjang. One of the most famous photographs of the emergency showed two blonde-haired toddlers in a rubber-plantation playroom with its windows protected by sandbags – the image of the outpost of civilisation under threat from the terrorist barbarians. The general attitude towards the CTs amongst the European population in Malaya was summed up by the anonymous refrain: 'Another Chinese bandit gone below/Praise God, from whom all blessings flow'.

The military campaign against the communists was initially restricted to aerial bombardments of the jungle, using napalm and defoliants. When these tactics proved ineffective, British servicemen and colonial troops were forced to enter the jungle themselves in search of what the authors of *Re-enter the SAS* described as 'the yellow-skinned zealot who killed from ambush or by booby trap'.[6] Often these expeditions failed to result in any contact with the enemy, but as the emergency progressed, the British troops became more effective, using small hunter-killer squads backed by native trackers, which penetrated deep into the jungle to ambush the CTs on their supply trails and destroy their camps.

The Oxbridge-educated officer Oliver Crawford wrote a vivid account of an encounter with the terrorist enemy during a 'long-term ambush' mounted on a jungle track. For three days Crawford waited with his men in concealment. On the third evening three guerrillas approached under cover of darkness and Crawford's patrol opened fire. Crawford then heard a 'low moan of agony' followed by silence:

> Afterwards I was badly shaken. Those few cries from the grass had been like a bucket of cold water in my face. I was awake, gasping with shock. This was real. This was happening. We were shooting people. We were killing them. At first I had been living from second to second, automatically, but now I was

awake. We had worked for this for months. This was raw, savage success. It was butchery. It was horror.[7]

It was through small skirmishes and ambushes like this that military progress was judged. Because of the scarcity of such engagements there was fierce regimental competition for CT 'kills,' with the Gurkhas topping the list at 300, followed by the Suffolks with 198. In 1953 Major Arthur Campbell of the Suffolks wrote a best-selling account of the war in Malaya called *Jungle Green*, thousands of copies of which were distributed to British troops in Malaya. *Jungle Green* received a less positive reception from the Chinese community in Malaya for its contemptuous references to 'yellow men' living in 'nauseating' hovels and Campbell's descriptions of the Chinese as 'two-faced beggars, sitting on the fence, waiting to see who was going to get the upper hand'. Its Bulldog Drummond viciousness and bare-knuckle descriptions of jungle warfare nevertheless struck a chord with the British reading public. The book describes the hunt for Liew Kim Bok, the Bearded Terror of Kajang, aka the King of Bastards, who carried out a string of executions and murders in the Kajang district before Campbell's platoon finally located and killed him:

> There was no doubt it was him. I had seen that cruel face so often in photographs that there was no mistaking it. The lips were drawn back in a snarl over his yellow teeth and his eyes were open wide; there was an expression of mixed fear and cowardice in them. His jacket was open in front, showing a narrow chest and a thin, flat stomach where Johnny had shot him twice. One of the bullets had ripped open his yellow skin and his guts were hanging out of the wound. As I looked about me I saw armies of ants coming down from the trees and advancing towards him over the sodden ground. I grinned at Johnny and said, 'Good shooting.'[8]

Because of his reputation, Liew Kim Bok's body was tied to a door and carted round the district on the back of a jeep as proof of his death. Other CT kills were registered by taking photographs of dead guerrillas or comparing them to already existing photographs of wanted terrorists. Whenever possible the corpses would then be tied to poles and dragged out of the jungle, but if this was too difficult the heads of dead guerrillas were sometimes considered sufficient evidence of a kill.

Hearts and minds

This brutal war of attrition was mostly concealed from the British public or presented in such a way that it seemed logical, legitimate and 'civilised' in comparison with CT barbarism. The image of the CTs also filtered back to Britain through novels set during the emergency, most of which were primarily concerned with exploring the European predicament in Malaya, from Anthony Burgess's magnificent Malayan trilogy *The Long Day Wanes* to Alan Sillitoe's *Key To the Door*, whose working-class communist squaddie engages in hand-to-hand combat with a CT in the jungle before he lets him go, recognizing him as a 'comrade'.

The most popular novel of the emergency was Leslie Thomas's best-seller *The Virgin Soldiers* (1966), which later became an equally successful film. Thomas was more concerned with the emotional and sexual experiences of his pimply national servicemen than with the enemy they were fighting. For the most part the CTs are a remote but threatening presence, hidden in the jungle beyond the palm trees and beaches, where the tawdry pleasures of dance halls and taxi girls are interrupted by sudden eruptions of violence, culminating in a communist ambush on a train in which the naive 'virgin soldier', Brigg, and his unit are travelling up country. Though Thomas based this scene on a real-life ambush, he embellished it for full dramatic effect as Brigg's wounded comrade wakes up to witness a rape in progress:

> One of the Chinese was standing in front of her, one hand carelessly holding a sub-machine gun and the other pulling open the front of the girl's dress. She stood still and weeping, unable to move for fright, while he casually tore the linen away from her body. Sinclair watched while the bandit unbuckled his belt and threw open the buttons on his trousers. The girl's body reflected the fire; it glowed on her fatty breasts and her young neck. She put her hands to her face, but still did not move away from the man. The bandit pushed out his free hand and quite gently threw her backwards on to the ground. There was a dead man in the ditch with Sinclair. Near his sightless head was a sten gun. "Dirty little dogs on leads," thought Sinclair. "They were all the same."

Perhaps to Thomas, and certainly to much of the British public, they were. Thomas's image of the CT 'bandit', straight from the bottom drawer of Fu Manchu stereotypes, replicates official British military propaganda of the day and is another illustration of the way in which popular fiction reinforced such images of oriental cruelty or native savagery in its construction of the terrorist 'Other'.

By the end of 1952 the guerrillas had largely been pushed back into the jungle. Over the next few years, the army also undertook a massive social-engineering experiment in which some half a million Chinese squatters were relocated in heavily guarded 'protected villages' surrounded by barbed wire and watchtowers. While these villages were advertised as safe havens for their inhabitants, their real purpose was to isolate the guerrillas from their civilian supporters and cut off their supply of food.

With the arrival of the forceful General Gerald Templer as C-in-C Malaya in 1952, military force was backed up by an increasingly sophisticated propaganda and psychological operations campaign which aimed to 'win the hearts and minds' of the population, as Templer described it in a phrase that would become a stalwart of the military lexicon. The carrot-and-stick approach was backed up by a range of coercive measures, from unlimited detention without trial to executions, arbitrary curfews and the deportation of some 34,000 Chinese to China. In 1952 Victor Purcell, a liberal critic of Templer and a former civil servant in pre-war Malaya, returned to the country for the first time since the war, where he described 'the over-powering dominance of the military machine. One felt numb in the middle of a huge armed camp … It was hard to believe that here was no army massing for a general offensive on a wide front but one combating a few thousand hidden terrorists.'[9]

These conditions prevailed for much of the twelve years of the emergency. Faced with such overwhelming force, the MRLA was gradually whittled down to some 2,000 half-starved and isolated guerrillas living deep in the jungle. At the same time, in a process that has been mirrored elsewhere, the violence forced Britain to negotiate with the non-communist Malay nationalist parties and establish a timetable for independence. In addition, the government took steps to ameliorate some of the grievances that had contributed to the revolt in the first place, including the extension of full citizenship to the non-Malay population. The fact that these reforms were carried out was itself a recognition that the rebellion had causes that were unconnected to international communism or local banditry. Had such reforms been implemented earlier, Malaya might well have been spared the trauma of the emergency, in which 6,711 guerrillas and 1,346 members of the security forces were killed, together with 2,473 civilians.[10]

The creation of Mau Mau

In the same period as the Malayan emergency the dynamic of terrorism and counter-terrorism unfolded in Kenya, the consequences of which were even more traumatic for the indigenous population. The crisis first came to international attention in 1952, when the governor of Kenya, Evelyn Baring, declared a state of emergency in order to combat a sinister movement known as the Mau Mau, which was believed to be responsible for a spate of grisly murders centred amongst the Kikuyu tribe, the most educated and politicised section of the indigenous African population. In Kenya, as in Malaya, the unrest in Kikuyuland was rooted in long-term historical grievances, most of them directly related to the political and economic domination of the colony by a white settler elite whose apartheid-style restrictions continued into the post-war period. From the late 1940s onwards Kikuyu resentment at the colonial system was sharpened by various factors, from growing population pressure on the limited available land in Kikuyuland to the evictions of rural squatters from European-owned farms and the continued refusal of the settler elite to allow African political representation.

Following the return of the charismatic Kikuyu leader Jomo Kenyatta from England and the formation of the Kenyan African Union (KAU), the Kikuyu increasingly took the lead in calling for African political representation and an end to racial discrimination in the colony. While the urban-based KAU continued to campaign legally, the Kikuyu Central Association (KCA), an organisation banned before the war, embarked on a new recruitment effort amongst its rural constituency, where resentment at the colonial system was already beginning to go beyond the KAU's reformist agenda.

In Kenya, as in Malaya, the drift from political radicalism to armed rebellion had causes that were rooted in the colonial system itself. But whereas in Malaya the indigenous roots of the MRLA's rebellion were obscured by the portrayal of the rebellion as an international communist plot, in Kenya the grievances that fuelled the revolt were obscured or denied by the official presentation of a murderous terrorist conspiracy of unparalleled evil and depravity. In 1948 police and district officers began to report the existence of a secret society whose members had supposedly taken an oath to exterminate the European settler population. The name given to this society was Mau Mau, after a chant allegedly used during its oath-taking ceremonies. Various explanations have been offered for the term, from an anagram based on a Kikuyu children's game to a corruption of the Kikuyu word *muma*, or oath, but the word was generally used by Europeans, not Africans, who referred to 'the Movement' or 'the Unity of the Community' whose goal was *wiyathi* – land and freedom.

To the outside world, 'Mau Mau' became synonymous with atavistic evil, encapsulated by a November 1952 issue of *Time* magazine featuring a photograph of a dead cat hanging from a tree to illustrate the Mau Mau custom of 'nailing headless cats to their victims' doors'. The image of Mau Mau as a demonic terrorist cult was relentlessly disseminated by officials in the colonial administration and by influential Kenyan settlers such as Elspeth Huxley and L. S. B. Leakey, a fluent Kikuyu speaker, who defined the Mau Mau as 'openly anti-White and also anti-Christian'. Other contemporary accounts of the Mau Mau phenomenon, such as C. T. Stoneham's *Mau Mau* (1953), were steeped in white settler prejudices, from its contemptuous references to 'the unusual secretiveness and mendacity' of the Kikuyu tribe to the salutary virtues of flogging natives with the *kiboko* or rhino-hide whip. In Stoneham's view, the Mau Mau had converted 'the timid unwarlike "Kuke" into the ferocious desperado who employs the methods of the modern American gangster'. The result was a new kind of terrorist, part clown, part murderer, as dangerous as he was deluded:

> The typical Mau Mau member grows a beard and moustache and cultivates a fierce demeanour. He is a killer, and proud of it. He has been reared on a diet of Hollywood violence and garbled accounts of underground warfare in Europe and the East. He sees himself a hero – with a wild-beast philosophy of profit and enjoyment for the strong – and is prepared to fight for the leaders who protect and direct him.[11]

For white supremacists like Stoneham there was no possibility that the unrest in Kikuyuland might stem from rational causes. Even more liberal Kenya settlers like Leakey argued that the Kikuyu had been 'manipulated' by unscrupulous leaders, while the *New York Times* attributed Mau Mau to 'the frustrations of a savage people neither mentally nor economically able to adjust itself to the swift pace of civilization'.

Crucial to the settler presentation of the Mau Mau as a depraved barbaric cult was the Mau Mau oathing ceremony. Oath taking was an established part of Kikuyu tradition, involving elaborate ceremonies and chants invoking a curse on the oath breaker, accompanied by the ritualistic tasting of goat's meat or blood. According to Stoneham, Leakey et al., however, the Mau Mau had debased these rituals to include a range of hideous obscene rites involving cannibalism, the drinking of menstrual blood and the sacrificial murder of children, in order to create a breed of soulless assassins. According to the British colonial secretary Alan Lennox-Boyd, the Mau Mau oaths 'had such a tremendous effect on the Kikuyu mind as to turn quite intelligent young Africans into entirely different human beings, into sub-human creatures without hope and with death as their only deliverance'.[12]

Former Mau Mau veterans have generally denied these claims or attributed the more lurid oathing stories to British propaganda or confessions
obtained by force. J. M. Kariuki, a detainee for seven years during the emergency, later dismissed 'stories of the widespread use of the menstrual blood
of women, of bestial intercourse with animals, of the eating of the embryos
of unborn children ripped from their mothers' wombs', claiming that such
stories were either deliberate fabrications or restricted to 'a minute number
of perverted individuals driven crazy by their isolation in the forests'.[13] Other
veterans have denied that such events ever occurred. Though the authorities
claimed that Mau Mau oaths were undertaken under duress, coercion alone
cannot account for the fact that some 80 per cent of the Kikuyu population
were estimated to have taken the basic oaths by the time the emergency
ended. Nor do white settler accounts of the insurgency as a collective descent
into depravity explain the extraordinary commitment shown by both Mau
Mau fighters and their supporters, in a rebellion that incorporated the whole
spectrum of Kikuyu society, from illiterate rural squatters and tribal traditionalists in rural areas to educated urban-based nationalists pursuing constitutional changes and impoverished inhabitants of the Nairobi slums.

Butchers

The depiction of Mau Mau as a manifestation of demonic possession or collective insanity ignored all these different facets of the rebellion and precluded any possibility of negotiation with its leaders. Yet despite Governor
Baring's claim that the colony was faced with 'a formidable organisation
of violence' it was only after the declaration of the state of emergency in
October 1952 that the first Europeans were killed, following the arrival of
British troops and the mass arrests of the KAU leaders, including Kenyatta
himself. Faced with this government clampdown and in imminent danger of
arrest themselves, thousands of KCA and KAU activists fled to the Aberdares
forests and the slopes of Mount Kenya and began to mount sporadic guerrilla attacks on isolated police stations and farms. Two weeks after the declaration a white farmer and two African servants were killed by a Mau Mau
gang. Other attacks soon followed. In January 1953 a settler couple and their
six-year-old son were hacked to death with machetes or *pangas*.

To the settler community one of the most disturbing aspects of these
gruesome killings was the fact that the attackers had gained entry with
the help of one of the family's farm labourers. Other attacks on Europeans
were similarly carried out with the help of trusted house servants, spreading panic amongst the settler community. While some European farmers

withdrew from the countryside to the relative security of Nairobi, others remained on their farms, keeping a revolver handy when they took a bath or warily watching their houseboys during dinner in case they threw soup in their faces and ushered in a Mau Mau murder gang.

Across Kenya white women took to wearing pistols in holsters while customers turned up in Nairobi bars and restaurants armed with sten guns and rifles. In one incident two female settlers on a remote farm were attacked by a Mau Mau gang aided by their houseboy. The pair fought off their assailants with a pistol and shotgun, killing three. The impression of a civilised society under siege was transmitted to the outside world by local and foreign correspondents, through books, and through films such as *Safari* and the Dirk Bogarde vehicle *Simba*. One of the most influential interpreters of the emergency was the American novelist and *Life* correspondent in Kenya, Robert Ruark, who wrote regular columns about the evil of the Mau Mau and the heroism of the white settlers.

Ruark turned his journalistic experiences into a sprawling 300,000-word colonial epic, *Something of Value* (1955). Despite a generally hostile critical reception, the novel became an international publishing phenomenon and remained on the *New York Times* best-seller list for forty-two weeks. As a writer, Ruark rarely rises above the level of a second-rate Hemingway with his pen dipped in blood and entrails, but his novel was published at a time when international fascination with the exotic evil of Mau Mau was at its height and Ruark more than fulfilled the expectations of his audience, so much so that a British Foreign Office official observed that the novel's US publication 'has done the British name more good than harm, by exposing the purely criminal nature of the Mau Mau conspiracy and exploding its claim to the distinction of a social and economic origin'.[14]

The novel tells the parallel stories of white settler Peter McKenzie and his Kikuyu childhood companion, Kimani. While McKenzie grows up to become a hunter and safari guide, the resentful Kimani falls out with his white boss and gets sucked into the bestial depravity of the Mau Mau. The unwitting Kimani descends deeper into the moral abyss, participating in an oathing ceremony where the recruits drink blood from the skull of a young child. In the face of such unbridled evil, even Ruark's potentially controversial revelations of the torture and execution of Mau Mau suspects by white settler paramilitaries appear reasonable and justifiable. Whereas Mau Mau terrorist atrocities are a confirmation of innate African savagery, McKenzie and his fellow torturers are decent chaps, forced to use horrific methods against an even more horrific enemy. Even when they inflict the most vile tortures on Mau Mau suspects Ruark invites the reader to sympathise not with their victims but with their torturers, who sink into alcoholism and depression under the weight of the white man's burden.

Though Ruark gave the impression that Europeans were being slaughtered in their thousands across the country, only thirty-two settlers were killed during the whole seven-year period of the emergency, while the official number of African victims of Mau Mau violence was just under 2,000. To the settler population and the outside world, however, the Mau Mau's dread reputation stemmed not just from the number of killings, but from the stories that their victims had first been disembowelled and mutilated with *pangas*. Such incidents certainly occurred, in a chaotic and uncoordinated rebellion, whose 'political' dimensions sometimes overlapped with violent criminality. Nevertheless, one European doctor who examined some 200 bodies of Mau Mau victims claimed that nearly all of them had died quickly as the result of blows to the head, rather than through slow torture, suggesting that the *panga* was a weapon of efficiency rather than an expression of native sadism.[15]

The motives behind these murders were often as mysterious as their perpetrators. Unlike other anti-colonial revolts of the period, the Mau Mau rebellion did not become an organised or coherent movement and the struggle for *wiyathi* overlapped with what amounted to a civil war within the Kikuyu, between Mau Mau and pro-British loyalists, between landless peasants and tribal chiefs. One of the most notorious Mau Mau atrocities was the Lari massacre of 1953, when an undefended village complex was attacked during the night, apparently by Mau Mau insurgents, and dozens of women and children were slaughtered. Photographs of the massacre were reproduced throughout the world and confirmed the Mau Mau as the embodiment of evil. But as historian David Anderson has shown, the massacre was the result of complex tensions and class conflicts within the Kikuyu community around Lari, and was followed within days by a second massacre in which even more people were killed by British loyalists seeking revenge.[16]

The Lari massacre coincided with a Mau Mau assault on a police station at Naivasha that same night. But such large-scale assaults on the security fences were rare. From the beginning, the poorly armed forest fighters who made up the 'Land and Freedom Army' were almost entirely on the defensive, faced with a formidable array of forces consisting of some 10,000 regular troops backed up by police, home guards and 6,000 part-time auxiliaries made up mostly of the settlers themselves. As the emergency wore on these forces were supplemented by the so-called 'pseudo gangs' comprising former Mau Mau and white settlers with blackened faces who penetrated deep into the forest in search of the Mau Mau 'hardcore'.

From the outset the barbarism and irrationality of the insurgent enemy was used to justify exceptional official violence as white settlers clamoured for the mass slaughter of Kikuyu and the *Kenya Sunday Post* called for the crushing of the Mau Mau terrorists 'with no considerations of sentiment'. As in Malaya, the guerrillas' hideouts were attacked from above, by RAF Harvards and Lincolns dropping 1,000lb bombs. At other times the security forces entered the forests like hunters on safari, with lines of native beaters leading the way followed by armed soldiers and police. The future British counter-insurgency specialist Frank Kitson was then a young liaison officer with the Special Branch and accompanied one of these expeditions, where he observed an African herdsman 'stalk and kill a terrorist' with a bow and arrow. According to Kitson, the herdsman spotted the Mau Mau 'gangster' lying in some reeds and crept up on him till he was about thirty yards away. Kitson watched with awestruck admiration as the herdsman drew his bow and fired:

> The arrow passed through the air with much less force than I had expected and I wondered whether it would do any damage on arrival. In fact it caught the gangster in the neck and cut through the jugular vein. He staggered to his feet clutching his throat from which blood poured forth in a dark crimson torrent painting the rushes round about so that they looked like the decorations some people keep in their house when flowers are out of season.[17]

To the settlers the forest 'hardcore' was made up of the most bestial and depraved Mau Mau terrorists, whose reversion to savagery was demonstrated by the physical appearance of captured members, in their animal-skin clothes, their stolen ill-fitting overcoats and their dreadlocked hair. Karari Njama, a member of the Land and Freedom Army, later recalled how wild animals 'became accustomed to our presence and smell and, after a few months in the forest, they treated us as simply another form of animal life and we in turn learnt all their habits and calls.'[18]

Even in these circumstances, the fighters with a military background tried to establish the rudiments of a modern military structure, under the leadership of 'Field Marshal' Dedan Kimathi, a former soldier in the British army. To the settlers Kimathi was the archetypal depraved Mau Mau terrorist, but the testimony of Karari Njama and others described a natural leader who tried to unify the different groups in the forest through the creation of a 'Kenya Defence Council' and an African 'Kenya Parliament'. To J. M. Kariuki, Kimathi was 'the greatest hero of us all'.[19] Karari Njama's own portrait of Kimathi depicts him as a courageous revolutionary Moses, inspiring his fighters with quotations from the Bible and Kikuyu 'levellation songs' in a doomed struggle for survival in the forests. Frozen and often half-starved, with the full might of the British counter-insurgency machine directed against them, the efforts of the Land and Freedom Army were increasingly devoted to their own survival rather than offensive operations. At the same time survival itself was considered a political victory, since according to Waruhiu Itote, a Mau Mau combatant known as 'General China', 'Our fight was not a single, organised campaign … It was not even a territorial battle to gain certain areas: it was a matter of keeping our struggle in the forefront of world opinion … Mere survival was victory.'[20]

This was the same strategy pursued by Michael Collins, Begin and Grivas, but the Land and Freedom Army was never able to transcend the demonic image of Mau Mau that dominated international perceptions of Kenya. As in Malaya the colonial government embarked on a policy of food denial by forcibly incorporating Kikuyu peasants into fortified settlements surrounded by barbed wire, bamboo stakes and trenches. In the course of the emergency more than a million Kikuyu were penned up in 800 new villages that were often little more than open detention centres. Conditions were little better in the rest of the country, as the suppression of the Mau Mau became a licence for rape, torture and arbitrary violence by the security forces.

The Kenyan political dissident Koigi wa Wamwere, a child during the emergency, describes an incident in which he and his mother encountered a friendly Mau Mau fighter named 'Elephant' hiding in a maize field. Six months later the inhabitants of his village were summoned to a meeting by a white forest officer and a group of armed police, who laid out four bodies on a table with their arms and heads chopped off. When the heads were produced as well, the young Wamwere recognised the Mau Mau who had sung to him in the maize field:

> When the white officer stood to speak, he said, 'Come forward, all of you. I want you to see well who is on the table. Here are the bodies of four dead Mau Mau terrorists.' Pointing to the armed men around him, he said, 'My men here and I just come from a hunt in the forest. Every time we come for night inspections, you people deny there are Mau Mau terrorists in this forest. But I have always known that all of you are liars. Yesterday a bird told me it had seen

some cowardly Mau Maus hiding in the forest … Now you see what Kimathi and all Mau Maus will harvest – death.'[21]

The cutting off of corpses' hands for fingerprinting was common practice. As in Malaya, bodies would be left in public places or strapped to jeeps and paraded round the villages to mock their inhabitants. And as in Malaya, British regiments kept scorecards of their kills, in some cases offering a £5 reward to the first soldier to bag a Mau Mau. Some of the worst abuses were carried out by settler paramilitaries, who tended to regard expeditions in search of Mau Mau as a kind of safari in which they were allowed to kill and torture with impunity.

Faced with such widespread violence, many Kikuyu began to believe that the British were intent on exterminating the entire Kikuyu population. On 20 October 1956 Dedan Kimathi was captured and wounded during an ambush and hanged the following year. By then the emphasis of the anti-Mau Mau campaign had shifted from the forests to the chain of detention camps known as 'the pipeline' where the colonial administration attempted to break the hundreds of thousands of Mau Mau suspects remaining in the camps by forcing them to confess their oaths and renounce the movement. Those who passed through the de-oathing process were gradually filtered through the camp system until they were declared fit for rehabilitation into society.

The official depiction of 'terrorism' as a metaphysical 'evil' has rarely been more explicit than it was during the Mau Mau rehabilitation process. While some detainees agreed to undergo a Christian 'cleansing' ceremony, in which they renounced Mau Mau by swearing on the Bible and professed their loyalty to the colonial government in return for 'loyalty certificates' authorising them to look for work, other released detainees remained suspect and liable to re-arrest. Ostensibly these procedures were intended to neutralise the occult power of Mau Mau, but the detainees recognised their political implications and the camps often became the scene of bitter conflict between the colonial administration and the more committed detainees who refused to renounce the oath. In the last years of the emergency this battle was often waged with extreme ferocity, as the administration sought to wear down the detainees' resistance using a range of coercive measures, which in some camps included beatings, floggings and summary executions.

By the time the emergency came to an end in 1960 the government estimated that 80,000 men and women had passed through 'the pipeline', though some historians have estimated the actual figure at 300,000. The statistics demonstrate the hugely unequal nature of the conflict. The official death toll was 11,503 Mau Mau, compared with 167 dead amongst the security forces, of whom 101 were Africans.[22] The actual death toll was almost certainly higher. David Anderson has estimated Mau Mau casualties at more than 20,000, in addition to more than 1,800 African civilians murdered by the Mau Mau themselves.[23] Some historians have estimated that up to 150,000 Kikuyu may have died through famine and violence while hundreds of thousands more were maimed or made homeless. As in Malaya, 'terrorism' became a pretext for the colonial presence and a justification for even greater violence in the name of counter-terrorism. At the same time the trauma of the emergency obliged Britain to seek alternative political arrangements with more 'moderate' nationalist politicians in order to prepare the way for independence. One of these moderates turned out to be none other than Kenyatta himself, who was released from prison in 1961 and went on to become the first president of independent Kenya two years later. In power, the terrorist leader once described by the *Nairobi Times* as 'stained with the mark of the beast' proved remarkably conciliatory towards the settlers, declaring that 'Mau Mau was a disease which had been eradicated, and must never be remembered again'.

Kenyatta's attitude angered many of his former supporters, who believed that their sacrifices had helped bring him to power.[24] The Kenyan novelist Ngugi wa Thiong'o later attempted to provide a fictional commemoration of the struggle for *wiyathi* that neither the British nor official Kenya have ever acknowledged in his novels *A Grain of Wheat* and *Petals of Blood*. For Ngugi the emergency was the Calvary of the Kikuyu people and the crucible of violence which brought about Kenya's political independence. This is not a view that the British public has become accustomed to, where the image of Mau Mau as a particularly dreadful and freakish manifestation of 'terrorism' continues to obscure what may well be one of the great deceptions of British imperial history.[25]

The terrors of Algiers
In both Malaya and Kenya, 'the terrorist' was a combination of bandit and wild beast, that the forces of order and civilisation were obliged to hunt down and destroy in his forest lair. It was a different matter in Algeria, where nationalist insurgents engaged in revolutionary terrorism with unprecedented ferocity on the urban stage. More than any other anti-colonial struggle of this period, Algeria was a crucial episode in the evolution of terrorism, in both the methods used by the insurgents and the techniques used by the French army against them. The bloodiest of all colonial wars began on All

Saints Day 1954, when 150 poorly armed Algerian Muslims spread out from a farm in the Aurès mountains and carried out a series of attacks in the surrounding area, including the murder of a French schoolteacher and his wife. The next day a previously unknown organisation calling itself the Front de Liberation National (FLN) issued a manifesto calling for negotiations on national independence based on 'the recognition of Algerian sovereignty'.

Neither the French government nor the 1 million settlers known as 'pieds noirs' or blackfeet were disposed to recognise anything of the kind. As the rebellion spread rapidly across the countryside, French troops poured into the country and began to carry out rural 'pacification' operations that bore all the hallmarks of Marshal Bugeaud's scorched earth campaigns during the conquest of Algeria in the nineteenth century, with the added destructive power of modern military technology. From the beginning the war was characterised by extreme brutality on both sides, though these events initially received little attention from the French public. It was partly in an attempt to shock French public opinion out of its indifference that the FLN launched a series of mass attacks on French towns and villages in the Constantine region in August 1955. In the coastal town of Phillippeville, Muslims poured through the streets throwing grenades into cafés and beating Europeans to death with axes and pitchforks.

Though the French garrison was forewarned and repelled the attack, an atrocious massacre took place at the nearby mining town of El-Halia in which 130 European civilians were hacked to death, many of them women and children. Afterwards the army and settlers exacted their own bloody vengeance as they roamed the area killing more than 5,000 Muslims. From the FLN's point of view these attacks had served their purpose. On the one hand they had forced French public opinion to pay attention to what was taking place in Algeria. At the same time the savage French response further radicalised their own Muslim constituency and helped polarise Algerian society still further. And the following year the organisation began to prepare for an even more spectacular campaign of urban terrorism in the capital itself, that would be unlike anything the world had previously witnessed.

The battle of Algiers
Like other revolutionary organisations of the era, the FLN used violence and intimidation as a means of establishing itself as a 'parallel hierarchy', killing informers and pro-French officials as well as rival nationalists. In addition, the FLN carried out killings and exemplary mutilations amongst the Muslim population to enforce its puritanical and authoritarian social rules regarding

practices such as smoking and drinking alcohol. In the summer of 1956, however, the decision was taken to launch a terrorist offensive in Algiers at the clandestine FLN summit in the Soummam valley, which marked the ascendancy of Ramdane Abbane, the 'Algerian Lenin'. On the one hand the FLN wanted to create a diversion from its besieged mountain strongholds where superior French military power was exacting a heavy toll. At the same time the organisation was determined to force the outside world to pay attention to the Algerian cause by whatever means it could.

Under the direction of Abbane and a former theatre student Larbi ben M'Hidi, the FLN began the conversion of the Algiers area known as the ZAA, or Autonomous Algiers Zone, into an urban battleground. The heart of the ZAA was the old Arab quarter known as the Kasbah, a densely packed mass of crumbling tenements and narrow labyrinthine streets, which housed a population of some 450,000 Muslims. The inhabitants of the Kasbah were subjected to the FLN's harsh revolutionary discipline, as its teeming underworld of gangsters, prostitutes, drug addicts and gamblers was systematically purged. Within a short time the Kasbah was turned into an urban revolutionary fortress, with a network of secret tunnels between houses, arms caches, bomb factories and hiding places that provided the base of operations for a terrorist wing some 1,400 strong.

The organisational brain behind the terrorist section was Yacef Saadi, the son of a baker, a football fan and ladies man, backed up by an illiterate former pimp called Ali la Pointe, about whom little is known, beyond his reputation for violence and the tattoos MARCH OR DIE on his feet and SHUT UP on his chest. At the core of Yacef's organisation was a bomb squad composed mostly of young women chosen for their physical attractiveness and Westernised appearance in order to pass through French checkpoints. The participation of Algerian women in urban warfare was not entirely new. Like the 'shawled women' who had carried guns for IRA assassins in Dublin, traditional Muslim women enclosed in the square veil known as the *haik* had already been used to smuggle weapons and explosives through the streets. But the decision to use women to carry out bomb attacks in the European city was a new strategy, which the Martinique-born psychiatrist and ideologue of the Algerian revolution Franz Fanon described at the time as an act of political and sexual liberation:

> Carrying revolvers, grenades, hundreds of false identity cards or bombs, the unveiled Algerian woman moves like a fish in the Western waters. The soldiers, the French patrols, smile to her as she passes, compliments on her

looks are heard here and there, but no one suspects that her suitcases contain the automatic pistol which will presently mow down four or five members of one of the patrols.[26]

The majority of the female members of the bomb squad were middle-class students, graduates of French lycées, recruited from the tiny portion of Algerian women who went to university, such as Zohra Drif, a law student at Algiers university, who later told the historian Alistair Horne how her decision to join 'an essentially terrorist group' was motivated by her anger at the continued repression of the Muslims in Algiers while the European population 'in its tranquil quarters ... lived peacefully, went to the beach, to the cinema, to *le dancing*, and prepared for their holidays'.[27]

Similar justifications would later be given for the first IRA bombings on the British mainland and the Palestinian suicide attacks on Israeli civilians. But there is no sign of anger in the two extraordinary photographs later published by the French showing Zohra Drif standing with the other key female members of Yacef's organisation, Samia Lakhdari, Djamila Bouhired and Hassiba ben Bouali. The photographs were both taken in an unknown room in Algiers, at a time when the members of Yacef's bomb squad were regarded in the Kasbah as national heroes and 'protectors of the people' who had defiantly opposed the might of the French army. In one of the photographs the women are posing with pistols and sub-machine guns. They are chic, smiling and playful, holding their weapons like toys. At the centre of the photograph Yacef is standing with his arms around Ben Bouali and Bouhired, with Ali la Pointe and his youthful nephew Petit Omar squatting down in front of them. The mood is similarly exuberant and carefree, with none of the formality and seriousness which revolutionaries often like to project when posing for photographs. These are more like holiday snaps, taken by a group of young people who have embarked on a great adventure together to a place where few people have ever been.

The immediate event that triggered the FLN's terrorist offensive was the execution of two FLN activists accused of murder in June 1956. These executions outraged the Muslim population and Yacef was given orders to kill any European male between the ages of 18 and 24 in response. In a three-day period Yacef's operatives roamed the city and shot and stabbed forty-nine Europeans in random attacks. The violence soon spiralled. In August a group of European *ultras* bombed the house of an FLN suspect in the Kasbah's rue de Thèbes, demolishing several surrounding buildings and killing fifty-three people. As was usually the case involving violence carried out by Europeans, no arrests were made and the explosion was barely reported in the French or European newspapers.

The following month, Yacef's female operatives set off two bombs on the same afternoon in the European quarter, in a family café called the Milk Bar and a popular hangout of young pieds noirs called the Caféteria. The total casualties were three dead and over fifty injured, including several children. Unlike the bombing in the rue de Thèbes, the attacks on Europeans generated huge publicity. As French and international journalists began to take up residence in Algiers hotels it seemed that the world was taking notice of the Algerian conflict at last, to the satisfaction of an FLN spokesman at the United Nations, who told the journalist Edward Behr, 'You must understand that every time a bomb goes off in Algiers we are taken more seriously here.'[28]

Over the next few months, civilians were deliberately targeted in public places as bombs exploded in school buses, brasseries, restaurants, bars, sports stadiums and the Algiers racecourse. No revolutionary organisation had engaged in such a systematic campaign of urban terror on such a scale, but Abbane was unrepentant, telling one FLN sympathiser who criticised the bombings, 'I see hardly any difference between the girl who places a bomb in the Milk Bar and the French aviator who bombards a *mechta* or drops napalm in a *zone interdite*.'[29] This rationale has been invoked in many subsequent episodes, from Northern Ireland to Iraq. Unable to defeat the French militarily, the FLN could nevertheless make political gains, by staging deliberate outrages that shocked French public opinion and forced the outside world to recognise the reality of the Algerian conflict. But if the FLN was prepared to go to new extremes to realise these objectives, France too was about to enter uncharted territory.

The city of terror

By the end of 1956 the beautiful whitewashed Mediterranean city where the youthful Camus and his friends had once constructed a 'house above the world' had become a battleground in a new kind of war, where FLN bombings and assassinations alternated with vicious *ratonnades*, or 'rat-hunts', in which Europeans killed any Muslim they could find, where Europeans took to carrying guns and nervously stopped when Muslims walked behind them in the streets and cinema audiences were forbidden to leave before the film was over to ensure that they had not left a bomb.[30] In January 1957 the governor-general, Robert Lacoste, officially handed responsibility for law and order in the city to the 10th Paratroop Regiment under General Jacques Massu, a veteran of the Indochina war.

The arrival of the 'paras' in their leopard fatigues and lizard hats marked the real beginning of what became known as the battle of Algiers, as Massu and his team of highly politicised officers introduced a series of exceptional measures aimed at 'winning back the night' from the FLN. For the first time in history an army was given complete control of a city with orders to use whatever methods were necessary to eradicate a clandestine terrorist organisation. Massu's officers were steeped in the theories of *la guerre révolutionnaire* elaborated during the Indochina war, which argued that the West was engaged in an unacknowledged 'Third World War' against international communism that could be won only by waging total war across the whole of society, a strategy that was sometimes known as 'the War on the Crowd'.

From the beginning, Massu's paratroopers took the view that normal police and legal procedures were inadequate to deal with the FLN offensive. Over the next few months the paratroopers interrogated scores of Muslim suspects, using torture as a systematic tool for gathering intelligence information. In luxurious suburban villas and other detention centres on the edges of the city, thousands of prisoners were beaten, burned with blowtorches, given electric shocks from field telephones or pumped full of water. Between 30 to 40 per cent of the population of the Kasbah were tortured by Massu's paras, of whom an estimated 3,000 either died during interrogation, were shot and buried in anonymous graves or tossed from helicopters. Other prisoners vanished in the invisible production line of interrogation centres, internment camps and execution centres established by the army.

The use of torture by the French army, many of whose members had only recently fought against the Nazi occupation, shocked French public opinion and aroused a storm of protest from French liberals. One of the few Europeans tortured was Henri Alleg, the editor of *Alger Républicain*, whose harrowing account of his experiences, *La Question*, became a bestseller in France, despite the attempts by the French military to suppress it. In Alleg's opinion, the army's use of torture was a double-edged weapon which dehumanised both torturers and their victims. To Colonel Roger Trinquier, one of the proponents of *la guerre révolutionnaire* and an intelligence officer under Massu's command, torture was an essential instrument of counter-terrorism:

No lawyer is present for such an interrogation. If the prisoner gives the information requested, the examination is quickly terminated; if not, specialists must force his secret from him. Then, as a soldier, he must face the suffering, and perhaps the death, he has heretofore managed to avoid. The terrorist must accept this as a condition inherent in his trade and the methods of warfare that, with full knowledge, his superiors and he himself have chosen. Once the interrogation is finished, however, the terrorist can take his place among soldiers.[31]

This is the stern voice of the counter-terrorist inquisitor, for whom torture is a route through which the 'unworthy opponent' can achieve moral redemption, even if he dies in the process. Other French officers justified torture on humanitarian grounds, arguing that it saved lives by enabling the army to prevent terrorist bomb plots. As a junior officer during the battle of Algiers, the future General Paul Aussaresses personally tortured numerous prisoners and carried out summary executions. In his memoir *The Battle of the Casbah*, Aussaresses was matter-of-fact about these procedures, insisting that the interrogations 'never lasted for more than one hour' and the suspects would speak in the hope of saving their own lives. They would therefore either talk quickly or never.'[32]

In 1971 General Massu defended the methods used by his paratroopers in *La Vrai Bataille d'Alger* on similar grounds, arguing that torture was not inherently cruel or sadistic provided it was restricted to extracting intelligence information.[33] The idea that torture might be required to defeat the 'terrorist with the ticking bomb' has been repeated in many different contexts, from the Argentinian 'dirty war' to the current War on Terror, but the Algerian war was the first time that a democratic state had used torture as an instrument of counter-terrorism on a systematic basis. The result, according to Henri Alleg, was the conversion of the 'Centre de Tri' into 'a school of perversion for young Frenchmen' which brutalised the soldiers who tortured him even as it 'broke' its Arab suspects.[34]

To the classical scholar Pierre Vidal-Naquet, torture was a 'cancer of democracy' which eroded French democratic institutions through the creation of a secret conspiratorial world of unaccountable power. Camus firmly rejected the utilitarian defence of torture as a means of saving lives, arguing that, 'Torture has perhaps saved some, at the expense of honour, by uncovering thirty bombs, but at the same time it arouses fifty new terrorists who, operating in some other way and in some other place, will cause the death of even more innocent people.'[35] In the short term, however, the army's methods began to make inroads into the FLN's urban network. In February ben M'hidi, joint leader of the FLN, was caught and secretly executed by Aussaresses himself, though his death was publicly described at the time as suicide. At night Algiers was placed under curfew and the city belonged to the paratroopers, who entered the Kasbah to take more suspects off for arrest or interrogation. By day the violence continued. In May two paratroopers were shot in the street and a group of their comrades machine-gunned a Turkish bath reputed to be an FLN hideout, killing up to eighty Muslims, most of them beggars who used the baths as a night shelter. In June the bombings began again, when four FLN operatives disguised as electricity and gas workers placed shrapnel bombs in lamp posts near bus stops around the city centre, which were deliberately timed to explode during rush hour, killing numerous pedestrians.

In the same month a bomb exploded in a popular European dance hall called Le Casino, killing nine people and wounding eighty-five, including the band's female singer, who lost both feet. Soon after this atrocity the liberal ethnologist Germaine Tillion met Yacef himself and her subsequent recollections provide some of the few insights into the inner world of Yacef and his circle. The meeting was arranged through a female Muslim friend, and Tillion was taken to a house in the Kasbah, expecting to engage in conversation with students about her writings.

Instead she found herself in a room with two young women, including Zohra Drif, before two heavily armed men entered. One of them was Yacef himself, whom Drif introduced only as *le grand frère* and the other was described as 'our glorious Ali la Pointe'. The former Resistance fighter and inmate of Ravensbruck concentration camp now found herself in a long political discussion with the two most wanted men in Algiers. Yacef and his compatriots questioned Tillion in detail about her experiences in the Resistance, when the following exchange occurred:

> After about two and a half hours of conversation, Yacef smiled faintly and said something like: 'You see that we are neither criminals nor murderers.' Very sadly, but very firmly, I answered: 'You are murderers.' He was so startled that he said nothing for a moment and seemed to be choking. Then his eyes filled with tears and he said: 'Yes, Madame Tillion, we are murderers.' Then he told me several details about the Casino bombing, adding that when he heard about it he wept for three days and three nights. In the second part of the conversation, he had tears in his eyes on several occasions, and when he spoke of the Casino incident the tears ran down his face.[36]

Tillion saw Yacef's outburst as evidence of 'a moral burden that had probably been weighing upon him for some time when I met him'. The idea that those responsible for atrocities such as Le Casino and the Milk Bar might be carrying a 'moral burden' does not fit well with the image of the universal terrorist, but Yacef's tears were clearly authentic as he told Tillion that the FLN bombs were 'our only way of expressing ourselves'. At the end of this extraordinary meeting Yacef made an unexpected promise to Tillion that no more civilians would be killed, provided no more executions of nationalists were carried out by the government. Though Tillion's subsequent overtures to influential members of the government failed to achieve this objective, Yacef kept his promise.

Tillion subsequently stated her belief that Yacef had ordered a halt to attacks on the French population not only in Algiers itself but across Algeria 'for specifically moral reasons – in order to spare the innocent'. But Yacef was not in a position to take such decisions for long. In September he was cornered in a house in the Kasbah and surrendered with Zohra Drif when a paratroop officer threatened to blow up the building. The following month Ali la Pointe, Petit Omar and the former nurse Hassiba ben Bouali were trapped behind a concealed partition in one of their Kasbah houses. Unlike Yacef they refused to surrender and the paratroopers took no chances, setting off a charge of plastic explosive so powerful that it destroyed the entire house and killed seventeen Muslims in neighbouring buildings.

The death of Ali la Pointe signified the end of the battle of Algiers. For all the publicity and international attention it had generated, it was a political and military disaster for the FLN, which failed to bring sufficient national or international pressure to get the French government to the negotiating table. In addition, the FLN lost credit with its own Muslim constituency for the horrendous repression which the violence had brought down on their heads. On the surface, the restoration of civil order in Algiers was a vindication of Massu's methods and the paras became the toast of the European city. But the tortures and executions left a profound legacy of bitterness and anger towards the French amongst the Muslim population that was far greater than their resentment at the FLN. Faced with such antipathy, French hopes of retaining Algeria through negotiations with a Muslim 'third force' made little headway. Instead there was increasingly no option beyond the search for an elusive military victory. Nor was the FLN ever completely eradicated from Algiers, as the triumphant nationalist demonstrations of December 1960 showed, when the residents of the Kasbah poured into the European quarter in their thousands waving green and white FLN flags, even as they were fired on by French soldiers and police.

The counter-terrorist hero

The idea that the explosion of violence in Algiers constituted a 'battle' was another indication of the degree to which conventional notions of warfare had changed on both sides during the Algerian 'events'. Whether the victims were French civilians blown up or maimed by FLN bombs, or Arabs tortured and killed in clandestine *centres de tri*, it was not like any battle that the world had previously seen. General de Gaulle coined the term *la sale guerre* – the dirty war – to describe the methods used by the French army. The new conception of warfare generated a new concept of military heroism, in which the counter-terrorist warrior is 'forced' to use the methods of the terrorist in order to defeat him. Once of the most popular exponents of the counter-terrorist mythology was the novelist and former paratrooper Jean Larteguy, whose novels on the paratroop regiment became best-sellers in France during the Algerian war. In his most popular novel, *The Centurions* (1961), Larteguy depicted his former comrades in Algeria as the modern-day equivalent of the Roman legionnaires, authentic heroes fighting against international communism, 'that monstrous brain that sought to reduce mankind to insects', on behalf of a decadent French society that has forgotten the meaning of heroism.

The novel follows the progress of the charismatic Colonel Raspéguy and his officers from their defeat at Dien Bien Phu to the mountains of Algeria. Though Raspéguy and his men are the epitome of martial purity, they are also intellectuals, familiar with Mao Zedong, Camus and Malraux, proponents of the new strategy of *la guerre révolutionnaire* that will save France and civilisation from the communist insectoid hordes. Once in Algeria in their new desert-combat fatigues, the modern-day 'centurions' are forced, like Robert Ruark's white settlers, to embrace the new methods of counter-terrorist warfare. When an FLN band kills and mutilates two paratroopers and leave their bodies facing Mecca, the paratroopers slaughter all the adult males in a nearby village with knives and line up the bodies with 'their throats cut, their heads turned towards the West, in the direction of Rome'.

After the massacre Raspéguy criticises his men for allowing themselves to descend to the same level as the natives, telling them: 'I should have preferred the grenades and sub-machine guns, and the whole lot wiped out. Knives turn warfare into murder. And here we are doing what they do, soiling our hands like them.' For Larteguy, the willingness of the paras to descend to such depths is proof of their moral superiority. Like the counter-terrorist warriors of our own era, Larteguy's paratrooper heroes were exemplary servants of the state in a new kind of war in which 'the rules of the game have changed' and his celebration of their achievements was matched by a withering contempt for a decadent French society which failed to appreciate the new parameters.

Writing terror

For Larteguy, the decadence of metropolitan France was epitomised more than anything else by the vocal criticism directed at the French army from French liberals and leftists. More than any political issue since the Dreyfus affair, the Algerian war galvanised and divided French writers and intellectuals, producing a flood of essays, articles, books and manifestos which analysed the ongoing violence from a variety of political and moral perspectives. The questions raised during the *guerre de l'écrit* remain pertinent to any discussion of the legitimacy of violence, both that of the state and of its enemies. Are there any moral limits that must be observed in the conduct of revolutionary violence? Can those who dominate and oppress another race or community dictate the methods used by the oppressed to defeat them? Can torture ever be a legitimate instrument of the state? If a revolutionary organisation is prepared to engage in the systematic killing of civilians in order to undermine the state, is the state not justified in using equally extreme measures to protect its citizens and defend itself?

All these issues were debated with passionate intensity in the course of the war and its aftermath. If liberals and leftists were sometimes able to find common cause with more conservative intellectuals in their denunciation of torture, there was less unanimity when it came to the violence of the FLN itself. While militant advocates of the Algerian revolution such as François Jeanson and Jean-Paul Sartre wanted the left to go beyond their criticism of the French conduct of the war and come out openly in favour of Algerian independence, others found the atrocities of the FLN as morally repugnant as the army's use of torture.

To the FLN and its leftist supporters these moralistic concerns smacked of bad faith, which failed to differentiate between the violence used to uphold an oppressive social system and the revolutionary violence used to overthrow it. In his hugely influential anti-colonial tract *The Wretched of the Earth*, Franz Fanon argued that violence could be a psychologically liberating process for the colonised native which, 'At the level of individuals ... is a cleansing force. It frees the native from his inferiority complex and from his despair and inaction; it makes him fearless and restores his self-respect.'[37]

For Fanon, violence is a transforming and redemptive process in which the colonised native finds an outlet for the bottled-up aggression that once found release in ecstatic dances, crime and domestic violence, and 'canalises in the direction of the occupying power all congenitally murderous acts'. The notion that revolutionary violence could be therapeutic was given even more strident expression in Sartre's famous preface to *The Wretched of the Earth*, which asserted that 'The rebel's weapon is the proof of his humanity. For in the first days of the revolt you must kill: to shoot down a European is to kill two birds with one stone, to destroy an oppressor and the man he oppresses at the same time; there remain a dead man, and a free man; the survivor, for the first time feels a *national* soil under his boot'.[38]

For Sartre, violence was the act of 'man re-creating himself', which opened the way to the socialist future that will unfold 'once the last settler is killed, shipped home or assimilated'. It is difficult to believe that Sartre or Fanon regarded the disembowelments and throatcuttings of European women and children at El-Halia and Phillippeville as psychologically liberating events. But Sartre's use of impersonal abstractions such as 'the settler' and 'the native' tends to distance the discussion of 'violence' from its real consequences. In his self-chosen role as the interpreter of the Third World revolution to a European audience, Sartre was determined to be provocative, and his statements on violence sound dangerously glib and shallow as a consequence.

Sartre has been variously criticised as a self-hating European intellectual and an armchair revolutionary theorist, but his support for the Algerian revolution was entirely coherent and consistent in his own terms. Having decided that the FLN was the legitimate representative of the Algerian revolution he gave it his full unconditional support and refused to criticise any of its actions. This was the position Sartre held throughout the conflict, in both his writings and his public interventions, a position which earned him the vilification of the French extreme right and a bomb attack on his Paris apartment.

The silence of Albert Camus

Sartre's militant advocacy of the Algerian revolution placed him at odds with his former friend and political ally Albert Camus. As the most prominent pied noir intellectual, and a writer and thinker whose work was strongly defined by a preoccupation with the relationship between morality and politics, Camus's views on the conflict were a subject of close scrutiny in both France and Algeria. Unlike Sartre, Camus had participated in the French Resistance and his attitude towards violence was always tempered by real experience. Though not a pacifist, he opposed what he called the 'deification' of violence and was wary of its potential to become an institutionalised instrument of state power.

Camus was particularly critical of intellectuals who advocated or toler-
ated what he called 'comfortable murder' from the safety of their studies
and his strongly moralistic approach to politics was severely tested by the
eruption of violence in his own homeland. Camus was not insensible to
the social causes of the revolt, but he nevertheless regarded Algeria as an
integral part of France and refused to accept the idea of Algerian independence. In January 1956 Camus, together with a small group of European and
Muslim liberals, formed a 'Committee for a Civil Truce in Algeria' which
aimed to promote the idea of a mutual 'civilian truce' in which both sides
would agree to refrain from 'the murder of the innocent'. By this time the
war had already passed the stage when either side was prepared to accept
a limitation on the level of violence, and the civil truce committee was dissolved following a stormy public meeting in Algiers.

Camus was bitterly disillusioned by the failure and made the decision
to refrain from any further public declarations or interventions concerning
Algeria. For the remaining years of his life he remained an absent presence in
the Algerian debate, restricting his involvement to behind-the-scenes interventions on behalf of Algerian Muslim friends who had been imprisoned or
condemned to death. The motivations behind this Achilles-like withdrawal
from the political arena were complicated and Camus often struggled to
understand them himself. But the refusal of the most prominent French-
Algerian intellectual to enter the most urgent national political debate of
the era mystified and angered his contemporaries. In December 1957, while
receiving the Nobel Prize for literature, he delivered a speech at Stockholm
University, where he was heckled by an Algerian student about his failure
to condemn French abuses in his native land. Camus lost his temper and
declared that, 'I have always condemned terror. I must also condemn a terrorism which is exercised blindly, in the streets of Algiers, for example, and
which one day could strike my mother or my daughter. I believe in justice,
but I would defend my mother before justice.'[39]

These comments brought a storm of criticism from leftist French and
Algerian intellectuals, who accused him of implicitly supporting the pacification campaigns of the French army by referring only to the 'terrorism'
of the FLN. To his critics, Camus was now revealed as a 'colonialist under
the skin', whose humanistic denunciation of FLN terrorism concealed more
partisan political sympathies. There was no doubt that Camus was genu-
inely appalled by the FLN's methods, but his reluctance to enter the Algerian
debate was never based entirely on humanitarian grounds. In a notebook
entry in February 1957 he wrote that 'My position has not varied on this

matter and if I am able to understand and to admire the liberation fighter, I have only disgust for the killer of women and children'.[40] The problem was that, in Algeria at least, the two concepts were not incompatible. Nor was the killing of women and children restricted to the insurgents. In 1958, shortly before the collapse of the Fourth Republic and de Gaulle's ascent to power, Camus broke his silence with the publication of *Actuelles*, a collection of his previous Algerian essays. In a new foreword he criticised pro-FLN French intellectuals who believed 'that the Arabs have acquired the right to slaughter and mutilate', and condemned once again 'the insane criminal who may throw his bomb into an innocent crowd that includes my family.'[41]

Camus's belief that such practices were restricted to 'the Arabs' carried more than a hint of pied-noir prejudice, as did his call for a federated political arrangement between France and Algeria as an alternative to 'an Algeria linked to an empire of Islam'. But as Sartre already realised, and de Gaulle himself would later come to accept from a very different political perspective, the FLN represented wider nationalist aspirations that could no longer be denied without an endless war of repression. For all his disgust with the FLN's methods, the logic of Camus's political position required a continuation of the war and an intensification of French repression. The alternative was to enter into political negotiations with the terrorist enemy, regardless of its methods. This was not a reality that Camus was able to accept and he effectively bowed out of the political arena in favour of the moral high ground.

The witness

Camus did not live to see the end of French Algeria. On 7 January 1960 he died in a car crash, without having broken his silence again. Among the many who paid tribute to him were his former friend, the Algerian novelist Mouloud Feraoun. As a teacher working with the liberal French educational institution the Centres Sociaux Educatifs, Feraoun watched the war unfold at first hand, in a small provincial town in his native Kabylia, where he continued to teach, think and write while compiling the notes, stories and newspaper clippings that would later be incorporated into his private journal.

Feraoun's wartime journal contains an unsparingly honest and agonised portrayal of a conflict that he saw as characterised by 'cruelty, egoism, ambition, arrogance, and stupidity' on all sides. Unlike Sartre and Fanon, Feraoun also addressed the subject of FLN violence towards other Muslims and he frequently expressed his outrage at the FLN's brutality and authoritarianism, such as the following entry, written on 9 March 1956 in response to reports that FLN units had machine gunned farmers and burned down their farms:

> Can people who kill innocents in cold blood be called liberators? If so, have they considered for a moment that their 'violence' will engender more 'violence', will legitimise it, and will hasten its terrible manifestation? They know that the people are unarmed, bunched together in their villages, immensely vulnerable. Are they knowingly preparing for the massacre of 'their brothers'?[42]

These were important questions, which the subsequent history of post-colonial Algeria would render even more pertinent. But even though Feraoun bitterly criticised the FLN, he nevertheless recognised the nationalist impetus behind the revolt in a way that Camus did not and saw that the organisation had come to embody an unstoppable collective will for independence, which he found simultaneously terrifying and awe inspiring. Such was the level of violence in Feraoun's native Kabylia that in 1957 he moved to Algiers for the safety of his family, even as the battle of Algiers was moving to its bloody conclusion. For the next five years he worked as a school inspector and continued to record the large and small events of the war with the same luminous intelligence, as Algiers became a murder zone once again and pied noir ultras of the Organisation de l'Armée Secrète (Secret Army Organisation), OAS, unleashed a sanguinary terrorist offensive that eclipsed the FLN's earlier efforts. In the last months of the war, the OAS killed Arabs at random and the murder rate climbed to forty deaths per day. On 15 March 1962 Feraoun attended the final planning meeting of the Serveis Sociales in the suburb of El Biar. In the middle of the meeting a group of OAS commandos entered the room and read out a list of seven names, including Feraoun's. The seven were taken into an adjoining courtyard and shot. The gunmen took their time, beginning in the legs to make the deaths as painful as possible. Thus the man who had criticised the authoritarianism and brutality of the FLN was himself murdered by the OAS on suspicion of being an FLN member. Feraoun's journal was in the editorial stage at the time of his death and was published shortly afterwards. More than four decades later, it remains a testament of supreme intellectual and moral courage and a stark counterpoint to Sartre's and Fanon's more abstract and ideological exaltation of revolutionary violence.

Gillo Pontecorvo and the Battle of Algiers

More than any other colonial conflict, the Algerian war epitomised the disparity between the supposedly humanistic aspirations of revolutionary violence and the inhuman nature of the violence itself. This contradiction was brilliantly addressed in the Italian director Gillo Pontecorvo's cinematic masterpiece *The Battle of Algiers* (1966). Shot in Algiers only a few years after independence with a mostly unknown cast, the film depicted the course of an anti-colonial struggle with a stunning combination of documentary realism and operatic emotional power that has never been equalled. The tone is set by an early scene in which Ali la Pointe and his collaborators are hidden in an alcove as French paratroopers line the entrance with explosives. The framed, almost painterly shot captures their faces illuminated in the darkness. They are faces of great beauty, serenely defiant and determined, refusing to answer when the French officer orders them to surrender or be blown up. No single image has ever captured more effectively the inner culture of heroic self-sacrifice and nobility of purpose at the heart of revolutionary terrorist violence.

Though the sympathies of Pontecorvo were clearly with the FLN, the film avoids caricature in its presentation of the French adversary. The paratrooper colonel, Mathieu, an amalgam of Massu's politicised colonels, is a suave, cultured intellectual, who defends the use of torture, as Massu did himself, on utilitarian grounds. When a journalist questions the paratroopers' methods at a press conference Mathieu replies, 'We are soldiers and our only duty is to win. Therefore, to be precise, I would now like to ask you a question: Should France remain in Algeria? If you answer "yes" then you must accept all the necessary consequences.'

In their depiction of FLN terrorism Pontecorvo and his scriptwriter, Franco Solinas, reverse the dilemma and ask their audience to agree that if France should be removed from Algeria then they too should accept all the necessary consequences. In the scene of Hassiba ben Bouali's bombing of the Milk Bar, the camera pans round the café, showing the European customers who are about to be killed and mutilated, including a child eating an ice cream. The audience is invited to suspend moral judgement and see the atrocity as a necessary tragedy, as logical in its context as the use of torture by the French. In this way Pontecorvo achieved a seemingly impossible feat, that no previous film director had even attempted, in which the deliberate killing and maiming of civilians appear to be morally acceptable acts of war.

In a subsequent interview Solinas rejected the idea that such methods were morally unacceptable, claiming that the notion of ethical standards in warfare was an anachronistic relic of a 'romantic, nineteenth-century attitude' that was inherently dishonest to begin with, since, 'For centuries they've tried to prove that war is fair play, just like duels; but war is not and therefore any method used to fight it is good ... It is not a question of ethics or fair play. What we must attack is war itself and the situations that lead to it, not the methods used to fight it.'[43] The *Battle of Algiers* is a dramatic exposition of this essential thesis. For all its grainy realism, the film contains an epic, almost mythological narrative of collective heroism in which suffering, sacrifice and violence pave the way for the triumphant eruption of popular power in the film's closing sequences.

Few accounts of the Algerian war have been as influential as Pontecorvo's film. In terms of its impact on revolutionary organisations across the world, it constituted a cinematic counterpart to Kravchinsky's *Underground Russia*. Many urban revolutionary groups have claimed Algeria as a tactical inspiration, but thousands of revolutionaries and would-be revolutionaries across the world derived their first impressions of the Algerian war from *The Battle of Algiers*. Police forces and armies everywhere have also referred to it for their own purposes, and within a few years of its making the film formed part of the curriculum at the International Police Academy in Washington, where Latin American police officers were being trained to deal with a new incarnation of the terrorist hero who had begun to appear in cities across the continent.

The Romance of the Urban Guerrilla

The words 'aggressor' and 'terrorist' no longer mean what they did. Instead of arousing fear or censure, they are a call to action. To be called an aggressor or a terrorist in Brazil is now an honour to any citizen, for it means that he is fighting, with a gun in his hand, against the monstrosity of the present dictatorship and the suffering it causes.

Carlos Marighela, Minimanual of the Urban Guerrilla, 1969

In November 1970 *Time* magazine devoted an alarming in-depth report to a new global phenomenon: 'The Urban Guerrillas'. It depicted an alarming upsurge in left-wing urban terrorism from Canada and Latin America to India and Northern Ireland that recalled 'the last decades of the nineteenth century, when an anarchistic reign of terror spread a blanket of fear all over Europe and the US'. *Time*'s coverage of these events itself recalled the nineteenth century, in its depiction of a peaceful and democratic world under assault from violent nihilistic cults whose members were impervious to rationality. As is so often the case in the establishment presentation of 'terrorism', *Time* presented the 'urban guerrillas' as a danger to democracy, even in countries where democracy was conspicuously absent. In the case of Brazil, for example, *Time* blamed terrorism for having 'set Latin America's most powerful country back by several political light years', even though Brazil had been ruled by a military dictatorship since 1964, three years *before* the emergence of the first Brazilian urban guerrilla group. By 1970, the regime had incarcerated some 12,000 political prisoners and had become a pioneer in the new 'scientific' methods of torture that would spread across Latin America over the next decade.

The *Time* reporters made no comment on these practices, except to observe that 'Brazil's tough response has put all but a few fanatics out of the terror business'. In an open letter published in *Le Monde* that same year, however, Dilma Borges Vieira, the wife of a Brazilian journalist arrested by the Brazilian army, gave more insight into the methods used against such 'fanatics'. The letter was addressed to the wife of the Brazilian consul in Uruguay,

Aloysio Gomides, whose husband had been kidnapped by Uruguayan revolutionaries. Senhora Vieira described how her own husband, a left-wing
journalist, had been tortured and literally flayed to death by his interrogators, before addressing the Brazilian consul's wife directly:

> I know, madam, that you are not in a position to understand my suffering,
> because each one's suffering is always greater than that of the rest. But you
> understand, I hope, that the conditions that brought about the kidnapping of
> your husband and the fatal torture of mine are the very same: that it is impor-
> tant to realise that hunger-violence, misery-violence, oppression-violence,
> underdevelopment-violence, torture-violence lead to kidnapping-violence, ter-
> rorism-violence, guerrilla-violence; and that it is very important to understand
> who puts the violence into practice: whether it is those who cause misery or
> those who fight against it.[1]

This letter was later quoted in full in the great Argentinian writer Julio Cortázar's novel *A Manual for Manuel*. Cortázar's most overtly political novel
was an attempt to align his own cultural preoccupations with the utopian
aspirations of the Latin American revolution, mixing contemporary newspaper reports on torture, guerrilla raids and the Cuban sugar-cane harvest
with playful meditations on Stockhausen, Joni Mitchell and sexual freedom.
The mood of playful new-left optimism is captured by one of Cortázar's
bohemian intellectuals, who declares that revolution 'has to be something
like wanting to go to bed or playing or going to the movies, something that
just comes out, like a cough or a curse'.

The English playwright Christopher Hampton also offered a sympathetic
portrait of the Latin American urban guerrillas in his play *Savages*, in which
a Brazilian urban guerrilla cell kidnaps a British diplomat in order to obtain
the release of political prisoners. Both Cortázar and Hampton were writing
at a period when the western world was becoming increasingly preoccupied
with the prospect of terrorism, 'subversion' and internal unrest. These fears
were especially prevalent in the United States, where the January 1968 issue
of *Army* magazine carried an article by Colonel Robert B. Rigg predicting
'scenes of destruction approaching those of Stalingrad in World War II', in
which 'at least one major metropolitan area could be faced with guerrilla
warfare requiring sizeable United States army elements'.[2]

The US government took such predictions sufficiently seriously to conduct
various hearings and investigations on the subject of 'internal security' in
the 1960s and early 1970s, as the spectre of a violent urban conflagration

continued to haunt political scientists, military and counter-insurgency analysts and writers throughout the decade. To some analysts the size and complexity of modern cities made them inherently fragile and vulnerable to internal assaults, so that even the smallest groups now possessed what the *Time* reporters called a 'disproportionate power to render society immobile'. These fears were not entirely new. In the nineteenth century, the 'anarchist terror' generated equally apocalyptic scenarios, in which anarchists were believed to have the capability and the intention to wipe out whole cities by poisoning reservoirs, blowing up dams or dropping bombs from the air. In its depiction of the urban guerrillas, *Time* demonstrated once again how official 'terrorism' narratives can reflect the perennial fears of violent implosion and civilisational collapse that are part of technological society. Once again it exaggerated the scale of the threat, while at the same time it fused complex and disparate violent conflicts into a single phenomenon, in which all acts of violence could be attributed to the same urge for destruction and the same nihilistic aversion to democracy and international 'order'.

Cities under siege

There were historical precedents for what would later be called urban guerrilla warfare, from Dublin to Algiers. But it was in Latin America where the concept of urban guerrilla warfare was first articulated into a coherent set of strategies and tactics, and where the image of the urban guerrilla acquired its glamorous and seductive aura. Though urban terrorism had played a minor role in the Cuban revolution, the Cuban guerrillas who overthrew the Batista dictatorship in 1959 regarded the city as 'the graveyard of the revolution', where the state forces were strongest and where any revolutionary activity was liable to draw high casualties. According to the theory of the *foco insurrectional* promulgated by Che Guevara, the natural revolutionary battlefield was the countryside, where mobile guerrilla 'columns' could act as an armed vanguard and make maximum use of the available space and topography. Inspired by Che's vision of revolutionary spontaneity amongst the peasantry, a generation of Latin American revolutionaries established such 'columns' in various countries, the majority of whom were destroyed by US-trained armies that were better equipped to deal with rural insurgencies than Batista's had been.

It was not until after Che Guevara's death in 1967 that urban guerrilla warfare really came into its own as a distinct revolutionary strategy. Its most prominent exponent was a former Brazilian communist congressman named Carlos Marighela, who summarised his theories in a detailed and influential handbook entitled *Minimanual of the Urban Guerrilla*. Like Kravchinsky's *Underground Russia*, the *Minimanual* offered a beguiling vision of urban revolutionary warfare, in which the anonymity and alienation of the modern city could be superseded by a new revolutionary hero, part bandit, part guerrilla, fighting in the name of 'a just cause, the cause of the people ... Though his arms are inferior to those of the enemy, his moral superiority is incontestable.' For Marighela the ideal urban guerrilla was a jack of all trades, able 'to drive a car, pilot a plane, handle both motor and sailing-boats, to know something of mechanics, radio, telephones, and even electronics'.

These revolutionary supermen were to be organised into 'firing groups' of four to five people, acting on their own initiative whenever possible, in order to 'baffle, discredit and harass the Brazilian military and other forces of repression', thus paving the way for a nationwide campaign of violence and sabotage. Like Nechaev before him, Marighela believed that 'the mistakes and the various calamities that fall upon the people' as a result of these activities would be attributed to the government rather than the revolutionaries themselves. Marighela's own attempts to practise these principles occurred when he was already in his fifties. In 1967 he broke with the Brazilian Communist Party and formed a broad movement called Action for National Liberation to begin armed struggle against the dictatorship. Two years later, on 3 September 1969, Marighela became involved in the kidnapping of the US ambassador in Brazil, Charles Elbrick, who was eventually released following the extradition of fifteen political prisoners.

Elbrick subsequently praised his captors for their idealism and commitment and their humane treatment of him. The events surrounding the Elbrick kidnapping later became the subject of the Brazilian director Luis Barreto's *4 Days In September* (1997). The young revolutionaries it depicts are mostly young middle-class students, with little conception of the forces ranged against them. They are courageous, idealistic and dangerously naive, unwitting players in a lethal game that begins as a heroic adventure and leads them to imprisonment, torture and death. Barreto's film was made in a different era, when the romantic image of the urban guerrilla had long since faded. Marighela himself outlived the kidnapping of Elbrick by less than a month. On 4 November 1969 he was shot dead in an ambush, wearing a wig and carrying a briefcase, by police agents disguised as building labourers and necking couples. The urban guerrillas were not the only ones, it seemed, who could make use of the topography of the modern city.

Che Guevara in the city

If Marighela was the tactician of urban guerrilla warfare, its most influential strategist was an exiled Spanish Civil War veteran named Abraham Guillén, who moved from Argentina to the Uruguayan capital of Montevideo in the 1960s. Unlike Marighela, Guillén's activist days were over by the time he began to elaborate his theories and he was a professorial figure, reliving battles from the Spanish Civil War on the plastic map of Spain which he used as a protector on his kitchen table. In *Strategy of the Urban Guerrilla* (1966), Guillén argued that in countries where the majority of the population lived in urban conglomerations the main focus of revolutionary war should be in the cities. To Guillén it was axiomatic that 'between a favourable territory and a favourable population the army must choose the population and not the terrain'.[3]

These wars would not be fought like previous urban wars in Stalingrad or the Warsaw uprising, where enemy forces had been able to use artillery or air power against fixed positions defended by the insurgents. Instead, the urban guerrilla columns would avoid major battles and 'slowly corrode the enemy, stripping him of his ability to unite his forces' by carrying out lightning attacks and melting back into the urban population that supported them. In Guillén's optimistic prognosis, the urban guerrillas would cede control of the streets by day and re-emerge at night to conduct their operations. Like Kravchinsky and Michael Collins before him, Guillén predicted that 'the war will be won by whoever endures longest'.[4]

These proposals ignored the experience of urban guerrilla warfare in Caracas and Algiers, where the insurgents had noticeably failed to achieve the level of invulnerability that Guillén predicted. For a generation of urbanised Latin American leftists, however, the proposals of Marighela and Guillén offered the chance to realise Che Guevara's call to create 'two, three many Vietnams' in an environment that they were familiar with. The men and women who answered this call were mostly middle-class graduates or students, products of the post-war expansion in higher education whose expectations the economic system was increasingly unable to satisfy. On the one hand these students belonged to the international youth culture of the sixties, brought up on protest music, sexual liberation, Sartre, rock and roll and films like *The Battle of Algiers*, *Zabriskie Point* and *The Hour of the Furnaces*. At the same time they were often painfully aware of their privileged isolation from the peasant masses and the working classes. In countries such as Uruguay, where the majority of the population lived in cities, the strategy of urban guerrilla warfare made a virtue out of necessity. And it was here, in Guillén's adopted home of Montevideo, that urban guerrilla warfare was practised with unrivalled skill and ingenuity.

Robin Hood in Uruguay

On the surface, a country known to the outside world largely as an exporter of meat and wool and Fray Bentos corned beef was an unlikely setting for a guerrilla campaign of any kind. In addition, the Uruguayan republic had a long tradition of democratic consensus and political stability that was summed up in the popular refrain *Como el Uruguay no hay* – there's no place like Uruguay. Uruguay's reputation as a Latin American exception was largely due to the pioneering reforms introduced at the beginning of the century by Uruguay's visionary president Jose Batlle y Ordoñez, whose two terms of office laid the basis for a modern welfare state that was unrivalled in Latin America and in advance of much of the industrialised world.

Throughout the 1960s the Batlle model began to unravel. The international prices of meat and wool fell and the Uruguayan economy began to stagnate accordingly. Stagnation turned to recession, fuelling an inflationary spiral that had reached 136 per cent by the late 1960s and ate into salaries and pensions, resulting in the pauperisation of the middle class and growing political unrest.[5] It was against this background of dizzying economic collapse and vanishing prosperity that a new revolutionary organisation calling itself the National Liberation Movement (NLM) emerged, under the leadership of a charismatic former student and trade union organiser named Raul Sendic. The organisation called itself the Tupamaros, after the rebellious eighteenth-century Inca chief Tupac Amaru, executed by the Spanish, and it rapidly acquired an unrivalled international reputation as the most skilful of all urban guerrilla organisations.

Though sporadic armed actions connected to the group could be traced back to 1963, it was not until August 1968 that the Tupamaros first established themselves as a national presence, with a series of politically astute and largely bloodless operations that increased their popularity even as they humiliated the government. On one occasion the Tupamaros robbed the offices of a loan company and photocopied pages from its account books, revealing massive fraud and malpractice in which government ministers and prominent business figures were implicated. In another operation the Tupamaros robbed the house of a local tobacco magnate and stole £25,000 worth of gold bullion, together with documents proving years of tax evasion, which they handed over to a judge. In February 1970 the Tupamaros carried out the biggest armed robbery in Uruguayan history, when guerrillas wearing police uniforms held up a casino in the Punta del Este beach resort and walked away with £7.5 million. When the croupiers complained in the newspapers that they had lost their tips the robbers mailed them back a few days later.

The Tupamaros also engaged in agitprop and 'armed propaganda', using inventive and unusual means that often seemed more appropriate to revolutionary theatre than guerrilla warfare. During the 1968 Book and Print Fair, a box gently exploded, showering revolutionary leaflets over the crowd. On the walls of an elite nightclub they wrote *O Bailan todos o no baila nadie* – Either everyone dances or no one dances. Across Montevideo armed guerrillas burst into cafés and public meeting places to deliver political lectures and entered cinemas to harangue their audiences or project their own short propaganda films onto the screen.

The verve and ingenuity of these operations made the government and the police seem inept by comparison and the organisation grew rapidly, acquiring some 3,000 active members and another 5,000 supporters, whose ranks included high-school pupils and students, professors of fine art, housewives, white-collar workers and even policemen and army officers. Like revolutionary superheroes, bank clerks would carry out robberies during their lunch-breaks and then return to their desks; office workers would take advantage of a faked appointment with the dentist to carry out an act of armed propaganda; primary school teachers would spend their free time guarding hostages in a 'people's prison'.

Few urban revolutionary organisations have ever exceeded the Tupamaros in their use of the modern city as a theatre of revolutionary warfare. In addition to an extensive network of safe houses, prisons and arms caches across Montevideo, they organised their own medical corps, the *commando sanitario*, with its own ambulance service for wounded guerrillas, a 24-hour switchboard and clandestine hospitals for short-term and long-term medical care, all of it completely secret. Their exploits and technical efficiency were celebrated beyond the national borders of Uruguay, to the point when even Uruguayans who did not support them took a certain patriotic pride in their reputation as the best urban guerrillas on the continent.

On 8 October 1969 the confrontation entered a new phase, when the Tupamaros decided to commemorate the second anniversary of Che Guevara's death with the occupation of Pando, a small town of 20,000 about fifteen minutes from Montevideo. The operation was carried out with characteristic theatrical flair, as a group of Tupamaros staged a faked funeral in the town to bury a deceased uncle. The mourners had hired a cortège of five cars and a van for the funeral and arrived bearing the coffin, together with two weeping black-clad women. As the cortège moved slowly through the streets of Pando, more mourners began to join the procession, while other guerrillas arrived in town in cars or on public transport. At a given signal, the mourners overpowered the hired chauffeurs and distributed a supply of weapons concealed in the coffin. Within fifteen minutes the various Tupamaros units had robbed two banks, taken over the police station, the fire station and the telephone exchange and distributed hundreds of leaflets to the stunned population.

As the guerrillas sped back towards the capital in high spirits, they found the road blocked by police and were forced to leave their cars. In the running gun-battles that followed, three Tupamaros were killed and twenty more captured and tortured. As a result, the organisation began to carry out exemplary 'deterrent' assassinations of notoriously brutal police officers and torturers, such as the police superintendent Moran Chaquero, the head of Montevideo's anti-terrorist brigade, who was shot dead in March 1970. And that same year the Tupamaros carried out an operation that brought the organisation for the first time into the emerging narrative of an international terrorist onslaught on the democratic world.

The advisor

The growing use of torture in Uruguayan police stations was further evidence of how far Uruguay was moving from its liberal traditions. Like the French Resistance, captured Tupamaros were expected to try to hold out for at least twenty-four hours. During and after that time they might be subjected to the full range of techniques being developed by the new twentieth-century inquisitors in Latin America, from beatings and burning with cigarettes, to the electric prod known as the *picana*. The new profession-alisation of torture required training and equipment, which the Uruguayan police and armed forces initially received from the military regime in Brazil. In 1969, however, an American FBI agent named Dan Mitrione arrived in Montevideo on assignment with the Agency for International Development (AID) as an advisor to the Uruguayan police. Mitrione had previously been an advisor to the Brazilian police in Belo Horizonte, where he had become an expert on the interrogation of political prisoners.

Based in an unmarked office in the central police station in Montevideo the advisor began to play a similar role in training the Uruguayan police. Among his innovations was the introduction of newer electrode needles for the *picana*, that could be inserted under the fingernails or the gums. The Uruguayan public was unaware of Mitrione's existence until he was kidnapped on 31 July 1970 by the Tupamaros, who demanded the release of 150 prisoners and promised to execute him in a week if their demands were not met. The kidnapping became a national emergency as the army combed Montevideo in a futile attempt to locate Mitrione and two other hostages kidnapped on the same day. For the first time in its history, Uruguay became the object of international media attention, as the US government rejected negotiations with the kidnappers and even the pope joined in the condemnation of the Tupamaros. On 10 August Mitrione's corpse was found in a car, shot by different calibre bullets in what appeared to be a collective execution. In death, the former Indiana policeman-turned-torturer became part of a ritual that has been repeated in other terrorist hostage episodes, in which the innocence and virtuousness of the 'victim of terrorism' serves to highlight the absolute evil and inhumanity of his killers. Thus the US secretary of state, William Rogers, condemned 'the spread of terrorism, which cloaks common crimes in political fanaticism' while the *New York Times* accused the Tupamaros of using the 'techniques of Hitler'. The outrage in the United States was such that even Frank Sinatra held a special benefit concert with Jerry Lewis for Mitrione's widow in Mitrione's home town in Richmond, where he told the audience, 'In my book of human beings worth knowing and remembering, Dan Mitrione is really something else.'[6]

Amid the outpouring of moral indignation, both Mitrione's actual role in Uruguay and the policies that he served were almost universally ignored. While Mitrione was presented as a humble policeman trying to assist a developing country on traffic control, the Tupamaros were cited again and again as embodying barbaric evil. For their part, Mitrione's kidnappers gained nothing from this episode. Not only did they fail to obtain the release of prisoners but they clearly miscalculated the importance of their hostage and locked themselves into a doomed negotiating process, in which they saw themselves obliged to choose between carrying out their threat of execution and losing face politically.

The Mitrione incident received a more sympathetic treatment in Costa Gavras's influential film *State of Siege* (1973). Scripted by Pontecorvo's scriptwriter Franco Solinas, the film depicts the kidnapping by an unnamed revolutionary organisation of an American police advisor, Philip Santore, played by Yves Montand as a suave and ruthless anti-communist ideologue. The film was intended as an indictment of American involvement with Latin American military dictatorship and it presents an essentially appealing image of urban guerrilla warfare which does not critique the Tupamaros' strategic choices. The urban guerrillas in the film are young, good-looking, committed and firmly implanted amongst the population. Unlike their thuggish police opponents, they use violence only as a reluctant and surgical necessity. Even when they use guns to hijack cars, their threats are not aggressive but firm and apologetic. When a young couple hijack a truck they tell the exasperated driver he will be able to reclaim it from the police. Throughout all these operations the urban guerrillas are calmly efficient, matching revolutionary idealism with technical proficiency, the embodiment of Costa Gavras's description of the Tupamaros as an organisation 'held together by serious, passionate idealism'.[7]

The British ambassador, Geoffrey Jackson, who was kidnapped by the Tupamaros in January 1971, offered a very different perspective and later wrote a powerful account of his imprisonment in two underground 'people's prisons' that began with a pistol whipping by a jumpy young guerrilla during the kidnapping and ended with his release eight months later. The devoutly Catholic ambassador was not enamoured of the hooded captors who maintained a 24-hour watch over his subterranean prison, among whom he occasionally distinguished 'some quite charming human beings, poised, it seemed to me, on the brink of transformation into robots'. But these glimpses of humanity were always tempered by the 'essential ferocity' of his captors, which at any moment could transform them into his executioners. Jackson was dismissive of the politics of the Tupamaros, which he attributed to a neurotic death wish derived 'from Sartre, Camus and their numerous River Plate emulators who seemed to provide much of my hosts' reading'.[8]

Coming from a man deprived of his freedom and under threat of death for eight months, Jackson's attitude towards his individual captors is remarkably generous and frequently perceptive, but it is also conditioned by a political conservatism that regarded left-wing politics as essentially neurotic and totalitarian. There is no evidence of this nihilistic rush towards death and annihilation in Heidi Specogna and Rainer Hoffman's sunny documentary *Tupamaros* (2002), in which a succession of veteran Tupamaros discuss their youthful participation in a movement for which many of them suffered torture and years of imprisonment. The collective story that Specogna's interviewees tell is one of courageous self-sacrifice in a thwarted revolutionary adventure, as middle-aged guerrillas whose faces once stared moodily from sixties wanted posters nostalgically recall their preference for Volkswagens during robberies, the failed attempts by doctors to change their faces through plastic surgery and the experience of clandestinity, torture and imprisonment.

The film does not explore the murkier areas of the Tupamaros' past, nor is there much analysis of their political or tactical mistakes, but its nostalgic reconstruction of a failed revolutionary offensive demonstrates once again how rarely the external perceptions of 'terrorist organisations' correspond to the way such organisations appear to their participants. Nevertheless the establishment view of the Tupamaros was not universally shared. Few urban guerrilla organisations were more influential in spreading a positive and romantic image of the urban guerrilla into the late sixties and early seventies. Their exploits were celebrated in a popular comic book by the Mexican cartoonist Ruis, and they were hailed as a tactical example by aspiring urban guerrilla organisations in both Europe and North America. But even as their reputation as the Robin Hood urban guerrillas continued to spread, the Tupamaros were already moving closer to their own destruction.

The end of Uruguayan democracy

Though the Tupamaros came into existence in a parliamentary democracy, the organisation always regarded the electoral process as a diversion from what they regarded as an inevitable revolutionary war. At the end of 1971, however, the Tupamaros leadership declared a truce, while a new coalition of leftists and trade unionists formed a Broad Front to participate in general elections, with a respected left-wing army general named Liber Serigny as the presidential candidate. In a campaign characterised by intimidation and right-wing violence, the Broad Front gained 20 per cent of the national vote, but failed to make any impact on the traditional two-party system.

The Tupamaros leadership now proposed an escalation of military activity and the extension of the war into the countryside through the construction of a VietCong-style tunnel system, which it called Operation Armadillo. But the armed forces had also taken advantage of the long truce to make their own plans. In April 1972 the truce came to an end in a day of bloody confrontations in which eight Tupamaros and four policemen belonging to right-wing death squads were shot dead in various gunfights. President Bordaberry declared a state of internal war and the armed forces launched an all-out offensive against the Tupamaros, carrying out hundreds of arrests and breaking suspects through the systematic use of 'energetic and forceful interrogation'. Within months the carefully maintained walls of secrecy that had braced the Tupamaros' organisation collapsed as police stations and military barracks experienced blackouts owing to the excessive use of electricity during interrogation sessions. Aided by information from high-level informers, the seemingly impregnable Tupamaros infrastructure of hospitals, prisons and safe houses was discovered and its rural tunnel network traced and destroyed.

By the end of the year the guerrillas were no longer capable of mounting offensive operations. Having crushed the Tupamaros, the armed forces had no intention of returning to the barracks. In June 1973, Bordaberry dissolved parliament and placed the country under the control of a National Security Council, with himself as president. In 1976, however, the armed forces dispensed with the civilian fig leaf and the country was ruled directly by a military junta. Batlle's utopia was now extinct and the great democracy of the southern cone was reduced to a claustrophobic fascist state. The collapse of Uruguayan democracy and the unravelling of the Tupamaros was powerfully depicted by an exiled Uruguayan novelist, Carlos Martínez Moreno, in his collection of linked short stories *El Infierno* (1981), based on affidavits and testimonies that he had collected as a lawyer. Moreno's stories provide glimpses of the Uruguayan battlefield not contained in political manifestos and newspaper reports, depicting a grotesque and nightmarish world of sadistic army officers, doomed and irresponsible guerrillas, torture and tragedy.

In 'Caraguas' he describes an incident that occurred in 1971 when an illiterate peon accidentally stumbled on the Tupamaros' underground firing range concealed on a ranch. After some anguished debate and consultation with the 'Orga' in Montevideo, the guerrillas were ordered to execute their captive, rather than risk letting him go and revealing the firing range to the police. In Moreno's account, one of the guerrillas, Marcos, an anarchist known to his comrades as 'the Priest', reminds his comrades that the Tupamaros came into existence in order to liberate the peasantry, not kill them. But the leadership's decision is final and the guerrillas are ordered to kill the peon by injection and bury him in an unmarked grave. Marcos also participates in the digging, meditating on the meaning of his actions even as he does so:

> At the beginning, when we robbed the Monty Finance Company and the San Rafael Casino, we were Robin Hoods, we wanted justice, we were crusaders against injustice, defenders of the poor. But after that, after we had been forced to kill, we became, in the minds of the majority, murderers, wild animals, cornered in their dens, teeth and claws at the ready. And now, for logistical reasons, that transformation was complete. We were digging the grave of a man whom we would never ever have reason to believe was anything but innocent.

'*Compañeros*, it is done. And I now realize who it is we are burying.'

'Who?' they asked, allowing him to exercise his fantasy for a moment (was he going mad?).

'We are burying Robin Hood,' he said.[9]

In 1973 novelist V. S. Naipaul visited a traumatised Montevideo and described 'a city where, as in a fairy story, a hidden calamity has occurred'. Naipaul was as contemptuous of the Tupamaros as he was of Uruguay itself, describing the organisation as 'destroyers. They had no program; they were like people provoking a reaction, challenging the hidden enemy to declare himself. In the end they picked on the armed forces and were speedily destroyed.'[10] Even the more sympathetic French leftist Régis Debray also described the Tupamaros as the gravediggers of Uruguayan democracy, though Debray also pointed out that the corpse had already 'died a natural death from economic asphyxia'.[11]

There is no doubt that the Tupamaros provided the pretext for the conversion of Uruguay into a 'national security state'. But the transformation of Batlle's liberal republic into the torture laboratory of Latin America was as much a matter of choice as the tactics of the Tupamaros themselves. While the Tupamaros certainly did not hold Uruguayan democracy in high regard, the organisation was a symptom and a consequence of a society in a state of unprecedented economic crisis, which Uruguay's political class elected to resolve through authoritarian means. The Uruguayan government had already taken its first steps towards dictatorship as early as 1965, in response to the wave of public sector strikes, at a time when the Tupamaros had hardly begun their operations.

The provocations of the urban guerrillas certainly accelerated this process, but not for the last time 'terrorism' provided a pretext for a political agenda that went far beyond the immediate objective of suppressing the terrorist conspiracy itself. Thus the 1973 coup brought an end to a prolonged period of labour unrest and enabled the military to freeze wages, ban strikes and trade unions, arrest dozens of labour leaders and dismiss thousands of private and public sector workers for union membership. In 1976 an Amnesty International report listed Uruguay as the country with the highest number of political prisoners per capita in the world. Though the regime never killed on the same scale as other Latin American 'national security states', it treated its political prisoners with relentless cruelty, isolating them from the world in barracks and detention centres across the country, where many remained in solitary confinement for years. Some went

mad, others survived by communicating with each other like the revolutionaries in tsarist Russia, tapping on the walls of their cells, gleaning snippets of
international events by reading fragments of newspaper left by the guards
as toilet paper.[12] It was not until 1985 that the military finally stepped down
and former Tupamaros were allowed to return to the world. Their organisation had paid a heavy price for their misplaced revolutionary optimism
and so too had Uruguayan civil society. But in neighbouring Argentina, the
consequences of urban guerrilla warfare were even more catastrophic.

Perón's legions

The counter-terrorist fantasy of the terrorist as a creature beyond the reach of
civilisation has often served as a licence for the abandonment of legality and
civilisation by the state, in which the counter-terrorist is obliged to 'become
like his enemies' in order to defeat them. There are few more horrendous
examples of this process than the political tragedy that unfolded in Argentina
during the 1970s, following the return of General Juan Domingo Perón to his
native land after eighteen years of exile. Perón had been an absent presence
in Argentinian politics since his overthrow in a military coup in 1955 and
the ageing general owed his return to some extent to the left-wing urban
guerrilla organisations that had emerged in Argentina from the late sixties
onwards, most of whom saw Perónism as the route to a socialist transformation of Argentina. The largest Perónist organisation was the Montoneros,
formed in 1970 by a small group of left-wing Perónists and Catholic students,
including a young student named Mario Firmenich, who became its leader.

In naming themselves after the nineteenth-century Gaucho volunteers
who had fought the British-backed liberal elite in Buenos Aires, the Montoneros were appealing to the same nationalist constituency that Perón
embodied. Adopting the slogan 'all or nothing', these twelve students began
their war on Argentina's military rulers with the sensational kidnapping of a
former president, Pedro Aramburu, the general who had originally deposed
Perón. In a communiqué the Montoneros accused Aramburu of 'crimes
against Perónism', including the deaths of twenty-seven Perónists during
the 1955 coup and the theft of Eva Perón's earthly remains. A few days later
the organisation announced that the general had been tried and executed,
and subsequently described how he had been shot in a cellar while one
of the kidnappers banged a hammer upstairs to hide the sound from the
neighbours.[13]

The execution of Perón's arch-enemy turned the 'boys of the M' into
Perónist heroes. With the indirect patronage of Perón himself, the organisa-

tion grew rapidly, until by the time of the general's return it had become the largest urban guerrilla group in Latin America. At their peak the Montoneros were capable of mobilising demonstrations of up to 100,000, but their active membership was probably only around 5,000, of whom just a few hundred engaged in armed operations.[14] The main non-Perónist urban guerrilla organisation was the People's Revolutionary Army (ERP), a fusion of Trotskyist and Guevarist groups led by a former accountant from a provincial bourgeois family named Roberto Santucho.

Like the Montoneros, the ERP was dominated by young men and women in their teens or early twenties, mostly from the middle or lower-middle classes, many of whom had experienced their first taste of military rule through the suppression of literary and satirical magazines and violent incursions by the police and army into the university campus. In the late 1960s there was a growing convergence between the student radicals and the industrial working class, culminating in a series of violent strikes and near-insurrections in various cities in 1969 that shook the military's grip on power. In this context the urban guerrillas came to see themselves as the armed vanguard of a broader revolutionary movement that was about to end nearly two decades of military rule and realise Che Guevara's aspirations in his native land.

The Peter Pan revolutionaries

The tactics of the Argentinian urban guerrillas were broadly similar to those of the Tupamaros, in their emphasis on exemplary feats of arms and 'Robin Hood' operations such as redistribution of food and clothing in poor areas and attacks on symbols of the Argentinian oligarchy, such as country clubs, jockey clubs and luxury apartments. Even more than their Uruguayan counterparts, the Argentinian urban guerrillas were prolific kidnappers. In 1973 alone, the different organisations carried out 190 kidnappings, including the executives of foreign and national companies. From the beginning the urban guerrilla struggle in Argentina was more violent than it was in Uruguay. Though the guerrillas generally tried to avoid civilian casualties, they had no compunction about assassinating army officers and policemen, especially when the security forces carried out killings and atrocities of their own, such as the execution of sixteen captured ERP prisoners who had tried to escape from a prison at Trelew in 1972, during which Santucho's wife was killed.

By the time the armed forces allowed Perón to return to Argentina, the Montoneros controlled an array of front organisations in universities, shanty towns and secondary schools, in addition to its grandiosely titled subdivisions such as the Department of War, the Department of Logistics and the Montonero Information Service. Former Montoneros later looked back on their early years in the organisation with great nostalgia as a period in which they were part of a shared adventure and a heroic war of national liberation that they believed would culminate in a socialist revolution in Argentina.

In this heady atmosphere, youthful urban guerrillas would jump on buses and deliver to the bewildered passengers political speeches on their willingness to fight and die for their country, and plant bombs overnight and then stay up till the next morning to read about their exploits in the newspapers, convinced, as one female Montonera later described it, that 'arms and social work were the way to achieve a better world'. Much of this radical idealistic fervour was centred on Perón's first wife Eva, who was celebrated in the Montonero anthem:

> With rifles in their hands
> And Evita in their hearts
> Montoneros 'Fatherland or Death'
> Are soldiers of Perón

Though she had died in 1952, before many of the Montoneros were even born, the urban guerrillas vied for the honour of carrying out operations with the prestigious fighting groups named after Evita herself. Many of them joined the ranks of Montoneros martyrs, whose names were given to new fighting units and celebrated in fulsome tributes, such as the following epitaph written for the guerrilla fighter Capuano Martinéz:

> He knew that if he died, it would be at the hands of the enemies of the people, of the enemies of Peronism, which is the most beautiful form of dying. It makes the comrades proud; it distresses our hearts, but makes us happy to know that sacrifice is no mere gesture but a form of life. Just as Evita, the owner of our revolutionary tenderness, would have wanted it.[15]

If the Montoneros were prepared to die, they could also kill. In one incident a female Montonera killed an Argentinian general by befriending his teenage daughter and planting a bomb under her father's bed. In another episode, in early 1976, a group of Montoneros stopped pedestrians on a Buenos Aires street and checked their identification until they found a policeman, whom they promptly shot dead. The idealistic revolutionary fervour that motivated many rank-and-file members was often manipulated by a leadership whose arrogance and cynicism mirrored that of Perón himself. In exile Perón had encouraged the Montonero leaders to think of themselves as Perón's heirs apparent, but neither the general nor his fanatically anti-communist secretary José López Rega, known as the Rasputin of the Pampas, had any intention of allowing the left anywhere near government. Following his return to Argentina Perón rapidly distanced himself from the movement which had helped him back to power, while the Montoneros put their armed operations on hold and waited for Perón to introduce a radical social programme. In September 1973 Perón was elected president by an overwhelming majority and his new government proceeded to unleash a clandestine death squad called the Argentine Anti-Communist Alliance or Triple A, composed of policemen, soldiers and right-wing Perónist hoodlums.

The rate of political homicides soared as men and women suspected of being 'Marxist subversives' were snatched from their homes and their bodies turned up dead in roadside ditches, in the picnic grounds alongside the Ezeiza airport and in burned-out cars in residential areas in Buenos Aires. Andrew Graham-Yooll, a journalist with the English-language *Buenos Aires Herald*, described a capital patrolled by the ubiquitous unmarked Ford Falcons, filled with 'men in dark glasses and half-open shirts, holding machine guns, wearing half a dozen chains around their necks, with Saint Christophers, crucifixes and Virgin Marys'.[16]

Initially, the Montoneros refused to believe that Perón was personally responsible for the violence being directed against them. In a massive May Day demonstration in the Plaza de Mayo in 1974, however, Montoneros demonstrators attempted to engage in 'dialogue' with the general, shouting slogans in praise of Evita and denouncing Perón's wife Isabel and López Rega. Perón flew into a rage and denounced the Montonero columns as idiots and *imberbes* – beardless wonders. This outburst was the signal for a mass exodus of Montoneros from the plaza, which marked an open breach between the general and his legions. In the wake of their excommunication, the Montoneros took the fateful decision to go underground and resume their revolutionary offensive, convinced that they were now a more authentic representation of Perónism than Perón himself.

The result was a chaotic explosion of violence, depicted in the novelist Osvaldo Soriano's breathless farce *A Funny, Dirty Little War*. The violence intensified following the death of Perón in July 1974, when the presidency passed into the hands of his ineffectual wife Isabel, who together with López Rega presided over a corrupt and repressive regime characterised by total ineptitude in everything but political homicide. Isolated from the Perónist orbit the Montoneros stepped up their armed campaign. In September 1974 the Montoneros kidnapped the Born brothers, of the export company Bunge y Born, and netted the huge sum of $60 million, the equivalent of one third of Argentina's annual military budget.

The world record ransom enabled the Montoneros to carry out increasingly sophisticated and audacious operations, including the assassination of the hated Buenos Aires police chief Alberto Villar, whose yacht was blown up by a scuba diver. A team of Montonero frogmen blew up the Argentinian navy's first missile-carrying frigate on the anniversary of the 1955 coup, destroying its electronic equipment. And on 5 October the guerrillas carried out a spectacular assault on the headquarters of the 29th Regiment of Mounted Infantry, in which an assault team attacked the base wearing the Montonero uniform of blue shirts, jeans and hiking boots, while another group hijacked an Aerolineas Argentinas passenger plane and landed it near the base. Though the guerrillas suffered heavy casualties the survivors fled in the plane with a number of captured weapons and landed at a rendezvous in the middle of the countryside, where they escaped in trucks.

This was the closest any urban guerrilla organisation had come to an open 'military' confrontation. At times the urban guerrillas appeared to be dazzled by their own achievements and convinced that they could conjure up a revolutionary movement through heroic feats of arms alone. This strategy was based on a dangerous underestimation of the forces ranged against them. In the middle of 1975 López Rega fell from grace and went into exile, and the repression passed more directly into the hands of the armed forces themselves. In the same period some 200 members of the ERP tried to establish a Cuban-style rural guerrilla column in the impoverished sugar-growing province of Tucumán. But the hapless collection of students and school children were isolated and slaughtered by some 6,000 soldiers under the fascistic general Luciano Menéndez, who subjected the province to a reign of violence and torture. At the end of the year the ERP compounded its tactical errors with a massed assault on a military arsenal at Monte Chingolo, in which poorly armed guerrillas attacked a military garrison with a primitive armoury that included home-made grenades in yoghurt cartons. The garrison had been forewarned and the assault group suffered over eighty casualties.

By the beginning of 1976 the ERP had been virtually annihilated. In the previous twelve months the *Buenos Aires Herald* estimated that 1,100 people had died in acts of political violence. On 24 March 1976, a military junta took control of the country, headed by General Jorge Videla, an unassuming military bureaucrat and devout Catholic, who had told a military conference in Montevideo the previous year that 'as many persons must die in Argentina as are necessary to guarantee the country's security'. At the time these words passed largely unnoticed, but the armed forces were already making plans to turn them into reality.

El Proceso

From the beginning the armed forces presented themselves as the neutral defenders of the state in a country besieged by the 'two demons' of left- and right-wing terrorism, even though both the armed forces and the police were already participating in the latter. The coup was initially welcomed by many Argentinians, particularly amongst the wealthy and privileged classes, but liberals also saw the junta as a positive development. In his account of his subsequent imprisonment and torture, *Prisoner without a Name, Cell without a Number*, the editor of *La Opinión*, Jacobo Timmerman, described pre-coup Argentina as a chaotic society under siege from terrorism at both ends of the political spectrum, whose youth were in thrall to what he called 'the eroticism of violence'.

Though liberals like Timmerman argued in favour of a 'legal' repression, it was already clear that the military had a very different agenda. Shortly after the coup Timmerman had lunch in a Buenos Aires hotel with a naval officer, Captain Carlos Bonino, a close collaborator of Admiral Emilio Massera, one of the key ideologues of the junta, who coolly informed him that Argentina's political problems could be resolved only through the extermination of some 20,000 people, including left-wing terrorists, their relatives 'and all those who remember their names'.

The military called this project El Proceso de Reorganización Nacional – the Process of National Reorganisation. In one of the high-flown rhetorical flourishes to which the junta leaders were prone, Videla defined its aims as 'a profound transformation of consciousness'. The savage governor of Buenos Aires province, General Ibérico Saint-Jean, was less philosophical, declaring: 'First we are going to kill all the subversives; then we kill their collaborators; then their sympathizers; then … those who remain indifferent; and finally we kill the timid.' This was the great service Argentina's new rulers intended to render to the nation. These 'delinquents' would disappear from the face of the earth and no trace of them would ever be found, precluding the possibility of trials or investigations. The groundwork for the implementation of the Argentinian 'Night and Fog' had already been laid with the establishment of a chain of clandestine concentration camps, torture chambers and detention centres across the country.

Much of this was modelled on the methods used by the French army in Algeria. As early as 1957 two French Indochina veterans were engaged by the Argentinian Superior War College to instruct Argentinian officers in 'anti-subversive warfare' and by 1964 one Argentinian colonel wrote that the Argentinian upper and lower ranks had been thoroughly inculcated with French counter-insurgency doctrines. Whereas the French army had remained subject to some democratic scrutiny, in Argentina the entire state machinery became an instrument of counter-terrorism, which enabled the junta to maintain an outward appearance of normality, even as the armed forces presided over a secret world of torture and extermination. Working their way through pre-prepared lists, 'task forces' made up of plainclothes soldiers and police carried out dozens of kidnappings each week, breaking into houses in the middle of the night, dragging away selected individuals or whole families to torture and death. No one was immune, nor was there any legal recourse, as female psychoanalysts were dragged screaming down hospital wards by their hair, as snatch squads burst into private homes, cinemas, bakeries and workplaces, as suspects were dragged off buses or shot dead on the spot in front of frightened witnesses.

The majority of killings were carried out in secret, as thousands of Argentinians were murdered with absolute impunity, their bodies tossed into the sea from planes and helicopters or buried in mass graves or public cemeteries. In 1995 Adolfo Scilingo, a former naval officer, detailed his participation in two separate flights from the Navy Mechanics School, the ESMA, in 1977, in which groups of between fifteen and thirty terrorist prisoners were tossed alive into the South Atlantic. Scilingo described how the prisoners were led hooded and shackled to the school's infirmary, where they were told that they were being transported to a prison in the south and that a vaccination was required. Instead the prisoners were drugged and led 'like zombies' onto a navy Skyvan plane, then stripped and laid out in rows before being tossed into the ocean one by one. A low-level and not particularly intelligent functionary, Scilingo was nevertheless sufficiently troubled by these procedures to consult a navy chaplain, who assured him that the prisoners had been given a 'Christian death' and that 'even the Bible provided for eliminating the weeds from the wheatfield'.[17]

Often counter-terrorism became an alibi for more conventional criminality, as army officers blackmailed the families of prisoners into selling their property to save their relatives' lives, and 'task forces' stripped the homes and apartments of people they had gone to kidnap, or returned afterwards with vans to carry away furniture and other possessions. Even the children of captured subversives could be turned to a profit. Pregnant guerrillas were kept in special wards, often in leg irons, where the progress of their pregnancies was carefully monitored. After giving birth the mothers were killed and their children sold or handed over to 'proper families', often amongst the military themselves, in order to prevent them fulfilling their 'genetic destiny' as guerrillas.

All the essential elements of the official anti-terrorist anathema are present in the Argentinian military's depiction of the terrorist as a denationalised creature beyond the reach of law, morality and religion. If El Proceso's combination of pious Catholic fanaticism and merciless state terror recall the holy wars of the Inquisition against heretics, its practical consequences are best represented by Goya's portrait of Cronus devouring his son, as the military set out to punish Argentina's delinquent children for having allowed themselves to be corrupted by the alien doctrines of Freud, Marx and Einstein. But the justification for the regime's barbarity was the Otherness of the 'terrorist'. In General Videla's definition, a terrorist was 'anyone who holds ideas contrary to Western civilisation' while the director of the Argentinian Military Academy, General Reynaldo Bignone, regarded subversives as 'anti-fatherland' and agents of the 'Antichrist'. The French military influence was also evident in the belief amongst the Argentinian officer corps that Argentina was in the midst of a 'Third World War' against a vast international subversive conspiracy promoted by Cuba and the Soviet Union. From the junta's point of view, the conspiracy was so far advanced that it could be removed only by using the most drastic methods.

Ideologues of El Proceso frequently invoked the familiar anti-terrorist metaphor of terrorism as a 'disease' or 'cancer' in which counter-terrorism was a surgical operation aimed at removing the 'contaminated flesh' from the Argentinian nation. In a famous speech in 1978, Admiral Massera described El Proceso as a noble enterprise 'against nihilists, against agents of destruction whose only objective is destruction itself, although they disguise it with social crusades'. Faced with this 'machine of horror', declared Massera, the armed forces had been obliged to engage in 'an oblique and different kind of war, primitive in its ways but sophisticated in its cruelty'.[18]

This grandiloquent rhetoric concealed a world of scarcely believable cruelty, depravity and criminality. Few regimes in history have tortured their own citizens on such a massive scale as the Argentinian junta. Abducted prisoners were routinely subjected to a range of savage practices, from karate kicks and beatings with clubs and whips to immersion in tubs of water filled with faeces to rape, mutilation and the extraction of finger- and toenails. Others were impaled on sticks or savaged by dogs. The favoured instrument of Argentinian torturers was the ubiquitous *picana* – the electric prod, which was used to administer electric shocks to the gums, genitals, nipples or ears.

Parents and grandparents were also tortured in front of their subversive offspring in order to make them talk. In Admiral Massera's 'Christian humanist' concentration camp at the ESMA a twenty-month-old baby was subjected to the *picana*, after consultation with a doctor. During his imprisonment Jacobo Timmerman heard whole families being tortured together in adjoining cells. Though these procedures allowed unlimited scope for individual sadism and pathology, even the worst torturers were taught to regard the interrogation process as a 'battlefield' in a brutal but essentially noble effort to defend the Argentinian nation from a vast subversive conspiracy.

In the face of this onslaught, the urban guerrilla organisations rapidly crumbled as their members were swallowed up in the nightmare world of El Proceso. Even veteran Montoneros became *quebrados* – broken ones – and gave their interrogators the names and addresses they wanted or went out into the streets to point out their former comrades. Whereas the Tupamaros had been expected to hold out for twenty-four hours, the Montonero leadership demanded that its members hold out under torture until death, on the grounds that failure to do so was 'not a problem of physical weakness but ideological firmness' that failed to fulfil the requirements of the socialist 'new man'.

To prevent such lapses the leadership issued cyanide pills to their members. Some Montoneros killed themselves in this way. Others died in desperate and isolated shootouts, trapped in their flats and houses, in the assignation hotels favoured by adulterous lovers where they had once held meetings and now sought refuge. One of those who died was Vicki Walsh, the daughter of Rodolfo Walsh, an investigative reporter and Montonero militant. A high-ranking member of the Montonero 'Political Secretariat', Vicki Walsh and four comrades were asleep in a house in Buenos Aires on 28 September 1976 when they were woken up by the sound of shots and loudspeakers outside. While three members of the group fired back Vicki went with the group's political secretary on to the roof, still wearing her nightdress, leaving her year-old daughter in the room. A fierce battle ensued, in which the 150 soldiers used a bazooka and a helicopter to dislodge the guerrillas. One of the soldiers later described the battle to Walsh himself and told him how his daughter had fired down at the soldiers with a Halcon machine gun, bursting into loud laughter every time the soldiers took cover. The battle lasted for an hour and a half, when there was a momentary lull in the fighting. In a letter to his friends Walsh related what happened next:

> 'Suddenly,' said the soldier, 'there was a silence. The woman put the machine gun down, she stood over the parapet and opened her arms. We stopped shooting without even being told and we took a good look at her. She was thin, with short hair and wore a nightdress. She began speaking to us in a loud but calm voice. I don't remember everything she said but I remember the last phrase: it keeps me awake at night. "You can't kill us", she said, "we choose to die." Then she and the guy with her put guns to their heads and killed themselves in front of us.'[19]

There was no more resistance down below and the soldiers found Vicki Walsh's baby daughter sitting on a bed, surrounded by five dead bodies. Walsh himself survived for just over six months, hiding out in his wooden cabin amid the marshlands adjoining the river Plate, sending out news reports on the disaster typed on his old Remington typewriter, before he was shot dead in an ambush in Buenos Aires in March 1977. That same year the Montonero leadership finally made a 'strategic withdrawal' abroad while their remaining cells were disbanded or left to fight a futile war they had no chance of winning. The inability of the Montonero leaders to comprehend what was happening in Argentina was demonstrated again in 1978–9, when hundreds of exiled members were ordered back into the country as part of its 'World Cup Tactical Offensive' in what Firmenich described at a Youth Festival in Cuba as a 'Normandy landing' to liberate Argentina. Nearly all the guerrillas who took part in this ill-conceived offensive were captured and killed, but 'Commandante' Firmenich was unrepentant, telling the Cuban magazine *Bohemia* in 1981 that 'our organisation is a means, merely a means, and therefore we have been prepared to sacrifice the organisation in combat in return for revolutionary prestige'.

Disillusioned Montonero survivors have variously described Firmenich as authoritarian and even 'psychotic', but in 1993 the American journalist Martin Erwin Andersen suggested another explanation for Firmenich's behaviour, with the publication of *Dossier Secreto,* in which he claimed that the Montonero leader had been an agent of the Argentinian military since the early days of the organisation. Andersen based his assertion on information received from unnamed US diplomatic and intelligence services, who claimed that it was taken for granted that Firmenich had been working for the military. These allegations have not been proven but they have continued to swirl around Firmenich and the Montonero leaders, many of whom have gone on to become successful businessmen or developed new careers within the Perónist political machine.

Whatever the truth, the fact that so many young Argentinians should have placed their trust in these pied pipers of the revolution adds one more bitter note to the tragedy and horror of Argentina's darkest years. By the time the junta withdrew from power in 1982, following Argentina's humiliating defeat by Britain in the Falklands/Malvinas, between 10,000 and 30,000 Argentinians had been killed or disappeared. Other regimes have killed their own citizens on an even greater scale than the Argentinian junta, but it was in Argentina where the official fantasy of the universal terrorist became a licence for a war of extermination fought on behalf of 'Western civilisation and Christianity'. The result, as the National Commission on the Disappeared (CONADEP) later observed in its final report, was the 'greatest and most savage tragedy of Argentine history', in which, 'To the crimes of the terrorists, the armed forces responded with an infinitely worse terrorism.'[20]

Once again, the tactics of Marighela and Guillén had brought about a disastrous political and military defeat, in which the limitations of the city as a revolutionary battleground were brutally exposed. Instead of providing sanctuary for the insurgents, as the urban guerrilla strategists had predicted, the concrete jungles of São Paulo, Buenos Aires and Montevideo turned into traps that favoured their more powerful enemies. Given this record, the strategy and tactics of the Latin American urban guerrillas might have seemed seriously flawed and unworthy of imitation. But even as the Tupamaros and the Montoneros were being destroyed, their tactics had already begun to spread beyond Latin America to the citadels of the industrialised world itself.

The Revolutionary Festival

Change your hatred into energy. Fight on the streets Saturday evening, create massive terror at every street corner the night before. Good targets are American industrial firms, banks, police stations, and everything which makes man into a slave. Show everyone who does not understand it yet that solidarity expresses itself in deeds, not just words.

Berlin anarchist pamphlet, 1969

Let's have a wargasm!

Weather Underground communiqué, 1969

Revolutionary terrorism may sometimes signal the early stages of a revolutionary upheaval, or it may occur when a mass political or revolutionary upheaval is in decline, at the point when heightened political expectations collide with a more mundane or disappointing reality. In the latter case, small armed groups may remain like isolated pools when the revolutionary tide has subsided, for whom violence is an attempt to restore the lost political momentum. This sense of anachronism was a feature of the urban guerrilla organisations that emerged in Europe, Japan and North America in the aftermath of the tumultuous upheavals of 1968. That year a chain of student-led demonstrations, campus occupations and mass protests erupted in cities across the world in the high-water mark of sixties radicalism. For many of the participants in those tumultuous events, the world seemed briefly poised on the brink of a new revolutionary era, in which the post-war international order was about to be permanently transformed into a utopian future that was often vaguely imagined but no less passionately felt. By the end of the year these rebellions had largely been suppressed, and their radical expectations had either failed to resonate with the wider population or were dissipated through the absence of any clear political mechanism for achieving them.

It was in this period that the first urban guerrilla groups began to emerge in the industrialised world. Like the Latin American urban guerrillas, their members were largely middle class, products of the post-war boom in higher education. Though university was instrumental in their political radicalisation, their conversion to revolutionary violence tended to be based on an abstract identification with revolutionary struggles far beyond their own borders, in Latin America, the Middle East and Africa.

Like the Russian nihilists in the mid-nineteenth century, the student urban guerrillas were products of a generational rebellion against conservative social mores that became increasingly political. But these organisations emerged at a period when the world was a smaller and more integrated place, when radicalising events such as the Vietnam war mixed feelings of outrage, impotence and guilt in a generation that felt itself to be part of an international culture of protest. At no point in history had the image of the revolutionary enjoyed such exalted moral status as it did in the late 1960s. Yet if the student urban guerrillas were inspired by images of distant revolutionary struggles in societies very different from their own, their revolutionary offensives unfolded in countries where post-war austerity was already becoming a distant memory and the consumer society was becoming the dominant economic model. These were not the most promising circumstances for a successful campaign of revolutionary violence, and the student urban guerrillas often displayed an excessive revolutionary optimism that was so removed from reality as to seem, in retrospect, almost suicidal. Even more than their Latin American counterparts, the student urban guerrillas were an armed vanguard in search of a revolutionary constituency, but in the industrialised societies of Europe, America and Japan these constituencies were always going to be considerably smaller. Such was the atmosphere of revolutionary fervour in the wake of 1968, however, that objective analysis was often eclipsed by wishful thinking, and even the smallest organisations declared war on their own governments, regardless of whether they had any possibility of winning.

Revolutionary suicide in Germany

There were few more unlikely settings for an urban guerrilla campaign than the West Germany of the early 1970s. To the outside world the Bundesrepublik was a political and economic triumph, in which the *wirschaftwunder*, or economic miracle, had laid the basis for a prosperous industrialised nation with one of the highest standards of living in the world and the former Nazi state had evolved into the gleaming technocratic model described with cool irony in the American writer Walter Abish's terrorist novel *How German Is*

It. To many young Germans born during or just before the war, however, the seamless transformation from Nazism to an Americanised consumer society merely confirmed the moral bankruptcy of their parents' generation.

Throughout the 1960s an increasingly radical student protest movement campaigned on a range of issues from the transformation of the university to the Vietnam war, which gradually coalesced into a loose formation called the Extra-Parliamentary Opposition (APO). The APO's main base was West Berlin, where an assortment of dropouts, rebels and outsiders set up squats and communes and experimented with alternative lifestyles. Among the flotsam and jetsam of the Berlin alternative scene in this period was a 20-year-old former art student called Andreas Baader, the son of a historian and archivist killed on the Russian front during the war. This loutish would-be gigolo was not the most obvious representative of the German national conscience. In 1967, however, Baader met Gudrun Ensslin, the daughter of a parson and a descendant of the philosopher Hegel. A willowy blonde with the gaunt features of a German expressionist heroine, Ensslin was considerably more intelligent than the resolutely unintellectual Baader. She was also more politically committed and contemptuous of the society she called 'the Raspberry Reich'. Her furious outrage struck a chord with Baader and the two of them left their respective partners and children to move in together, thus beginning a relationship whose consequences would shake German society.

Their union coincided with an increasingly violent escalation in the confrontation between the authorities and the APO, culminating in the death of a pacifist student named Benno Ohnesorg on 2 June 1967, shot by police during an angry demonstration against the Shah of Iran outside the Berlin Opera House. The refusal of the authorities even to investigate the circumstances of Ohnesorg's death reinforced the conviction amongst the more militant elements of the APO, including Ensslin, that the limits of protest had been reached and that the 'generation of Auschwitz' was once again revealing itself beneath the façade of democracy. That same month the leftist student leader Rudi Dutschke was shot and seriously wounded by a lone right-wing fanatic, after a virulent campaign against him by the Springer newspaper chain, igniting riots, arson attacks and fire-bombings across Germany.

In October Ensslin, Baader and two co-defendants were sentenced to three years' imprisonment for an arson attack on a Frankfurt department store, which they described as an attempt to bring the recent American bombing of North Vietnam to the attention of the German public. The contemptuous disdain with which they treated the court proceedings converted them into minor celebrities and earned them the attention of Germany's most famous female journalist, Ulrike Meinhof, the star columnist for the left-wing magazine *Konkret*. Meinhof's strong left-wing views slotted seamlessly into a conventional bourgeois lifestyle, with parties amongst Germany's radical chic middle class known as the *Schili* and holidays in Italy with Inge Feltrinelli, the wife of a millionaire Italian leftist publisher. But her successful career concealed a fragile, insecure personality with a tendency to depression and a nagging sense of her own inauthenticity.

By the late sixties her marriage was unravelling and she had come to loathe her philandering husband. Meinhof's personal existential crisis was exacerbated by the intensity and passion of the youth revolt, as organisations with such names as Tupamaros West Berlin, the Roaming Hash Rebels, the Mescaleros and the Black Front began to emerge in Berlin and other cities, many of whose members were nearly ten years younger than she was. Meinhof became increasingly mesmerised by the youth counter-culture and by Ensslin and Baader's plans to establish an urban guerrilla organisation on the Latin American model. And on 14 May 1970, the German public received the sensational news that she had participated in an armed jailbreak to spring Baader from prison by an organisation calling itself the Red Army Faction (Rote Arme Fraktion or RAF). An RAF communiqué written shortly afterwards exudes a mood of triumph that the great leap into the revolutionary underworld had finally been undertaken. The RAF exhorted the alternative movement to follow their example while at the same time attempting to appeal to a wider constituency in its indictment of the German economic miracle, in which: 'Those who don't defend themselves die. Those who don't die are buried alive in prisons, in reform schools, in the slums of worker districts, in the stone coffins of the new housing developments, in the crowded kindergartens and schools, in brand-new kitchens and bedrooms filled with fancy furniture bought on credit.'[1] This diatribe closed with a flurry of inane slogans to 'Start the armed resistance now! Build up the Red Army!'

At this point the RAF's active membership barely ran into double figures and the organisation had barely made any preparations for an underground war on the West German government. Nevertheless, the would-be revolutionaries travelled to Jordan to undergo military training in a Palestinian refugee camp and escape the attentions of the police. In Margarethe von Trotta's film *Marianne and Julianne*, based loosely on the relationship between Ensslin and her sister, the group's arrival in the Palestinian refugee camp is a joyous confirmation of revolutionary internationalism. But their

Palestinian hosts were scandalised by the sight of the German women nude sunbathing on the roof and by Baader's insistence that the male and female comrades should be allowed to sleep together on the grounds that 'fucking is like shooting'.

The war of six against sixty million

Eventually the group was asked to leave and returned to Germany, where they belatedly began to construct an urban guerrilla infrastructure of safe houses and false identities, getting weapons and radio equipment, stealing cars, forging identities and robbing banks to finance themselves. Much of their time was spent driving back and forth across the autobahns in the stolen Alfa Romeos and BMWs that became popularly known as 'Baader Meinhof wagons' to a soundtrack of rock and roll and country songs on US armed forces radio. The group drove the way they did everything else, carelessly and too fast, frequently crashing their expensive vehicles, while they relied for accommodation and shelter on Meinhof's radical chic contacts.

At this stage the RAF still had an aura of romantic outlaws amongst sections of the left as the group became the focus of intense media interest. The press obsessively followed the progress of Germany's 'Bonnie and Clyde' terrorists and *Der Spiegel* even included a regular Baader Meinhof column alongside its international and culture sections. Much of this interest was focused on Ulrike Meinhof herself, the celebrity outlaw whose moody features were included in the 7 million wanted posters bearing the title 'Anarchist Violent Criminals – Baader/Meinhof gang' stuck on petrol pumps, lamp posts, walls and trees across the Federal Republic in the summer of 1971.

That summer the first casualties occurred, when two urban guerrillas and a policeman were shot dead in separate incidents. Amid the reports of shootouts, bank robberies and discoveries of weapons caches, the German government placed the overall anti-terrorist investigation under the jurisdiction of the Federal Criminal Investigation Office (BKA), which for the first time began to operate as a national organisation similar to the FBI. Under its new chief commissioner, Horst Herold, the BKA began to accumulate a national computerised data base on suspected terrorists while right-wing politicians once again invoked the fantasy of the ubiquitous terrorist conspiracy as a pretext for an ideological offensive against the intellectual 'fellow-travellers' in universities and elsewhere, who helped spread 'ideologies of hatred'.

In January 1972 the German parliament unanimously approved the Berufsverbot or Radicals' Decree, which banned civil service employment to people with 'unconstitutional attitudes'. This new law was strongly criticised by German liberals such as the Nobel Prize-winning novelist Heinrich Boll, who famously coined the phrase the 'war of six against sixty million' in an attempt to place the terrorist threat in perspective. By this time Meinhof and her companions were locked on a collision course with the West German state from which they were not prepared to divert. In *The Urban Guerrilla Concept*, probably written by Meinhof herself, the RAF echoed the tactical conception of nineteenth-century revolutionary terrorism in its insistence that the urban guerrillas could 'attack the state's apparatus of control at certain points and put them out of action, to destroy the myth of the system's omnipresence and invulnerability', even though Germany's revolutionary traditions were 'broken and feeble'.[2]

In the German context this strategy was essentially a fantasy, devoid of any political reality. Nevertheless in May 1972 the organisation finally launched its anti-imperialist offensive, with a string of bomb attacks across the Federal Republic to coincide with the US mining of North Vietnamese harbours, using explosive devices made with the help of a Frankfurt metal sculptor who later told police he believed he had been creating film props for 'a piece of revolutionary fiction'. The casualties, however, were real. Two bomb attacks on US military installations in Frankfurt and Heidelberg killed three US soldiers and wounded several others. The RAF also set off two bombs at the Springer offices in Hamburg, injuring seventeen typesetters, an incident which did little to improve the organisation's already low status amongst the working class.

On 31 May 1972 the authorities launched a nationwide dragnet in which virtually the entire police force was deployed across the Federal Republic, setting up hundreds of roadblocks and buzzing the autobahns with helicopters. The next day Baader was discovered in a Frankfurt garage, together with a former film student called Holger Meins, following a tip-off from the public. By the end of June the entire RAF leadership was in prison, including Meinhof herself, and the rest of its revolutionary campaign would now be fought from behind prison walls.

Plague carriers
At this point the West German authorities embarked on a contradictory policy that has often been repeated in other terrorist episodes. On the one hand the authorities insisted that the RAF were ordinary criminals; on the other they were subjected to unusual terms of imprisonment that belied such claims. For months the RAF prisoners were kept in isolation in separate cells in conditions of almost complete aural isolation known as 'the dead

zone'. As exceptional as these conditions were, they still fell short of the comparisons to Auschwitz and Buchenwald made by Ensslin, who wrote in one of her letters, 'Those of us in there, to put it bluntly, can only be surprised they don't spray the gas in.'

The prisoners protested these terms of imprisonment with a series of debilitating hunger strikes, which were also intended to galvanise their supporters and place themselves at the centre of the German left. With the help of their lawyers, the prisoners established an 'info-system', by which news and letters were copied and sent to individual members of the group via a 'secretariat' composed of Ensslin and Baader. The prisoners also engaged in 'criticism and self crit' sessions in which they examined their attitudes and behaviour in letters that were circulated among the group. The harshest self-critic was Ulrike Meinhof, who regularly abased herself before her comrades, to the point when an exasperated Baader told her 'not to lower yourself to something like a fawning dog'.

The masochistic self-hatred in Meinhof's self-crit letters contrasted with the occasional flashes of ordinary humanity in her letters to her children, who visited their mother in prison for the first time in October 1972. But the tenderness that Meinhof expressed in these letters was increasingly absent as the RAF prisoners continued their grim political struggle against what they called the state's 'policy of annihilation'. In April 1974 Meinhof and Ensslin became the first residents of an entire wing given over to the RAF prisoners in the top-security Stammheim prison in Stuttgart, where they were joined in October by Baader and another prisoner, Jan-Carl Raspe. The following month the film student Holger Meins died as the result of a hunger strike that had reduced him to a grotesque emaciated skeleton weighing just under seven stone. Meins's self-imposed martyrdom ignited another chain of riots, demonstrations, bombings and arson attacks across Germany.

On 25 April 1975 an armed group calling itself the Holger Meins Commando took over the West German embassy in Stockholm and held its staff hostage while they wired the building with explosives and threatened to blow themselves up if the police intervened. The kidnappers originated from the Socialist Patients Collective (SPK), one of the strangest organisations in the German terrorist underworld, whose members consisted of mental patients drawn from the group therapy sessions run by Dr Wolfgang Huber, a psychiatrist at Heidelberg University. Dr Huber believed that all mental illness was caused by capitalist society and that violent revolutionary action could be therapeutic. Though the collective had dissolved, some of its members became involved with the RAF and the kidnappers now demanded the release of twenty-six RAF prisoners, including the four at Stammheim.

In a demonstration of intent, they prodded the German military attaché out onto a balcony and shot him dead. When the German and Swedish governments rejected these demands, the kidnappers shot the 64-year-old economics attaché and threatened to kill more hostages. The Swedish police were preparing to carry out an armed assault when the kidnappers accidentally set off their explosives, killing one of their members. As flames poured out of the embassy windows both the badly burned attackers and hostages stumbled out into the street, bringing the siege to a chaotic end.

Germany's worst terrorist incident since the deaths of eleven members of the Israeli Olympic team in Munich in 1972 fuelled right-wing pressure for an extension of the existing emergency laws to prevent the terrorist 'plague' from spreading and root out the sympathisers within the universities where the terrorists had acquired their 'psycho-social poison' and 'ideological ammunition'. Heinrich Boll attacked the witch-hunt mentality in his terse novel *The Lost Honour of Katherina Blum* (1975), in which a female domestic servant has a one-night stand with a wanted terrorist, knowing nothing about his background, and finds herself hounded by the tabloid press as a 'terrorist whore'.

On the surface the drift towards an 'aggressive democracy' seemed to bear out the RAF's thesis concerning the latent fascist tendencies of the West German state, but there was a great difference between an authoritarian democracy and fascism, even if the RAF failed to see it. In May 1975, after nearly three years of imprisonment, the RAF leaders finally appeared in court. The trial was characterised by numerous delays, disruptions and angry outbursts from the defendants, who variously denounced the judge as a 'swine' and a 'fascist arsehole' and the impartiality of the legal process was called into question by the introduction of the so-called 'Baader Meinhof laws' that enabled the court to try the defendants in their absence.

Behind the façade of unity, Meinhof's self-abasement was compounded by the relentless and vicious criticism she received from Ensslin and Baader. In May 1976 she made her last appearance in court. Five days later, on Mother's Day, Meinhof was found dead in her cell, having hanged herself using wire mesh from her cell window. Though Ensslin and Baader claimed she had been murdered, it was almost certainly an act of suicide, for which they themselves bore much of the responsibility. Thousands attended her funeral, where a pastor described her as 'the most significant woman in German politics since Rosa Luxemburg'. That year the SPD published an electoral poster showing a smiling young couple on a motorbike with the slogan: *Modell Deutschland – a good future for us.* For many Germans this message already seemed anachronistic, but the events of the coming year would strain the cosy optimism still further.

The 'German Autumn'

On 28 April 1977, after 192 days in court, the RAF defendants were sentenced to several terms of life imprisonment. But even as the Stammheim prisoners slipped from public view, new RAF recruits were emerging from the network of defence lawyers, Red Aid groups and 'committees against torture' that had sprung up in various German cities. Many of these recruits came from a privileged background, such as 19-year-old Susanne Albrecht, the daughter of a wealthy lawyer, who once told a friend, 'I was tired of all that caviare.' Albrecht took part in the botched kidnapping and murder of her own godfather, Jurgen Ponto, the chairman of the Dresden Bank, in July 1977, by pretending to be on a family visit to his home.

Albrecht was so devastated by the murder of 'Uncle Jurgen' that she had a nervous breakdown and had to be resettled in East Germany, where she ceased to play any further part in the RAF's activities. But the RAF 'second generation' proved itself to be considerably more effective than the organisation's founders. On 4 September an RAF team kidnapped the president of the German Employers Association, Martin Schleyer, in an audacious commando-style ambush in the streets of Cologne. A former SS officer and a member of Heydrich's staff in Czechoslovakia during World War II, Schleyer embodied the continuity between the Third Reich and the post-war capitalist state that the RAF had always denounced. The kidnap was carried out with military precision, as three members of Schleyer's security escort were killed in a fusillade of more than 300 bullets, which left Schleyer unscathed.

When the kidnappers released a photograph of their captive, together with a communiqué demanding the release of eleven RAF prisoners, including those at Stammheim, the government established an all-party 'crisis group' which secretly agreed on a policy of no concessions to terrorism and imposed a news blackout on the affair. Anti-terrorist hysteria reached new heights as the far-right president of Bavaria, Franz-Josef Strauss, called for a terrorist hostage to be shot for every prisoner killed by the RAF and the Christian Democrat CDU published a 'blacklist' of prominent 'terrorist sympathisers', including the novelist Gunter Grass.

While the government feigned negotiations to play for time, the crisis worsened on 13 October, when four RAF guerrillas and a Palestinian hijacked a Lufthansa jet in Majorca and threatened to blow it up unless the Stammheim prisoners were released. After five days of flying between Europe, the Middle East and Africa, the hijackers landed in Mogadishu, where the plane was stormed on 18 October by the German government's elite anti-terrorist GSG-9 unit, who killed four of the hijackers and freed the passengers. The next day it was announced that Baader and Ensslin and Jan-Carl Raspe had been found dead in their cells. Baader and Raspe had been shot while Ensslin had hanged herself. Though the authorities reported their deaths as suicide, the RAF's supporters once again claimed they had been murdered and asked how guns could have been smuggled into a maximum security prison. In fact, security conditions at Stammheim were more lax than they appeared and despite some anomalies in the official account the evidence of state murder is not convincing. Whether the Stammheim 'Death Night' was an expression of despair at the failure of Mogadishu, or an act of 'revolutionary suicide' aimed at proving their absolute sincerity and galvanising the RAF's supporters once again, cannot be known, since the prisoners left no explanations.

There was still one more death to come. On 19 October an RAF communiqué announced that 'after 43 days of captivity we have put an end to the corrupt and miserable existence of Hans Martin Schleyer'. Police were directed to a green Audi near the German border, where Schleyer's body was found in the boot with three bullet wounds to the head, in what Peter Jürgen Boock, a morphine addict who conducted the operation, later described as an act of revenge.

The bloody sequence of events closed with two funerals, which symbolised the unfolding confrontation. Whereas Schleyer, the former SS officer, was given a televised state funeral attended by leading politicians and former army officers, and accompanied by a three-minute silence in the Daimler car works, Baader, Ensslin and Raspe were interred only after the mayor of Stuttgart courageously ignored protests against the burial of terrorists in 'sacred ground'. Their funerals were attended by some 3,000 mourners, many of them with their faces covered or wearing Palestinian keffiyahs and waving clenched fists, watched by dozens of police.

The chain of deaths and funerals that marked the 'German Autumn' represented a watershed in the history of the Federal Republic, when the economic miracle seemed to be faltering and the country seemed to be caught in an apparently inexorable spiral of violence and counter-violence, with echoes of its fascist past. While conservative politicians called for further repression, liberals compared the current situation to the Weimar Republic and saw in it a confirmation of Germany's 'tragic destiny'. This mood of pessimism and foreboding was eloquently portrayed in the film *Germany in Autumn*, a collaborative meditation on German politics and history by various German directors including Rainer Fassbinder and Volker Schlondorff.

One of the film's contributors was Heinrich Boll, who subsequently offered a nightmarish portrait of a society traumatised by terrorism in *The Safety Net* (1979). The novel describes the claustrophobic world of a wealthy newspaper owner and his family, living largely under permanent police protection, trapped by their own paranoid fear of terrorists, most of whom come from the same social class and even the same family as themselves. This grim dystopia did not materialise and other German liberals were beginning to come round to Boll's view that the anti-terrorist offensive had gone too far. In 1978 an investigation by the Bertrand Russell Tribunal listed numerous infringements of civil rights resulting from the emergency laws, from excessive surveillance by the intelligence services to harassment of individuals and organisations deemed to be 'disloyal to the state'. By this time the BKA's computer system had accumulated data on 3,100 organisations and 4,700,000 individuals. Between 1971 and 1979 some 1.5 million citizens were interrogated about their political beliefs and another 4,000 banned from state employment, often on the most tenuous grounds.[3]

No democratic country had previously undertaken such drastic measures in response to terrorism. The counter-terrorist campaign had effectively transformed the relationship between the state and its citizens, fostering an atmosphere of suspicion and paranoia in which any political opposition or dissent could be interpreted as support for terrorism. The drastic response of the West German state to what was essentially a marginal revolutionary threat was in marked contrast to the complacent official reaction to the even greater explosion of neo-Nazi violence in the 1990s.[4] To some extent the contrast can be explained by the fact that the Red Army Faction and its offshoots were directly attacking the state, rather than immigrants and asylum seekers, but the determination with which German conservatives set out to uproot the terrorists' 'intellectual sympathisers' was another example of how a particular version of 'terrorism' can be used to justify a broader ideological agenda.

In the wake of Stammheim, the West German left was also beginning to reassess the impact of terrorism from its own perspective, as articles began to appear in left-wing publications criticising the Red Army Faction and accusing it of harming the left politically. In a review of *Germany in Autumn* the French 'anti-psychiatrist' Felix Guattari rejected 'the altogether absurd confrontation between a monstrous State power and pitiful politico-military machines' and described the RAF as 'mistaken in its target, mistaken in its method, mistaken in its strategy, mistaken in its theory, mistaken in its dreams.'[5] Criticisms were also coming from within the terrorist milieu itself. In an interview with *Liberation* in 1980, Hans Joachim Klein, a member of the Revolutionary Cells, denounced what he called the 'slaughter politics' of his former comrades in which 'The connection between the objective and the means gets screwed up ... sooner or later you've got to get rid of a lot of baggage. From your humanity to your political ideals. You sink deeper and deeper into shit.'[6]

On the run from his former comrades and the police, Klein joined in the calls for a general amnesty to bring the terrorist era to an end. This was not a step the authorities were then willing to take and the RAF continued to show a surprising ability to reproduce itself. The second generation was followed by a third, believed to consist of no more than twenty members. In his savage burlesque *The Third Generation*, Rainer Werner Fassbinder portrayed them on film as decadent thrill seekers for whom terrorism had become a psychological addiction. But the RAF was a far more effective organisation than Fassbinder's camp terrorist caricatures suggest and it continued to carry out occasional bombings and high-profile assassinations even after the reunification of Germany. It was not until 1998, thirty years after the momentous events of 1968, that the RAF finally announced its official dissolution, in a long statement which declared that 'the RAF was born from an act of liberation: today we are ending this project. The urban guerrilla in the form of the RAF is now history.'[7]

'Armed existentialism'

What lured so many young men and women into a doomed and futile war that they never had any chance of winning? The East German spymaster Markus Wolf later described the RAF members who had taken refuge in East Germany as 'spoiled, hysterical children of mainly middle- and upper-class backgrounds'.[8] To the right-wing South African novelist Jillian Becker, author of the best-known biography of the early RAF, *Hitler's Children* (1978), the RAF leaders were proto-Nazis in leftist guise, whose shallow political judgements and individual neuroses led them to seek 'personal relief through acts of violence and blood and terror, and always with a grandiose moral justification'.[9]

Becker's shrill moralistic judgements do not stand up to objective scrutiny. Though Meinhof had certainly moved a long way from her original pacifist position by the time she joined the RAF, there is no evidence that she gained any personal satisfaction from acts of 'blood and terror'. On the contrary, even her own comrades commented on her aversion to bloodshed and her preference for non-violent operations. In *Journeys From Berlin/1971* (1980), the avant-garde filmmaker Yvonne Rainer saw Meinhof's involvement in the terrorist underworld as an expression of personal and political despair and placed her in a tradition of self-destructive female revolt stretching back to Sofia Perovskaya in nineteenth-century Russia.

Whether Meinhof was intent on suicide or personal liberation, the illusion of political authenticity and the imagined companionship of the revolutionary underworld were clearly more attractive to her than the prospect of bombs and bullets. Others were motivated by similar illusions. In 1977 Christof Wackernagel and Gert Schneider, two second-generation RAF members, were arrested in Amsterdam after a gunfight with Dutch police. In 1981 the two prisoners began an intensive process of political study and self-criticism in order to 'examine whether we had done anything wrong'. As a result of this process, both renounced their previous activities, on the grounds that 'the more we read, the more difficult it became to justify our armed struggle.'[10]

On the evidence of these statements, both Wackernagel and Schneider had been prepared to kill and die without any clear idea why they were doing either. A successful child actor before joining a Stuttgart commune, Wackernagel described the armed struggle as an attempt to find out 'whether you can find freedom if you completely break with society'. Astrid Proll similarly described the revolutionary underground as an expression of 'armed existentialism'. To Michael 'Bommi' Baumann, a member of the anarchist June 2 organisation, urban guerrilla warfare offered a seductive lifestyle, in which, 'You lead a life without a past, living without a personal history … You can't be integrated into the bourgeois system anymore, you're always outside.'[11] Disillusionment set in as Baumann found himself and his friends turning into reflections of the consumer society they once aimed to destroy, accumulating records, televisions, radios and new cars with money from bank robberies, and disguising themselves in smart velvet suits that 'look like you've jumped right out of *Playboy*'.

These trajectories make it tempting to regard the entire German terrorist underworld as an existential rebellion that had nothing to do with politics. But if the RAF's politics were incoherent and confused, their leap into revolutionary violence reflected the political frustration of a protest movement that found itself increasingly at odds with a conservative German society which regarded them as 'freaks', '*die Chaoten*' (violent anarchists) and a 'cancerous sore'. Their depiction of the Bundesrepublik as an 'SS state' in thrall to 'consumer fascism' may have been exaggerated and histrionic, but the continuity between the West German political and financial establishment and the fascist era was not a paranoid fantasy.

Should we regard the RAF and its offshoots as misguided idealists who sought to awaken their country's dormant conscience? There is too much blinkered rage and narcissism to reach such conclusions, but Becker's suggestion that they were crypto-Nazis motivated by an illiberal hatred of a 'free society' is an anti-terrorist cliché rather than an explanation. In 1988 the German painter Gerhard Richter revisited the Stammheim 'Death Night' with a series of documentary-style paintings entitled *October 18, 1977* based on photographs published in the German press showing Baader, Ensslin and Meinhof dead in their cells. One painting is based on a photograph of Ulrike Meinhof as a young woman, fresh-faced, serious and earnest. Another shows her lying in her cell with a wire noose around her neck. In juxtaposing these images Richter seemed to ask how one could lead to the other, and hinted at a complexity of cause and motivation behind a historical tragedy that the official presentation of the German terrorists as 'plague carriers' did not even begin to explain.

Italy's terrorist emergency

The legacy of fascism was also instrumental in the even more virulent and extensive explosion of left-wing violence in Italy in the same period. Unlike their West German counterparts, the Italian urban guerrillas were drawn from a much broader constituency and did achieve some working-class support, in a society where radical leftist politics were not as marginal as they were in Germany. Italy was the base of the most powerful communist party in Europe, the Italian Communist Party (PCI), which had been kept from power largely by the unstinting financial and political support, both overt and covert, which the ruling Christian Democracy (DC) received from the United States. The DC's long years in power were characterised by gross levels of corruption and mismanagement and punctuated by obscure fascist and far-right plots that often emanated from within the Italian military and secret services.

From the mid-1960s onwards, the post-war system was challenged by an increasingly militant student movement in the country's overcrowded and antiquated universities. Student militancy reached a peak in 1968, with a wave of sit-ins and occupations on most Italian campuses protesting a range of issues, from the narrow curriculum to the Vietnam war. Unlike similar events elsewhere in Europe, the Italian student protests turned in some cases to what amounted to permanent occupations, and coincided with a new mood of working-class militancy that culminated in the wave of wildcat strikes in 1969 during a period that came to be known as the 'Hot Autumn'. These events coincided with a resurgence of neo-fascist violence, dubbed the 'strategy of tension', in which fascist groups linked to the Italian secret services bombed civilian targets in order to destabilise Italian society and mobilise popular support for a strong authoritarian government. In December 1969 a bomb exploded at a bank in the Piazza Fontana in Milan, killing sixteen people and wounding another eighty-eight.

In a country where the wartime anti-fascist partisans remained both a heroic memory and an unfinished political project, the more militant sectors of the Italian left called for armed resistance under the slogan 'Ni mai più sin fucile' – 'Never again without a rifle'. These radical sectors emerged mostly outside the PCI, which was committed to the 'Eurocommunist' project of gaining power through elections and was as wary of working-class 'spontaneity' as it was of the unrest in the universities. Throughout the 1960s a new generation of Marxist intellectuals increasingly called for a more revolutionary form of Marxism to replace the 'reformism' of the PCI. In the turbulent aftermath of the Hot Autumn there were many on the left who believed that the PCI had become an essentially conservative political force and that the revolution would take place outside its ranks. Others saw the collusion between Italy's democratic institutions and neo-fascism as justification for an all-out assault on the bourgeois state itself.

Renato and Margherita
The unlikely seedbed of left-wing terrorism was the conservative university of Trento, where Christian Democrats established a new institute of social studies in the early sixties. One of the first batch of sociology students was a 23-year-old named Renato Curcio, who arrived in 1964. Curcio came to the university a practising Catholic, an introspective and lonely young man from a modest lower-middle-class background with no obvious interest in politics. Within two years of his arrival, however, he underwent a profound and passionate conversion to Marxism, immersing himself in the writings of Lenin, Marx and Mao, whose precepts he received like holy writ. At Trento he also met the love of his life, an earnest young sociology student named Margherita Cagol, who came from a stable conservative family in a nearby town.

Before going to university Cagol had been a promising classical guitarist who had performed in public. Amongst her family and friends she was known for her modesty and generosity and a concern with what her sister called 'the great problems of life' which expressed itself in charitable work and visits to hospitals. Cagol also embraced revolutionary politics with evangelical fervour. The pair were married, and in July 1969 left for Milan, where the newlyweds immersed themselves in the city's turbulent revolutionary politics. At the height of the Hot Autumn Margherita wrote to her mother describing how

> this great city, which at first seemed to me luminous, full of attractions, increasingly seems to me a ferocious monster that devours all that is natural, human, essential in life. Milan is barbarity: it is the true face of the society in which we live ... This society, which violates all of us every moment, taking from us anything that might in some way emancipate us or make us feel truly what we are ... has extreme need of being transformed by a profound revolutionary process.[12]

The rejection of the materialism and soullessness of modern urban living, the vaguely imagined but intensely felt possibility of a different way of life based on the collective rather than the individual, the inherent nobility and generosity of the revolutionary calling – all the ingredients of 'armed existentialism' are present in Cagol's conception of herself. Her mother could have little inkling where this 'profound revolutionary process' would lead. For both Cagol and Curcio were already involved in trying to build a new revolutionary organisation amongst the 'study groups' and factory-based committees that had sprung up in the wake of the revolutionary ferment in Milan.

Out of these efforts came the formation of a new armed revolutionary organisation in 1971 to represent 'the most decisive and conscious part of the proletariat in struggle' that would soon become known to millions of Italians as the Brigate Rosse – the Red Brigade (BR), usually translated in the plural. Its founders included Mario Moretti, a former right-wing Catholic student activist from a radical Milan commune, and Alberto Franceschini, a Bologna university student from a traditionally communist family, whose parents and grandparents had been active anti-fascists. Unlike the Red Army Faction, the BR engaged in a long period of political preparation before entering into armed struggle, slowly gathering recruits in factories such as the gigantic Fiat Mirafiori auto works in Turin for what it called 'an armed underground state that prepares for war'.

'Strike one to educate one hundred'

The *brigatisti* soon turned to low-level acts of violence intended to 'educate' the workforce, fire-bombing management cars, beating up and temporarily abducting company officials and supervisors. In May 1974 the organisation kidnapped the attorney-general of Genoa, Mario Sossi, known as 'Doctor Handcuffs' for his vigorous persecution of the left. After thirty-five days the BR released their prisoner, without having realised their demands, showing a magnanimity which they would not often repeat. In June that year the *brigatisti* killed for the first time, shooting two members of the neo-fascist MSI Party during a raid on its offices in Padua in response to another bloody bombing of an anti-fascist demonstration in Brescia. Soon afterwards the *brigatisti* suffered a major setback, when the BR leadership was infiltrated by a police agent provocateur, whose efforts resulted in the arrest of a number of high-level members, including Franceschini and Curcio.

At this point the Red Brigades might easily have collapsed, but in February 1975 Margherita Cagol personally led a Red Brigade commando unit to spring her husband from prison. Two months later the reconstituted 'Strategic Direction' published a resolution outlining its political and military strategy. Though much of the document was steeped in the impenetrable Marxist jargon known to the carabinieri and police agents who penetrated the organisation as 'brigadese', it contained a number of key Red Brigades concepts. For the first time the BR described Italy as the 'Imperialist State of the Multinationals' (SIM) – an entity that was to occupy a dominant position in the organisation's political demonology. The main allies of the SIM were the ruling Christian Democrats, whom the *brigatisti* accused of instigating a 'counter-revolutionary civil war' on behalf of international capital. To combat these developments, the Red Brigades proposed to build a 'fighting party' that would 'raise every partial expression of proletarian antagonism in a convergent assault on the heart of the state'. But it was the state that struck first, when Margherita Cagol was shot dead during a carabinieri raid on a Red Brigades safe house. The loss of 'Mara' devastated Curcio, who wrote an elegaic communiqué celebrating her life and exemplary death. In January 1976 Curcio was recaptured and the remnants of the organisation passed into the hands of Mario Moretti, under whose leadership the *brigatisti* proved to be more efficient and sanguinary than before.

In June that year the organisation carried out the mafia-style assassination of the prosecutor general, Francesco Coco, on the eve of national parliamentary elections in which the communists made major gains. Even as the left edged closer to government the number of violent incidents continued to soar as dozens of revolutionary groups sprang up across the country under such names as Senza Tregua (Without Truce), the Armed Proletarian Nuclei (NAP) and Prima Linea (Frontline). Membership of these groups was fluid and often interchangeable, as new factions formed and dissolved or collaborated in joint operations. Between them, these armed groups carried out a sustained campaign of bombings, arson attacks, assassinations and kneecappings as a warning or punishment to their class enemies. In some northern factories the practice of kneecapping was so widespread that company officials took to carrying tourniquets to make sure they did not bleed to death when shot.

The result was an almost daily level of violence that marked the *anni di pliombi* – the years of lead. In general the targets of left-wing violence were chosen for their perceived symbolic function within the Italian state or business establishment, such as magistrates, prison officials, policemen and factory managers. But journalists, academics and factory foremen were also killed or crippled as the *brigatisti* and the other armed organisations waged their anti-imperialist class war with pitiless ferocity against anybody who challenged or criticised them. Many members of the armed organisations were drawn from the loose movement known as the 'Autonomia', or autonomous area, a heterogenous collection of groups and organisations that incorporated anarchist squatters, feminists, students, factory workers and revolutionary Marxist intellectuals opposed to the PCI's 'reformism'.

Autonomia was known for its innovative tactics, from the looting of supermarkets (known as 'proletarian holidays') to the refusal to pay public transport fares or rents considered excessive. On the surface there was little in common between the doctrinaire Marxism of the Red Brigades and the libertarian anarchism of Autonomia, with its rejection of the work ethic and its stated intention 'to make the revolution, then disappear'. But many *autonomi* shared the same exaltation of revolutionary violence, and regularly turned up at demonstrations in their black ski-masks and crash helmets armed with 'comrade P-38', where they engaged in gun battles with the police and fascist groups.

Some university campuses had virtually slipped from official control, as students wrote the curriculum and professors delivered their lectures in classrooms covered in revolutionary graffiti proclaiming the 'proletarian assault on the sky' and *mitra è bello* – the machine gun is beautiful. In the university of Padua, the base of the charismatic Marxist professor of politics Tony Negri and a leading Autonomia intellectual, graffiti affirmed the 'right' to shoot professors in the mouth and academic staff with politically unsound views were routinely threatened with assassination.

In keeping with their conception of themselves as ordinary members of the proletariat, the full-time urban guerrillas, or *clandestini*, who lived in hiding in communal safe houses, were paid monthly salaries of $450, based on the minimum wage of workers on the Fiat assembly line. The *clandestini* also took regular summer holidays every August, paid for out of their wages or through bank robberies that were often carried out in the same seaside towns where they rented holiday homes. The rest of the year they lived together in their safe houses under false identities. For security reasons, contacts with family and outsiders were discouraged or forbidden and the *clandestini* spent most of their time with each other, following the strict rules advocated in the BR manuals, which advised them to go to bed no later than midnight and to maintain themselves in a state of alertness by constantly looking over their shoulders and checking their rear-view mirrors. Such was the lifestyle that many urban guerrillas maintained for years.

For some there were compensations for this austere and difficult existence in the grandeur of the revolutionary cause, and the sense of shared hardship in which one Prima Linea remembered, 'this sensation of never feeling alone because ... there was always somewhere to sleep, and there was always this thing about sharing everything we had.'[13] Most insider accounts of the Italian terrorist underground have come from the *pentiti* – former revolutionaries who co-operated with the state in return for reduced sentences – and the *dissociati* – those who renounced the armed struggle following their imprisonment without actually betraying their former comrades. As a result their recollections tend to be negative or tempered by experience. Nevertheless, one former Prima Linea member recalled the armed struggle as 'a break with a castrated and obsolete world of politics, the old and unresponsive world', while another member of the same organisation spoke of his adolescent awe for the resistance fighters of his youth who represented 'the fact of risking something serious ... determining like your own life'.[14]

If the revolutionary underworld offered a sense of solidarity and heroic purpose, its actions were frequently appalling. In one operation in December 1979 ten Prima Linea members held up a classroom of students in a graduate business school at the university of Turin. When a student jokingly asked one of the female guerrillas if he should address her 'formally or informally', the *piellina* replied, 'Please address me formally', and shot him in the leg. The group then shot five professors and five students in the kneecaps, and left them writhing in pools of blood. Before leaving, the avengers of the proletariat exhorted the hysterical survivors to 'do as we do, we are ready to welcome you'.

What explained this extraordinary combination of savagery and naivety? A photograph taken at one of the terrorist 'maxi-trials' shows a group of female Prima Linea members laughing in a large cage. The women are all wearing cardigans and ponchos and look more like a women's conscious-ness-raising group than the routine Italian press depictions of terrorists as 'beasts', 'delinquents' and 'desperate criminals'. In an essay entitled 'Why Are They Laughing in Those Cages?' Umberto Eco compared the Red Brigades to the Manson family, claiming that their members displayed 'the same psychology, the same lack of remorse, the same sense of having done something that gave meaning to a life that … was too boring and peaceful'.[15] In his last novel, *Time of Desecration*, Alberto Moravia compared the left-wing revolutionaries to the barbarians who had once sacked Rome. To Moravia the terrorist underworld was the culmination of an escalating revolt against bourgeois sexual and cultural norms and the expression of an age-old 'dream of a heroic community' that was 'heroic not merely because it was danger-ous but also because it was dedicated to certain failure'.

Needless to say, this was not how the urban guerrillas saw their own actions. Some of them, such as the millionaire leftist publisher Giangiacomo Feltrinelli, saw themselves as the heirs of the wartime partisan resistance against a resurgent fascist threat in which Italy's democratic institutions were deeply complicit.[16] Others were convinced that capitalism was a 'dying dinosaur', needing only one last violent push before what Curcio once called 'the happy island' of revolutionary socialism was within Italy's grasp. A number of *dissociati* later attributed the armed struggle to a super-ficial analysis of the political situation in Italy, while Alberto Franceschini subsequently described himself and his comrades as 'addicts of ideology. A fatal drug, worse than heroin. A few cubic centimetres of it and you're done for life'.[17] There is no doubt that the Red Brigades' belief in an imminent revolutionary civil war was based to some extent on a narrow and dogmatic application of Marxist theory to the Italian situation. Yet even though the BR continued to churn out a prolific stream of earnest communiqués to explain the political meaning of each kneecapping or act of 'annihilation' of the class enemy, its violence was often stunningly frivolous.

In one incident the BR shot and wounded a Fiat manager whom they had mistaken for a Siemens director living in the same block of flats. On realising their error, the *brigatisti* simply rewrote the original communiqué to make it look as if the Fiat official was their intended target. On another occasion they

asked an employee at the Ercole Marelli company for biographical information on a company director they had already killed so that they could write
a communiqué to explain why they had shot him.

Both the left and the far right had a mutual interest in destabilising Italian
society for their own different reasons. In 1984 a far-right activist named
Vincenzo Vinciguerra admitted to an Italian judge, Felice Casson, that he had
planted a bomb in a booby-trapped car which killed two carabinieri near the
town of Peteano in May 1972. Vinciguerra claimed in sworn testimony that
it was one of various 'false flag' bombings carried out by the far right, using
materials supplied from the NATO 'stay behind' networks known as Operation Gladio. The Gladio networks had originally been created to engage
in guerrilla warfare in the event of a Soviet invasion in various European
countries, but Vinciguerra told Casson that some of its members had participated in the 'strategy of tension' under the protection of the Italian secret
services. According to Vinciguerra, the aim of these bombings was to 'force
… the Italian public to turn to the state to ask for greater security'. Therefore
'You had to attack civilians, the people, women, children, innocent people,
unknown people far removed from any political game.'[18]

Whether it came from the left or right, the ongoing violence coincided
with a period in which the PCI was making steady electoral gains, which
led some theorists to wonder whether the Red Brigades were also being
manipulated by obscure elements within the Italian secret services. Some
commentators, most notably the pro-PCI judge Pietro Calogero and the journalist Philip Willan, have argued that the Red Brigades were penetrated
by Italian and foreign intelligence agencies from its early origins in Milan
and subsequently used to undermine and discredit the PCI.[19] In the baroque
conspiratorial world of Cold War Italian politics, few possibilities are out-
landish enough to discount entirely.[20] Both Moretti and Curcio have always
denied accusations of external manipulation, but the 'puppetmasters' thesis
reached a crescendo in 1978, when the Red Brigades carried out their most
audacious blow to the heart of the state and the operation with which they
have most widely been associated.

In the catacombs – the destruction of Aldo Moro
On the surface there are few more illustrative examples of the 'terrorism'
versus 'democracy' narrative than the extraordinary drama which followed
the kidnapping of the president of the Christian Democrat Party, Aldo
Moro. On 16 March 1978 Moro left his home on his way to present the new
government to parliament, the first in Italian history to receive the support

of the PCI. More than any other politician, Moro was the architect of the 'historic compromise' – an arrangement that the dour pragmatist known as the 'Master Weaver' considered essential to the stability of what he called a 'difficult democracy'. Moro's convoy of two cars and five bodyguards was passing along the Via Fani towards the Via Stresa when a Fiat 128 reversed into his car and the driver and his female passenger came running towards them, firing at Moro's chauffeur, Corporal Ricci. In the same moment four uniformed airline pilots who had been standing nearby raked the two cars with machine-gun fire, skilfully angling their line of fire in order to avoid hitting Moro himself. Only one bodyguard managed to reach his weapon and get out of the vehicle, where he was shot dead by another attacker who had been waiting in readiness. The terrified Moro was dragged from the car and driven away, leaving behind five corpses and Italy's gravest political crisis of the post-war era.

Within hours the prime minister, Giulio Andreotti, and his cabinet agreed that there would be no negotiations or concessions with Moro's kidnappers. The *linea della fermezza* (policy of firmness) was supported by all the other parties, including the communists. It also received immediate international approval, particularly from the US and West German governments. From the outset both the government and the Italian press presented the kidnapping as an attack on the Italian republic itself and Moro became a symbolic pawn in a cruel and complex political game. Two days after the kidnapping the Red Brigades released a communiqué announcing that Moro was a 'political prisoner'. Though the kidnappers issued no demands, Moro was already being treated by his own party and the Italian media as condemned to death. Then, on 29 March, a letter apparently written by Moro was sent to his friend and colleague Francesco Cossiga, the interior minister, urging him not to reject the possibility of negotiations with his kidnappers. The letter caused consternation in the DC ranks. Not only was Moro refusing to accept the mantle of sacrificial victim that they had conferred upon him, but he also used words like 'political prisoner' and 'guerrilla war' to describe his situation, thereby conferring a degree of legitimacy on his terrorist kidnappers that his party had never accepted.

Faced with such a direct challenge to the policy of firmness by the captive himself, the party leadership claimed that Moro had become a tool of the Red Brigades and that 'the letter was not morally imputable to its subject'. Using their extensive media contacts, the government and their supporters set out to show that 'Moro no è Moro', using a procession of handwriting experts, pharmacologists and cryptologists who suggested that Moro's letter showed evidence of coercion, sleep deprivation and the use of mind-altering drugs. The bad faith of these manoeuvres did not go unnoticed by the captive himself, who continued to issue a stream of correspondence to his party colleagues, his wife, the Communist Party secretary, Enrico Berlinguer, and the Socialist Party leader, Bettino Craxi, in an effort to breach the hardline consensus.

A grotesque spectacle now unfolded, in which at times Moro's kidnappers appeared to be more interested than the leaders of his own party in keeping him alive. The more Moro manoeuvred to save his life, the more the DC party leaders continued their attempt to neutralize his arguments by presenting him as an infantilised mouthpiece of the Red Brigades. For nearly two months the kidnapping dominated the news in Italy, as analysts pored over the meaning of Red Brigades' communiqués and the authorities continued to turn the country upside down in a massive police operation involving some 16,000 carabinieri, 18,000 police, 4,000 frontier guards and hundreds of army units. In the course of the crisis nearly 7 million Italians were checked, 3.3 million cars and houses were examined at 62,000 roadblocks and 35,000 houses were searched. At the same time the investigation was characterised by numerous police failures, which further fuelled rumours of a conspiracy involving the CIA, NATO and/or the KGB. The national drama also became an international media spectacle, as Amnesty International, the pope and UN secretary-general Kurt Waldheim appealed at various times to the BR for clemency. Various governments and international media commentators presented the episode as a crucial test of the will of Western governments to confront terrorism and urged the Christian Democrats to stand firm against a threat whose consequences were no longer limited to Italy itself. Such exhortations were based partly on the assumption that any concession to Moro's kidnappers would encourage further kidnappings, both in Italy and elsewhere. But the Italian government was also charged with upholding an inviolable moral principle, by which democratic governments could never succumb to terrorist 'blackmail'.

The high moral tone of this debate concealed the fact that there were sectors within the Christian Democrat Party and the United States government that had always opposed the 'historic compromise' and were determined to exclude the communists from government. Though rarely spoken outright, the policy of firmness made it virtually inevitable that the principal architect of the historic compromise would have to become a sacrificial victim. For the Christian Democrat hardliners, a martyred Moro far outweighed any political benefits that might accrue from his release, by discrediting the left and enabling the party to identify itself with the survival of the republic. Not surprisingly, the Christian Democrat position received the strongest support from the US government, whose overriding policy in Italy during the previous three decades had been to ensure that the PCI did not take power. Not everyone was prepared to go as far as the conservative American columnist William Buckley, who described Moro's attitude to his party as 'unchristian' and advised him to 'die like a man, not a coward', but official opinion was virtually unanimous that any concessions to the Red Brigades would constitute a political catastrophe.

What did the Red Brigades themselves hope to gain from the macabre drama they had presented to the nation? The kidnappers' intentions were not always clear, even to themselves. In the mammoth 'Strategic Resolution' that accompanied communiqué number 4 the BR ranted once again against the diabolical machinations of the SIM ('the greatest multinational of crime that humanity has ever known') and identified the Christian Democrats as its main instruments. Some students of Red Brigades theology assumed that the kidnapping was intended to undermine the SIM by wrecking the historic rapprochement between Italy's two largest parties, but the same objective could have been achieved by killing Moro along with his bodyguards. Instead, the *brigatisti* entered into a tortuous and protracted process that could easily have resulted in the discovery and arrest of their own members. Despite the much-vaunted 'trial' of Christian Democracy and the man they called 'the demiurge of bourgeois power, present in the decisive moments, meditations, choices', the Red Brigades did not even make the transcriptions of his interrogations public, which suggested that Moro's revelations did not support their narrow formulations.

Throughout his ordeal Moro behaved with courage and dignity and sought the meaning and value of his life in terms of his relationships with his family rather than with the party that he believed had betrayed him. On Tuesday 9 May, fifty-four days after the kidnapping, Moro was dressed by his captors and ordered to lie down in the boot of a Renault, where he was shot in the chest with the BR's favoured Skorpion machine gun, before another *brigatisti* completed the job with a pistol. In a final theatrical flourish the Renault was then driven through the centre of Rome, which was swarming with some 50,000 police, and left at a point exactly halfway between the Christian Democrat and the Communist Party headquarters. The photograph of Moro's corpse was flashed round the world: wearing a suit, his head tilted to one side, half-covered with a blanket, an iconic sacrificial victim crushed between two rival abstract notions of power – the state and the revolution.

On 10 May Moro was buried at a small family funeral in his native village. As he had requested, there were no members of his party present. Four days later the politicians he derided as 'the men of power' held their own symbolic service for the unwilling martyr, in a special mass given by the pope and attended by a host of national and international political leaders. The next day the national election results saw the Christian Democrats reach 40 per cent for the first time in years. The PCI, which had so fervently defended the hard line throughout the crisis, saw its share of the vote decline by almost 25 per cent from its historic gains in 1976. The historic compromise was effectively null and void as the DC now sought its political alliances elsewhere. Italian democracy had been 'saved' and the communists would never again come as close to power as they had during the brief period of expectation that ended in the Via Fani. In 1991 the senate commission investigating the Gladio networks found that the majority of official documents regarding the Moro case had vanished from the Ministry of the Interior. The commission subsequently concluded that the Moro kidnapping was 'a criminal project in which the Red Brigades most probably were instruments of a larger political framework'.[21]

Failure and defeat

The Moro tragedy was a pivotal episode in the confrontation between the state and the Red Brigades, one which finally galvanised the government into a more systematic anti-terrorist campaign under the direction of the carabinieri general Carlo Alberto Dalla Chiesa. A swathe of emergency laws granted the police new powers of search and arrest, enabling the government to suppress the Autonomia movement, banning its demonstrations and closing its journals and radio stations. As the jails filled up with some 5,000 terrorist suspects another 500 fled abroad, including Toni Negri and other Autonomia leaders. In 1979 Dalla Chiesa made a major breakthrough when a captured Prima Linea member turned state's evidence, resulting in a string of arrests that virtually destroyed Prima Linea as an organisation. In August 1980 a massive bomb exploded in the second-class waiting room at the railway station in the communist-controlled city of Bologna, killing 85 people and injuring another 200.

Once again police investigations pointed to Italian neo-fascists, though no arrests were made. The Bolgna atrocity occurred at a period when the tide of left-wing terrorism was beginning to ebb, and Dalla Chiesa scored his biggest breakthrough so far with the arrest of a high-ranking *brigatista*, Patrizio Peci. Disillusioned with the armed struggle and disgusted with his own actions, Peci revealed names and information that led to some eighty arrests. At the end of the year the *brigatisti* kidnapped General James L. Dozier, a high-ranking officer in NATO's Southern Europe headquarters. But on 27 January 1982 Dozier's place of imprisonment was revealed by an informer and the police freed the general and arrested his captors. Further arrests crippled the organisation. By this time the Red Brigades had become largely isolated from the constituencies that might once have enabled them to recover from these losses. In 1983 Curcio announced that 'the armed struggle has been short-circuited, it did not succeed in making the great leap forward, it fell to the ground. Its protagonists can only mourn, liberating themselves from its ghost'.[22]

Freaks, deviants, fantasists

In 1985 the novelist Doris Lessing delivered a withering indictment of middle-class terrorism in *The Good Terrorist*, in which a group of English squatters become involved with the IRA and the KGB and carry out a terrorist bomb attack in London. The main character, Alice, who gives the novel its ironic title, is a spoiled, dysfunctional hysteric who vents her hollow rage at bourgeois society while simultaneously engaging in guilt-free sponging off the state and her parents. Though written much later, Lessing's vicious troglodytes encapsulated the conservative view of the student urban guerrillas in the 1970s as the 'spoiled children of affluence' and the products of liberal 'excess'.

If the phenomenon of middle-class terrorism was regarded as a bewildering manifestation of social deviancy, it was also a source of prurient fascination. The nearest English equivalent to a left-wing urban guerrilla organisation was a London-based anarchist group called the Angry Brigade, which carried out a number of bomb attacks in Britain in the early 1970s, including a BBC television van filming the Miss World competition and the house of the Tory home secretary, Robert Carr. The group emanated from a similar student/squatter subculture to the Red Army Faction and its members were strongly influenced by the French Situationists, with their critique of capitalist society as a media-generated 'spectacle'. This philosophy resulted in an apparently eccentric choice of targets, such as the firebombing of the trendy Biba clothing emporium, which was accompanied by a communiqué complaining that

> Life is so boring there is nothing to do except spend all our wages on the latest skirt or shirt. Brothers and sisters, what are your real desires? Sit in the drug-

store, look distant, empty, bored, drinking some tasteless coffee? Or perhaps BLOW IT UP or BURN IT DOWN.[23]

Though their bombs claimed no casualties, the Angry Brigade was regarded by the Tory government as 'Public Enemy Number 1' and the subsequent police investigation resulted in eight arrests, including four former students from Cambridge and Essex universities. In May 1972 the defendants went on trial at the Old Bailey, in what became the longest conspiracy trial in British legal history. The proceedings were the subject of intense media interest, which brought back distant memories of the anarchist bomber as the term 'infernal devices' was used in a British court for the first time since the nineteenth century. Despite scoring numerous points regarding the forensic evidence which resulted in four acquittals, a quartet of students known as the Amhurst Four were found guilty and given ten-year sentences after the judge blamed their deviant behaviour on a 'warped understanding of sociology'.

The reaction to the verdict and sentences in the British press echoed the official belief that a Baader-Meinhof-style terrorist conspiracy had been uncovered. The *Daily Mirror* celebrated the 'Downfall of the bighead brigade' while the *Sun* wrote a lurid and almost entirely fictitious article entitled 'Sex orgies at the cottage of blood', describing how the 'communist' Amhurst Four had supposedly gathered 'for drugs, and conspiracies and sex' in an Essex farmhouse. Though the *Daily Express* described the Angry Brigade as an authentic terrorist conspiracy intent on 'anarchy on a grand scale – amassing bombs and machine guns to destroy anything that came to mind', its home-made bombs never amounted to a coherent urban guerrilla campaign and would soon be eclipsed by the far more destructive IRA bombing campaigns on the English mainland.

Sex, drugs and dynamite

In the United States, left-wing terrorism tended to be a similarly ad hoc and spontaneous phenomenon. In the late sixties and early seventies dozens of bombings and arson attacks were carried out by anonymous groups and individuals, usually during periods of particularly intense campus unrest or anti-Vietnam war protests. The most notorious 'terrorist' organisation of the era was called the Weathermen, whose unlikely name was taken from the line 'you don't need a weatherman to know which way the wind blows' in Bob Dylan's 'Subterranean Homesick Blues'. The group originated from a militant faction within the Students for a Democratic Society (SDS), the main radical organisation on US campuses, and its members espoused an improbable mixture of Maoism, Black Power and hippiedom. The majority of its leaders came from well-connected white families, such as Bill Ayers, a former civil rights activist whose father was the chairman of the board at Commonwealth Edison, and Bernardine Dohrn, the charismatic and attractive daughter of an appliance dealership owner and a law-school student, who was memorably described by the FBI director J. Edgar Hoover as 'La Passionaria of the lunatic Left'.

The Weathermen first became the centre of national attention following the 'Days of Rage' in October 1969 in Chicago, when some 400 Weathermen and Weatherwomen armed with baseball bats fought pitched battles over a four-day period with 4,000 police and national guardsmen in the city's financial district in an attempt to draw attention to the Vietnam war and demonstrate their revolutionary commitment. In December that year some 400 Weathermen held a 'war council' in Flint, Michigan, where the leadership, the 'Weather Bureau', officially declared war on the United States government. In a hall lined with giant pictures of Ho Chi Minh, Malcolm X and Fidel Castro, the delegates danced, practised karate moves and heard speeches from their leaders, including Bernardine Dohrn in knee-high leather boots and mini-skirt, who exhorted the delegates to behave like 'crazy motherfuckers' and 'scare the shit out of honky America'. Dohrn hailed the recent murders of Sharon Tate and her entourage by the Charles Manson family, telling the delegates, 'Dig it. First they killed those pigs and ate dinner in the same room with them. Then they even shoved a fork into a victim's stomach! Wild!'[24]

To their supporters the Weathermen were sexy and hip. To their critics on the left, such as the SDS leader Todd Gittlin, they were destructive sectarians, hijacking the anti-war movement in pursuit of a doomed revolutionary offensive. The feminist writer Robin Morgan later recalled the 'longing for catastrophe' which characterised the period and described an SDS milieu in which 'Swaggering and strutting, the Weathermen dominate meetings, define priorities, regard all unarmed struggle as irrelevant or reactionary'.[25]

The sectarian politics, puerile Maoism and narcissism are mostly absent from Bill Ayers's lyrical memoir *Fugitive Days*. For Ayers the Weathermen were a flawed but essentially noble gesture, which aimed to overcome 'white skin privilege' by aligning themselves with the Black Panthers and the VietCong. Ayers paints an apocalyptic picture of a violent era in which

The world was in flames ... little Vietnam bearing the brunt and racism at home paralleling most of the horrors visited upon the third world. Human existence itself seemed in grave doubt as, armed to the teeth with nuclear weapons and the masters of war at the controls, the world raced at warp speed towards oblivion. We imagined that the survival of humanity depended on the kids alone. And, from the edges, we were entirely inflexible, maybe even a bit goofy.[26]

There is more nostalgia than regret in Ayers's evocation of the strange world of the Weathermen, where LSD and dope-smoking sessions alternated with karate exercises as a preparation for urban guerrilla warfare, where refrigerators were filled with Vietnamese fish sauce and food was eaten with chopsticks as a matter of political principle, and members showed a collective predilection for a multi-purpose liquid known as Dr. Bronner's Magic Soap. Even as the Weathermen prepared for revolutionary war they continued to enact mass polygamous encounters and orgies in fulfilment of the organisation's pledge to 'smash monogamy'. Despite its dim-witted celebration of the Chinese Cultural Revolution, the organisation had more in common with Robert Crumb's Furry Freak Brothers comic than Mao Zedong. Like the Angry Brigade, the Weathermen claimed to represent a wider movement whose members, according to Dohrn, were to be found 'wherever kids are making love, smoking dope and loading guns'.

This was the subculture to which the Weathermen belonged and which they hoped to lead as they rushed to meet the revolutionary wave. But their attempts to unleash urban guerrilla warfare in the heart of the 'oppressor nation' received a disastrous setback in March 1970, when three members of the group were killed while preparing a bomb in a Greenwich Village townhouse in New York, which they intended to use at an army dance at Fort Dix, New Jersey. The explosion blew the front off the townhouse, and brought the Weathermen national publicity, in which Dohrn was described by *Newsweek* as 'America's most dangerous woman' and her striking good looks were reproduced in wanted posters across the country, together with those of the other leading Weather activists. In the American media the Weathermen were variously presented as Mansonesque killers, the members of a left-wing 'terror gang' and a 'gang of hate' with possible links to the Soviet Union.

In fact the Weathermen killed no one but themselves, and their acts of violence, as Bernardine Dohrn later admitted, amounted to no more than 'bee stings'. In the aftermath of the Greenwich Village explosion the remnants of the organisation opted for clandestinity, changing their name to the Weather Underground. According to Ayers they also decided to restrict their bombing campaigns to property to avoid casualties. Over the next few years the organisation carried out some twenty-five bombings in which no one was killed, including attacks on the Senate and the Pentagon. In 1974 the Weather Underground helped free the LSD guru Timothy Leary from jail and into exile in Algeria on behalf of an organisation called the Brotherhood of the Free Spirit, but this operation was carried out for money rather than for revolutionary purposes and it was not one to make the hearts of the proletariat beat faster.

By the end of the decade the majority of its members had been arrested. A few, including Dohrn and Ayers, managed to stay on the run until the early eighties, when they negotiated their way back from the underground in return for reduced sentences. The novelist Marge Piercy wrote an idealised account of the fugitive underground in her novel *Vida*, whose flame-haired bisexual heroine remains on the run more than a decade later, still clinging on to the radical values of the sixties even as the society around her changes. In the early 1980s the group's name made a brief reappearance, when two ex-Weathermen participated in an armoured car hold-up by a previously unknown group called the Black Liberation Army in which two security guards were killed. Despite a flurry of sensational headlines, the organisation itself did not reappear, and it soon became clear that it had long since ceased to exist.

The search for sincerity – the Japanese Red Army

The Weathermen, like so many student urban guerrilla groups, were fixated by the notion of revolutionary violence as the ultimate proof of political commitment and moral coherence. The obsession with authenticity was a major factor in the evolution in Japan of the United Red Army, the Sekigun-ha, one of the most violent left-wing urban guerrilla groups of the post-1968 era, which emerged from the left-wing student organisation the Zengakuren. From its inception the Red Army leadership was fixated with a narrow concept of revolutionary 'sincerity', defined almost entirely in terms of the willingness to face death.

In December 1971 its leaders conducted a ferocious experimental attempt at 'communist transformation' in a mountain lodge near Tokyo, which rapidly descended into a vortex of violence and sadism as members of the group were beaten to death and tied to stakes in freezing weather as a punishment for their 'spiritual weakness' and for 'bourgeois tendencies' such as wearing jewellery and make-up. By the time police tracked the group down to a nearby lodge in January 1972, fourteen people had been cruelly murdered for such transgressions. When the five remaining members took the lodge owner hostage, a nine-day siege ensued in sub-zero temperatures, watched by over 700 reporters and photographers and television cameramen who circled overhead in helicopters, before the police mounted an assault and took possession of the building floor by floor.

The 'snow murders' stunned the Japanese public, causing the father of one of the group's members to hang himself in shame and the country's minister of education to question whether 'the existence of national universities may be harmful to the nation'. With the organisation utterly discredited inside Japan, the leadership of the Red Army passed to a female member named Shigenobu Fusako, who had flown to Beirut the previous year with her husband in order to forge links with leftist Palestinians. In May 1972 Shigenobu helped to organise one of the worst terrorist atrocities of the modern era, when three members of the Red Army, including her own husband, volunteered to carry out a suicidal assault on Tel Aviv's Lod airport on behalf of the Popular Front for the Liberation of Palestine (PFLP). After receiving military training at a Palestinian camp near Beirut, the team flew to Rome, where they were given machine guns and grenades before flying to Israel on 30 May posing as Japanese businessmen. In preparing to sacrifice themselves on behalf of the revolution, the three men were self-consciously enacting a very specific Japanese national drama, drawing on the example of the kamikaze pilots and the warrior tradition of *bushido*.

On reaching the airport the team calmly retrieved their cases, unpacked their weapons and began shooting and throwing grenades at the passengers and airport staff. The attack coincided with the arrival of a party of Puerto Rican Christian tourists on a tour of the Holy Land. It was these tourists who bore the full brunt of the Red Army assault. In less than three minutes twenty-six of the party lay dead while another eighty-five people were wounded and the airport had become a scene of carnage. One of the attackers was accidentally shot dead by his own comrades while another blew himself up with one of his own grenades. The only survivor was a former student named Kozo Okamoto, who was so ashamed at having lived that he refused to speak to his interrogators until an Israeli officer promised to allow him to shoot himself in exchange for a confession.

The officer subsequently reneged on his promise and Okamoto was denied the death he craved. Instead, he went to court, where the judge ignored his own father's request to execute him and gave him a life sentence. The massacre was the bloodiest single operation carried out by any of the student urban guerrilla groups and it received widespread international condemnation, in language that was already becoming part of a ritualistic response to terrorist events, as a 'senseless' and 'cowardly' terrorist attack on innocent civilians. As horrendous as it was, the Lod massacre was neither senseless nor cowardly. To the Red Army and the PFLP, Lod airport provided Israel's main connection to the outside world and therefore constituted an economic target. At the same time the operation was intended, as Okomoto explained at his trial, to 'instil the Arab masses with spiritual fervour'.

As always, the morality of the operation was determined by the justice of the revolutionary cause itself and by the nature of the imperialist enemy. To the PFLP and the Red Army revolutionary violence could not be subject to ethical constraints, and anyone who visited Israel for whatever reason was indirectly supporting the Zionist state and therefore could not be 'innocent'. To the Libyan leader Colonel Qaddafi, who called for the Palestinians themselves to carry out similar operations, the Lod airport massacre was a heroic act of revolutionary solidarity. The Red Army took the same view. In an interview with a Japanese newspaper, Okamoto paid tribute to the kamikaze pilots of World War II and to Yukio Mishima, the right-wing Japanese novelist who killed himself during a failed military coup in 1970, claiming that 'Even though Mishima and other Japanese suicide heroes believed in anti-revolutionary or reactionary ideologies, their emotions were the same as those of revolutionaries.' Within Japan, however, the massacre provoked the same shocked incredulity and shame that had greeted the snow murders. Okamoto was released in 1985, following a prisoner exchange with Palestinians. By that time the Red Army was already on its way to becoming a footnote in history, and the post-1968 student urban guerrillas had long since been eclipsed by organisations with a very different agenda and a far greater capacity for mayhem.

Patriots

O heroes!
Where are the revolutionaries of yesterday?
Where are the companions of the mujahideen?
Where are the sons of Shaikh Qassam,
The brethren of Abdul Qadir … ?

Our Palestine, March 1961[1]

Life springs from death; and from the graves of patriot men and women spring living nations.

Padraig Pearse, 1915

In September 2003 the 151st San Sebastián film festival became the scene of an acrimonious political controversy when the festival screened the documentary *The Basque Ball – the Skin against the Stone* by the acclaimed Basque director Julio Medem, which examined the long conflict between the Basque separatist organisation ETA and the Spanish state. Medem defined his film as an invitation to dialogue and it contained interviews with more than seventy writers, intellectuals, politicians and ordinary Basques, offering a broad range of views on the Basque conflict. Two perspectives were conspicuously absent: those of ETA itself and of the conservative governing party the Partido Popular. ETA could not participate in the film because Spanish anti-terrorism laws prohibited any direct representation of ETA's views, while the Partido Popular leadership refused to participate in what the Spanish minister of culture described as 'a suspicious enterprise'.

Medem's arrival at the festival was greeted with a noisy demonstration by an organisation called the Association of Victims of Terrorism, which accused him of supporting ETA and insulting the 'victims of terrorism'. No objective viewing of Medem's documentary could possibly interpret it as an apology for terrorist violence. The father of one of the film's co-producers had been murdered by ETA and the film contained interviews with a young

Socialist Party member in the Basque country who lost his leg in an ETA car bomb attack, and the widow of a socialist politician murdered by ETA, both of whom called for a negotiated solution to the conflict. In addition, the film included interviews with Basques who had suffered at the hands of the Spanish security forces, including a young woman tortured by Spanish police. Both the calls for negotiation and Medem's suggestion of a degree of mutuality in the violence effectively breached the 'closed' anti-terrorist anathema which has prevailed in Spain for so many years.

The same dictum has been pronounced on other violent nationalist organisations that employed revolutionary terrorism as a tactic, such as the Provisional IRA and the PLO. All these organisations were products of the same revolutionary era that produced the student urban guerrillas. But where the student urban guerrillas acted in the name of an abstract revolutionary constituency, the nationalist insurgents represented organic communities that shared their aspirations and supported their use of violence. Not only did these organisations represent a historical tradition of armed resistance, but their violence was directed towards the more limited goal of national independence and self-determination rather than social revolution.

In this sense their objectives were clearly recognisable and far more coherent than those of the post-1968 leftist revolutionaries. Yet even more than the student urban guerrillas, the nationalist insurgents have given rise to some of the key concepts of the anti-terrorist malediction, with its godfathers of terror, criminal mafias, gangsters and gunmen. In 1989 the British home secretary Douglas Hurd declared that 'with the Provisional IRA and some of the Middle-Eastern groups, it is really nothing to do with a political cause any more. They are professional killers. That is their occupation and their pleasure and they will go on doing just that. No political solution will cope with that. They just have to be extirpated.'[2]

As an explanation for either the IRA or the PLO, Hurd's declarations were patently ridiculous. Spanish officials have used very similar language in its depictions of ETA. But no matter how much their enemies insisted that they were criminals, gangsters and terrorists, all three organisations continued to describe themselves as patriots, fighting wars on behalf of nations-in-waiting, but wars none the less.

The Irish Troubles
Few conflicts has become more associated with terrorism than the three decades of violence in Northern Ireland which began in 1966, with the killing of two Catholics by a Protestant paramilitary group, the Ulster Volunteer

Force (UVF). By the time the Good Friday Agreement brought the conflict to a tentative conclusion more than three decades later in 1998, 3,636 people had been killed out of a population of one and a half million, while thousands more had been maimed and seriously injured. Of these, 2,139 were killed by the IRA and other republican groups, 1,050 by loyalist paramilitaries and 367 by the Northern Irish security forces and the British army.[3]

The statistics merely sketch out the devastating impact on Irish society of a vicious conflict in which the more spectacular atrocities alternated with a routine barbarity that often attracted little attention from the outside world, in which men were shot dead watching television, buying groceries or driving cement trucks to work or standing on the doorstep in their slippers, in which Protestant hit squads with sledgehammers, known as the 'Loyalist skeleton key', broke down doors in the middle of the night to shoot their victims in their beds in front of their children. Such was the level of everyday obscenity that transformed this previously ignored and little known province of the United Kingdom into the definitive terrorist battleground of the post-war era. In the beginning, the explosion of violence in Ulster was sometimes regarded in the outside world as an atavistic retreat from civilisation that was racial in origin. As early as August 1969 a *New York Times* reporter in London commented on 'a sense of something dark, inexplicable and strange in the Irish soul that foreigners cannot explain – or quite ignore', while a cartoon in the London *Evening Standard* in 1982 showed a man walking past a giant poster for a film entitled THE IRISH – THE ULTIMATE IN PSYCHOPATHIC HORROR, depicting brutish Irish murderers in a graveyard armed with an array of ghastly weapons, who might have stepped from the nineteenth-century caricatures of the Fenians in *Punch*.

The unexpected return of the 'Irish question' also came as a shock to the British government and public, which had paid little attention to the decades of sectarian misrule that preceded the violence. In the early stages of the conflict the British government presented itself as a neutral arbiter attempting to separate the warring Irish tribes. Once the British army found itself in direct conflict with the IRA, however, the official presentation of the violence was dictated by the imperatives of counter-insurgency, which sought to portray the IRA as an evil and extraneous presence in Northern Ireland. In 1971 the Northern Ireland information office produced a gory leaflet entitled 'The Terror and the Tears', showing photographs of IRA atrocities as evidence that the IRA were 'thugs with blood dripping from their hands'.[4]

The victims were real, though the propaganda narrative ignored the fact that the IRA was supported by a broad swathe of the Catholic population. From the outset the British government and much of the media presented the IRA as a 'criminal' rather than a 'political' organisation. The IRA certainly engaged in various 'ordinary' criminal activities, including bank robberies and smuggling, the sale of stolen goods and extortion. That the gains from such activities were generally directed towards the IRA's armed campaign rather than personal enrichment was a detail that rarely featured in the British portrayal of the IRA as 'thugs' and 'a terrorist Mafia-type conspiracy'. This presentation was part of the anti-terrorist malediction that prevailed throughout the Troubles. If the IRA were gangsters, they were also morally corrupt and degenerate. As late as 1989, when the British government was already engaged in secret diplomacy with Sinn Fein, the Northern Ireland Information Service issued a booklet in which it attributed the continuing violence in Ulster to 'the evil dreams of evil men' and 'the wickedness of terrorism' – of which only the IRA was mentioned as an example of either.

The British media tended to follow the official lead in their identification of the IRA as the incarnation of barbaric evil and 'hatred'. In 1971 the *Sun* reported from Belfast that 'IRA terror leaders here are now sending their shock troops to war – their own children. Bomb-throwing eight-year-olds are in the front line. They steal out at dusk to play games with death, trained to hate and kill.'[5] These terrorist children of the damned were one of many fabricated stories devised by army 'black propaganda' specialists and fed to the press in order to discredit the IRA. But the tabloids often needed little encouragement, reaching into their own stock of stereotypes and hate figures, such as Maire Drumm, the fiery vice-president of Sinn Fein, described by the British press as 'the granny of hate' and 'Grandma Venom'.

The idea that Catholic violence was a product of irrational and groundless 'hatred' tended to ignore the reality of Protestant bigotry, embodied in graffiti declaring 'Any taig [Catholic] will do' and loyalist literature describing Catholics as 'slimy excreta that pass for human beings'. In the course of the Troubles loyalist paramilitaries randomly murdered hundreds of Catholics. Loyalist groups also engaged in the practice known as 'rompering', in which Catholics were snatched off the streets and tortured to death in after-hours drinking clubs known as 'Romper rooms' – a practice that was taken to its most depraved extremes by the sectarian murder gang the Shankhill Butchers. The killing of 'taigs' was justified by the UDA magazine *Combat* on the grounds that 'There is only one way to control an area or ghetto that harbours terrorists and insurgents and that is to reduce its population to fear by inflicting upon them all the horror of terrorist warfare.'[6]

Though the British media occasionally acknowledged these events, it was generally the IRA that was portrayed as the terrorist aggressor, whose violence was as absurd as it was unjustified. When the IRA blew up ten members of a British military band in Kent in 1989 Prince Charles wondered 'what sort of mentality can contemplate such meaningless acts. It is appalling.' IRA atrocities tended to elicit the same ritual response, in which politicians and press commentators reiterated their common commitment to the democratic process and their refusal to submit to terrorist barbarism. On the one hand, the terrorism versus democracy framework misrepresented the political causes of violence in Northern Ireland to the point when the IRA appeared almost incomprehensible to the British public. At the same time the moralistic subtext of good versus evil, civilisation versus barbarism denied any degree of responsibility or mutuality on the part of the British government in the conflict. In the course of the Troubles many Catholics were shot dead by the British army or the RUC in disputed circumstances. In addition there was evidence to suggest that a number of loyalist paramilitary killings were carried out on the basis of intelligence information emanating from the security forces themselves. But in wars between good and evil, there can only be victims on one side. When British soldiers killed Catholic civilians, such incidents generally received little publicity in the British press, while the collusion of the security forces in loyalist violence was accompanied by official cover-ups, denials and contradictory testimony and rarely resulted in prosecutions.

The British government's presentation of the IRA as murderous thugs echoed the official portrayal of Michael Collins and his 'murder gang' during the 1919–21 Tan war and its public depiction of the Provisionals was similarly at odds with the internal views of its own officials. Thus, in 1979 a secret report written by a senior intelligence officer, Brigadier James Glover, declared

> Our evidence of the calibre of the rank-and-file terrorists does not support the view that they are merely mindless hooligans drawn from the ranks of the unemployed and unemployable. PIRA (Provisional IRA) now trains and uses its members with some care. The mature terrorists ... are constantly learning from mistakes and developing their expertise ... The Movement will retain popular support sufficient to maintain secure bases in the traditional republican areas.[7]

The 'Glover Report' fell into the hands of the IRA, and its release caused some embarrassment to the Labour government, which was at the time committed to a policy of removing political status from republican prisoners in order to support the 'mafia-terrorist conspiracy' thesis. In 1976 the government replaced the phasing out of internment with the construction of a newly built H-Block complex in the Maze prison, in which all prisoners were obliged to wear prison clothes. By portraying violent republicanism as a criminal enterprise, the Labour government hoped to marginalise and isolate the IRA politically and reduce the problem of terrorism to a law-and-order issue. The republican prisoners immediately recognised the political implications and embarked on a series of militant protests within the prison, in which they refused to wear prison clothes and smeared their cell walls with their own excrement. For three years prisoners wore only blankets and refused to shave or cut their hair in conditions that one visiting priest compared to a 'Calcutta slum'.

The continued British intransigence culminated in the traumatic hunger strikes of 1980–81, when ten IRA prisoners died one after another in a failed attempt to pressure Whitehall into restoring special category status. In the end the government won the short-term battle when the prisoners called off the hunger strike without achieving their aims, following intervention from their families. But it was the IRA who reaped the political harvest as the episode proved to be a catalyst in the evolution of the 'bullet and the ballot' strategy pursued by the Gerry Adams faction, which paved the way for the rise of Sinn Fein as an electoral force in both north and south.[8]

It would take another seventeen years of secret negotiation and bloodshed before the signing of the Good Friday Agreement in 1998. But behind the scenes things had already begun to change. On 19 March 1993, the British government responded to another IRA bombing offensive by sending Sinn Fein a secret memo stating that 'All those involved have responsibility to end the conflict. No one has the monopoly of suffering. There is need for a healing process.' Even then it was years before the official anathema was revoked. In an interview with the *Observer* journalist Anthony Bevins in 1993, an unnamed government official even conceded that the IRA 'was imbued with an ideology and a theology' and that its ideology contained 'an ethical dimension' – an admission that Bevins rightly described as 'breathtaking.'[9] This was a direct contradiction of everything the British government had argued for years, and only when it recognised that the IRA could not be defeated was it prepared to jettison the anti-terrorist anathema and recognise publicly what many of its officials already knew, namely that IRA violence was political in character. Without that recognition the secret diplomacy between the British and Irish governments and Sinn Fein would never have taken place, and the British army would still be patrolling the streets of Belfast and the fields of South Armagh, trying to slay the terrorist monsters that its own propaganda had helped to create.

Armed struggle

The return of physical force republicanism in its most lethal incarnation originally emerged in response to the loyalist violence unleashed against the Catholic civil rights movement in the late 1960s. But the arrival of British troops in the Six Counties in 1969 quickly changed the nature of the conflict into an armed confrontation between an occupying army and the newly formed Provisional IRA, which had taken on the role of protector of the Catholic community. Though the army arrived as the neutral upholder of constitutional authority, it found itself facing a resurgent republican movement that regarded the British government as ultimately responsible for the violence directed against Catholics. At the time the IRA believed that the British would disengage politically as soon as British casualties reached double figures, as they had in other colonial conflicts. Fuelled by these expectations, the Provisionals unleashed a storm of violence that soon outstripped that of their predecessors in the 1919–21 Tan war. While IRA volunteers, many of them still in their teens, ambushed British soldiers in the countryside, the Provisionals engaged in urban guerrilla warfare with ruthless ingenuity, as snipers opened fire on military patrols from walkways and sitting rooms and cars known as 'floats' filled with heavily armed IRA operatives roamed the streets of Belfast in search of British army patrols.

At the same time home-made fertiliser bombs exploded in hotels, offices, warehouses and city streets across the province in a devastating campaign of economic sabotage. The IRA bombing campaign reached a peak of destructive intensity in 1972, the most violent year of the Troubles, when 436 people were killed, more than half of them by loyalist paramilitaries. On 21 July the IRA set off twenty-one bombs in Belfast city centre in a single afternoon and a terrified population careered from one explosion to the next in what became known as 'Bloody Friday'. By the end of the day nine people had been killed and more than 130 maimed and wounded, as television viewers watched appalling footage of body parts being scraped with shovels off roads and walls and shovelled into plastic rubbish sacks. These events provoked so many angry protests that the Provisionals tried to evade responsibility, claiming that the authorities had deliberately ignored its telephone warnings. It was not till years later that organisation admitted that the bombings had been badly planned and that the city centre had been too small for such a wild assault.

As the Troubles turned into a protracted conflict, there were many other 'bad bombs', the majority of them the result of careless planning and faulty execution. The IRA was not always the implacably efficient organisation portrayed in the British gangster film *The Long Good Friday* and some IRA operations were reckless and incompetent. In Northern Ireland the Provisionals often placed bombs in public places with little regard for the consequences, such as the incendiary device that exploded in February 1978 at the La Mon Country House, where members of the Irish Collie Club were having their annual dinner. The active service unit responsible had intended to phone a warning, but failed to notice there was no phone box nearby until after the bomb had been placed. The warning came too late to evacuate the building, and the bomb exploded, creating a napalm-like fireball that incinerated twelve people, including seven women.

The IRA apologised profusely, with the usual caveat that 'All killings stem from British interference and from their denial of Irish sovereignty'. This argument ignored the fact that it was the IRA, not the British, who had chosen to bomb a meeting of the Irish Collie Club in the first place. The IRA was always sensitive to accusations of terrorism and insisted that it did not deliberately target civilians and non-combatants. Nevertheless, the recklessness with which IRA operations were sometimes carried out, and the fact that these operations were generally conducted in built-up urban areas, multiplied the possibility that civilians would be killed. In the worst 'accidents' the IRA simply denied responsibility. In other cases the leadership issued apologies or declared civilian casualties to be an inevitable consequence of 'war'. A number of republican bombs were clearly intended to kill civilians, from the Birmingham pub bombings in 1974 to the bombing of two Mayfair restaurants in October 1975, by the London-based cell known as the 'Balcombe Street gang', which killed four customers.

Nevertheless, such attacks were not as common as was sometimes imagined. The most lethal terrorist attack of the Troubles was not carried out by the IRA, but by the loyalist UVF, which exploded two no-warning bombs in busy shopping streets in Dublin and Monaghan in the Irish Republic on a single day in 1974, killing thirty-three passers by and wounding dozens of others. These bombs were deliberately intended to kill as many people as possible, as part of a policy of pressuring the Irish government to take action against the IRA that the UVF called 'returning the serve'. In theory, there was nothing to stop the IRA from emulating these methods and killing British civilians en masse, but the Provisionals had a constituency both in Ireland and in the United States that was not prepared to accept such actions. The main aim of bombing campaigns on the British mainland was to ensure that the conflict was not allowed to settle down into the 'acceptable level of violence' that the British government hoped to achieve.

In addition to attacks on 'soft targets' the IRA also engaged in a more overtly 'military' war of attrition against the 40–50,000 soldiers, police and part-time members of the Ulster Defence Regiment (UDR) comprising the 'Crown Forces' inside Northern Ireland itself. It was total war on an intimate scale, a war fought with stealth and cunning, in which targets were attacked at their points of greatest vulnerability, from army tea boys and brass bands to building contractors working for the military and judges, to businessmen and prison officers.

The ultimate aim of all IRA violence was to wear down the will of the British population to maintain its military presence in Northern Ireland. But the inherent coherence and rationality of the IRA's violence was often concealed from the British public, partly by the shocking nature of the violence itself and also by the way it was represented by British politicians and the media. From the IRA's point of view, one of its most successful days in the entire Troubles was the assassination of Lord Mountbatten at his holiday home in southern Ireland on 27 March 1979, the same day that another IRA unit ambushed and blew up eighteen British soldiers at Warrenpoint in a more conventional guerrilla operation. But it was the killing of Mountbatten that dominated the headlines. In a front-page article headlined 'THESE EVIL BASTARDS', the *Daily Express* condemned the 'cowardly psychopaths' responsible for Mountbatten's death and invoked the bulldog spirit of the British who 'have never yielded to terror' while the *Daily Telegraph* denounced the assassination as a product of 'diseased minds rather than political calculation'.

In fact, the killing of Mountbatten had as coherent a political rationale as the killing of the eighteen soldiers. Both actions helped revive the morale of the IRA's members at a period when the armed struggle had shown signs of stalling. In addition, the killing of a high-profile member of the British establishment propelled the conflict back into the headlines, thereby undermining the attempts by the British government to present the IRA as an increasingly marginal phenomenon. From the IRA's perspective the assassination of Mountbatten was a legitimate act of resistance against a military occupation, comparable to the killing of Heydrich by the Resistance. The fact that Britain was a parliamentary democracy did not alter the IRA's perception of Ulster as an artificially created 'fascist' statelet, propped up by the British army. Whatever else could be said about these arguments, they bore no relation to the motivations and rationale attributed to the assassination by the British media. Not only was the presentation of the IRA as an organisation of 'cowardly psychopaths' inaccurate and misleading, but it was an explanation that made no rational sense. As a result it served only to confirm the existence of an organisation that was mysterious, unfathomable and fundamentally alien, even as the Provisionals continued to insist, like their predecessors, that they were no more than soldiers.

The secret army

Throughout the three decades of the Troubles the IRA never ceased to regard itself as a legitimate military force, engaged in a valiant war of resistance against overwhelmingly powerful enemy forces. The IRA's concept of warfare was often one-sided. Even though the Provisionals protested loudly when its own members were ambushed by the SAS or ill treated by the security forces, they were merciless towards their enemies, generally choosing to kill even when other options were available. Nevertheless, the notion that the Provisionals were 'at war' provided a moral context in which killing and violence could be justified, as well as a chain of command and a disciplined organisational structure in which individual responsibility for such actions could be subsumed within the organisation as a whole. In the playwright Ron Hutchinson's plague-on-both-their houses drama *Rat in the Skull*, the RUC officer Nelson pours scorn on the IRA's military pretensions, telling the republican prisoner Roche:

> Don't tell me you're just a simple soldier, Roche. You blow the arms and legs off the language too. You torture the meaning of things, like you've cut into every part of us that thinks and feels. 'Active service units – simple soldiers – execution – collaboration' – How sick I am of your cheap and easy rhetoric and how easy it is for you to grab the monopoly of love for Ireland, while you're wading through the blood of Irishmen.'[10]

Though it sometimes seemed like fraudulent posturing to outsiders, this military culture was an integral part of the IRA's identity. But if the IRA was a secret army, it was an army in pursuit of the political objective of a united Ireland. In the late 1970s the Provisionals produced a *Green Book*, modelled on Colonel Qaddafi's book of the same title, which explained the IRA's tactics, objectives and rules of engagement to its new recruits. The *Green Book* explained to all IRA 'volunteers' that they were soldiers in a people's army, whose legal and moral legitimacy stemmed directly from the 1918 Daíl Eireann, the only Irish parliament based on the participation of all the twenty-six counties. As members of 'one of the oldest and surviving guerrilla armies in the world' volunteers faced an enemy that

> kills people, it jails people, it consistently repeats that it will not give way to the IRA, it ridicules one's objectives as being unrealistic and unachievable. It attacks the methods such as the commandeering of cars, the taking over of houses, fighting a war in the streets in which people live, the execution of informers, etc. All this is so much hypocrisy compared to the commandeering of a country and British institutionalised violence and sectarianism.[11]

The publication of the *Green Book* coincided with a period in which the IRA was replacing its structure of battalions and companies with independent, self-contained cells using the classic urban guerrilla model. Though a hierarchical chain of command still existed, these cells were expected to operate as autonomous units, thus reducing the risk of British penetration. In this context it was more important than ever that individual members were aware of why they were fighting. But IRA members were not merely soldiers, they were soldiers who had volunteered, heirs to a living tradition of patriotism and self-sacrifice that was reiterated and celebrated continuously in murals, songs and literature, in graveside orations at the funerals of IRA volunteers 'fallen in active service' and engraved on tombstones with quotations from Pearse and nationalist poets to commemorate the 'warriors of the Gael'.

As always, this heroic ideal was often in stark contrast to the sordid and brutal actions that the IRA's patriotic war required, a campaign in which progress was measured not by military victories but by a steady accumulation of corpses. And as always, the notion of the symbolic target helped to rationalise and neutralise the brutality required. Language was also an important element in the dehumanisation of the enemy. To the IRA all members of the Crown Forces in Northern Ireland were 'symbols of the uniform' and therefore equally eligible to be 'hit', 'whacked' or 'stiffed'. There were further subdivisions into 'good hits' or 'good stiffs' depending on the political or military significance of the target. For some IRA members, brutality undoubtedly came more easily than others. Others became conditioned to it or accepted it as a regrettable necessity, according to the broader framework described in the popular nationalist song 'Sniper's Promise':

> The night was icy cold I stood alone
> Waiting for an army foot patrol.
> When at last they came into my sight
> I squeezed the trigger of my Armalite.
>
> Oh mamma, oh mamma comfort me
> For I know these dreadful things have got to be
> But when the war for freedom has been won
> I promise you I'll put away my gun.
>
> A shot rang out, I heard a soldier cry,
> 'Please don't leave me here alone to die.'
> I realised his patrol had gone away
> And left a wounded comrade for me to slay.

This is the tragic revolutionary hero with 'dirty hands' once again, forced to carry out barbaric acts to make a more human world. Even as the song indicts the cowardly Brits who have abandoned one of their own comrades, the sniper feels pity for the wounded enemy he is about to 'slay' while assuring himself and his mother that peace and normality will again be possible when victory has been achieved. All wars represent a conscious descent into barbarism, but the face-to-face intimacy of the Troubles demanded a particular kind of violence, and not all IRA volunteers were able to reconcile the discrepancy between the glorious image of the patriotic volunteer and the actions such men were expected to carry out.

Dirty hands

One of the most honest and compelling insider accounts of the IRA was provided by Eamon Collins, a British customs official who served as an IRA intelligence officer in County Tyrone in the early eighties. Collins was politically on the left before joining the IRA and his drift towards the more conservative nationalism of the IRA was partly the result of a childhood fascination with the romantic 1916 Easter Rising. In his compelling memoir, *Killing Rage*, he recalled watching the fiftieth anniversary celebrations of the Easter Rising in Dundalk in 1966, where he experienced a moment of nationalist epiphany:

I saw lines of marching men carrying banners, tricolours and symbols that spoke of a heroic Ireland, an Ireland of great deeds, courage and self-sacrifice. The ghosts of the great heroes Pearse and Connolly were invoked, their deified spirits provoking reverence ... I saw medals and ribbons awarded by the Old IRA, the force that fought the War of Independence between 1919 and 1921. It dawned on me that I was not looking at a dead history of insurrection, I was looking at an alternative society, government and army.[12]

These memories were rekindled by the hunger strikes and Collins was put through his *Green Book* training and began to combine his job at the Customs and Excise office in Warrenpoint with his work as an IRA intelligence officer. Though Collins did not kill anyone himself, he planned and organised at least five murders. In one incident he helped plan the murder of a suspected UDR man, who was shot dead in the street in front of his three-year-old daughter. Afterwards it emerged that the victim had left the UDR five years before. Though Collins tried to rationalise such mistakes on the grounds that 'this savagery was the necessary price of our struggle to create a more just society', these arguments became increasingly difficult to sustain. One night, after returning home from a police interrogation, he looked at his sleeping six-month-old son and contemplated the killing of Sean McShane, a Catholic whom he had mistaken for an RUC officer:

I was suddenly nauseated by my lack of feeling for other human beings. There seemed to be a void inside me where my conscience had been. Was it over for me? Had I lost my nerve? This was surely just exhaustion ... I traced my finger gently over my son's face. Was I preparing him too for the sacrificial altar of republicanism?[13]

Eventually Collins was arrested and agreed to become to become a 'supergrass' and testify against his former comrades. Despised by his own movement and rejected by his wife as a traitor, Collins retracted his testimony and was allowed to rejoin the republican prisoners. At his trial he was found not guilty on a technicality and released. Because Collins had retracted his testimony, the usual IRA death penalty was not administered, but his former comrades were vengeful and suspicious, summoning him to a series of threatening debriefings in Dundalk. Spiritually and psychologically broken, Collins left the IRA and lived in the Irish Republic before returning to Newry to inherit the family farm, where he was reconciled with his wife.

In returning to live so close to South Armagh Collins was re-entering a community where he was held in suspicion and even despised. At times he seemed to be deliberately defying the IRA, voluntarily offering to appear at a libel case in the South to act as a witness against the former IRA chief of staff and millionaire smuggler Tom 'Slab' Murphy. Collins was angered at what he regarded as Murphy's 'hypocrisy' in denying his IRA past and suing for loss of income following allegations about his activities. As a result of Collins's testimony Murphy was ordered to pay costs of £1.5 million. The undermining of a senior IRA figure did nothing to endear Collins to his enemies. Even when his farm was burned down he refused to leave, and in July 1999 he was savagely beaten to death while out walking his dogs in what the RUC described as 'more like something done by primitive cavemen than an act of the twentieth century'.[14]

The leftist, middle-class Collins was in many ways atypical IRA material, although there is no archetypal member of an organisation of violence that included some 10,000 members in the course of the Troubles. Its ranks included violent men like 'Slab' Murphy and Jim Bryson, a Belfast volunteer shot dead by a British army undercover unit in 1973, who liked to roam the streets of the city armed with an antiquated Lewis gun, in search of a random confrontation with British soldiers. Though Bryson was described by one of his own comrades as a 'psychopath', such men were rare. The IRA delegation that met the British home secretary William Whitelaw for secret talks in 1972 included a butcher's assistant, a former barman, a bookmaker's runner, a solicitor and a teacher – a microcosm, in other words, of the constituency that supported the organisation.

The majority of IRA members were working-class men from urban Catholic ghettos, such as Patrick Magee, the so-called 'Brighton bomber', who grew up in the fiercely republican Unity Flats estate in Belfast in the early 1970s. For republicans like Magee, joining the IRA in this period was an entirely logical and even inevitable process. Magee's IRA career came to an end when he attempted to blow up the entire Tory government at their party conference in Brighton in 1984, for which he was jailed for life two years later. At his trial Magee was described by the judge as 'a man of exceptional cruelty and inhumanity' who 'enjoyed' terrorist activities, but his subsequent trajectory suggests a very different profile. During his years in prison, he wrote a PhD thesis on portrayals of the Troubles in popular fiction, which was eventually published under the title *Gangsters or Guerrillas?*

Magee's own position on the familiar either/or question in the title is clear throughout and he has remained unrepentant about his participation in the armed struggle. His thesis is simultaneously a defence of republican-ism and a demystification of the stereotypes contained in novels such as Tom Clancy's *Patriot Games*. For Magee, the terrorist stereotypes of Irish republicans in popular fiction were another manifestation of anti-Irish racism or an extension of propaganda, both of which denied the humanity of the community he came from. Magee did not address the inhumanity that so often characterised the IRA's armed struggle, but in the aftermath of the Good Friday Agreement he was released from prison, where he founded the Causeway Project, a charity which aimed to facilitate meetings between perpetrators and victims of the Troubles. In the course of these encoun-ters Magee met Jo Berry, the daughter of the Tory minister Sir Anthony Berry, who had been killed in the Brighton bombing. Astonishingly, the two became friends and appeared together in public as advocates of reconcili-ation and a mutual healing process. Magee has said that he hoped in this way to try and regain his own lost humanity. We cannot know if he has succeeded, or what this cryptic declaration meant in practice, but it would be unwise to attribute his actions, or the actions of the IRA in general to the 'evil dreams of evil men'.

The Seminarians

The Irish peace process was made possible when all sides recognised the impossibility of winning an outright military victory. This process has not occurred in the long-running conflict between the Basque separatist organi-sation ETA and the Spanish state, the onset of which roughly coincided with the outbreak of the Troubles. In the 1950s a new generation of Basque nation-alists began to question the political passivity of the mainstream nation-alist party, the PNV, exiled by Franco after the Spanish Civil War. These discussions led to the formation of Euskadi ta Askatasuna (ETA) – Basque Homeland and Freedom – on 31 July 1959, the Saints Day of the founder of the Jesuits, Ignatius Loyola. Initially ETA's activities were mostly dedicated towards the preservation of Basque cultural identity rather than armed struggle. Like Irish republicanism, Basque nationalism has always been closely linked to the Catholic Church, particularly the rural Catholic clergy, which provided ETA with meeting places in churches and monasteries.

A number of future *etarras* were ex-seminarians who participated as pupils in the clandestine study groups established by Basque priests for the preservation and diffusion of Euskera, the Basque language. Many experi-enced their introduction to nationalist politics in church-run scout groups, in religious pilgrimages or hiking trips to the mountains, often the only place where the Basque language could be spoken and political ideas discussed freely.

Others came to the organisation through their local *cuadrilla* – groups of friends from the same town or village who grew up together. In some cases members of the same *cuadrilla* joined ETA en masse and remained a close-knit group within the organisation. Though ETA carried out some operations against symbols of the Franco regime during the 1960s it was not until after 1968 that its armed struggle began in earnest. This was the beginning of ETA's heroic period, when the organisation confronted the Franco dictatorship in an unequal David and Goliath struggle for national independence. In 1973 the Madrid commando carried out what still remains ETA's most spectacular operation, when it blew up Franco's trusted political confidant Admiral Luis Carrero Blanco, by mining a tunnel under the Madrid street where he passed on his way to mass. The explosion blew Carrero Blanco's car seven storeys into the air, an event that is still celebrated in a popular Basque song entitled 'the Carrero Waltz', in which the singers joyously throw loaves of bread, scarves and other assorted objects in imitation of the admiral's 'flight'.

From patriots to terrorists?
The Carrero Blanco assassination was painstakingly recreated in Gillo Pontecorvo's *Operation Ogro* (1981). Pontecorvo presented the assassination as an entirely legitimate and even heroic operation in the context of the Franco dictatorship. By telling the story in flashback and juxtaposing it with ETA operations in the early 1980s, however, Pontecorvo critiqued the use of such methods in a democratic society, where other political options were available. In his central character Txabi, an ex-seminarian, Pontecorvo traced the fine line between idealism and fanaticism that has also been part of ETA's trajectory. Throughout the Carrero Blanco operation Txabi is a courageous and idealistic Basque patriot. But Txabi is temperamentally unable to accept small political changes and continues to engage in the armed struggle, even after the return to democratic rule.

Pontecorvo described Txabi as 'someone who, on one hand, has a desire to remake man and society – a noble and generous desire – and, on the other hand, someone who has the capacity for a violence that can become savage'.[15] The same could be said of ETA itself. The same year that Pontecorvo's film was released a Civil Guard officer, Lieutenant-Colonel Antonio Tejero, led an abortive military coup, which was partly motivated by the anger at ETA's continued attacks. In the wake of the failed coup the more 'political' ETA faction known as 'ETA –pm' formally dissolved itself, leaving only 'ETA militar', the most militant advocates of armed struggle in the field. From ETA's point of view Spain's evolution from dictatorship to democracy had not changed the fundamental relationship between the Basque country and the Spanish state, therefore there was no reason to end the armed struggle. In the early eighties the organisation embarked on a campaign of bombings and assassinations that would soon outstrip its activities during the Franco era. As the death toll continued to rise, the new Socialist government went on the offensive, using mercenary hit squads to assassinate exiled ETA leaders in France while simultaneously offering an amnesty policy intended to induce other ETA members to abandon the armed struggle. For ETA the policy of 'social reinsertion' was even more politically dangerous than the Spanish government's death squads, and its attempts to reverse it led to one of the cruellest acts in its history.

The tragedy of Yoyes

In 1979 the BBC current affairs programme *Panorama* interviewed a female leader of ETA militar codenamed 'Yoyes'. Asked whether she believed the cause of Basque independence was worth dying for, Yoyes told the interviewer: 'Either we fight or die anyway. If we die fighting, well, that's the way it goes. But if we don't fight, the Basques will certainly perish as a people.'[16] This was the conventional public narrative of the indomitable freedom fighter, to be expected from one of the leaders of ETA's most militant faction. But the nationalist discourse concealed a complex personality with a far more ambivalent motivation than a short political interview was likely to reveal.

Yoyes' real name was Dolores Maria Katurain. She was born in 1954 in the small Basque town of Ordizia, in the province of Guipozcoa, and like many future *etarras* remained a fervent Catholic until her late teens. In 1971 she was considering becoming a missionary in South America, but she was also tormented by self-doubt at her ability to 'do something for Jesus'. By the end of the following year she had abandoned her religious aspirations and joined ETA, where she acquired her nom de guerre. Despite her doubts, Yoyes proved herself to be a dedicated and committed combatant, participating in numerous ETA operations. In 1976 Yoyes was obliged to go into exile in France, where she opted to join the ETA military faction during the transition to democracy. This was an unusual decision from a woman who was already beginning to distance herself internally from the violent struggle to which she had dedicated the last few years of her life. A fan of Virginia Woolf and Emily Dickinson, her diaries and poems reveal a sensitive and thought-ful woman, with a tendency to melancholy and introspection.

Removed from the tension and political turbulence within the Basque country, Yoyes felt increasingly oppressed by the life of armed political mili-tancy she had chosen. In September 1979 she wrote of her need to 'escape from this tomb, this living death that was beginning to suffocate me and in which I was physically dying.'[17] Though she felt increasingly estranged from ETA, she was also aware of the difficulty of breaking away from the organi-sation and establishing a separate identity from the nationalist community that she came from. In 1980 she went into exile in Mexico, where she took a degree in sociology and became pregnant. By this time she had ceased to play any role in ETA but the birth of her son, Akaitz, intensified her nostalgia for her country and her family, while the experience of maternity was an important episode in her disenchantment with politics.

In 1983 she began to consider the possibility of returning to the Basque country and taking advantage of the Spanish government's amnesty policy. Even as she planned this she was aware of the difficulties in returning to ordinary life in a country divided by a violent political struggle that she no longer felt part of. In April 1984 she wrote of her former comrades:

> To the government they are 'killing machines', to the nationalist left they are 'heroes of the people'… Neither interpretation is true and each one only serves to define fixed positions and confirm established assumptions. I don't like this hero nonsense. I've never felt like a hero, I don't believe in heroes, because these ideas lead only to an absurd mystification that impedes personal and therefore collective development, and I believe in the former, not the latter.[18]

At the end of the year Yoyes returned to France, where she succeeded in negotiating an amnesty for herself that did not require any public renuncia-tion of her political past. At the same time she obtained guarantees from one of her contacts in the ETA leadership that the organisation would not try to kill her if she returned to the Basque country. In 1985 she returned to Ordizia to live with her family, where she immediately found herself the object of unwanted media attention. As a leading former *etarra* who had abandoned the armed struggle, Yoyes was a triumph for the Spanish government's amnesty policy. Precisely for this reason, she represented a political danger to ETA. On the walls of her town ominous graffiti began to appear on the walls, calling her a traitor and a *chivata* – stool pigeon, one of the worst insults in the nationalist vocabulary. Yoyes found these insults coming from within her own community particularly painful. In November 1985 the former *etarra* wrote in her diary of an armed struggle that 'has degenerated into something terrible, dictatorial and mythical' and described the radical nationalist organisation Herri Batasuna, which broadly supported ETA's activities, as 'a puppet of fascistic militarism'.

Yet even as Yoyes remained insistent that she did not belong to either side, she felt herself under constant pressure in a country where 'only the community matters, and to stand out from it isn't just to run the risk of death, it's the most contemptible crime that exists, a crime that you have to pay for'. In October 1985 she wrote a public letter to *El País*, in which she tried to assert her personal autonomy and distance herself from the political game that she knew was leading her to disaster. But no matter what Yoyes said or did, she had become a symbol in a political game that was beyond her control. The following year a change in the ETA leadership removed her protector from the organisation, and on Wednesday 10 September 1986 Yoyes was walking with her son during the annual town fête in Ordizia when an ETA assassin named 'Kubati' approached her in the street. According to his later testimony in court:

I went up to Yoyes and said, 'Are you Yoyes?' She asked me who I was. I said, 'I am from ETA and I have come to execute you.' Immediately, I fired two shots from my pistol into her breast. She fell to the ground and I finished her off with another shot to the head.[19]

Even ETA's own supporters were appalled by the murder. In the wake of her death another letter was found amongst her possessions, addressed to 'public opinion', in which she declared that in the event of her death, it was ETA and not the Spanish security forces who should be held responsible. Nevertheless, the assassination served its political purpose in deterring others from following her example, and the policy of social reinsertion soon withered away.

In the ensuing years, some 800 deaths have been attributed to ETA, including more high-ranking officers in the Spanish armed forces than have been killed in any of Spain's wars. In addition to attacks on the military, police and Civil Guard, ETA has assassinated local politicians and critical journalists. In keeping with its puritanical Catholic ethos, it has placed bombs in cinemas showing pornographic films and bars where drugs are sold. It has issued death threats to local journalists, bombed radio stations and even attacked a Bilbao leftist bookshop, the owner of which had criticised ETA's refusal to abandon the armed struggle. The organisation also extracts 'revolutionary taxes' from wealthy Basque businessmen, usually preceded by polite letters spelling out the sum required and warning that failure to comply may result in 'painful consequences', including 'repressive measures against your property and person'.

Today few Spaniards know what ETA's political demands are, partly because the Spanish media habitually ignores or distorts them, but also because ETA's violence seems as anachronistic as it is relentlessly brutal. ETA is not the only source of violence in the Basque country. In the late seventies and early eighties dozens of Basques were killed by mercenaries and death squads organised by the Spanish security forces. Since 1980 some 8,000 Basques have been arrested and detained on suspicion of terrorism. Many have been subjected to some kind of torture or ill-treatment. In addition, hundreds of ETA prisoners continue to serve their sentences in prisons far from the Basque homeland, in a deliberate ploy to limit their access to their families and relatives.

Few Spaniards are aware of these events, yet they remain a source of anger and bitterness in the Basque country itself and have helped give legitimacy to ETA's violence in some sectors of the Basque nationalist community. ETA would not have lasted as long as it has had it not represented a constituency that shared its political aspirations, even if it did not always approve of its methods. Neither ETA's actions, nor the official invocation of the antiterrorist anathema have changed that equation. Behind the bitter drama of terrorism and counter-terrorism, and the regular street clashes between hooded nationalist youth and hooded Basque police, flow years of history and the unresolved question of the Basque country's relationship with Spain. The inability to resolve that question is one reason why attempts to negotiate an end to Europe's oldest separatist conflict have always failed. While the Spanish government has always insisted that ETA abandon violence as a precondition to formal political discussions, ETA has always refused to do so without a recognition from the Spanish government of the right to self-determination in the Basque country. The result has been a dialogue of the deaf, in which successive governments continue to invoke the anti-terrorist malediction in the hope that ETA will cease to send its monotonous but increasingly sporadic 'messages'. In March 2006 ETA declared a 'permanent ceasefire', raising hopes across Spain and the Basque country that an end to the violence might finally be in sight. Whether there is sufficient mutual political will to bring these expectations to fruition remains to be seen.

Nothing personal: the moral economy of political homicide
In July 1997 ETA kidnapped Miguel Angel Blanco, a 24-year-old Partido Popular councillor from a small provincial Basque town, and threatened to kill their captive unless the government agreed to relocate ETA prisoners to prisons inside the Basque country. The immediate reaction to the kidnapping was a spontaneous eruption of anti-ETA demonstrations across Spain and the Basque country, in which more than a million people took to the streets. Bolstered by this popular outrage, the Partido Popular government reiterated the familiar refusal to negotiate with 'terrorism' and the crisis moved inexorably towards its inevitable conclusion. When the ultimatum expired without any concessions, ETA shot dead the young councillor and dumped his body by a roadside, prompting widespread fury and anguish across Spain.

Miguel Angel Blanco was not an 'illustrious corpse', like Aldo Moro or Lord Mountbatten, and the very fact that he was so ordinary and insignificant made the murder seem even more incomprehensible to the Spanish population, particularly when more than a million Spaniards had taken part in dignified appeals to spare his life. From ETA's point of view the size of the demonstrations were as irrelevant as the moral arguments they represented. Traditional Basque culture contains the concept of *joko* – a word used to refer to any competitive game or wager. From the moment he was kidnapped Miguel Angel Blanco became a bargaining chip in a political *joko* between ETA and the Spanish government – a conservative government with a clear lineage to the Francoist state. In the absence of a political outcome, ETA saw itself as obliged to kill their captive in order to maintain the organisation's credibility.

As always, it would be convenient to regard those responsible as gangsters and psychopaths, but the reality is almost certainly more disconcerting. In her interviews with anonymous ETA militants, Miren Alcedo, a Spanish anthropologist, found men and women united by 'a shared concern with the meaning of life' and the sense of comradeship that came from the pursuit of a great cause. A number of her interviewees described their membership of the organisation as an existential revolt against the boredom and mediocrity of everyday life, in which participation in the armed struggle was a means of conquering death by deliberately seeking and courting it. One former *etarra* similarly described ETA to the Basque ethnologist Joseba Zulaika as 'heroism and adventure'.

Zulaika tells the chilling story of the kidnapping of a nationalist Basque industrialist, Angel Berazadi Urbe, by ETA activists from the village of Itziar in 1976 in order to extort 'revolutionary taxes' to help finance the organisation's activities. While Berazadi's family negotiated with the ETA leadership in southern France, the industrialist was held captive in a barn in Itziar by four teenage ETA activists. For weeks the captive and his young kidnappers were closeted together, eating and sleeping in the same room. In the process the kidnappers and their hostage became friends and even made plans to meet in southern France for a celebratory dinner when negotiations were concluded. When the mother of one of the teenage kidnappers accidentally discovered what was going on, the ETA leadership took a collective vote to decide their captive's fate.

After two tied votes, a single abstention swung the vote in favour of Berazadi's execution and the four activists were ordered to kill their prisoner, who was shot and dumped in a ditch. All but one of the kidnappers were captured soon afterwards and Zulaika later interviewed two of them in prison. Both men denied that they were personally responsible for Berazadi's death. When asked in reference to a recent ETA killing whether the killers were likely to feel remorse, one of the prisoners told Zulaika:

> They will never have any burden of conscience. As an example, the other day in San Sebastián there were 40,000 people demonstrating against them; well, they should say to that: 'Forty thousand sons of bitches deceived by their political parties.' You just accept the decision taken by the organisation without question.[20]

When Zulaika suggested that the taking of a life was 'logically and ethically' different from simply carrying out orders, the ETA prisoner insisted that the relationship between assassin and victim was always dictated by broader political interests that precluded individual pangs of conscience: 'What matters is what ideology you represent and which one he represents. I don't think that normally there is any hate or anything like that. If in former times I had killed ten or fifteen Civil Guards I would never have had the slightest hatred. It is their symbolism, what they represent, period.'[21]

A member of the IRA Army Council later invoked the same rationale for the assassination of Lord Mountbatten in an interview with a French newspaper in which he explained, 'Given his personal importance there was inevitably going to be enormous publicity attached to this operation … we had no hatred for him as a person. It is the society, the military and political machine he symbolised, that we were aiming at.'[22] This ability to convert human beings into political symbols is the essence of revolutionary terrorism as a 'technique of violence', whatever its ideology. The Red Brigades leader Mario Moretti once justified the killing of Aldo Moro on the grounds that they 'did not kidnap and kill Moro the man, but his function'.[23] The same logic undoubtedly dictated ETA's killing of a low-ranking government official. This rationale was partly a self-deception since ETA was certainly aware that the violent death of a human being was a tragic and painful event. Were this not the case then political homicide would have no ability to transmit any message at all. By transferring such events onto a symbolic plane, however, even the most brutal acts of violence can be transformed into abstract political confrontations in which anyone can be killed and no one is ever personally responsible. And if the nationalist insurgents regarded such actions as a brutal necessity in times of 'war', they were also willing to convert their own deaths into symbolic representations of the cause they fought for, thus imbuing their organisations with a further aura of heroism.

The exemplary sacrifice

The glorification of the soldier who dies for his country is a universal element of patriotic mythology and the nationalist insurgents were no exception. In Ireland, the veneration of martyrdom has always been an integral element of the republican tradition, from the execution of Robert Emmett, the leader of the 1803 rebellion against British rule, to the IRA hunger strikers. The notion of the exemplary revolutionary sacrifice was equally important in the Basque country. One of the decisive episodes in the early history of ETA was the execution of the ETA militant 'Txiki' in 1975 by a Spanish firing squad. The execution was witnessed by his mother and brother, who later recounted how Txiki raised his clenched fist and sang a Basque patriotic song as he faced the firing squad. Even after being shot he continued to sing while lying on the ground. Joseba Zulaika has written how the location of the bullet wounds in Txiki's body was afterwards 'recounted with precision, as if it were the exact map of heroic martyrdom'.[24]

Txiki's exemplary death passed into posterity, fusing the religious notion of sacrificial martyrdom with the mythological warrior-hero who fights on behalf of the tribe. For violent revolutionary organisations lacking official legitimacy, such deaths are the ultimate validation of the revolutionary cause. In a 1991 article commemorating the tenth anniversary of the Irish hunger strikes, the *Andersonstown News* observed that 'a slow lingering death by starvation ... in an effort to rectify what they perceived to be a wrong, takes a special courage and a spirituality seldom found in the human race'.[25] The anthropologist Marianne Heiberg also recalled interviews with ETA leaders and supporters in which photographs of 'bloodied, violated bodies' of nationalists killed by the Spanish security forces were 'reverently shown – like fine art – as an inevitable preface to the presentation of "The Cause".'[26]

This iconography of pain and death generates not only outrage and a desire for vengeance, it also becomes an inspiration to fulfil the political aims that led to the martyr's death in the first place. Whether they die in front of the firing squad, on the battlefield on in the prison cell, revolutionary martyrs are martyrs in the eyes of their supporters not just because they die bravely, but because they die for an idea. In countries where the political aims of violent nationalism are shared by a wider community, revolutionary martyrdom may resonate for generations and become part of a tradition of resistance, which binds the present to the past and acts as a permanent repudiation of accusations of terrorism.

The rise of the fedayeen

The notion of the exemplary sacrifice was an integral component in the armed Palestinian organisations that emerged from the mid-1960s onwards, the largest of which was al-Fatah, whose nucleus was formed in 1957, by a group of Kuwait-based Palestinian students including Yasser Arafat. Though the Fatah journal *Our Palestine* was filled with grandiose exhortations calling for acts of resistance against Israel, it was not until New Year's Eve 1965 that Fatah's military wing al-Asifah finally began its armed struggle, with a failed act of sabotage inside Israeli territory. From Fatah's point of view, even failure was better than nothing at a period when Israel appeared to be invincible and unchallengeable. The collective name for the guerrillas was 'fedayeen' – those who sacrifice themselves, and the idea that their acts of violence could have an exemplary and even redemptive impact on the humiliated Palestinian diaspora was embodied in a Fatah hymn:

> Farewell, tears and sorrow,
> Farewell, sighs and grief,
> Our people has come to loathe you;
> Welcome, blood and heroic death,
> Welcome, 'El-Asifah', who brings death and ruin to our enemies,
> And shatters the designs of Imperialism and Zionism

Other Palestinian guerrilla organisations emerged in the same period and began to carry out cross-border raids into Israel. The majority of their operations were costly failures, in which guerrillas were easily killed or captured while inflicting only negligible damage. This situation began to change following the comprehensive destruction of the Arab armies during the 1967 Six-Day War. In March 1968 Fatah salvaged some Arab pride when a contingent of its guerrillas and Jordanian soldiers repelled a heavily armed Israeli military incursion at the town of Karameh in Jordan. Overnight Fatah and Yasser Arafat became the toast of the Arab world, prompting a huge influx of weapons and financial support from the Arab regimes, as well as a burgeoning supply of new recruits from the Palestinian refugee camps.

By the end of 1968 Fatah contained some 12,000 full-time soldiers and had become the dominant organisation within the Palestine Liberation Organisation (PLO), a body originally created under the auspices of the charismatic Egyptian strongman Gemal abd Nasser to rein in Palestinian radicalism rather than encourage it. The main political rival to Fatah in this period was the Popular Front for the Liberation of Palestine (PFLP), created in December 1967 by the Orthodox Christian doctor George Habash, a late convert to Marxism, who believed that the liberation of Palestine would be achieved only through a wider revolution across the Arab world.

Between 1967 and 1970 the number of border incidents between Israel and Jordan climbed from 916 to 2,432, as the fedayeen filtered into the West Bank and Gaza in an attempt to instigate a guerrilla war against the Israeli occupation. These hopes soon faded, as Israel tightened its control over the Arab population and sealed its new borders more effectively. It was in this period that the fedayeen began to carry out attacks on the Israeli civilian population itself, placing bombs in public places and carrying out raids on apartment blocks, bus terminals, beaches and cinemas in an attempt to take the armed struggle 'to the heart of the occupied homeland in a confrontation in which the Israeli invasion finds itself solitary and alone and without protection, facing the Arab fighter at home, on the land, on the road, in the coffee house, the cinema and army camps'.[27]

The adoption of explicitly terrorist attacks on civilians was partly due to military failure and the inability of the fedayeen to challenge the Israeli army itself. At the same time some fedayeen outrages were deliberate provocations that were intended to invite Israeli reprisals and draw the surrounding Arab countries into the conflict. This objective was not difficult to achieve, since Israeli policy was always predicated on retaliation with overwhelming force against the Arab countries that sheltered the guerrillas. The worst fedayeen outrages occurred after the 1973 Yom Kippur War, when Arab military weakness was once again revealed. In April 1974 three members of the PFLP general command crossed the border from Lebanon and shot their way into an apartment block in the town of Kiryat Shmona, killing eighteen residents before blowing themselves up. The following day the Israeli army crossed into Lebanon and raided numerous villages, blowing up houses and taking Arab civilian hostages back to Israel.

Over the next few weeks, Israeli jets, artillery and gunboats blasted Palestinian refugee camps across southern Lebanon, using massive firepower including napalm, bombs and anti-personnel weapons that killed at least 200 and drove thousands of Lebanese refugees into Beirut. The following month three fedayeen crossed over from Lebanon once again and rampaged through the town of Ma'a lot, shooting at a bus and killing a family in a private house before taking over a high school, where ninety young students on an excursion were asleep. The guerrillas took some seventy teenagers and students hostage and demanded the release of twenty Arab prisoners in exchange. The negotiations broke down when Israel refused to comply and Israeli troops under the command of Moshe Dayan finally stormed the building. In the ensuing gunfight the guerrillas and twenty-five hostages were killed, the majority of them teenagers. In the aftermath of Ma'a lot, the Israeli prime minister Golda Meir promised to 'cut off the hands' of those responsible and the Israeli air force carried out its heaviest air strikes so far against 'Palestinian targets' in south Lebanon. As the casualties mounted on both sides, the conflict sank deeper into the cycle of violence and counter-violence that has characterised it ever since.

The villa in the jungle

Wherever it occurs, terrorism tends to be depicted as a barbarous assault on a benevolent and peace-loving society. The roots of Palestinian violence lay in the violent dispossession of 700,000 Palestinian refugees during the 1948 war and the subsequent emergence of a Palestinian national movement, centred in the impoverished refugee camps in the surrounding Arab countries. From the late sixties onwards, however, Israel presented itself as an outpost of Western civilisation facing a murderous onslaught that had no origins beyond the bloodthirstiness of its terrorist perpetrators. In doing so, Israeli propaganda was instrumental in propagating the notion of 'terrorism' as a uniquely evil form of violence inimical to Western civilisation. But the methods used by the fedayeen were not entirely alien to Zionist practice. Before World War II the Irgun placed bombs in Arab buses and markets during the Arab revolt against the British, and both the Irgun and the so-called 'Stern Gang' terrorised and killed Palestinian civilians during the 1948 war in order to make them abandon their towns and villages. Even after the establishment of the state of Israel the Israeli army carried out cross-border raids, massacres and violent reprisals against Arab civilians, such as the killing of forty-nine inhabitants in the village of Kafr Qasim in 1956, who were shot for disobeying a curfew which they did not realise had been ordered, by the Israeli army's Unit 101, commanded by a young Ariel Sharon.

These tactics were a source of considerable anguish to the dovish Moshe Sharett, the Israeli foreign minister from 1948 to 1956 and prime minister in 1954 and 1955. On 12 December 1954 Israeli fighter planes forced a Syrian civilian plane to land in Israel and its passengers and crew were held prisoner for two days while Moshe Dayan demanded the release of five Israeli soldiers captured inside Syria. In a letter to his defence minister, Pinhas Lavon, an outraged Sharett denounced the military leaders responsible who 'seem to presume that the State of Israel may – or even must – behave in the realm of international relations according to the laws of the jungle.'[28]

That same year an Israeli spy ring in Egypt carried out a string of bombings of British and American cultural institutions, as well as cinemas and Egyptian public buildings, in order to prevent a rapprochement between Nasser's regime and the West. When ten members of the group were arrested and put on trial, Israeli propaganda accused the Egyptian government of extracting confessions under torture. Though Sharett remained publicly silent, he was privately appalled at the machinations of the Israeli military, accusing the hawkish Lavon of having 'taught the army leadership the diabolic lesson of how to set the Middle East on fire, how to cause friction, cause bloody confrontations, sabotage targets and property of the powers and perform acts of despair and suicide'.[29]

Sharett's views were increasingly out of step with his own cabinet. In March 1955 off-duty paratroopers carried out a revenge attack in Jordan in response to the killing of an Israeli couple by unknown assailants, in which the soldiers kidnapped five Bedouin and stabbed four of them to death. An infuriated Sharett demanded that those responsible be put on trial, only to be opposed by Lavon's successor in the Ministry of Defence, David Ben-Gurion, and the army high command. In his diary Sharett lamented the fact that his countrymen had transformed revenge into a 'sacred principle' and speculated that such acts 'must make the State appear in the eyes of the world as a savage state that does not recognise the principles of justice as they have been established and accepted by contemporary society'.[30]

Sharett's dovish Zionism eventually cost him his political career, but the aggressive militarism that he privately denounced has remained the dominant force in Israeli foreign policy. In the same period as the PLO was first acquiring its bloodthirsty terrorist reputation, the Israeli armed forces carried out numerous military operations against their Arab neighbours that were often vastly more destructive than the actions that supposedly provoked them. According to Israeli police statistics published in 1982 in *Ha'aretz*, the total number of Israelis killed by different PLO groups between 1968 and 1981 was 284.[31] Yet between 1968 and 1975 alone, the United Nations estimated that Israel killed some 3,500 Arab civilians during its 'punitive' raids on Lebanon, Syria and Jordan.

In the Western world, Palestinian and Israeli violence were generally interpreted in very different ways. Where the killing of Israeli civilians was greeted with horror and condemnation by Western politicians, the victims of Israeli air strikes and cross-border military incursions tended to be routinised in brief news items or subsumed in the euphemistic vocabulary of counter-terrorism. Where such attacks were presented as retaliations or punitive counter-insurgency operations, Palestinian violence confirmed the savagery and visceral brutality of its 'Arab terrorist' perpetrators. There is no doubt that Palestinian attacks on Israeli civilians were cruel and merciless, but Israeli artillery bombardments and air strikes were not noted for their humanity or their discrimination regarding the 'innocent' and the 'guilty'. In 1982, the Likud prime minister Menachem Begin angrily responded to what he regarded as hypocritical denunciations from the Labour opposition of civilian casualties in Lebanon by listing various incidents in which civilians had been killed in Lebanon under Labour governments during the 1970s. The former Labour diplomat Abba Eban did not deny Begin's accusations but claimed that such attacks were justified since 'there was a rational prospect, ultimately fulfilled, that affected populations would exert pressure for the cessation of hostilities.'[32]

The killing of civilians in order to bring about political consequences is normally included within the consensual understanding of terrorism, but such actions have rarely dented Israeli's anti-terrorist credentials in the Western world. Begin subscribed to the same logic when he ordered the Israeli invasion of Lebanon in 1982 as a 'counter-terrorist' operation in response to cross-border rocket attacks on Israel, even though there had been no such attacks for months beforehand. The ultimate goal of the invasion was the destruction of the PLO and its expulsion from Lebanon. This objective was partly achieved, but not before some 18,000 Lebanese and Palestinians had been killed, the majority of them civilians. In one of the worst episodes of the invasion, Israeli army units entrusted with the protection of the Palestinian refugee camps of Sabra and Chatila allowed Phalangist militias to embark on a wild orgy of rape, murder and mutilation in which some 2,000 defenceless civilians were killed. Though the then defence minister Ariel Sharon claimed that the camps were infested with PLO 'terrorists', the majority of those killed were old men, women and children, many of whom were hacked to death with knives and axes while the Israeli army fired flares to light their killers' way.

The horrific slaughter at Sabra and Chatila dwarfed any of the outrages carried out by the fedayeen. Yet four years later, the defence minister, deemed by an Israeli inquiry to be 'personally responsible' for the massacres, could be found dispensing advice to readers of the *Washington Post* on how to stop 'the slaughter of innocents' by terrorists. The history of terrorism is filled with similar quirks and ironies, but the Israeli–Palestinian conflict has more of them than most. Israel has often portrayed itself as a lone pioneer in the front line against terrorism, fighting the common enemy of the West long before Western governments had become alert to the danger. In the late 1960s this situation changed, as the fedayeen erupted onto the international stage with a new set of tactics that confirmed the evolution of terrorism into a menace to the civilised world.

PART III

The Terrorist Decades

The Dawn of International Terrorism

In the world today, no one is innocent.

George Habash, 1970

At the end of the 1960s 'terrorism' was still generally regarded in the West as a localised and conflict-specific phenomenon, whose barbaric methods were mostly restricted to the colonial battlefields of the Third World. Over the next decade these perceptions were drastically changed by the advent of revolutionary terrorist organisations in the industrialised world. In the same period the Israeli-Palestinian conflict spilled over beyond the Middle East, as various Palestinian groups attacked Israeli facilities and other international targets in different parts of the world. The occasional participation of Japanese, German and Latin American revolutionaries in these events suggested a new process of cross-fertilisation and mutual co-operation between disparate groups. Events such as the Lod airport massacre, where Puerto Rican tourists were killed in Israel by Japanese, and the OPEC conference in Vienna in 1975, where oil ministers were taken hostage by a team containing two Germans, a Venezuelan and a Palestinian, all pointed towards a new internationalism and a shared political agenda.

All these events were increasingly incorporated into a single overarching narrative of 'international terrorism'. In theory, the term referred to acts of terrorist violence occurring outside the national territory where a specific conflict was taking place or whose targets involved foreign nationals. But in practice international terrorism was often used as a catch-all category to include any act of 'terrorist' violence taking place anywhere in the world. As the decade wore on even unconnected terrorist events were portrayed as expressions of the same sinister international phenomenon. Where 'terrorism' had previously been a threat to colonial societies and individual governments, 'international terrorism' was regarded as a danger to world order and a sinister conspiracy against the free world. If the concept echoed the transnational anarchist networks of the nineteenth century, the international terrorist was also presented as a modern-day pirate, preying on the vulnerable lines of transport and communication that bound the modern world together, in order to project media-driven spectacles onto an unwilling audience.

The hijacking era begins

On 29 August 1969 a TWA Boeing 707 jet en route from Los Angeles to Tel Aviv stopped at Rome to refuel and pick up more passengers. Half an hour after the plane had taken off, a young Palestinian woman named Leila Khaled and her companion Salem Issawi ran towards the cockpit brandishing grenades, and ordered the pilot to fly to Lod airport without making its planned stop in Athens. The two passengers were both members of the Popular Front for the Liberation of Palestine (PFLP) and they had trained for this mission for months beforehand. As the plane approached Lod airport, the ebullient Khaled taunted the Israeli control tower, telling them, 'This is no longer TWA 840, this is Flight PFLP Free Arab Palestine. What can you do about it?' When three Israeli jet fighters buzzed the plane, Khaled switched on the intercom so that the passengers could hear and announced that she would blow up the cockpit if the fighters did not withdraw. The Israelis complied and Khaled then ordered the plane to descend, so low that she could see the tanks and soldiers lined up across the Lod airport runway to prevent them from landing. As the impotent Israeli ground staff yelled abuse at her, Khaled ordered the plane to fly north to Damascus, accompanied by Israeli jet fighters, where the passengers disembarked and Issawi blew up the cockpit with explosives.

Her Syrian hosts were anxious at the prospect of Israeli retaliation and kept the two hijackers under house arrest for forty-five days. By the time they were released, Khaled found herself acclaimed as a heroine throughout the Middle East, and the PFLP sent her on a regional tour, where she was fêted 'like a visiting astronaut', as one British businessman in Qatar described it. Khaled's celebrity status was greatly enhanced by the PFLP publicity photographs taken in October 1969, showing her in military uniform and holding a Kalashnikov, her jet-black hair half-covered by a Palestinian keffiyah. To supporters of the Palestinian cause, Khaled was a photogenic heroine, an iconic female revolutionary to rival Che Guevara. To governments who did not support either the Palestinian cause or the methods she used, Khaled was a terrorist, whose actions heralded a new and unwelcome tactic.

Wadi Haddad's war

Hijacking, or 'air piracy', was not a Palestinian invention. The heyday of aeroplane hijacking coincided with the dawn of the jet age and the boom in civilian air traffic from 1958 onwards, when Boeing 707 and Comet 4 jet airliners began to make regular flights across the Atlantic. Over the next fourteen years some 400 hijacking incidents took place across the world, the majority of which were associated with Cuba, as a variety of different aeroplanes were hijacked by opponents of the Castro regime seeking political asylum in the US or by Cubans and Americans fleeing the United States in the opposite direction. According to the PFLP's media spokesman, Bassam Abu-Sharif, the idea of hijacking civilian jets was first proposed at a meeting in late 1967 by the head of the PFLP's Special Operations Group, Wadi Haddad, who proposed that the fedayeen undertake a series of 'spectacular, one-off operations' in different parts of the world. Abu-Sharif later recalled the impact on the meeting as Haddad proposed hijacking an El Al airliner in mid-air and holding its passengers for ransom:

> This was breathtaking stuff. When he had finished speaking, I felt like standing up and applauding, and I could tell the others round the table felt the same way. The world had tilted slightly on its axis, and it had tilted in our direction. Here, at last, was a new way forward – a chance to get the Israeli boot off the back of the Arab neck. From now on, we would carry the attack to Israel. We would take – and keep – the initiative. I felt exhilarated. It was from this moment that Haddad became known as 'The Master'.[1]

The main focus of the Master's 'foreign operations' was the Israeli El Al airline's fleet of seven Boeing 707 jumbo jets. Though El Al was a civilian airline, Haddad considered it a vital communications link between Israel and the outside world and a symbol of Israeli national prestige. If the El Al fleet was a legitimate 'military' target, hijackings were also seen as a means of forcing international opinion to recognise the Palestinian cause and drawing other Arab countries into the struggle by inviting Israeli retaliation. Last but not least, hijacking constituted a variant on the old strategy of 'propaganda by deed', in which, as one of Khaled's comrades described it, 'We act heroically in a cowardly world to prove that the enemy is not invincible.'[2] Over the next three years, the PFLP and other fedayeen organisations struck at El Al planes, offices and other Israeli commercial and diplomatic facilities across Europe.

In the wake of these attacks some European airports began to improve their security procedures, while at least two international airlines and a number of Arab governments made large payments to Haddad's organisation in return for not attacking their aircraft, which Haddad invested in further terrorist spectaculars. Ever the innovator, Haddad recruited a team of chemistry and engineering graduates from Arab universities who experimented with new metal alloys that could evade airport security checks. According to Abu-Sharif, Haddad also considered the possibility of aerial suicide missions in which pilots would fly planes filled with explosives into Israeli buildings. One plan to fly a twin-engined light plane into the Shalom Tower in Tel Aviv was eventually abandoned when the pilot crashed during his final training flight.

Not surprisingly, Israel was very keen to see Haddad dead and tried on various occasions to eliminate him. On 11 July 1970 Mossad agents fired six remote-controlled Katyusha rockets at Haddad's Beirut apartment. Unknown to Mossad, Haddad and Leila Khaled were planning the PFLP's next hijacking operation while Haddad's wife and eight-year-old son were sleeping in the bedroom. No one was killed in the attack and the operation that Haddad and Khaled were planning turned out to be the apotheosis of the hijacking era, when the PFLP hijacked three international jets from different countries on Sunday 6 September 1970. The first two planes were successfully diverted to a former Royal Air Force airstrip in the Jordanian desert known as Dawson's Field, where they were greeted by armed fedayeen led by Bassam Abu-Sharif. Khaled was also a participant in the operation, her face reconfigured by plastic surgery as a result of her high media profile, but her attempt to hijack an El Al plane from Amsterdam was foiled when she was overcome by passengers and crew and her Nicaraguan accomplice was mortally wounded. The plane was forced to make an emergency landing in London, where Khaled was arrested by British police after an unseemly tug o'war between the Israeli cabin crew and Scotland Yard detectives.

In the course of 'Skyjack Sunday' Haddad's teams had hijacked three jumbo jets and obliged four different governments to engage in complex hostage negotiations regarding Palestinian prisoners in order to prevent the threatened destruction of the two planes in Jordan, together with their passengers and crew. Though the UN general-secretary, U Thant, condemned these events as 'a return to the law of the jungle', the PFLP proceeded to hijack a BOAC VC-10 en route from Bahrain to London, which joined the others at Dawson's Field as the PFLP now added the release of Leila Khaled to their list of demands. For nearly two weeks the negotiations continued as the fedayeen removed the hostages to the Intercontinental Hotel in Amman and blew up the three planes, with a collective value of some $30 million, in full view of the world's television cameras. The hostages were released and the PFLP achieved most of its demands, but Haddad's 'hijacking carnival' finally prompted Jordan's King Hussein to take action against the fedayeen organisations, whose power had come to rival his own.

In three weeks of savage fighting the Palestinian guerrillas were defeated and some 3,000 Palestinians killed. In the aftermath of these events the fedayeen began to re-evaluate hijacking as a strategy. By the end of 1972 most international airports had installed X-ray luggage scanners and compulsory security checks with magnetometers and body searches, thus making hijackings more difficult to carry out. Not only had the hijacking programme failed to cut off Israel's contact with the outside world but the El Al fleet had actually expanded. For a brief period Haddad's operatives had forced the world to pay attention to the Palestinian cause, but the resulting attention had not resulted in clear political benefits for the Palestinians and had directly contributed to the loss of the fedayeen's principal base in Jordan. The PFLP leader, George Habash, was more ambivalent about hijackings than his public statements sometimes indicated, declaring in 1972 that such operations were inimical to 'Marxist-Leninist tactics'. But no sooner had the hijacking era come to an end than a new Palestinian organisation emerged whose actions would do even more to herald the advent of the terrorist evil.

The 'scum of the earth'

On 28 November 1971 Palestinian gunmen shot dead the Jordanian prime minister and former defence minister Wasfi Tal, in the lobby of the Sheraton Hotel in Cairo. The assassination was claimed by an organisation called Black September, named after the events in Jordan, whose origins have never been entirely clear. Though Israel described Black September as a Fatah terrorist front created on Yasser Arafat's orders, Fatah never officially took responsibility for its actions, despite the fact that some high-ranking Fatah members were involved in some its operations. Whatever its origins, over the next three years Black September carried out a string of bloody operations in different parts of the world, culminating in the deaths of eleven members of the Israeli Olympic team during the Munich Games in September 1972.

The Olympiad was the first that Germany had hosted since the Berlin games of 1936, and it received more extensive media coverage than any previous sporting event, with some 6,700 journalists and the most advanced technology to ensure that the proceedings were seen by more than 670 million viewers worldwide. For the first eleven days the games projected as the 'carefree games' lived up to their expectations. But on the evening of 6 September, eight members of Black September forced their way into the Israeli pavilion, killing an Israeli weightlifter and a wrestler who tried to resist them before taking nine other members of the team hostage. The kidnappers then threatened to shoot their captives unless 200 Palestinian prisoners from Israeli jails were released, in addition to the recently arrested members of the Red Army Faction.

As the games ground to a halt, the ongoing crisis was broadcast live to the largest audience in history. One of the most famous images of Munich showed one of the kidnappers standing on the balcony of the flat where the Israeli athletes were held hostage. The Palestinian is crouching slightly, his face entirely covered by a makeshift mask that appears to have been cut from a tracksuit leg and tied at the top. The eye sockets are completely black, adding to his inhuman, freakish appearance, the very image of the terrorist as *hosti generis humani* – the enemy of mankind. In the evening the kidnappers asked for two helicopters to take them and their hostages to an airport and an aeroplane to fly them to an unnamed Arab country. The German authorities agreed, then staged an ambush at the airport, which was badly planned and clumsily executed. A chaotic two-hour gunfight ended in tragedy when the kidnappers killed all their hostages. By the end of the night five of the eight-man Black September team and one policeman were also dead and the three surviving kidnappers had been arrested.

Though the operation had failed to achieve its specific objectives, Black September hailed it as a publicity success, declaring in a communiqué that 'A bomb in the White House, a mine in the Vatican, the death of Mao Tse Tung, an earthquake in Paris could not have echoed through the conscious-ness of every man in the world like the operation at Munich … It was like painting the name of Palestine on a mountain that can be seen from the four corners of the earth.'[3] Across the world the bloody violation of the 'Olympic Peace' was greeted with horrified revulsion and an outpouring of sympathy towards Israel. The attitude towards the kidnappers was summed up by a letter to *Time* magazine describing Black September as 'the scum of the earth' and 'degenerate "heroes of the sewers" '.

In Palestinian refugee camps across the Middle East, however, the Black September team were hailed as heroes who had struck Israel a painful blow. After the three survivors were freed a few weeks later following a Black-September organised hijacking they were given a rapturous welcome in Libya. Within the United Nations, the events at Munich prompted the first major international debate on the subject of terrorism since the 1937 League of Nations Convention, with similarly inconclusive results.[4] Within the Israeli-Palestinian conflict itself, the Munich massacre was another link in the endless chain of violence and retaliation as Israeli air strikes pounded Palestinian refugee camps in Lebanon, killing some 200 people, none of whom was known to have any connection with Munich. Israel also undertook a secret campaign of assassinations in Europe and the Middle East directed against those it believed to be responsible, culminating in a car bomb in Beirut in January 1979 which killed Ali Hassan Salameh, the head of Arafat's personal security unit whom Israel believed had masterminded the Munich operation.

The PLO – Murder Inc.?

Though fedayeen 'foreign operations' certainly succeeded in attracting international attention to the Palestinian cause, they also established an association between the Palestinian struggle and terrorism which has often proved to be a political liability. In the wake of Arafat's historic appearance at the United Nations in 1974, the PLO was given observer status at the UN and soon achieved the de facto status of a government in exile. Increasingly, Fatah's hopes were concentrated on winning a Palestinian state through diplomatic means rather than through armed struggle. But the more Arafat attempted to steer his own Palestinian constituency towards diplomacy, the more Israel portrayed the PLO as a murderous terrorist organisation, financed by Arab oil and Moscow gold.

To Israeli prime minister Menachem Begin, the PLO was 'the blackest organisation – other than the Nazi murder organisations – ever to arise in the annals of humanity', while a brochure published by the Zionist Centre for Information and Documentation on Israel and the Middle East (CEDIP) described the PLO as 'the wealthiest terrorist organisation in history', whose 'chartered killers' were taught to murder at the age of 12 and given drugs and pornography 'as a reward for the completion of their training'. Such propaganda was intended to undermine the credibility of the PLO as a political organisation and the credibility of Arafat in particular. There is no doubt that the PLO chairman sanctioned 'terrorist' attacks on Israelis, but the portrayal of Arafat as a duplicitous 'terror master' ignored the fact that the PLO was a broad amalgam of different groups and personalities, whose actions were not always in accordance with the diplomatic path which Fatah was embarked on, and which sometimes actively hindered it. Some of the bloodiest fedayeen operations were deliberately designed to sabotage Fatah's diplomatic progress, such as the murderous activities of the renegade Fatah member Sabri al-Banna, more commonly known as Abu Nidal, whose operatives left a trail of death and mayhem across Europe and the Middle East. The majority of these operations did more harm to Arafat and Fatah than they did to Israel, so much so that Fatah's intelligence service believed that Abu Nidal was actively working in collusion with Mossad.[5]

The paranoid, whisky-drinking Abu Nidal embodied the 'terrorist godfather' image which Israeli propaganda tried for so many years to pin on Arafat himself. As always, the anti-terrorist anathema was determined by political rather than moral priorities. What made Arafat really dangerous to Israel was not the terrorist acts for which he was deemed responsible, but the fact that he was the only Palestinian leader with the ability to persuade the PLO to accept a negotiated settlement to the Israeli-Palestinian conflict. By presenting Palestinian 'terrorism' as a threat to the West as well as to Israel itself, Israeli propaganda aimed to halt the drift towards diplomacy and exclude the PLO from serious political consideration.

This strategy was particularly effective in the United States. In 1987, the first intifada erupted across the Occupied Territories and an astonished world watched the almost daily confrontations between Palestinian schoolchildren and the Israeli army. The revolt brought new hope to the flagging Palestinian cause and in 1988 the Palestine National Council called for an independent Palestinian state in the West Bank and Gaza and an international conference to find a political solution to the conflict. Instead, the US government demanded that Arafat reject 'terrorism in all its forms' and declared the PLO leader persona non grata in the United States.

Desperate to convert the intifada into tangible political achievements, Arafat agreed to jump through the hoop and announced at the Palais des Nations in Geneva that the PLO was ready to recognise Israel and rejected 'all forms of terrorism, including individual, group and state terrorism'. This was still not explicit enough for the US. During the US–PLO discussions held in Tunis later that month, the Palestinian delegates were told that 'the internal struggle that we are witnessing in the Occupied Territories aims to undermine the security and stability of the State of Israel, and we therefore demand cessation of those riots, which we view as terrorist acts against Israel'.[6]

Even as the PLO delegates were being lectured on the 'terrorist' activities of stone-throwing children, the Israeli army was trying to crush the revolt, using innovative new practices such as breaking the arms and legs of teenage rioters. While these actions received no criticism from the US government, Arafat was now asked to halt a 'terrorist' rebellion which he had not even started, simply in order to win the right to enter into a dialogue with Israel's most powerful ally and protector. Even Arafat could not do this without committing political suicide. And so he was condemned to remain a terrorist as Israel tried to put down the uprising which had saved him from political oblivion. It was only when these attempts had failed that the PLO chairman was deemed fit for civilised consumption by the arbiters of international morality. So the long process began which would lead to the famous handshakes on the White House lawn and Arafat's temporary conversion from terrorist godfather to statesman.

The modern plague

Throughout the 1970s the chain of embassy sieges, aeroplane hijackings, bombings and assassinations continued to unfold, even in countries where such events had never before been imagined, such as the spate of train hijackings carried out by Moluccan separatists in Holland. The confluence of so many terrorist events in the 1970s was a historical novelty and their impact was magnified by an increasingly pervasive mass media, whose coverage enhanced the impression that the world had now entered a new 'age of terror'. Not for the first time, the publicity that these events aroused was deceptive. Even in the United States, where 'international terrorism' became a foreign-policy obsession during the 1970s, the State Department listed 913 incidents of transnational terrorism between 1968 and 1975, in which 800 people were killed and 1,700 injured.[7]

These figures constituted a minuscule proportion of the number of people killed by war, famine, preventable disease and natural disasters in the same period. The average annual domestic homicide rate in the United States in the 1970s was nearly three times higher than all the deaths resulting from acts of international terrorism in the same decade. Then, as now, the majority of people in the Western world were far more likely to die in a car crash or a domestic accident than an act of terrorist violence, yet a succession of pundits continued to insist that terrorism represented a fundamental threat to international security, and even to the survival of civilisation itself.

Why did this happen? The belief that terrorism was getting inexorably worse was crucial to the attention it received. Where the statistics did not bear out the thesis, they could always be manipulated. Thus a 1979 CIA report listed 3,336 incidents of international terrorism since 1968. The following year another CIA report listed 6,714 incidents for the same period.[8] The reason for the disparity lay in a deliberate widening of the categorisation of terrorist incidents to include 'threats' and 'hoaxes', thereby painting an even bleaker picture in order to suit the administration's depiction of a terrorist onslaught on the West.

The fear of terrorism was also magnified by alarmist speculation about what terrorists *might* do. 'Nobody knows where the terrorists will strike next or just how far they will go. We are all in the firing line,' warned Christopher Dobson and Ronald Payne in *The Weapons of Terror: International Terrorism at Work* (1979). The Payne/Dobson tandem produced a number of influential books and articles on the subject of terrorism and *The Weapons of Terror* is a period piece, with its chilling portrayal of the lethal arsenal now available to an assortment of nihilists, left-wing fanatics and middle-class idealists, 'deluded by their gurus into thinking that violence provides the only true road to salvation'. Inside colour plates display a gleaming array of weapons from the Armalite AR-18 and the Heckler & Koch MP-5, to the Czech Skorpion VS-61 machine pistol used by the Italian Red Brigades.

That such weaponry should now be available to terrorists was dangerous enough, but another chapter lists more destructive ways in which 'nations can be held to ransom or even dealt crippling blows by terrorists and individual madmen', from poisoning the water supplies and stealing nerve gas to 'agricultural terrorism' and nuclear weapons – the 'ultimate weapon of terror'. Like many purveyors of apocalyptic terrorist scenarios, Dobson and Payne do not question the legitimacy of these 'weapons of terror' in the hands of governments, but only in their possible use by terrorists. Other analysts offered similarly grim predictions, in which terrorists might manufacture a nuclear bomb, take over a nuclear facility, unleash nerve gas or poisonous chemicals, or blow up gas pipelines and cut communications and transportation systems, thereby unleashing a series of 'cascading failures' that would reduce whole countries to chaos.

For the majority of the Western public, the only way that terrorism intruded on their lives was through the baggage searches and security checks that were becoming increasingly routine at most international airports. Less visible was the growing investment in computer and surveillance technology by the police and intelligence services in various countries, which aimed at preventing terrorist activity and monitoring its potential sources. In the same period governments began to invest in anti-terrorist training programmes for diplomatic staff and military personnel and increased the physical security of embassies and other public buildings, from CCTV and electronic sensors to detection and screening devices. By 1985 the United States was spending an estimated $4.2 billion per year and employing some 18,000 people on a range of anti-terrorist measures, from intelligence gathering and research to protection for diplomats and embassy officials abroad.[9]

Much of this protection was supplied by the private security industry, which entered a boom period in the security-obsessed world of the terror-

ism era, providing a range of anti-terrorist services from guarding and electronic security to government buildings at home and abroad, to bodyguard
protection for business executives and diplomats. Other companies offered
risk-analysis profiles of foreign trouble spots to potential Western investors,
seminars for executives fearful of being kidnapped and residential courses
on 'executive survival' and 'urban combat' techniques in anti-terrorism
training camps. The private security sector was dominated by former police
and military officers or ex-intelligence agents; for example the Wackenhut
Corporation in the United States, one of the largest private security firms in
the world, and the British company Control Risks, whose subsidiary KMS,
or 'Kini Mini Services', was staffed almost entirely by former members of
the SAS.[10]

In the militarised South Africa of the late 1970s, private security consultants
offered 'counter-terrorism' courses, including training in unarmed combat,
'crisis management' and abseiling, while electronics companies advertised state-of-the art security cameras providing permanent surveillance
to anxious homeowners.[11] In Israel the private security industry frequently
acted in tandem with the Ministry of Defence in providing 'counter-terrorist' training to a range of repressive Third World regimes, from the military
governments of Guatemala and Honduras to the Marcos dictatorship in the
Philippines. In the same period most Western governments formed elite
anti-terrorist military units that were trained to respond to the new forms
of violence, from aircraft hijackings to hostage taking. Some of these units,
such as Israel's Sayeret Matkal, had a glamour and mystique of their own.
All these developments were part of what Dobson and Payne called 'democracy's fightback' against the ubiquitous invisible enemy, but at the same
time the enemy needed to be analysed and explained.

The interpreters

It has often been observed that terrorism 'uses' the media to communicate
its message. But the publicity given to international terrorism was never
simply due to the terrorist events themselves. The perception that the world
had entered an 'age of terrorism' was partly due to the increasing attention
given to the subject by Western governments, but it also reflected a new
tendency to identify disparate acts of violence as manifestations of the same
phenomenon.[12] Since the 'terrorists' had not changed their methods or their
conception of themselves, this new categorisation depended entirely on
external interpretations of their actions. Before the 1970s 'terrorism' had generally been studied within the context of political science, history or military

history, rather than as a separate category in its own right. From the mid-seventies onwards, however, the number of books, articles and academic studies devoted to terrorist phenomena turned from a trickle to a flood.

The more terrorism became a central policy concern of Western governments, the more it became the subject of research for both governmental and privately funded think tanks, institutions and university departments. In the United States, various universities began to carry out research into the linked tributaries of terrorism, insurgency and 'political violence', while the Rand Corporation, a US Air Force-funded think tank, organised seminars, conferences, articles and publications on terrorism, and established the first comprehensive international chronology of terrorist incidents. In the same period a number of private institutions and think tanks came into existence whose purpose was to study the terrorist phenomenon, such as the London-based Institute for the Study of Terrorism, directed by the Baader-Meinhof biographer Jillian Becker, and the Jaffee Centre for Strategic Studies in Israel. Like the security industry, many of these institutions were established and/or staffed by former intelligence agents, police and military officers, who tended to regard terrorism from a narrow pro-Western perspective, such as the Jonathan Institute in Israel, founded by Benjamin Netanyahu in 1979 and named after his brother, an Israeli colonel killed in the Entebbe airport raid in Uganda. The Jonathan Institute was not so much a research institute as a highly effective conduit for the dissemination of Israeli anti-PLO propaganda, whose two international conferences on terrorism in the 1970s and 1980s received widespread publicity.

Other private terrorism think tanks were little more than vehicles for Cold War propaganda and disinformation, such as the London-based Institute for the Study of Conflict (ISC), founded by an Australian journalist, Brian Crozier. A self-confessed conduit for the CIA and other Western intelligence services, Crozier was an indefatigable anti-communist propagandist and Cold War conspirator, who regularly contributed to *The Economist* and several newspapers, in addition to writing numerous books on terrorism and Third World insurgencies, including the pioneering *The Rebels* (1960), an early study of left-wing revolutionary and anti-colonial movements that was used by the US military in its counter-insurgency courses at Fort Bragg.

The ISC's activities included the publication of a regular monthly newsletter and annual review containing updates on international subversive and terrorist activity for a select list of clients, including Margaret Thatcher and Ronald Reagan. Though Crozier described himself as a liberal defender of the free society against Soviet 'totalism', his profoundly anti-democratic politics were evident in his warm apologias for Franco, Pinochet and the Shah of Iran and his far-right connections in Britain itself. In 1975 Crozier appeared before a US senatorial subcommittee, where he was introduced as 'one of the free world's foremost experts on international terrorism'. As Crozier later admitted, 'My role, although it was not spelt out, was to define various types of terrorism and above all to produce the evidence … of the key role of the Soviet Union and its satellites in the recruiting, training and financing of terrorist gangs.'[13] Throughout the seventies and eighties Crozier continued to perform the same function, providing what he called a 'very, very restricted list' of some 160 politicians and world leaders with his monthly updates on terrorist and subversive activity around the world.

Other prominent terrorism pundits included Ray Cline, a former deputy director of the CIA and co-author with Alexander Yonah of *Terrorism: the Soviet Connection*, and Michael Ledeen, an American journalist with murky intelligence connections in Italy and the United States.[14] Nearly all the leading terrorist experts were similarly situated on the conservative to far-right end of the political spectrum. The more successful became media pundits, appearing on television and writing regular commentaries on the subject. Many of these experts were part of the same interlocking network. They attended the same international conferences, they cited each other as sources in their books, they contributed articles to the same journals and chapters to terrorism anthologies.

All these individuals and institutions helped shape the way that terrorism was perceived and understood by governments and the public in the terrorist decades. Within this vast output there were many serious and objective studies of the role of terror and violence in international politics, but much Western analysis of terrorism tended to fall within the pseudo-discipline of 'terrorology' and focused on revolutionary violence directed against Western governments or societies. Though terrorologists varied in their emphases and their fields of study, they generally shared certain core beliefs. Nearly all of them agreed that terrorism was a uniquely barbaric and immoral form of violence, which Western democracies did not support or engage in; a number argued that terrorism was not just a technique of violence but an 'ideology' that was antithetical to liberal democracy and the 'free society'. For most terrorologists, 'political violence' was a concept that referred to violence used against governments, rather than violence directed by them, unless it was to prove that enemies of the West were engaging in 'state-sponsored terrorism'. Terrorologists were often suspicious of what they regarded as a promiscuous relationship between the media and terrorism, echoing the views of police and politicians that media coverage of terrorist events was politically irresponsible, that it 'glamorised' terrorism and played into the hands of terrorists by providing them with the 'oxygen of publicity'.

Terrorology covered a broad spectrum, from academia to the media, but even the most apparently academic analyses of terrorism were often matched by strident moral condemnation of terrorist violence, coupled with warnings that such violence was getting steadily worse. In his seminal terrorological work *Terrorism and the Liberal State* (1986), the English political scientist Paul Wilkinson criticised those who pointed out the relatively low number of deaths caused by the kind of violence he described, asking 'Have we become so indifferent to the value of an individual human life that we can no longer hear the cries of the victims, the suffering of the dying and injured, the anguish of the bereaved? Is it not a crime against God and humanity that these innocent lives have been taken by terrorist guns and bombs?'[15]

The 'innocent' is a key terrorological concept, but Wilkinson's cri de coeur would have more resonance were it not for the more muted indignation that he tends to show when innocent lives are taken by governments he considers to be on his own side. For Wilkinson terrorism is uniquely and irredeemably evil, its 'rejection of all moral constraints ... reflected in particularly hideous and barbarous cruelties and weapons', such as the IRA's use of bombs filled with ball bearings and shrapnel during one of its London bombing campaigns. It is not necessary to condone the IRA's use of such tactics to point out that these weapons were crude imitations of the cluster bombs routinely used by the United States, one of the great liberal democracies, on a massive scale during the Vietnam war.

But for Wilkinson, the idea that liberal states can also engage in 'hideous and barbarous cruelties' is incompatible with the shallow notion of an irreconcilable philosophical and moral distinction between 'terrorism' and 'democracy'. Wilkinson also articulated another core concept of 1970s terrorology, arguing that the Western world had failed in its moral 'duty' to treat the terrorist evil with the severity and seriousness it demanded. In Wilkinson's view, the 'moral weakness and cowardice of modern governments' had emboldened terrorists and allowed the phenomenon to spread unchecked. In the second half of the decade these accusations of 'moral weakness' became increasingly strident and alarmist, and helped create one of the great myths of modern terrorist history.

The hydra

The advent of terrorology coincided with a period in which the Soviet Union and the Western world were beginning to establish a new modus vivendi in the détente era. From the mid-1970s onwards, the spectre of international terrorism became part of a sophisticated and wide-ranging right-wing propaganda offensive, which aimed to convince the Western public that the Soviet Union was still pursuing its dream of world conquest even as it edged towards peaceful coexistence. Instead of seeking a nuclear confrontation, argued Jillian Becker, the Soviets were secretly orchestrating an international terrorist offensive in which 'the little bombs, the hand guns, the grenades go off instead, killing innocent people by tens rather than millions, but at the same time weakening the foundations of our world to bring about our downfall'.[16]

The Dobson–Payne tandem similarly described 'a worldwide network of revolutionaries determined ... to destroy the fabric of modern society', behind which the intrepid reporters invariably detected 'the footprints of the heavy-booted men of the KGB – for the Kremlin, even when it is not involved, wants to know what is going on'.[17] Evidence to support these allegations was generally scant and circumstantial, and much of it emanated from Western intelligence services or defectors of dubious probity. Though the Soviet Union certainly provided some assistance to Third World revolutionary organisations, such support could be construed as support for terrorism only if it was accepted that such movements were 'terrorist' in the first place.

Even when it did occur, such support tended to be opportunistic and piecemeal. Even though Libya received shipments of Soviet weapons, some of which found their way into the hands of the IRA, it was not at all clear whether the Soviets had any knowledge of these transactions, nor was there any obvious reason why a Catholic state in Ireland should have favoured Soviet interests. Nevertheless, right-wing politicians and terrorism analysts continued to depict the dread hand of the Soviets behind any violent upheaval, such as the Australian journalist Robert Moss, a protégé of Brian Crozier, who also found his way to the US congressional hearings on terrorism in the late 1970s.

Like Crozier, Moss saw the shadow of the Soviets behind every insurgency or revolution from Nicaragua to Iran. The notion of a sinister Soviet-backed Terrorist International was often accompanied by an equally delusional McCarthyite fantasy, that the Soviets had penetrated the media, the political establishment and even the intelligence services themselves in order to conceal the threat from the public. Thus, Jillian Becker warned that World War III had already begun and that 'most of us in the West, our governments, our press and news analysts remain blind to the nature of the aggression ...

while it threatens to destroy our world piecemeal'.[18] In 1980 Richard Nixon entered the fray, arguing in *The Real War* that 'An international fraternity of terrorists, with the Soviet Union as the chairman of the Rush Committee, has enabled the Russians to engage ... in "warfare by remote control" all over the world.'[19] The disgraced ex-president issued a stirring call to the free world to defend itself, in a narrative that drew heavily on Robert Moss, Brian Crozier and Ray Cline. Nixon also referred to the most notorious 'international terrorist' of the era, who more than any single individual had come to embody the Soviet terrorist hydra.

The man known as Carlos

From the mid-1970s onwards, the Venezuelan Illich Ramírez Sánchez, more commonly known as Carlos or Carlos the Jackal after the Frederick Forsyth thriller *The Day of the Jackal* that was supposedly found amongst his possessions in London, was the world's most wanted man. Like so much about Carlos, even this minor detail was a myth, since the novel in fact belonged to an Australian flatmate, but the apparent interplay between the real-life terrorist and Forsyth's professional assassin only added to Carlos's media appeal. One of the most widely reproduced photographs of him shows a chubby dark-haired Latin with tinted shades, his fleshy sensual lips stretched in a faintly ironic smirk. The face looks slightly unreal, like a police artist's impression or an Andy Warhol silkscreen.

The artificiality is appropriate in a man whose status as the iconic international terrorist of the media age owed as much to what was said and written about him as it did to his actual deeds. At the height of his notoriety, it was not even clear whether the man in the photograph was the only Carlos. For a time Israeli Intelligence agents speculated that there were at least four separate Carloses, all using the same name. Other intelligence services confused him with Antoine Bouvier, an Ecuadorian KGB agent believed to have recruited Carlos in Cuba. In the second half of the 1970s Carlos became a cipher, into which various terrorism experts wove their nebulous international 'linkages'. According to the standard biography which circulated in those years, Carlos was a Red assassin straight out of Ian Fleming: the son of a communist millionaire, recruited by the Venezuelan communist party at the age of 14 and sent to a training camp in Cuba, where he was spotted by a KGB liaison officer called Viktor Semenov and sent for further training in the dark arts of terrorism and guerrilla warfare in the Soviet Union.

This biography was almost entirely based on circumstantial evidence, speculation or outright fiction. One of the most influential proponents of the Carlos–KGB connection was the ubiquitous Brian Crozier, who wrote various articles about Carlos that were subsequently quoted by other mainstream sources, including *Time* and *Newsweek*. Crozier was also a source for Dobson and Payne's classic terrorological account *The Carlos Complex* (1977), which portrayed a murderous communist anti-hero who, 'by means of the bomb and the machine-pistol … captured the public imagination. People may be horrified by him, but they are also enthralled by his exploits. His eagerness to kill, his contempt for the normal rules of civilised behaviour, his sexuality, are all a part of his spell.'[20]

Dobson and Payne do not address the extent to which this 'spell' was artificially created by terrorologists like themselves. It is difficult, if not impossible, to locate the 'real' Carlos in a man who became the object of so many fantasies and stories, and who to some extent collaborated in the construction of his own mythology. Ilich Ramírez Sánchez was born in Venezuela, the son of a Marxist lawyer, in 1949. Though he become peripherally involved in student politics in Caracas he did not go to Cuba, but to London with his family. In the years 1966–68, when he was supposedly receiving his terrorist training in Cuba, he was studying for his A levels at a tutorial college. Though he was sent by his father to study at Patrice Lumumba university in Moscow, there is no evidence that he went on to study 'killer karate' and other terrorist black arts. On the contrary he was expelled from the university in 1969 for indiscipline and a predilection for womanising and drunken partying which did not endear him to the university administrators.

Despite his hedonistic inclinations, Ilich inherited his father's leftist political affiliations and in 1969 he volunteered to join the PFLP in Beirut, where he was sent for military training in one of the PFLP's Jordanian training camps by Bassam Abu-Sharif, who gave him the nom de guerre Carlos. Though Carlos took part in the fighting between the PLO and King Hussein's troops and subsequently joined Wadi Haddad's organisation in Europe, he proved himself to be a surprisingly amateurish assassin. In 1973 he attempted to kill Joseph Edward Sieff, the head of Marks and Spencer and a well-known Zionist supporter. Carlos gained entry to Sieff's home in London and shot him in the face, but the bullet was deflected by his victim's teeth and failed to kill him. In 1974 a Japanese Red Army cell took hostages at the French embassy in The Hague in an attempt to gain the release of one of their comrades arrested in France. Carlos supported the operation by coolly tossing a fragmentation grenade into a Parisian shopping complex called Le Drugstore, killing two people and seriously injuring more than two dozen, including a child whose hands were blown off.

The operation succeeded, though Carlos's savage contribution was not revealed. Carlos was also involved in a failed attempt to shoot down an El Al plane with a bazooka that same year, but he did not emerge as a media terrorist icon until June 1975, when he shot dead two unarmed French policemen at his Paris flat in the rue Toullier, together with a member of his own organisation who had led them there. Though the destruction of his Paris-based cell did not please Wadi Haddad, it nevertheless turned Carlos into a media phenomenon, who was henceforth referred to as 'the famous Carlos' or 'the famous terrorist Carlos'. Carlos even introduced himself as 'the famous Carlos' when he led a German–Palestinian team in an assault on the OPEC oil ministers' conference in Vienna in December that year, killing two guards and a Libyan diplomat. The ensuing hostage crisis confirmed Carlos's celebrity status, as the Venezuelan held some of the most powerful representatives of the capitalist world hostage and conducted negotiations with the Austrian authorities with arrogant sangfroid.

In the wake of the Vienna operation, Carlos became an ubiquitous media presence. In the summer of 1976 he seemed to be everywhere at once. In May he was reported to have blown himself up in Tel Aviv. In June the Royal Canadian Mounted Police issued a nationwide alert amid reports that he was in Canada to disrupt the Montreal Olympics. That same month Italian newspaper reports linked him to the Red Brigades killing of the Italian attorney-general, Francesco Coco. In September he was reported by Egyptian intelligence and Crozier to be still alive and in possession of 'a small nuclear bomb'.

All this was fantasy. Following the OPEC raid, Carlos fell out with Haddad and formed his own organisation, called 'The Organisation of Arab Armed Struggle', which carried out various operations on behalf of the various regimes and intelligence services that gave him temporary protection. These operations are inevitably obscure, but the evidence compiled by the investigative writer David Yallop suggests that he functioned as a hitman and mercenary rather than a revolutionary.[21]

The East German espionage chief Markus Wolf later admitted that Carlos was given a temporary base in East Germany. But Wolf's intelligence reports described the Jackal as 'a loudmouth, a spoiled bourgeois-turned-terrorist who disregarded all the basic rules of discretion, thereby endangering those who worked with him'.[22] Other opinions of Carlos are equally unflattering. The only Palestinian member of the OPEC kidnap team later described him as 'bourgeois. A revolutionary only with his mouth, never with his heart' with a fondness for 'big cars and Hiltons'. Hans-Joachim Klein, who took part in the same operation, described Carlos as a 'very anal kind of guy, a cleanliness nut', whose favourite reading was *Playboy*, who once declared, 'in order to get anywhere you have to step over a lot of dead bodies'.[23] In the course of his career, Carlos stepped over many corpses, but where he was trying to get to was not always clear. In 1994 his career came to an end, when French intelligence agents tracked him to his latest refuge in Sudan, where he was betrayed by his Sudanese protectors and handed over to the French authorities. In 1997 the Jackal went on trial for the rue Toullier murders and another bombing in Paris. Though he insisted that he had fought 'for humanity, for the people of Palestine, for the people of France', he was sentenced to life imprisonment. Since then the former face of international terrorism has lived a more obscure existence as Detainee 8726861X in La Sante prison, where he has issued statements calling on revolutionaries across the world to accept the 'leadership' of Osama bin Laden.

Terrorism as entertainment

In Don de Lillo's novel *Mao II* (1991), the reclusive writer Bill Gray tells a photographer: 'Years ago I used to think it was possible for a novelist to alter the inner life of the culture. Now bomb-makers and gunmen have taken over that territory. They make raids on human consciousness.' In the stable democracies of the industrialised world, the terrorist events of the 1970s provided a constant procession of ready-made dramas and telegenic spectacles that were constantly newsworthy. Terrorologists might accuse the media of complicity in terrorism, but bombings, kidnappings, embassy sieges and aeroplane hijackings were dramatic events that could not be ignored. They were intended to command attention and they usually succeeded. If the protagonists of these events were objects of fear and loathing, they were also interesting. The media image of Carlos as a terrorist James Bond, combining his murderous activities with a playboy lifestyle in a variety of exotic locations, reflected a wider cultural fascination that was intrinsic to the terrorist decades, in which media representations of terrorism were frequently drawn from fiction and at the same time generated new fictional narratives of their own.

Carlos himself featured in various films and novels, from Robert Ludlum's *The Bourne Identity* (1980) to the Sylvester Stallone vehicle *Nighthawks* (1981), in which he was an obvious inspiration for the amoral Euroterrorist 'Wulfgar', played by Rutger Hauer, who leaves a trail of mayhem across New York. In the Hollywood thriller *The Assignment* (1997), made after his arrest, the image of the bedroom athlete and ruthless superkiller, able to shoot his way out of any situation, remained intact. The terrorist decades continued to produce a stream of thrillers, featuring terrorists and terrorism plots, which had reached such heights by 1980 that *Time* magazine wrote an article entitled 'Terrorists take over thrillers'. The plots and characters in many of these novels were often snatched from newspaper headlines or based on actual events. In some cases they were situated in contemporary locations, such as Northern Ireland or the Middle East, and the fact that they were sometimes written by journalists and foreign correspondents gave them a behind-the-scenes authenticity which enhanced their fascination.

Other terrorism novels were extrapolations on the more catastrophic scenarios of terrorism experts. In Richard Graves's *Cobalt 60* (1975), a Middle Eastern terrorist emir tries to infiltrate radioactive material into the White House. In *Hazard* (1973) by Gerald Browne, terrorists attempt to unleash bacteriological warfare against Israel using sound-waves. In *Frogs at the Bottom of the Well* (Ken Edgar, 1979), a group of revolutionary feminists threaten to explode an atom bomb. In Thomas Harris's *Black Sunday* (1977), later made into a film, Palestinian terrorists attempt to murder 80,000 spectators at a US Super Bowl football game.

In general, popular terrorist fiction was concerned not so much with the fictional exploration of violent conflict as it was with the spectacle of violence-as-entertainment. Both novels and films provided an imaginative space where the reader could safely contemplate the evil and insanity of terrorism knowing that it would be defeated and its protagonists destroyed. Many were outlets for recreational violence and fantasies of extermination, in which melodramatic villains and eminently killable terrorist psychopaths receive their just deserts at the hands of tough-guy heroes like Tom Clancy's Jack Ryan, or Hank Frost, the one-eyed mercenary hero of Axel Kilgore's *They Call Me Mercenary* series.

One of the best-selling novels of the terrorist decades was a thriller by 'Trevanian', *Shibumi* (1980), whose hero is Nicholai Hel, a freelance counter-terrorist assassin. Hel is no ordinary mercenary. Half German, half Russian, brought up by a Japanese general, he is a mystic, a martial-arts expert and a mathematical genius who speaks six languages and practises advanced Zen lovemaking techniques with his Japanese mistress. Between missions Hel lives in an eighteenth-century château in the Basque country, where he perfects his esoteric sex-life, meditates and indulges his favourite pastime of potholing. Hel is not enamoured with the modern world. He loathes Liberation Theology priests and revolutionaries of all kinds. But most of all he despises terrorists, from the 'thrill-seeking middle-class muffins tickling themselves with the thrill of terror and revolution' to the inept and brutal Palestinian 'goat-herds' whom he exterminates on behalf of various governments.

Variants on the counter-terrorist exterminator featured regularly in novels and films about terrorism, and reflected a cultural fascination with special forces that was also part of the terrorist decades. The soldier-of-fortune glamorisation of 'secret armies' and 'elite forces' became a nonfictional subgenre in itself, from the mercenary 'Gayle Rivers', the pseudonymous author of *The Specialist: the Personal Story of an Elite Specialist in Covert Operations* (1985) to Tom Clancy's *Shadow Warriors*. Other novels aspired to pseudo-authenticity, extrapolating the fictions already generated by governments and terrorologists, such as *The Fifth Horseman* (1981) by the best-selling 'reconstruction' journalists Larry Collins and Dominique La Pierre, which featured a host of characters from contemporary terrorist demonology, from Colonel Qaddafi to the KGB, in a malignant plot to explode an atomic bomb in the United States. Robert Moss also made a more overt foray into terrorism fiction, in collaboration with Arnaud de Borchgrave, the editor of the *Washington Times*, owned by the far-right Korean cult leader Sun Myung Moon, with the publication of *The Spike* (1980). Billed by its publishers as a story 'so explosive it can only be told as fiction', this absurd novel describes a plot by the KGB to manipulate the US liberal media and political establishment by feeding supposedly fraudulent stories concerning CIA assassinations and American massacres in Vietnam to credulous journalists.

The novel also includes a sinister international terrorist network, STAR, led by an utterly evil German 'playboy-guerrilla' named Sigismund von Klopp, who orders his organisation to carry out a frontal lobotomy on a kidnapped industrialist and seduces a radical American movie star before chaining her up in a basement, where she is fed on gruel, raped and injected with heroin in order to turn her into a terrorist zombie called 'Ulrike'.

The fact that such crudely manipulative Cold War propaganda could be praised by one reviewer for its 'aura of authenticity' is itself a tribute to the pervasive influence of terrorology. John le Carré attempted a more highbrow rendition of terrorism in his overwrought exploration of the Israeli-Palestinian conflict, *The Little Drummer Girl*, in which Mossad recruits a British stage actress to join 'the theatre of the real' and act as bait to catch a Palestinian terrorist. Despite its air of literary gravitas, le Carré's portentous journey into the dark heart of Palestinian terrorism fails to transcend its clichés or the inconsistencies in its central character, but it was high art by comparison with the portrayals of terrorism that began to feature in television and cinema in the terrorist decades. On both large and small screens the terrorist was typically an agent of irrational mayhem and gratuitous cruelty, often with a hint of sadism and sexual deviancy, such as the psychopathic Irish terrorist played by Sean Bean in the film version of Tom Clancy's *Patriot Games*.

The same terrorist 'character' appeared in dozens of Hollywood action films during the terrorist decades, with only accent and nationality differentiating them from Sigismund von Klopp. A few films did attempt to portray terrorism as an activity conducted by human beings, particularly in Italy, where directors such as Gillo Pontecorvo and Giuseppe Ferrara addressed the subject with real intelligence and sensitivity. But such films were aimed at minority audiences and were almost non-existent within mainstream cinema, where a procession of murderous assassins steadily advanced through the terrorist decades, fit only for the violent retribution they inevitably received.

Claire Sterling's terror networks

If terrorist fiction borrowed from real events, supposedly factual accounts of terrorism often drew heavily on fictional stereotypes and clichés. The biggest selling non-fiction book on 1970s terrorism was *The Terror Network: the Secret War of International Terrorism* by Claire Sterling, an American journalist based in Italy. With its smug moralising and breathless *Reader's Digest*-style accounts of the bloody terrorist events of the decade, *The Terror Network* was intended to entertain as well as alarm the reader. Its thrilleresque rendition of what Sterling called 'Fright Decade Number 1' depicted a vast international terrorist conspiracy involving the PLO, the IRA, the Red Brigades, ETA, the Japanese Red Army and the Weathermen, all of whom, according to Sterling, 'had … come to see themselves as elite battalions in a worldwide Army of Communist Combat' that could ultimately be traced back to the Soviet Union.

Though Sterling assures the reader in the introduction that her book 'deals with facts, not fiction', much of her information originated from European and other intelligence sources, and from terrorologists such as Crozier, Moss, and the Dobson–Payne tandem, all of which she accepts without question. In one characteristic episode she refers to the discovery of the 'Tucumán Plan', documents recovered in a police raid on an ERP safehouse in Argentina in the winter of 1976, which supposedly proved the existence of a 'Latin American Europe Brigade' consisting of '1,500 qualified Latin American terrorists' intent on wreaking havoc in Europe, with the backing of Cuba and the KGB. The fact that these documents were discovered by the police force in a military dictatorship might give many objective researchers pause to doubt their authenticity, but not Sterling, who received the story via the *Economist Foreign Report*, itself written by Brian Crozier and Robert Moss.

This was what Irish historian Conor Cruise O'Brien called the 'echo chamber effect' that often characterised terrological circles, in which unproven assertions and outright lies achieved the status of unchallenged facts through the incestuous exchange of sources and continual repetition. The acts of violence that Sterling described were not invented, but the 'fictional' qualities of *The Terror Network* lie not so much in the facts themselves, but in the way Sterling assembled them to support her apocalyptic vision of a world under siege from 'bands of professional practitioners dispensing violent death' who could be counted in their 'tens of thousands', all of them trained in Cuba, North Korea, the Soviet Union or Eastern Europe.

According to Sterling, these invisible armies were 'Methodically trained, massively armed, immensely rich, and assured powerful patronage, they move with remarkable confidence across national frontiers, from floodlit state to stage, able at a word to command the planet's riveted attention.'[24] Sterling does not even begin to prove these assertions and seems oblivious of the disparity between this awesome fighting force and its actual achievements. If this international terrorist army had been as well armed and well trained as she maintains, then British helicopters would have been shot down in Northern Ireland on a daily basis and half of Europe and the United States would have been in flames. Though Sterling presents herself as a fearless investigator, delving into the dark terrorist labyrinth that even cowed intelligence services refuse to recognise, her portrait of a unified 'terror network' is essentially a terrorological fantasy dressed up as reportage. The book's 'fictional' qualities were nevertheless part of its appeal. As one enthusiastic reviewer put it, 'Avid readers of the spy novels, such as those written by Robert Ludlum and John le Carré, should find this informational book both terrifying and fascinating.'

The Terror Network was similarly described by *Business Week* as 'important, disturbing' and 'studded with a gruesomely fascinating cast of characters'. This was exactly what Sterling's terrorists were – 'characters' in a horror-comic version of the official 'terrorism' narrative that was beginning to emerge from the first terrorist decade. For all its methodological flaws *The Terror Network* became a huge international success and Sterling found herself transformed into one of the foremost 'terrorism experts' of the era.

International terrorism – other networks

If Sterling's depiction of a democratic Western world besieged by a vast army of international terrorist was a grotesque exaggeration, it also ignored the fact that the kind of violence she describes was not exclusively directed at the Western democracies and their allies. Between 1973 and 1976 Cuba, one of the countries identified by Sterling and other terrorologists as one of the main sponsors of terrorism, listed seventy-three attacks on its installations and personnel by US-based exile groups. A number of these attacks were carried out by the Cuban paediatrician Orlando Bosch, a violent anti-Castro activist and a veteran of CIA covert operations against Cuba. In October 1976 Bosch and another anti-Castro veteran named Luis Posada Carriles were arrested in Venezuela for their involvement in the bombing of Cubana Airlines Flight 455, which was blown out of the sky en route from Venezuela to Havana, killing fifty-seven Cubans, including the Cuban gold medal-winning fencing team, and sixteen foreign nationals. Bosch and Posada were eventually released on a technicality, and continued to direct or carry out attacks on Cuban targets for many years afterwards.[25]

Some of these operations were carried out on behalf of Latin American military regimes in the context of Operation Condor, an international network founded by the Chilean intelligence agency DINA in 1975, in order to co-ordinate the inter-governmental war on left-wing 'subversion' across the continent. Over the next three years an estimated 13,000 people were killed, 'disappeared' or tortured as a result of the Condor system in Europe, the United States and Latin America. Although Operation Condor was supposedly a secret 'counter-terrorist' operation directed against Latin American revolutionary groups, it was essentially an instrument of international state terror which allowed security forces in one country to kill and torture foreign citizens and political refugees on their own soil as part of a reciprocal arrangement.

One of the most prominent assassinations carried out by the Condor network was the killing of a former Chilean chargé d'affaires, Orlando Letelier, and an American colleague, Ronni Moffitt, whose car was blown up in Washington on 21 September 1976. There was some irony in the fact that the most significant act of 'international terrorism' carried out in the United States during 'Fright Decade Number 1' was carried out by an American-born assassin on the orders of Chile, a key US ally, with the help of Cubans trained by the CIA to carry out terrorist operations against the Castro regime in Cuba. The irony is missed by Sterling, however, who does not mention the incident at all.

Operation Condor was only one of various anti-communist operations spawned by the Cold War, which regarded clandestine counter-revolutionary violence as a legitimate instrument of 'World War III', such as the Aginter Press, a fake news agency formed by former French veterans of the Algerian war in Portugal, whose activities, according to Portuguese intelligence sources, included 'the recruitment and training of mercenaries and terrorists specialising in sabotage and assassination' of leftists in Europe and Latin America.[26] According to the Swiss researcher Daniele Ganser, the Aginter Press was also linked to the European 'stay behind' Gladio networks created by NATO, whose components would later be implicated in bombings and other acts of violence in various countries.[27]

One of the most influential members of this far-right nexus was the ubiquitous Italian conspirator Liceo Gelli, the founder of the Masonic Propaganda Due organisation and a key figure in the various covert operations against the Italian Communist Party. In addition to his activities on behalf of the Gladio network inside Italy, Gelli enjoyed a close relationship with various Latin American dictatorships and military regimes, particularly in Argentina, where he helped fund the Triple A death squads. Gelli also collaborated closely with the Italian fascist Stefano delle Chaie, whose name was linked to some of the worst fascist atrocities of the 'strategy of tension' in Italy, including the Bologna bombing. From the mid-1970s onwards delle Chaie acted as a freelance torturer and assassin within the Condor network, and eventually based himself in Bolivia, where he worked alongside the former Nazi torturer Klaus Barbie, assassinating and torturing leftists and trade unionists on behalf of the country's military rulers.

All these 'networks' were part of 'Fright Decade Number 1'. Yet none of them are mentioned in Sterling's 'terrorism' narrative. Nor did they feature in the Jonathan Institute's 'International Conference on International Terrorism' held in Jerusalem in 1979, in which Sterling participated, together with an array of Israeli ex-army and intelligence officers and international terrorologists. The conference was partly sponsored by the Israeli government and took place against the background of the American hostage crisis in Teheran and the final stages of the Sandinista revolution in Nicaragua, in which another US satrap was being overthrown. In this context the collective presentation of 'terrorism' that emerged at the conference was essentially Sterlingesque. Various speakers depicted these events as part of the same sinister international conspiracy and argued that the West should adopt the Israeli policy of aggressive military retaliation in order to deal with 'the terrorists' and their sponsors. And in 1981 a new administration came to power in the United States that made this principle the cornerstone of its foreign policy and launched the first international counter-terrorist offensive of the terrorist decades.

The First War on Terror

Let terrorists beware that when the rules of international behaviour are violated, our policy will be one of swift and effective retribution.

Ronald Reagan, 1981

We are warriors!
Warriors all!
We are going forth to kill
A mountain of terrorists!
'Somos Guerreros', marching song of the Salvadoran Atlacatl Batallion

From the moment Ronald Reagan took office in January 1981, it was clear that the terrorologists had at last found an American president who shared their concerns. At his first press conference, Reagan's pugnacious secretary of state, Alexander Haig, accused the Soviet Union directly of 'the training, funding and equipping of international terrorists', an accusation that surprised his own department. When a State Department official protested afterwards that these assertions were not borne out by intelligence assessments, Haig brandished galley proofs of *The Terror Network* as evidence. State Department researchers then carried out their own analysis of this previously unknown book and produced a report refuting Sterling's allegations, only to be told by Haig that the authors of the report had been 'brainwashed'.

The new CIA director, William Casey, shared Haig's fervent admiration for Sterling's book and ordered the Agency's analysts to find out whether a little-known foreign correspondent had indeed discovered compelling new evidence that his own intelligence experts had overlooked. Once again the Agency's initial reports concluded that there was no hard evidence to support Soviet involvement in international terrorism. The CIA's analysts also found that a number of Sterling's facts originated in fabricated propaganda stories originally planted in the European press by the CIA itself, which had been treated by Sterling as real events, a process known in intelligence circles as 'blowback'.

Further intelligence evaluations were made of the terror network thesis, both for and against, before a final report took an intermediate position, claiming that although the Soviet Union supported national liberation movements, there was no evidence that it was co-ordinating global terrorism, and that on various occasions the Soviets had actually warned American officials of impending terrorist attacks.[1] These findings were never made public, nor were Haig's allegations ever retracted. Sterling's terror fantasies had found an influential audience at an opportune historical moment. Before taking office, a document prepared for the Reagan transition team by a right-wing think tank, the Heritage Foundation, recommended continual presidential emphasis on 'the escalation of Soviet bloc intelligence activities, the nature of the terrorist threat and its international dimensions and the reality of subversion'.[2] The new administration followed this advice to the letter, constantly blurring the distinction between 'terrorism' and left-wing revolutionary violence and presenting both as evidence of an aggressive conspiracy by the Soviet 'Evil Empire' stretching from Nicaragua and the Middle East to the tiny island of Grenada, which was described by Reagan as 'a Soviet–Cuban colony being readied as a major military bastion to export terror and undermine democracy' in order to justify the US invasion of the island in 1983. There was little evidence that the few hundred Cuban construction workers helping to build a new airport in Grenada had either the intention or the capability to realise any such objectives. But the effectiveness of propaganda, as Goebbels once observed, is rarely dependent on its relationship to the truth and by this time the fantasy of the Terrorist International had become so prevalent that Reagan's assertions went largely unchallenged.

At war with the hydra

The main object of US wrath in the Reagan era was Libya, whose mercurial leader Colonel Muammar Qaddafi was deemed to be a primary sponsor of international terrorism. It was never entirely clear why a small Arab country with a population of less than 5 million was elevated to the status of a major security threat to the United States. Sterling and other terrorologists had identified Libya as a key Soviet proxy, funnelling weapons and cash to terrorist groups around the world. There were certainly links between Libya and some Palestinian groups, and also with the IRA, but such links did not 'prove' Soviet knowledge or involvement. Nor was Libyan foreign policy consistent or coherent. For all Qaddafi's Arab nationalist rhetoric, Libya occupied a relatively isolated position within the Arab world, and his support for the Palestinians was generally opportunistic and self-serving. Nevertheless, the Libyan leader's anti-Western diatribes made him a convenient hate figure in the US media, where he was routinely portrayed as a strutting megalomaniac dictator and a 'mad dog' who needed to be muzzled.

Libyophobia reached a peak in the winter of 1981, when the US government issued warnings that a team of Libyan-backed terrorists, including Carlos himself, had entered the United States to assassinate the president. Such was the level of paranoia that snipers were placed on the White House roof in November, and the building was ringed with ground-to-air missiles, while decoy presidential motorcades were driven round Washington to draw the fire of the would-be killers. But despite Reagan's assertion that 'we have the evidence and Qaddafi knows it', no such evidence was produced, nor were any assassination attempts made as the Libyan hit squad vanished into the propaganda ether.

Over the next few years, the war of words moved closer to a more direct military confrontation, as the US navy carried out provocative exercises in the disputed Gulf of Sidra, resulting in a series of skirmishes with Libyan fighter planes. In December 1985 the United States blamed Libya for the vicious Abu Nidal atrocities at Rome and Vienna air terminals, in which eighteen people were shot dead. The confrontation reached a peak in April 1986, when US fighter planes bombed Tripoli and Benghazi in retaliation for a bomb attack on La Belle discotheque in Berlin, in which one US soldier and a Turk were killed. Qaddafi survived the attacks, but some thirty-seven civilians were killed, including the Libyan leader's fifteen-month-old adopted daughter.

This was a classic 'retaliatory' attack on the Israeli model. The next day Reagan announced that the United States had won 'but a single engagement in the war against terrorism' and informed the American public that, 'We will not end that struggle until the free and decent people of this planet unite to eradicate the scourge of terror from the modern world.' Though the US media exulted in Reagan's display of toughness and resolution, the bombings prompted widespread protests abroad. Afterwards supporters of the administration insisted that the bombings had deterred Libya from carrying out further attacks, but the evidence suggests that the air strikes may well have provoked Qaddafi to seek his own retaliation through more circuitous routes, using the Japanese Red Army and Abu Nidal as surrogates to carry out attacks that could not be directly traced back to Libya.

Certainly the Rand–St Andrews Chronology of International Terrorism recorded fifteen Libyan-sponsored acts of terrorism in 1987, including the bombing of a US military club in Naples by the Japanese Red Army in which five soldiers were killed. For all Reagan's insistence that there could be 'no appeasement of evil ... no sanctuary for terror', the United States increasingly resembled a lumbering beast, lashing out at irritating terrorist insects that it could neither see nor identify.

Disaster in Beirut

The limitations of the first War on Terror were even more glaringly revealed in Lebanon, where American troops arrived in 1983 as part of a multinational peacekeeping force, following the Israeli withdrawal from Beirut. The Reagan administration's support for the pro-Israeli Maronite Christian administration soon aroused the hostility of the radicalised Shia Muslim population, who saw the multinational forces as an instrument of Israeli foreign policy sent to uphold a despised sectarian government. Sniper attacks on US troops were followed by the bombing of the American embassy in Beirut in April 1983, and in October that year a suicide bomber drove a truck into the US marine barracks at Beirut airport, killing 241 soldiers in one of the most devastating single attacks ever carried out on the US army.

In February 1984 the peacekeeping forces withdrew from Lebanon, after a nine-hour bombardment of Shia mountain villages by the US battleship *New Jersey*. In a display of military power as futile as it was destructive, the *New Jersey* disgorged 40 per cent of all the 16-inch ammunition in the entire European theatre at an enemy it could not even see. How many people died in the bombardment is not known. But US revenge was not complete. In March 1985 a massive car bomb exploded in a Beirut street, which killed eighty people and wounded 246, including forty women and girls emerging from Friday prayers at a nearby mosque. The bombing had been aimed at Sheikh Fadlallah, the Shia cleric believed to be responsible for sanctioning attacks on US forces, who nevertheless survived. According to the *Washington Post* journalist Bob Woodward, the bombing was carried out by a team led by an English ex-SAS member recruited through the Saudi Arabian intelligence services on behalf of the CIA.

The collusion of the United States in a car bomb attack was not the finest advertisement for liberal democracy in the fight against terrorist barbarity. Nor was there any evidence that it had any deterrent effect. On the contrary, on 14 June that year, two Shia hijackers diverted an American TWA 847 en route from Athens to Rome and subjected the 153 passengers and crew to a terrifying seventeen-day ordeal, as the plane was flown back and forth between Algiers and Beirut. The hijackers' main demand was the release of Shia prisoners rounded up by the Israeli army in south Lebanon and taken to an Israeli prison, but they also called on the US government to take responsibility for the car bomb in Beirut. One of the hijackers had come from a village destroyed in the *New Jersey* bombardment, in which his wife and child had been killed, and shouted 'New Jersey! New Jersey!' at his bewildered and terrified captives.

Both men vented their anger on the helpless passengers, savagely beating a US Navy Seal diver named Robert Stethem, who was on the plane by chance. In the TWA's second and final touchdown at Beirut airport, Stethem was shot dead and pushed out of the plane when the authorities refused to allow the hijackers to speak to Nabih Berri, leader of Amal, the Shia militia. The authorities gave way and the negotiations were henceforth handled by the Amal leader and his team, who staged press conferences with hostages and allowed the crew to be interviewed by an international army of press reporters and television crews. The unfolding crisis dominated the major US television networks, drawing stern criticisms from a number of terrorologists and US politicians, who accused the media of playing into the hands of the terrorists.

What was it about the coverage of the TWA crisis that so offended these critics, to the point where one columnist described the coverage as 'terrorvision'? Some commentators were irritated by the focus on 'human interest' stories connected with the hostages and their relatives, which reinforced expectations of a negotiated solution to the crisis. Others accused the media of indirectly serving a terrorist agenda by broadcasting interviews with the hostages, some of whom compared their own situation to that of Lebanese Shia prisoners illegally held in Israel as 'terrorist suspects'. In doing so the media was breaching the 'closed' official presentation of terrorism that normally surrounds such events and strips them of any rational context. Thus the official consensus rejected any comparisons between the taking of hostages by terrorists and the forced removal of Shia villagers from south Lebanon to Israeli prisons. Instead, the hijackers were presented as the products of religious fanaticism and 'hatred', whose sole desire, according to Reagan, was to 'expel America from the world'. But even though the US government insisted that such an enemy could not be placated or negotiated with, the crisis was finally resolved with the assistance of the Syrian president Hafez al-Assad, and the hostages were released in return for the release of most of the Shia prisoners in Israel. On the day the last US hostages were released, Reagan appeared on television to assure the American public that 'The United States gives terrorists no reward and no guarantees. We make no concessions. We make no deals.'

But the message already sounded hollow. If the Beirut bombings revealed the limitations of blunt military force as an instrument of counter-terrorism, the TWA crisis demonstrated that there were occasions when even the most 'evil' and 'fanatical' terrorists could be negotiated with, without bringing about the expulsion of America from the earth. Subsequent events would make the disparity between the administration's public rhetoric and its actual practice even more glaringly apparent.

The Iran-Contra scandal

Nowhere was this gulf more striking than in the administration's relationship with Iran. Publicly the US government regarded Iran as one of the primary 'sponsors' of terrorism in the world and the epitome of Islamic fundamentalist fanaticism. Not only was Iran responsible for the American embassy hostage crisis, but the Khomeini regime was also accused of responsibility for a number of terrorist incidents in the Middle East, particularly in Lebanon, where Iranian agents were believed to have been complicit in attacks on Israeli and multinational forces in Beirut and the kidnappings of Western civilians.[3] Such a regime, the Reagan administration insisted, was worthy only of international quarantine. Yet even as the administration publicly denounced Iran as a terrorist-sponsoring state, US officials were secretly selling missiles and other military equipment to the Iranians, who were then embroiled in a bloody war with Iraq – whose regime the United States was also supporting. When the Iranian arms deals first became public in 1986, the administration attempted to portray them as a humanitarian gesture intended to facilitate the release of US hostages in Lebanon, by persuading Iran to exert pressure over its Lebanese protégés.

In fact, the weapons sales had begun before any Western hostages had even been taken and their profits formed part of an ingenious scheme cobbled together by a US Marine officer, Colonel Oliver North, together with a clique of officials in the Reagan administration itself, to raise money for the CIA-sponsored 'Contra war' against the Sandinistas in Nicaragua (see p. 235). A bewildered American public now found itself confronted with the startling revelation that elements within the Reagan administration had been secretly selling weapons to a regime that the US government had consistently denounced as one of the major sponsors of international terrorism.

Only the previous year a second conference of Benjamin Netanyahu's

Jonathan Institute had taken place in Washington, the proceedings of which were published in 1986 in Netanyahu's name under the title *Terrorism: How the West Can Win*. One participant was the American Secretary of State George Schultz, who condemned Libya, Syria, Iran and North Korea as 'full-fledged sponsors and supporters of indiscriminate, and not so indiscriminate murder', and insisted that 'the nations of the free world must stand together against terrorism to demonstrate our enduring commitment to our shared vision'.

That same year the congressional 'Irangate' hearings revealed just how enduring that commitment had been. Though the hearings concluded that Reagan himself had been unaware of the negotiations carried on by his own officials, the Majority Report of the Iran-Contra Committee accused the administration of undermining the international credibility of the United States, of conducting a secret foreign policy without informing Congress and of involving itself with 'an unknown number of shadowy intermediaries and financiers' across the world. Though the US media attempted to turn the proceedings into a soap opera with the disreputable anti-communist zealot North in the role of flawed patriotic hero, the disclosures fatally undermined the credibility of the administration's global anti-terrorist offensive. Not only had the United States acted in clear breach of its own principles regarding negotiations with terrorists and the states that 'harboured' them, but the arms sales may even have encouraged pro-Iranian elements in Lebanon to carry out more kidnappings in order to get hold of more weapons. As Schultz himself bitterly admitted:

> After years of work, the keystone of our counterterrorism policy was set: No deals with terrorists. Now we have fallen into the trap. We have voluntarily made ourselves the victims of the terrorist extortion racket. We have spawned a hostage-taking industry. Every principle that the president praised in Netanyahu's book on terrorism has been dealt a terrible blow by what has been done.[4]

Lockerbie

Though Schultz did not mention it, there was no evidence that the administration's policy of aggressive military retaliation had brought about any noticeable reduction in the kind of violence it was intended to prevent. On the contrary, the last decade of the Cold War was marked by a number of spectacularly vicious terrorist events. In September 1985 a group calling itself the Revolutionary Organisation of Socialist Muslims carried out a grenade attack on a Rome café, injuring forty people. In October that year a Palestinian group hijacked the cruise ship *Achille Lauro* and shot dead a wheelchair-bound Jewish pensioner, Leon Klinghoffer, who was thrown overboard. In April 1986 a Jordanian named Nezar Hindawi attempted to blow up an El Al plane departing from London by planting a bomb on his pregnant Irish girlfriend. On 5 September that year members of Abu Nidal's organisation hijacked a passenger plane in Karachi on its way from Bombay to New York and killed twenty passengers in a gunfight with security forces.

As always, such violence was not exclusively directed against Western targets. In 1986, the same year that the European Community agreed to impose sanctions on Syria for its involvement in terrorist acts abroad, a series of unclaimed bombs exploded on trains across Syria, killing 141 people. The single worst act of aircraft sabotage in history occurred on 23 June 1985, when militant Sikhs blew up an Air India 747 bound for London from Montreal over the Irish sea, killing all 329 passengers and crew in revenge for the storming of the Golden Temple by the Indian army in 1984.

On 3 July 1988 the USS *Vincennes* shot down an Iranian Airbus flying from Iran to Dubai, killing all 290 passengers and crew, while on patrol in the Persian Gulf. Though Reagan declared the incident 'a terrible human tragedy', the US government refused to apologise and the crew of the *Vincennes* were all awarded combat action medals, while the ship's air-warfare commander was given a commendation medal for 'heroic achievement'. On 21 December that same year a bomb exploded on Pan Am Flight 103 over the Scottish town of Lockerbie, killing all on board and several inhabitants of the town whose houses were hit by falling wreckage. In total, 270 people died.

The majority of the victims were Americans returning to the United States for Christmas, and initial investigations carried out by the CIA suggested that a Palestinian organisation called the PFLP – General Command had been recruited by Iran to carry out the bombing, in retaliation for the shooting down of its own airliner by the *Vincennes*. Other investigators claimed that Syria had been involved or even that the atrocity was the work of various governments and organisations acting together.

In 1991, to the surprise of many investigators and the families of the Flight 103 victims who had campaigned for an independent investigation into the Lockerbie bombing, the American and British governments accused Libya of sole responsibility for the bombing. Though the Libyan government consistently denied any involvement, Qaddafi eventually agreed to hand over two Libyan intelligence agents for trial in Scotland, after years of economic sanctions and diplomatic pressure. The crucial evidence of Libyan involvement was a tiny component of a circuit board used to activate the bomb, which the agents were believed to have planted in Malta. In January 2001 one of the two Libyans was found guilty and sentenced to life imprisonment. The trial failed to clarify why the bombing had been carried out or whether the agent found responsible had acted on the orders of his own government. One Scottish policeman later claimed that the incriminating evidence had been planted.[5]

The Lockerbie atrocity suggested a new and terrifying trend, in which anonymous actors could engage in the random mass murder of civilians for reasons which were not even explained. In 1989, following the execution of a kidnapped American Marine officer, William Higgins, in Lebanon, the Israeli ambassador to the United States once again called upon the civilised nations of the world to stand together in the 'confrontation between human concerns and the forces of darkness'. But in the explosion of international violence that marked the last decade of the Cold War, the moral parameters were never that straightforward.

How the West was won – the terrorism of the strong

To the Western public, incidents such as the murder aboard the *Achille Lauro* and the bombing of Pan Am 103 were emblematic crimes that confirmed the barbarity and horror of 'terrorist' violence. But as barbarous and horrific as these incidents undoubtedly were, they represented a tiny fraction of the civilians killed by governments in the last decade of the Cold War. Many of these casualties were inflicted in the course of counter-terrorist campaigns, by regimes that used the same rhetoric as the Reagan administration to justify their actions. In South Africa, the apartheid regime unleashed a devastating series of military assaults against the neighbouring 'Frontline' states accused of harbouring the ANC, whose impact was magnified by drought and famine, causing an estimated 1 million deaths and creating millions more refugees. The devastation was greatest in Mozambique, where the South African-backed Mozambique National Resistance (Renamo) waged a scorched-earth guerrilla campaign against the leftist Frelimo government with merciless ferocity.

Unlike most guerrilla organisations, Renamo made no attempt to win the support of the population and left a trail of murder and devastation across rural Mozambique whose atrocities shocked even Margaret Thatcher.[6] In April 1988 Roy Stacey, US Deputy Assistant of State for African Affairs, accused Renamo of perpetrating 'one of the most brutal holocausts against ordinary human beings since World War II'.[7] Though Renamo received no official support from the United States government, it nevertheless maintained an office at the headquarters of the Heritage Foundation in Washington, where the Reagan administration's favourite think tank lobbied energetically on its behalf. Jillian Becker's Institute for the Study of Terrorism was also supportive of Renamo, as was Brian Crozier, who wrote to Reagan to urge US support for the 'much maligned resistance fighters who, if helped, could yield a pro-Western, and certainly an anti-Communist, government in Maputo'.[8] From South Africa's point of view, Renamo terror was a means to an end, which forced the Frelimo government to choose between social and political collapse and their support for the ANC. These tactics eventually forced the government in Mozambique to sign the Nkomatai Agreement removing ANC bases from the country in 1984.

Even after Nkomatai Renamo continued its activities with ongoing South African support. In addition to its use of surrogates such as Renamo and Unita in Angola, South Africa also engaged in more conventionally 'terrorist' attacks on anti-apartheid activists and ANC members in Mozambique and other neighbouring countries, using letter bombs, car bombs and hit squads. These activities received no criticism from the Reagan administration, which selected South Africa for a policy of 'constructive engagement' throughout the decade. And while a 1988 Pentagon report described Nelson Mandela's African National Congress as one of the world's 'most notorious terrorist groups', Renamo was classified as an 'indigenous insurgent group'.[9]

In Israel the Likud government similarly presented its bloody invasion of Lebanon as a response to a PLO terrorist assault backed by the Soviet Union. The expulsion of the PLO from Beirut and Israel's subsequent occupation of South Lebanon brought the Israeli army into a confrontation with a new and more formidable enemy, in the shape of Hezbollah and the Shia resistance. A further local 'war on terror' then ensued, as the Israeli army tried to bludgeon the Shia guerrilla organisations into submission by punishing the 'terrorist villagers' who provided their base of support. Under its 'iron fist' policy in the mid-1980s, the Israeli Defence Forces bombed Shia villages with phosphorus and napalm, carried out mass arrests and summary executions, transported villagers to Israeli prisons as hostages and tortured suspects, turning schools and other buildings into makeshift interrogation centres. These activities attracted little media attention in the West, where they were regarded by most governments as a response to 'terrorism' and therefore legitimate.

The death toll caused by acts of official 'counter-terrorism' was even higher in Central America, where more than 200,000 people died as the US and its allies sought to roll back the tide of 'Cuban-backed subversion'. In

Guatemala one of the most brutal armies on the continent unleashed what the Human Rights Office of the Archdiocese of Guatemala later called 'a maniacal windstorm' of repressive violence, in which whole villages were massacred and thousands of civilians tortured and killed. In El Salvador security forces and death squads waged a war of extermination against the leftist FMLN and its real or imagined supporters. The worst abuses took place in the early 1980s, when hundreds of mutilated bodies were tossed on rubbish heaps or dumped by the roadsides each month.

One of the agents of this carnage was a dentist named Hector Regalado, known as 'Doctor Death', who once described to a US Drug Enforcement agent, Celerino Castillo III, how his paramilitary groups snatched their victims off the street in a van and tortured them on the spot by pulling their teeth out. According to Castillo,

> As the torture began, they wrote down every name their victim cried out. Regalado practised his impromptu dentristy on the unfortunate victims with a pair of pliers. I could see these doomed, bleeding men, screaming names with faint hope their pain would end if they fed their captors with enough future victims. The pain usually ended with a bullet or the edge of a blade.[10]

Regalado's ferocious reputation was well known to the US military advisors in El Salvador, who nevertheless recognised his usefulness. For Lawrence Bailey, a former US marine working as a mercenary in El Salvador, such violence represented 'a beautiful technique. By terrorising civilians, the army is crushing the rebellion without the need to directly confront the guerrillas'.[11] Neil Livingstone, a counter-terrorist advisor to the US National Security Council, similarly regarded the death squads as 'an extremely effective tool, however odious, in combating terrorism and revolutionary challenges'.[12] Though some US officials had qualms about such methods, the Reagan administration continued to provide political and military support to the Salvadoran security forces responsible and frequently attempted to conceal some of their worst abuses, such as the massacre carried out at El Mozote in 1981, when some 900 unarmed civilians, including women and infants, were slaughtered in the course of an anti-terrorist *limpieza* – a clean up of the area ordered by the US-trained Atlacatl Battalion.

Such actions were not the result of perverse Hispanic cruelty. In 1987, a unit of the Atlacatl Battalion murdered six Jesuits from the University of Central America, together with their housekeeper and her daughter. Of the twenty-six officers involved in organising the killings, nineteen were graduates of the US Army's School of the Americas (SOA), also known as the 'school of assassins', one of the main institutions through which US counter-insurgency doctrines were disseminated through Latin America. Between its establishment in Panama in 1946 and its relocation to Fort Benning, Georgia, in 1984, the SOA trained some 60,000 Latin American military officers, many of whom went on to play leading roles in the 'national security states' of the post-war era.

In 1996, declassified Spanish-language manuals revealed that techniques taught at the school included torture, murder, sabotage, and bribery of or extortion from internal dissidents. All these techniques were routinely employed by the military regimes that took control of much of Latin America and reflected a common approach to Third World counter-insurgency and 'low-intensity conflicts' by the United States and its allies during the Cold War. The use of such methods was entirely in keeping with the rationale defined by Sam Sarkesian, a US low-intensity warfare theorist, that 'low-intensity conflicts do not conform to democratic notions or tactics. Revolution and counterrevolution develop their own morality and ethics that justify any means to achieve success.'[13] Neither the methods nor the philosophy that supported them were unique to the United States, but few countries have so consistently disseminated the use of terror as an instrument of counter-insurgency while simultaneously engaging in a strident moralistic condemnation of 'terrorism'. And the disparity has rarely been more glaring than it was during the Reagan era.

Covert operations

In 1986 the Israeli terrorism analyst Uri Ra'anan and the Fletcher School of Law and Diplomacy published a collection of essays and documents entitled *Hydra of Carnage: International Linkages – the Witnesses Speak* (1986). A seminal work of eighties terrorology, with contributions from Claire Sterling, Michael Ledeen and other luminaries from the field, the anthology was essentially a propaganda platform for the war on terrorism dressed up as a scholarly investigation. One of these 'witnesses' was CIA director William Casey, who warned of a terrorist onslaught at 'the very heart of our civilisation' which aimed to 'undermine our values, to shatter our self-confidence, and to blunt our response'. Casey did not define terrorism as a concept, though he did explain helpfully that 'What the terrorist does is kill, maim, kidnap and torture'.[14]

At the time both the US government and its allies were involved in financing and training various organisations in different parts of the world that were routinely carrying out the acts that Casey described. In the CIA-sponsored Contra war against the Sandinista government in Nicaragua, Contra rebels carried out systematic attacks on health clinics, rural schools and rural co-operatives, whose 'dual-military purpose' made them legitimate military targets, according to one US State Department official. In 1985 a disillusioned Contra leader, Edgar Chamorro, told the World Court of 'routine' atrocities in Nicaragua: 'Many civilians were killed in cold blood. Many others were tortured, mutilated, raped, robbed, or otherwise abused.' According to Chamorro, these actions were carried out by the Contras with the full knowledge of their CIA trainers, who also provided recruits with large commando knives which were much sought after, since 'everybody wanted to have a knife like that, to kill people, to slit their throats.'[15]

The CBS news journalist Leslie Cockburn found graphic evidence of Contra atrocities in rural Nicaragua, including two sets of children, one of whom had lost a father and the other a mother. In both cases the victims had had their faces peeled off. Other journalists and human rights organisations recorded incidents in which peasants and local militiamen had their eyes gouged out, crosses carved into their bodies or their testicles cut off and women were raped and mutilated before being killed. One Contra victim was flayed alive and his skin stretched out on a rock. Often these tortures were enacted in front of the victims' families or other witnesses in order to magnify their impact. Like the atrocities carried out by Renamo, the surreal cruelty of the Contras was part of the deliberate psychological use of terror as an instrument of counter-revolution – a tactic whose broad outlines were described in CIA training manuals with sections covering 'Implicit and Explicit Terror' and 'Psychological Operations in Guerrilla Warfare'.

Though such tactics were accepted by the covert operations specialists and 'national security managers' who oversaw the secret wars of the Reagan era, they were unlikely to appeal to the American public. Democratic governments cannot use the language of Machiavelli to address their own populations, who generally prefer to believe that foreign policy is being conducted according to the universal moral principles that their leaders claim to embody. Fraudulent in principle, dishonest and incompetent in practice, the Reagan counter-terrorist crusade nevertheless marked a defining episode in the history of terrorism, in which the United States attempted for the first time to act as the world's policeman against the enemies of mankind. In its presentation of anti-terrorism as a war against evil and barbarism, the Reagan administration established a propaganda smokescreen in which the projection of US military force against an array of enemies could be justified as a moral crusade in defence of civilisation. The same moralistic rhetoric would later be invoked in a subsequent 'War on Terror' involving a combination of covert operations and conventional military power against a new set of enemies, who were already beginning to appear on the horizon even as the Cold War was coming to an end.

The Armies of God

History does not write its lines except with blood. Glory does not build its lofty edifice except with skulls. Honour and respect cannot be established except on a foundation of cripples and corpses ... Indeed, those who think they can change reality, or change societies, without blood sacrifices and wounds, without pure, innocent souls, do not understand the essence of our religion.

Abdullah Azzam, *Martyrs: the Building Block of Nations*, date unknown

When the Reagan administration began its anti-terrorist offensive, terrorism was primarily associated with secular nationalist or leftist organisations. By the end of the Cold War, however, the 'technique of terrorism' was being employed by a number of insurgent groups across the world claiming religious inspiration. In 1980 the US State Department included virtually no religious organisations in its annual list of international terrorist groups. Yet by 1995, the Rand–St Andrews chronology attributed 58 per cent of all international terrorist casualties that year to religiously motivated groups or organisations.[1] In some cases, such as the Sikh insurgency in the Punjab, or the armed Islamist groups in the Palestinian Occupied Territories, 'religious' violence was an offshoot or a continuation of already-existing nationalist conflicts. These movements reflected a broader spirit of religious revivalism at the end of the twentieth century, in which the goal of national independence had become inseparable from the defence of the faith itself.

Other groups pursued a more idiosyncratic theological agenda that was often steeped in apocalyptic prophecy, millenarian expectation and the fantasy of a violent purification of a defiled world. In the West Bank in the early 1980s, a group of Jewish settlers was discovered plotting to blow up the Temple Mount and the al-Aqsa mosque with the aim of starting World War III between Israel and the Islamic world. In doing so the settlers hoped to pave the way for the resurrection of the Jewish Third Temple in Jerusalem and the coming of the Messiah, as prophesied in the Old Testament and the writings of the medieval Jewish scholar Moses Maimonides. In the same period a proliferation of sects and churches in the United States connected to the racist Christian Identity movement fused neo-Nazi ideology with a yearning for the 'Endtimes' and the 'Tribulations' – an objective which drew some of them into violent conflict with the US authorities.

Whatever their different faiths and socio-political origins, these groups shared a common hostility to secularism and liberalism. As the defenders of the pure faith in an increasingly godless world they regarded violence as divinely sanctioned, or even as a sacred obligation. This unexpected combination of religion and revolutionary violence resulted in the elaboration of a new subcategory of terrorism, which some writers called 'holy terror' or 'sacred terror'. Where Cold War studies had once depicted terrorism as a modern phenomenon, derived from nineteenth-century anarchism and the Russian nihilists, terrorism writers now found pre-modern antecedents to contemporary religious terrorists, such as the Jewish Zealots in Roman-occupied Palestine and the Indian sect the Thugees.

The imprecision of 'sacred terror' made it theoretically capable of incorporating a wide range of violent movements and organisations, from the Holy Inquisition to the Gunpowder Plotters to the Ku Klux Klan. In general, however, the search for a tradition of sacred terror tended to focus on historical examples that fitted the contemporary understanding of what constituted terrorism. One of the most commonly cited examples of sacred terror was the heretical Ismaili sect known as the Assassins, which killed a number of Muslim dignitaries and Crusader knights in the twelfth century. According to the legends that percolated through Europe in the Middle Ages, the sect was created by a mysterious leader called Hassan-I-Sabbah, known as the Old Man of the Mountains, who supposedly prepared his men by giving them hashish and taking them to a lush garden filled with beautiful women. On awakening, the would-be killers were told they had been to paradise and they would enter it permanently after assassinating their victims, usually with a knife or dagger.

The exotic legend of the Assassins resurfaced following the Iranian revolution in 1979, when Ayatollah Khomeini was often depicted as a modern incarnation of Hassan-I-Sabbah, sending suicidal assassins in search of death and martyrdom. In the years that followed the image of the Old Man of the Mountains was often applied to any manifestation of 'Islamic' terrorism, from Colonel Qaddafi to Osama bin Laden. The fact that no contemporary organisation in the Middle East ever claimed the Assassins as an ideological or tactical inspiration did nothing to diminish their appeal to the Western imagination, with its suggestion of a cultural predisposition towards assassination, religious fanaticism and martyrdom that leapt across the centuries.

In this way the invented tradition of sacred terror provided a convenient explanation for the unfolding mayhem in the contemporary Middle East, which obscured its more recent political and historical causes within a much older narrative about Islam itself. And it was Islam, more than any other religion, that was seen in the West as the most threatening manifestation of sacred terror in the last years of the twentieth century.

The modern jihad

The concept of the Islamic terrorist first began to displace the 'Arab terrorist' in Western media portrayals of the Middle East in the late seventies and early eighties. If the standard image of the 'Arab' terrorist with glittering eyes, keffiyah and Kalashnikov epitomised native barbarism and cruelty, the depiction of 'Islamic' terrorism echoed an older conflict between Islam and Christendom, whose essential contours could be traced back to medieval perceptions of the 'Moors' and 'Saracens'. In these new narratives, bombs, kidnappings and hijackings were increasingly seen as the contemporary instruments of an aggressive Islamic holy war whose ultimate aim was global religious domination. It was in this period that the European and American press began to write of 'the return of Islam' and Muslim 'rage' or 'wrath'. To the Western imagination the convergence of terrorism and Islam was an alarming new development. The decisive event in these narratives was the Iranian revolution in 1979, which fuelled Western fears of a revolutionary Islamist movement spreading across the Gulf states, toppling the monarchies and sheikhdoms on whom the West's supply of oil depended. This new sense of vulnerability was reflected at the Jonathan Conference in Jerusalem that same year, where a number of participants identified Islamic fundamentalism as an emerging terrorist threat to the West that rivalled that of the Soviet Union.

The idea that terrorism represented the cutting edge of a looming fundamentalist threat was a misleading and inadequate explanation for Islamist violence in the Arab world. Not only did this presentation obscure the very real differences between Islamist organisations in different countries, but it failed to distinguish between religion as a *cause* of violence and the role of religion in justifying and mobilising popular support for revolutionary violence. Nor was 'fundamentalism' synonymous with political radicalism. In religious terms, the most 'fundamentalist' state in the Middle East was Saudi Arabia, a longtime strategic ally of the West and a vital component of the international capitalist economy. Though the ultra-conservative Wahhabi doctrines of the House of Saud indirectly influenced a number of violent Islamist organisations across the Middle East and beyond, Saudi 'religious imperialism' often complemented American foreign policy in the Middle East by promoting its purist version of Islam as an ideological counterweight to the influence of the left and the Soviet Union.

The roots of 'political Islam' or 'Islamism' could be traced back to the late nineteenth century, when a number of scholars and intellectuals in the Middle East had attributed the waning of Muslim power and the growing penetration of European colonialism to a general decline of religious faith. In the first half of the twentieth century, these arguments were mostly marginalised by the rise of secular Arab nationalism. It was not until the post-colonial era, when the dictators, military cliques and authoritarian regimes that dominated the Arab world proved themselves unable to fulfil the political and economic expectations of their populations, that political Islam began to emerge as a potentially revolutionary doctrine. It was against this background of political and military failure, of economic stagnation and cultural dislocation, that the Islamist critique of secular nationalism began to find a wider audience. And it was in the country that more than any other had come to symbolise the frustrated hopes of Arab nationalism that the Islamist combination of nostalgia and utopianism found one of its most influential spokesmen.

The trials of Sayyid Qutb

In the wake of the September 11 attacks, the Egyptian writer Sayyid Qutb has often been depicted in the West as the spiritual father of Islamic terrorism. Born in 1906, the son of a pious teacher in Upper Egypt, Qutb was a prolific author, churning out a stream of novels, short stories, political essays and literary criticism. As a young man he was briefly involved in nationalist agitation against British rule, but it was not until after World War II that his politics began to assume an Islamist hue. In 1948 he was sent by the Egyptian Ministry of Education to study the American education system. On the same voyage a tipsy American woman attempted to seduce him and the prudish Qutb later described his outrage and revulsion at these unwanted overtures. His puritanical sensibilities were further outraged during his two-year stay in the United States, where he was repelled by the brash materialism of American society, by its 'evil and fanatic racial discrimination' and the sexual promiscuity that he detected all around him.

In one episode, which he later recounted in his travel journals, Qutb was invited to a church social in Greeley, Colorado, where members of the congregation danced together in a hall adjoining the church. This juxtaposition of hedonism and religious devotion was offensive enough to the devout Qutb, but it was made even worse when the church pastor played a current hit, 'Baby, It's Cold Outside', and turned the lights down in order to create a suitably romantic atmosphere. Qutb watched aghast as 'The dancing intensified … The hall swarmed with legs … Arms circled arms, lips met lips, chests met chests, and the atmosphere was full of love.'[2]

The cultural incomprehension is total. The orgiastic atmosphere that Qutb imputed to a provincial church social was clearly a projection of his own repressed imagination, but if his unhappy visit to America confirmed his rejection of Western decadence, his revolutionary brand of Islam was forged above all in his own homeland. On returning to Egypt he joined the Muslim Brotherhood, perhaps the single most influential Islamist organisation in the Middle East. Though Qutb initially supported the nationalist military regime that brought Gamal Abdel Nasser to power in 1952, he became disillusioned with the regime's secular direction and in 1954 he was arrested along with hundreds of Muslim Brothers and sentenced to twenty-five years' hard labour.

It was during his time in prison that he wrote his most influential works. Qutb's brutal treatment at the hands of fellow Muslims helped forge his unforgiving analysis of contemporary Muslim society in his last book, *Milestones on the Road to Islam* (1965), an extended essay and political testament in which he savagely condemned the Muslim world for its abandonment of religion and spelt out his vision of a future Islamist society. In it, Qutb argued that the contemporary Muslim world was in *jahiliyya* – the pre-Islamic state of ignorance that had preceded the appearance of the Prophet, and that this situation could be reversed only by a political and religious transformation of society. The term that Qutb used to describe this process was 'jihad' – a word that has generally been associated in the Western world with the idea of aggressive religious war. Within Islam, however, jihad can refer either to the individual spiritual struggle known as 'greater jihad', or a war in defence of Muslims or Muslim territory known as 'little jihad'.

Not all wars in the Islamic world have been fought as jihads, since the jihad was theoretically fought against non-Muslims, but the understanding of the term has never been fixed or constant. In the thirteenth century the Islamic jurist Ibn Taymiyya challenged the notion that jihad could be fought only against non-Muslims and issued fatwas that allowed Arab Muslim leaders to declare a jihad against the 'apostate' Mongol rulers who had overrun much of the Muslim world, some of whom had converted to Islam. Ibn Taymiyya was reinventing the concept of jihad in response to the specific political needs of his own era. Qutb engaged in a similar process, arguing that jihad was justified against the contemporary apostate regimes who ruled the Muslim world.

Qutb's vision of jihad was not specific about the methods or tactics required, but his fierce indictment of the 'apostate' regimes always had revolutionary implications. The task that he envisaged for his generation was to clear away the obstacles, political and moral, that prevented the dawa, or call to Islam, from being heard. From this perspective a jihad against the secular 'apostate' regimes in the Arab world could be presented as a defence of Islam, and was therefore theologically justifiable. Once political sovereignty was returned to the Almighty, the Islamic nation would move seamlessly towards perfection and the social, economic and moral problems that afflicted his own era would find a solution. This process required an initial spiritual vanguard that would withdraw from *jahili* society and undergo exemplary torment and persecution in the name of the faith, as Qutb had done himself. This was the utopian goal that Qutb meditated upon during his years in Nasser's penal colonies. It was a project that left many practical questions unanswered, which Qutb himself did not live long enough to address. In 1964 he was released from prison only to be arrested and hanged two years later, indicted on trumped-up charges of a Muslim Brotherhood plot to assassinate Nasser. Though his death passed virtually unnoticed in the Western world, Qutb's quasi-anarchist vision of a perfect Islamic society would inspire a generation of jihadists, including Osama bin Laden, who was tutored by Qutb's brother in Saudi Arabia.[3] But it was in Qutb's own homeland, where the reformulation of Ibn Taymiyya's jihad was first harnessed to the methods and tactics of modern revolutionary violence.

Killing Pharaoh – jihad in Egypt

The emergence of revolutionary terrorism in Egypt was the result of a collision between a powerful Islamist movement, centred around the Muslim Brotherhood, and a one-party state that remained intransigently authoritarian under Nasser's successor, Anwar Sadat. The outside world did not become aware of this ongoing struggle until the assassination of Sadat in October 1981 by members of his own army while reviewing a military parade. In Europe and America Sadat was regarded as the peacemaker who signed the historic Camp David Accords with Israeli prime minister Menachem Begin. Though these US-brokered negotiations had brought American military and economic aid flooding into Egypt, Sadat was widely despised by his own population, particularly within Islamist circles, where he was given the title of 'Pharaoh' – the unjust and tyrannical ruler.

The growth of radical Islam had initially been encouraged by Sadat himself, who had provided state sponsorship to the Muslim Brotherhood and other Islamist organisations in an attempt to diminish communist and Nasserite influence in the universities. This strategy had succeeded, but the Islamists had grown more powerful than Sadat had counted on, extending their influence beyond the university system to the point when the more radical elements believed that the time had come for an Islamist version of 'propaganda by deed'.

Sadat's assassins were all members of a previously unknown organisation called al-Jihad or Islamic Jihad, whose essential doctrines were contained in a pamphlet called 'The Absent Obligation', written by an electrical engineer and a former Muslim Brother named Muhammad Faraj. Like Qutb and Ibn Taymiyya, Faraj argued that jihad was a religious obligation, the neglect of which in the contemporary Islamic world was 'the cause of the humiliation and division in which the Muslims live today'. Unlike Qutb, however, Faraj unambiguously defined jihad as 'fighting' and quoted selectively from the Koran and the hadith in order to demonstrate that jihad could include deception, lying, raiding and even killing women and children under certain conditions. As arcane as these references appeared, Faraj's text was an attempt to harness the formidable emotive power of jihad behind the new methods of revolutionary violence practised by his organisation.

Despite its ultimate objective of a religious state, al-Jihad had much in common with Latin American urban guerrilla organisations, with its code words and cover names and its divisions into self-contained urban cells known as *anquds*, the Arabic word for a bunch of grapes. Like the Latin American urban guerrillas also, the majority of al-Jihad's members were drawn from the Egyptian middle classes and saw themselves as a devout revolutionary vanguard. Unlike its secular counterparts, however, al-Jihad's operations were always carried out in keeping with religious directives issued by the organisation's spiritual mentors, such as the blind cleric Sheikh Omar Abd al-Rahman.[4]

Though Sadat's assassination was intended to bring the Islamists to power through a military coup d'état, it was a classic 'blow at the centre' in the Russian mould, aimed at the symbolic representative of a tyrannical political order. The belief that the killing of 'Pharaoh' would open the floodgates of revolt turned out to be premature, however, and Faraj and the other leading conspirators were subsequently hanged, without provoking any significant protests.

For more than a decade after Sadat's assassination the confrontation remained largely dormant, as Sadat's successor Hosni Mubarak adopted a policy of repressing Islamist organisations such as the Muslim Brotherhood and the Gama'a Islamiyya, the Islamic Group. In the wake of the first Gulf War, the latent conflict came out into the open once again, with the assassination of the journalist and writer Farag Foda by the Gama'a Islamiyya in June 1992. In November that year 12,000 Egyptian troops laid siege to the Islamist 'liberated zone' of Imbaba, a sprawling slum on the outskirts of Cairo where the Islamists had established a rudimentary social welfare network and established a template of the devout Islamic state. For more than six weeks, the population of nearly a million inhabitants was under the control of the army, which destroyed the area's Islamist infrastructure and carried out some 5,000 arrests. The Islamists responded with an all-out revolutionary offensive, carrying out dozens of attacks on government officials, police and army officers and prominent secular intellectuals, such as the octogenarian Nobel Prize-winning novelist Naguib Mahfouz, who was badly wounded in a knife attack.

Islamist violence was also directed against foreign tourists, as militants set off bombs in cafés, carried out commando-style assaults on cruise ships on the Nile, machine-gunned buses and hotels and even threw acid at the bare legs of foreign women. The campaign against the Egyptian tourist industry was partly an attempt to destabilise the Egyptian economy, though one Gama'a spokesman also described tourism as 'an abomination: it is a means by which prostitution and AIDs are spread by Jewish women tourists, and it is a source of all manner of depravities'.[5]

Though the Mubarak regime presented Egypt as a secular society under siege from an aggressive fundamentalist onslaught, the Egyptian regime had little to recommend it from the point of view of tolerance or democracy, as the security forces responded to the violence with a brutal counter-terrorist offensive, arresting and imprisoning some 20,000 Islamist militants and suspects, many of whom were tortured and kept in prison for years awaiting trial. Hundreds of militants were shot dead in gun battles with the security forces, while more than a hundred militants were executed following military trials that allowed no right of appeal. Others were 'disappeared', Latin American-style, or killed by the security forces in extra-judicial executions. These brutal and repressive tactics confirmed the Islamists' perceptions of themselves as heroes and martyrs, fighting a sacred war on behalf of the faith against a corrupt tyrannical regime. In massed trials that recalled the Italian 'maxi-trials' of the Red Brigades, bearded Islamist militants waved the Koran and shouted prayers and defiant slogans as they faced death or imprisonment. In parts of Upper Egypt, the confrontation came close to a full-scale guerrilla war, as mud-walled villages were patrolled by armoured cars and soldiers and sugar-cane fields burned by the army to deny cover to their enemies. By the late 1990s, however, the Islamist groups were clearly losing the confrontation. In July 1997 the state felt confident enough that its policy of repression was working to reject the offer of a unilateral truce from a group of imprisoned Gama'a Islamiyya leaders. The result was the most horrific atrocity of the conflict.

Luxor

On 17 November 1997, six Islamist militants calling themselves the 'Battalion of Havoc and Destruction' slaughtered fifty-eight foreign and four Egyptian tourists at the Hatshepsut Temple in Luxor. The group gained entry to the temple by disguising themselves as policemen and opened fire with machine guns on the unprotected tourists. Survivors later testified how the killers sang and danced as they hunted down their victims through the temple and shot them at point-blank range or stabbed them with knives. Among the dead were women, children and elderly tourists, including three honeymooning Japanese couples and three generations from the same British family: a grandmother, her daughter and grand-daughter. The majority of the tourists were Swiss, and all were killed with the same delirious insouciance before their murderers fled from the police into the surrounding countryside. Though the police initially claimed they had been killed in a gun battle, it subsequently emerged that the team had shot themselves in a nearby cave.

The perpetrators of this horrendous slaughter were university or high-school students from the Islamist stronghold of Asyut, led by a 31-year-old Islamist militant named Medhat Abderrahman, known to the Egyptian police as 'Moustache Sammy', who had fought in Afghanistan after the Soviet withdrawal. With the exception of their leader, none of the students had a record of Islamist militancy or violence, and they appeared to have been recently recruited for the task. All of them were in their late teens or early twenties and shared a middle-class or lower-middle-class background and technical education that was common to many Islamist militants in Egypt. On the surface, the savage killing of defenceless tourists in an ancient temple was the epitome of 'sacred terror'. Eyewitness descriptions of the killers cheerfully shouting, 'Allahu Akbar, we killed all the tourists', complete the image of religious fanaticism. Yet survivors also testified that the killers appeared to be high on drugs, while the fact that they fled the scene afterwards and committed suicide instead of dying in 'battle' suggest that this horrific crime was motivated by something more than religion.

Were the students manipulated and 'brainwashed' by Islamist preachers like Sheikh Rahman and Abu Hamza, as some of their families claimed? Were the killings a desperate attempt by a failing insurrectionary movement to attack the regime by destroying the Egyptian economy's main source of income? According to the demands on the attackers' leaflets, the slaughter was aimed at freeing Sheikh Rahman, who was then serving a life sentence in the United States for his part in the bombing of the World Trade Center. But survivors later claimed that no attempt was made to take hostages, while another bloodstained pamphlet stuffed into a pocket of one of the victims proclaimed: 'No to tourism in Egypt'. The massacre took place only a month after a lavish performance of Verdi's *Aida* on the same site that had been attended by President Mubarak and a host of national and foreign VIPs. At the time the performance had been widely criticised for its ostentatiousness, but the fact that it had taken place at all was seen by some commentators as another sign that the regime believed it had won the anti-terrorist battle. Was the massacre intended to demonstrate that this was not the case, by attacking civilian 'soft targets' in the most spectacular and bloody fashion?

All these possibilities remain purely speculative. Though the Egyptian government accused Egyptian veterans of the Afghan anti-Soviet war based in London of organising the massacre, the logistical structure responsible for Luxor has never been fully established. But whatever the motivations behind it, the slaughter of Western tourists drew a level of international attention that obscured the even greater massacres of Algerian civilians attributed to Islamist groups in the same period. One Swiss tour guide in Egypt summed up the sentiments of many observers in describing Luxor as 'beyond understanding', while the *Boston Globe* pointed out 'the terrible irony of an attack coming at a place that represented the pinnacle of civilisation 4,500 years ago' and insisted that 'governments must stand up to terrorists'. But the Egyptian government was already 'standing up' to terrorism, even if its methods were often as savage and barbaric as those used by the Islamists themselves.

If nothing else, Luxor provided the most horrific and irrefutable evidence that these methods had failed. But this 'fury for God' did not benefit the Islamist insurgency. On the contrary, within Egypt the 'catastrophe on the

Nile' was universally condemned. The academic and journalist Geneive Abdo later described how she left the American University in Cairo on the afternoon of the massacre and found that 'All around me, Egyptians were cursing the violence. They stood in crowds in the middle of downtown, waving their hands in the air and looking past one another as they shouted in anger and frustration.'[6]

Though the massacre struck a devastating blow to the Egyptian tourist economy, from which it would take a long time to recover, it proved to be a turning point in the bloody confrontation between the Islamists and the Egyptian state. So great was the public revulsion that the Gama'a announced that it would no longer target the tourism industry or foreign tourists. In the wake of Luxor the Islamist revolutionary offensive in Egypt abated, and the state also made some concessions to the Islamists by releasing some political detainees. In the ensuing years a grassroots Islamist movement embarked on a non-violent strategy of 'Islam from below' which has steadily gained influence in key areas of Egyptian society, despite the Mubarak regime's continued monopoly of political power. The standoff has yet to be resolved.[7]

Algeria – terror is the health of the state

The Mubarak regime often presented itself as the defender of tolerance and secularism against the fundamentalist hordes in order to ensure continued Western support for its brutal counter-terrorist offensive. But while the Islamist aspiration of cleansing Egyptian society of 'evil' often lent itself to brutal authoritarianism, intolerance and even murder, the presentation of a secular society threatened by totalitarian Islamic fascists is misleading. If the Islamist movement was hostile to aspects of Western secularism, it was also a response to political tyranny and the corruption and incompetence of the regime itself. The spectre of 'Islamo-fascism' was also invoked to justify an even bloodier counter-terrorist campaign in Algeria, following the cancellation by the army of the second round of national elections in January 1991, which the Islamic Salvation Front (FIS), a coalition of Islamist organisations, looked certain to win by a huge majority. As in Egypt, the Islamist movement was fuelled by various factors, from popular discontent at economic stagnation, corruption and years of authoritarian rule, to the unresolved role of Islam in post-colonial Algerian society. In Algeria, however, anger towards the ruling FLN was even more widespread following the October bread riots in 1988, in which the Algerian army shot dead some 600 civilians. In the wake of the 'Algerian intifada' various Islamist organisations mobilised a powerful grassroots mass movement that took advantage of the tentative democratic experiment by the FLN. The FIS competed in municipal and national elections with such success that it appeared to be on the brink of ushering in the Islamist 'reign of justice' through an indisputable democratic mandate.

For the armed forces, which constituted the real power in Algeria, the experiment with democracy had gone too far and the cancellation of the elections was followed by the arrest of thousands of FIS activists. The result was an explosion of violence which recalled the bloody years of the war of independence. On the surface the conflict was a civil war between an autocratic secular government and a popular Islamist movement that called for revolutionary jihad against a regime that it regarded as *taghut* – idolatrous and blasphemous. But these parameters do not reflect the brutal unravelling of Algerian society, as the initial confrontation between the Islamist organisations and the security forces fragmented into multiple conflicts.

The Islamists had never been a homogeneous movement and the differences between their various factions became even more apparent as the violence spiralled and several groups competed with each other for leadership of the jihad. As in Egypt, the Islamists targeted secular intellectuals, such as Tahar Djaout, one of Algeria's most prominent poets and novelists and the author of a powerful indictment of Islamist philistinism, *The Last Summer of Reason*, that was published posthumously after Djaout was shot dead while leaving his house for work on 26 May 1993. Djaout was movingly remembered by the Algerian novelist and film-maker Assia Djebar in *Algerian White*, a searing lament for the intellectuals and writers killed because of what they thought and wrote in Algeria's two wars, many of whom were Djebar's friends. Scores of journalists, writers and playwrights considered to be 'communists' or 'agents of Satan' were similarly assassinated.

The assault on the Francophone intelligentsia was only one element in a more wide-ranging purge of French and foreign influence, whose targets included Rai musicians, teachers and even schoolchildren at French-speaking schools. Women were also frequently victims of Islamist violence. Many were abducted from their homes and taken to the mountains to service the sexual needs of the Islamist guerrillas. Others were found guilty of 'immoral' or 'un-Islamic' behaviour – such as divorce, living alone, or going out with their heads uncovered – and were shot dead or had their throats cut.[8]

If women could be killed for not wearing the veil, they could also be killed when they did wear it by anti-Islamist vigilantes who saw any outward sign of piety as a sign of Islamist sympathies. As in contemporary Iraq, the violence formed new tributaries, in which the distinction between 'criminal', 'political' and 'religious' dimensions of the jihad became blurred or non-existent. For some local Islamist groups, the war became a route to wealth and social prestige, as various local 'emirs' or 'princes' engaged in black marketeering, drug trafficking, the sale of stolen property, raising protection money or 'war taxes' and even the formation of import–export companies.[9] The various Islamist organisations often differed radically in their conception of the jihad. In 1994 the FIS formed a military wing, the Islamic Salvation Army (AIS), which attempted to give the jihad a more ostensibly 'political' direction, concentrating on attacks on the regime itself, rather than civilians.

Other groups, such as the ferocious Armed Islamic Group (GIA), considered the jihad to be an 'absolute religious obligation' for all Algerians and divided the civilian population into 'enemies of Islam' and 'supporters of the jihad'. A shadowy organisation initially created by veterans of the Afghan war, the GIA soon established an unrivalled reputation for cruelty and massacre, killing Algerian civilians on a scale that appalled even its de facto allies amongst the FIS. GIA activity reached a peak in September 1997, when hundreds of people were slaughtered in the suburbs of Algiers and other villages in the most atrocious fashion. In the town of Benthala 600 men, women and children were killed with knives, machetes, saws and axes in an appalling six-hour rampage that was attributed to the GIA. But there was also an equally disturbing explanation for at least some of the violence. An Amnesty International report on the massacres noted that 'large groups of men have been able to come from their supposed hiding places in the mountains and forests into the villages … carry out killings lasting several hours, and leave to return – undisturbed – to their hiding places', even in areas with a strong military or police presence.[10]

In 2000 Nesroulah Yous, an entrepreneur from Benthala exiled in France, published *Who Killed in Benthala?* in France, in which he claimed that the massacres were carried out by members of the security forces themselves, disguised as terrorists. In *La Sale Guerre* (The Dirty War) published the following year, Habib Souaidia, a former Algerian special-forces soldier exiled in France, also claimed that his colleagues carried out massacres in order to discredit the Islamists. Other former members of the security forces painted a similarly grim picture. Nor were Algerians the only victims. In July 1994 seven Italian seamen had their throats cut while sleeping in a ship docked in a port near Algiers. Three years later an Algerian secret policeman named 'Yusuf' told the *Observer* that the killings had been carried out by the regime in order to rouse Western support against the 'Islamo-fascist' menace. Yusuf also claimed that a series of bombings on the Paris Métro in 1995 had also been carried out by agents provocateurs linked to the regime for the same reason.[11]

The deliberate staging of 'terrorist' atrocities was only one element in Algeria's war on terrorism, as the regime tortured and killed with impunity. As in Argentina, 'terrorist' suspects were snatched from their homes by the balaclava-clad anti-terrorist forces known as the 'Ninjas', and some 7,000 were never seen again. The security forces also resorted to a policy of indiscriminate reprisals, randomly selecting young men off the streets in Islamist districts for summary execution in response to the killing of soldiers and policemen in order to 'terrorise the terrorists.'

As always, the regime invoked the familiar anti-terrorist vocabulary to justify these measures, presenting the Islamists as 'devils' and the 'forces of evil' who were leading the nation into a state of *fitnah* – chaos. Within the neighbourhoods they controlled, the Islamists were regarded as 'heroes, protectors and avengers', in the words of the French sociologist Luis Martinez, at least initially. As the violence continued, many Algerians retreated from their initial enthusiasm for the FIS to resigned passivity, concentrating on daily survival. One of the most compelling chroniclers of the Algerian nightmare was the novelist Yasmina Khadra, the pseudonym of an exiled former Algerian army officer, Mohammed Moulessehoul. Khadra's work is a bleak and unflinching dissection of an Algerian society wrecked by official and unofficial terrorism, where 'the light at the end of the tunnel is only the reflection of Hell' and the revolutionary aspirations of the war of independence have given way to a society in which the most elementary notions of justice can no longer exist.

In *Morituri*, Khadra's acid, Chandleresque prose depicts contemporary Algiers as a city riddled with corruption and violence, where Islamists, drug dealers and gangsters collaborate with members of the politico-financial elite and everyday life for the majority of the population unfolds against a constant background of car bombs and assassinations. Khadra's suggestion of a symbiotic relationship between the Islamists and elements of the Algerian elite was shared by many Algerian commentators, who noted that Islamist violence tended to target state-owned factories and businesses that were being lined up for privatisation, while doing nothing to disrupt the export of oil and gas on which the regime depended for its survival. In 2002 one Algerian government official admitted to the American journalist Adam Shatz that the pace of privatisation tended to quicken during the periods of most intense violence, while another told Shatz, 'The state can't let terrorism die. It's the only thing keeping it afloat.'[12]

By the end of the century the Islamist offensive was no longer able to generate the same levels of mayhem and the clique of army officers, bureaucrats and businessmen known to Algerians as *le pouvoir* (those in power) remained precisely that. Within the FLN itself there were tensions between the 'eradicators' who wanted to destroy the Islamists completely and the 'conciliators' who sought to incorporate the more domesticated Islamist parties into the political mainstream. Following the election of the army's latest representative, Abdelaziz Bouteflika, as president in 1999, the conciliators began to gain the upper hand and the regime passed the 'Civil Concord' law offering amnesties and pardons to all Islamist guerrillas observing a ceasefire.

By this time Algeria was a traumatised society on the verge of a collective nervous breakdown, after years of violence in which an estimated 100,000 people had been killed, another million displaced and 7,000 disappeared. All this suggested a more complex pattern of violence than the image of a beleaguered secular government standing up to an 'Islamo-fascist' assault. The effect of terrorism often resembles a double-handled saw, on which both terrorists and counter-terrorists are pulling in opposite directions to fulfil their own particular agendas, but in few countries has this tendency been more horrifically demonstrated than Algeria.

The American jihad

In both Egypt and Algeria 'religious' violence was a product of specific historical and social circumstances, rather than a consequence of an ageless tradition of sacred terror. If the failed Islamist offensives demonstrated that terror was not a one-way process, the fact that these offensives were directed against a one-party state and a military regime contradicted previous terrorological clichés regarding an existential conflict between 'terrorism' and 'democracy'. It is one of the bitterest ironies in the history of 'Islamo-fascism' that the most violent fundamentalist organisations often received at least some support from the same 'secular' regimes they went on to attack. In both Egypt and Algeria Islamism was initially seen by the state as a means of countering the influence of the left. A similar process occurred elsewhere in the Middle East. Even in the occupied Gaza Strip, Israel granted considerable political leeway to the Muslim Brotherhood in the 1970s and 1980s in order to divide the Palestinian nationalist movement. This strategy was partially successful, but it also resulted in the creation of the Islamic Resistance

Movement (Hamas) during the first Palestinian intifada, which went on to prove a far more implacable and sanguinary opponent of the Israeli occupation than its secular nationalist counterparts.

In terms of its long-term international consequences, the most decisive episode in the evolution of the modern jihad occurred in Afghanistan, where the US government undertook a massive covert operation to support the Islamic resistance organisations fighting Soviet occupation. The Carter administration had already begun to provide assistance to Islamist groups in Afghanistan even before the Soviet invasion in 1979, with the aim of undermining the pro-Soviet Afghan government to the point where the Soviets would be obliged to intervene to prop up its protégé. The Soviets fell into the trap and the CIA undertook the largest covert operation in its history in order to 'make Russia bleed'. The fact that the majority of the organisations in the Afghan resistance were led by reactionary religious zealots intent on the construction of a theocratic state was always a secondary consideration, as the United States set out to convert Afghanistan into a Soviet 'Vietnam'. In order to maintain the façade of 'plausible deniability', however, US military and financial assistance to the Afghan resistance was largely channelled through Pakistan's powerful intelligence agency, the Inter-Service Intelligence (ISI). In addition to Stinger missiles and other weapons, the US government commissioned school textbooks from the University of Nebraska for use in Afghan refugee camps and Pakistani religious schools, in which children learned addition by counting dead Soviet soldiers, tanks and Kalashnikovs. The same materials were still in use in Afghan schools during the 2001 invasion of the country by the US-led coalition, when the same schools were accused by George W. Bush of 'indoctrinating students with fanaticism and bigotry'.[13] Bush did not mention where the schools' textbooks were produced.

Back in the eighties, however, fanaticism and bigotry against the Soviets were seen as positive attributes to be encouraged. A CBS television producer, George Crile, in his hagiographic biography of the congressman and arms lobbyist for the jihad, Charlie Wilson, summed up the prevailing view in the United States at the time when he described the mujahideen as 'mythological characters out of a legend, with their long beards, their burning eyes, their refusal to admit pain or fear or doubt ... they symbolized the raw essence of freedom and self-determination.'[14]

From Ronald Reagan downwards, US government officials often hailed the Afghan resistance as exemplary 'freedom fighters' to distinguish their struggle from the moral depravity of 'terrorism'. Needless to say, Western eulogies to the mujahideen tended to overlook the darker side of the Afghan holy war, from the routine practice of killing and mutilating Russian prisoners to the adoption of captured Russian soldiers as homosexual 'concubines' or sex slaves. In addition to conventional military targets, the Islamic Resistance also attacked primary- and secondary-school teachers, university lecturers and other civilian targets. As Brigadier Mohammad Yousaf, the head of the ISI's Afghan Bureau, later described it, 'Educational institutions were considered fair game, as the staff were all communists indoctrinating their students with Marxist dogma'.[15] Such 'Marxist dogma' included female literacy, considered to be anathema by the reactionary mujahideen leaders such as the 'engineer' Gulbuddin Hekmatyar.

Some 2,000 Afghan teachers were killed and another 15,000 driven from the profession in the course of this ideological offensive. The presentation of the Afghan resistance as a holy war in defence of Muslim territory brought thousands of volunteers to Afghanistan from across the Islamic world, in what one Pakistani general called 'the first Islamic international brigade in the modern era.' For the first time since Salah al-Din's defeat of the medieval Crusading armies, jihad became a truly international enterprise, which drew thousands of Muslims from across the world to drive out the infidel invaders or achieve glorious martyrdom on behalf of the faith.

One of the most charismatic and influential members of this Muslim 'international brigade' was a Jordanian-Palestinian doctor of Islamic science named Abdullah Azzam, who established the 'Services Bureau' which acted as a fundraising and recruitment office for the international jihad. To Azzam, the Arab volunteers were a spiritual vanguard, whose participation in the Afghan jihad was the first step in a broader religious revival that would lead to the restoration of the defunct Muslim caliphate, whose borders stretched from Andalusia to Indonesia. Thousands of 'Arab-Afghans' would seek to extend the jihad to their own countries. Others would spread out across the world, to a range of conflicts from Chechnya and Kashmir to Bosnia, Somalia and the Philippines. They took with them not only the heady atmosphere of martyrdom and religious fervour that characterised the Afghan jihad, but combat experience and training in the techniques of unconventional warfare, taught to them by the Saudi and Pakistani intelligence services that functioned as US surrogates. Many of these techniques would later appear in the 1,000-page *Encyclopedia of the Jihad*, which became known as the 'al-Qaeda manual'.

All this was a consequence of the biggest covert operation in CIA history, where the holy war against the infidel invaders coexisted seamlessly with drug dealing, arms smuggling, money laundering and the complex liaisons between various foreign governments and the BCCI 'outlaw bank'.[16] Nevertheless, Russia did bleed. By the time the Soviets finally withdrew in 1989, some 14,500 Soviet troops had been killed and hundreds of thousands wounded. The damage to Afghanistan was much worse. Some of the worst destruction occurred after the Soviet withdrawal, when Afghan warlords fought a ferocious battle for the control of Kabul, which reduced nearly 80 per cent of the city to ruins and killed 45,000 civilians. By this time few Western governments were interested in the fate of a country that had served its purpose. To the international volunteers, however, the collapse of the Soviet Union was a triumphant vindication of the jihad. By fighting under the banner of Islam rather than national flags, the mujahideen believed that they had indirectly brought about the collapse of the communist superpower, while their American sponsors remained equally convinced that their actions had forced the Soviet withdrawal and led directly to the end of the Cold War.

Few of the US officials have ever acknowledged any responsibility for their role in these events. In 1998 former secretary of state Zbigniew Brzezinski was asked whether he regretted 'having supported Islamic fundamentalism, which has given arms and advice to future terrorists', to which Brzezinski replied, 'What is more important in world history? The Taliban or the collapse of the Soviet empire? Some agitated Islamists or the liberation of Central Europe and the end of the Cold War?'[17] By that time these 'agitated Islamists' had already begun to make their presence felt elsewhere, but their connections to the American jihad were rarely made apparent in the depiction of the fundamentalist threat to civilisation. The historian Chalmers Johnson later reformulated the old CIA concept of 'blowback' to describe the 'unexpected consequences' of covert operations and foreign-policy decisions that the US public was unaware of. Originally intended as internal intelligence jargon, Johnson has cited various forms of blowback, to bear out the general principle that 'a nation reaps what it sows'.[18] There have been various manifestations of this process, but rarely has 'blowback' rebounded with such spectacular viciousness as it would later do on the sponsors of the Afghan jihad.

The Party of God
Afghanistan was not the only country in the Muslim world where religion was incorporated into a successful struggle against foreign occupation. In Lebanon the Israeli invasion of 1982 resulted in the creation of Hezbollah, the

Party of God, one of the most formidable politico-military organisations in the Middle East. Like the anti-Soviet Islamic resistance coalition in Afghanistan, Hezbollah regarded its war as a jihad in defence of Muslim territory, but the fact that Hezbollah was closely linked to Iran, and the main target of its violence was Israel, meant that the two movements were regarded very differently in the West. Where the Afghan 'muj' were celebrated by right-wing Texan socialites and Republican politicians as freedom fighters and Kiplingesque warriors, valiantly fighting the Soviet foe in the name of their religion, Hezbollah was portrayed in Israel and the United States as a fanatical terrorist organisation and a particularly virulent expression of Islamic fundamentalist irrationality.

Hezbollah's notoriety stemmed initially from the suicide bomb attacks on the multinational forces in Beirut in 1984. In addition, the organisation was accused of responsibility for the kidnappings of Western hostages during the 1980s, accusations which Hezbollah has always denied. Within Lebanon itself, Hezbollah's tenacious resistance to the Israeli occupation over nearly two decades earned the organisation a respect and popularity that transcended the party's Shia constituency. This reached a peak in April 1996, when Israel launched its 'Operation Grapes of Wrath' offensive against the 'Hezbollah terrorist bases' in southern Lebanon. In the middle of a ferocious aerial and land assault which drove some 200,000 people from their homes, Israeli tanks attacked a UN base in the village of Qana and killed 109 refugees. While Western politicians, including the British defence secretary, Michael Portillo, declared the offensive a legitimate and proportionate response to Hezbollah 'terror', the Party of God was acclaimed in Beirut by Christians and Muslims alike as the embodiment of national resistance to foreign occupation.

It was not until May 2000 that Israeli forces finally withdrew from Lebanon, retaining control only over the tiny Shebaa farms. For the first time the previously invincible Israeli army had suffered a major reversal and Hezbollah was the toast of Lebanon. It was the stuff of Islamist legend, the story of a small group of pious men who had forced the Zionist enemy to withdraw from occupied territory. Though Hezbollah relied heavily on Iranian support, its leaders showed a pragmatism and political flexibility in negotiating their way through Lebanon's sectarian minefield which bore little relation to former Israeli prime minister Shimon Peres's description of the Party of God as an organisation 'defined by jihad, not logic'.[19]

Unlike the Islamist organisations in Afghanistan, Hezbollah's leaders accepted the secular and democratic basis of the Lebanese state and declared that an Islamic society could not be created in Lebanon without the consent of the Lebanese population. The Party of God further demonstrated its commitment to the democratic process by standing as a political party in parliamentary elections, where it won twelve seats. In a country still recovering from civil war, whose political class was tarnished by years of corruption, venality and sectarian warfare, Hezbollah earned itself an enviable reputation for political and moral integrity, with a network of supermarket co-operatives, school and university committees, bookshops, factories and bakeries, and its own radio and television stations that were as much part of its political identity as its military wing.

Nevertheless, the organisation continued to appear each year in the US State Department's *Patterns of Global Terrorism* and in the early 1990s Hezbollah was accused of bombing the Israeli embassy in Argentina in 1992 and the even more destructive bombing of the Israeli-Argentinian Mutual Association in Buenos Aires two years later, in which eighty-five people were killed. Though US and Israeli intelligence agencies have always alleged that the bombings were carried out by an Iranian-Hezbollah terror network centred in the 'triborder' intersection of Argentina, Paraguay and Brazil, both Iran and Hezbollah denied responsibility and evidence of Hezbollah involvement is patchy and unreliable. In the wake of the September 11 attacks, however, influential voices in the United States and Israel called for air strikes on Hezbollah bases as part of the War on Terror, even though Hezbollah has condemned both the attacks and al-Qaeda itself. If nearly two decades of Israeli military force had failed to crush Hezbollah, it is difficult to see what foreign military action might achieve against an organisation that is now firmly embedded amongst the Lebanese Shia population. But for both Israel and the United States, the dream of total military supremacy over the Middle East remains a beguiling fantasy, and the world may yet see the bombers flying over the Bekaa valley once again in another attempt to eradicate 'terror'.

Martyrs and suicides

There is no doubt that religion played a powerful role in the mobilisation of the Lebanese resistance, as it did in Afghanistan. By presenting its actions as a defence of the faith as well as a patriotic liberation struggle against an occupying army, Hezbollah transformed the idea of resistance into a religious duty. Nevertheless, this use of religion did not equate with Western depictions of Hezbollah as a particularly virulent and fanatical embodiment of Islamic 'sacred terror'. To the organisation's enemies, the ultimate confirmation of Hezbollah's fanatical irrationality was its exaltation of religious martyrdom. This glorification of martyrdom was not unique to Hezbollah or Islam. One of the consequences of the resurgence in religious violence was the re-emergence of the concept of the religious martyr who 'bears witness' to the faith. But the new religious martyrs were not only prepared to sacrifice their own lives. In 1994 Baruch Goldstein, a Jewish doctor from the West Bank settlement of Kiryat Arba, entered the Tomb of the Patriarchs in Hebron and shot dead twenty-nine Muslim congregants praying in the mosque, before he was beaten to death by the enraged survivors. To the embarrassment of the Israeli government, Goldstein was hailed as a martyr by the racist zealots of Kiryat Arba and his tomb became a shrine and a site of pilgrimage for members of the settler movement.[20]

To those who did not regard the presence of Arabs in Hebron as a religious defilement, Goldstein's 'martyrdom' was cancelled out by the act of mass murder that he committed. But martyrdom, like terrorism, tends to be a question of subjective belief rather than an objective phenomenon. To the Indian government the radical Sikh leader Sant Bhindranwale, who died fighting with his followers during the Indian army's siege of the Golden Temple in Amritsar, was a terrorist bandit. To many Sikhs, however, Bhindranwale's exemplary death in the spiritual heart of Sikhism confirmed him as a warrior-martyr in the tradition of the Sikh founding gurus. Other religions have their own tradition of the warrior-martyr. In Islamic tradition any Muslim who dies fighting in defence of Islam or Muslim territory is venerated as a *shahid*, a martyr, a word stemming from the root word *shahida*, to witness or testify. In addition to the certainty of everlasting life in paradise, martyrdom in Islam also confers absolution from sin, enabling martyrs to bypass the post-mortem interrogation by the angels Nakir and Munkar and proceed directly to heaven. According to some traditions, martyrs who die on the battlefield are greeted by a beautiful angel who bathes their wounds and leads them to paradise. Other traditions cite that the bodies of martyrs fail to decompose, that they will be able to marry seventy-two beautiful 'houris' or virgins, that they can absolve seventy family members from sin, that a 'crown of glory' will be placed on the martyr's head of which a single ruby 'is worth more than the world and all that is in it'.

The veneration of martyrdom is a particularly powerful emotional component of Shia religious tradition, and can be traced back to the death of Hussein, the Prophet's grandson, at the battle of Karbala in AD 680. The Khomeini regime appealed to the memory of Hussein during the Iran–Iraq war, in recruiting legions of shock troops, many of them young adolescent boys, who charged Iraqi machine guns wearing the red scarves that signified martyrdom and the plastic keys that would open the gates of paradise. The Iranian example resonated strongly through the Shia resistance in Lebanon, where Hezbollah's secretary-general, Sheikh Nasrullah, hailed martyrdom as 'the greatest thing about our resistance, greater than victory and liberation'.[21] As in Iran, the glorification of martyrdom was reinforced in speeches by Hezbollah leaders, in radio and television programmes and in anniversaries commemorating its fallen fighters. All this was part of the propaganda of the resistance, through which Hezbollah sought to rouse the Shia community to further acts of self-sacrifice. At the same time this propaganda was aimed outwards and Hezbollah's celebration of its fighters' 'lust' and 'yearning' for martyrdom was intended to project an image of collective psychological strength at the enemy. And in the early 1980s, the Islamic resistance demonstrated its 'martyrological will' with a new and terrifying weapon.

The coming of the suicide bomber

In November 1982 a teenage Hezbollah operative named Ahmad Qasir drove a white Mercedes loaded with explosives into the Israeli military headquarters in Tyre, killing 141 people, including Israeli soldiers and other military personnel, as well as a number of Palestinian and Lebanese prisoners. Qasir's lethal assault heralded the even more devastating suicide attacks on the French and US multinational forces carried out the following year by Islamic Jihad, which Hezbollah celebrated as 'unprecedented in the history of mankind'. The Israeli defence minister, Moshe Arens, summed up the prevailing view in the West in attributing these attacks to 'a cruel and oppressive enemy who does not work with logical methods, at least with regards to the general basis and principles acknowledged in the civilised world'.[22]

Whatever else they were, the use of suicide attacks was entirely 'logical' and the withdrawal of the multinational forces from Lebanon demonstrated that they could also be effective. Though some Western analysts saw these attacks as further evidence of the Islamic infatuation with death and martyrdom, suicide bombings were not always carried out by Shia or even Islamist organisations. A number of attacks on Israeli forces were carried out by secular nationalists, such as Sanaa Muhaidily, a 17-year-old member of the Syrian Social Nationalist Party, who became known as the 'Bride of the South' after she drove her Peugeot car at an Israeli roadblock and killed two soldiers. Before the attack Muhaidily recorded the customary valedictory video, in which she asked her mother to regard her death as a 'wedding' and closed with a lyrical celebration of the martyr's death:

I have not died, but am moving alive among you. I sing, I dance, and I am fulfilling all my dreams. How happy and joyful I am with this heroic martyrdom
that I give. I plead with you, I kiss your hands one by one, do not cry for me, do
not be sad for me, but be happy and smile. I am now planted in the earth of the
South irrigating and quenching her with my blood and my love for her.[23]

Nevertheless, it was Hezbollah that became most associated with the new
tactics and which claimed responsibility for eighteen of the fifty-odd suicide
attacks carried out against Israeli forces in Lebanon. Hezbollah rejected
criticisms that 'human bombs' were uniquely barbaric, arguing that they
were the only way of countering the overwhelming military superiority of
Israel and its allies. Since suicide was forbidden by Islam, these operations
were called *al-amalyiat al istishadiya*, or 'self-martyrdom operations'. In the
opinion of some Hezbollah clerics, the fact that the perpetrators killed their
enemies as well as themselves made their actions a form of heroic self-sacrifice, rather than suicide. The theological status of martyrdom operations was
never definitively settled, but those who carried them out were nevertheless
acclaimed as *istishaadi* or 'esteemed self- martyrs' and accorded a special
status which distinguished them from the martyrs who died in battle.

For Hezbollah, the *istishaadi* were the ultimate expression of the self-sacrificial spirit of the resistance. Whenever possible their operations were filmed
and broadcast on Hezbollah's television station, together with pictures of the
martyrs accompanied by Koranic verses and video recordings of their last
statements. Yet even though Hezbollah claimed to have a limitless supply
of potential *istishaadi* willing to sacrifice themselves, the tactic of suicide
bombings was used sparingly. From 1987 onwards such operations were
rarely carried out at all as the resistance concentrated on more orthodox
guerrilla tactics against the Israeli army. But the example of the Lebanese
'laboratory of martyrdom' had not gone unnoticed.

The 'journey of honour' – suicide and martyrdom in Palestine
In *The Secret Agent*, Joseph Conrad depicted a crazed anarchist called the
Professor who wires himself up with explosives and walks the streets of
London exulting in the inability of the police to arrest him as he dreams
of the 'perfect detonator'. By the end of the twentieth century the freakish
creation of an Edwardian novelist had become a routine phenomenon, as the
modern world continued to produce a seemingly endless procession of men
and women prepared to blow themselves up in order to kill their enemies.
Between 1980 and 2003, suicide bombings accounted for more than a quarter

of all casualties attributed to international terrorism, even before the 9/11 attacks. The political scientist Robert Pape lists 315 separate incidents of suicide bombings around the world in this period, more than half of which were carried out by Islamist groups.[24] In some cases suicide bombers used cars, trucks, motorcycles and boats. But the majority of attacks were carried out by individuals carrying explosive belts or home-made bombs known in military jargon as IEDs, or 'improvised explosive devices'.

The proliferation of 'human bombs' in different conflicts bore little relation to the nihilistic insanity of Conrad's lone anarchist. As in Lebanon they represented a cost-effective weapon that generally followed a coherent political and tactical rationale. Nowhere else in the world have suicide bombings received more international attention than during the Israeli-Palestinian conflict. The most intense period of suicide bombings occurred following the outbreak of the second Palestinian intifada in 2000, when 103 incidents took place between 2000 and 2003, resulting in 440 deaths and 3,076 injuries. The attacks were carried out in supermarkets, cafés, pizza restaurants and night clubs, and at weddings and parties, on buses, in crowded streets and a university canteen.[25] To ensure maximum carnage, bombs were often packed with nails, metal and shrapnel. On 2 December 2001, a *Washington Post* reporter described a suicide bomb attack on a bus in Haifa, that killed fifteen people and wounded dozens more:

> In an instant, the bus became an inferno of death and blood. Corpses and frag-
> ments of bodies were strewn across the seats and aisles, and the wounded
> staggered out the doors and tumbled from the shattered windows. The bomb
> tore apart students and retirees, Filipino workers and Russian immigrants,
> soldiers and civilians – a random sampling of this working-class city's diverse
> population.[26]

Similar scenes became a regular feature of international television news, as the world became accustomed to the sight of scorched buses, the wailing of ambulances, police sirens and the bereaved, and Orthodox Jewish salvage crews in yellow smocks gathering up body parts. Not since the battle of Algiers had a civilian population been subjected to such a systematic and bloody bombing campaign. But for all the carnage wrought by suicide bombers, the overall number of victims was considerably less than the death toll inflicted on the Palestinian population by the Israeli army in the same period.

During the first three years of the intifada, 2,400 Palestinians were killed and tens of thousands injured, compared with 700 Israeli casualties. These incidents rarely generated the same level of international coverage as a bombed café or bus in Jerusalem or Tel Aviv. Such attacks represented an intrusion of alien violence into an everyday world of cafés, discotheques and restaurants that was recognizably Western and civilised, whereas Palestinian civilians died in a war zone in what the Israeli army inevitably described as accidents or unavoidable consequences of war. In these circumstances, suicide attacks on Israeli civilians were broadly supported by the Palestinian population, though approval was not unanimous or consistent. The very fact that Israeli society was able to function normally in the midst of violent conflict was a source of anger and indignation to many Palestinians, who saw these 'letters to Israel' as both a means of equalizing the conflict and a counterweight to Israeli military superiority. In this sense suicide attacks fitted Robert Pape's definition of suicide bombings as a 'strategy for weak actors' rather than an expression of 'sacred terror'.[27] At the same time they were intended to demoralise the Israeli civilian population and recreate the sense of permanent siege to which much of the Palestinian population felt itself subjected to by the Israeli army.

The happy martyr

As in Lebanon, the use of suicide bombing was not restricted to organisations with an explicitly religious ideology. Amongst the Islamist groups, however, the 'holy explosions' of the *istishaadi* were presented as a cause for particular joy and celebration, not only because of the damage they inflicted on the enemy but because they marked the ascension of the martyr into paradise. According to one Hamas leader, 'the bodies of the exploding martyrs smell of musk' and the image of a painless and beautiful death was exemplified by the *bassamat al-Farah*, or 'smile of joy' which suicide bombers supposedly wore in the moment before they blew themselves up. The *istishaadi* were celebrated in a consciously created culture of martyrdom, which hailed their actions as an expression of the collective will of the Palestinian resistance. In the Islamist stronghold of the Gaza Strip, units of potential martyrs paraded in white capes and masks with sticks of imitation dynamite strapped to their waists and some refugee camps were plastered with iconic posters of young suicide bombers smiling sweetly against a background of the al-Aqsa mosque, or paintings of birds against a crimson background, symbolising the ascent of their souls to heaven.

From the moment they volunteered for an operation, recruits began their inner separation from the everyday world and their metamorphosis into mythological heroes and future instruments of propaganda. In general, recruits were instructed not to tell their families, in order to avoid the risk of being dissuaded, and told to settle their worldly affairs unobtrusively, writing private valedictory letters and recording on video the public statements that would be broadcast or circulated by the organisation afterwards. These statements were usually recorded with the Palestinian flag or the insignia of the organisation or faction responsible in the background.

As soon as the operation had been successfully carried out, a delegation from the faction responsible would visit the family of the martyr to congratulate them on having a child or relative who had undertaken 'the journey of honour'. Ideally, the parents and relatives of the *istishaadi* were expected to make public declarations of approval and pride, such as the father of one suicide bomber who told an Arab television channel that if he had twenty children he would like to see them all become martyrs. The funerals of martyrs were celebrated like weddings, with sweetened coffee and sweets and wedding songs, though not all families were willing or able to rise to the occasion. These families were given an honoured place in the community and their sitting rooms often turned into shrines, filled with pictures and mementos of their dead children.

In September 2002 Islamist students at the al-Jah University in Nablus staged a particularly repugnant celebration of the new weapon, when they commemorated the Sbarro Pizza Hut bombing, in which fifteen Israeli teenagers died, with a public exhibition in which photographs of the carnage were accompanied papier-mâché body parts and pizza slices and fake blood. Though this grotesque montage was promptly closed down, it has been cited by some Western and Israeli commentators as further evidence of a debased Palestinian 'culture of death'. In this corrupted world, some analysts have argued, Palestinian parents have become indifferent even to the deaths of their own children. But the Palestinian response to martyrdom was not straightforward. Palestinian psychologists have reported incidents in which parents have come to them asking how to detect warning signs that their children might be aspiring to martyrdom in order to prevent them. Even parents who expressed pride in their children's actions have often made contradictory statements to journalists, insisting that they would have stopped them had they known their intentions.

In most cases parents had no indication beforehand that their children were set to become martyrs and their immediate reactions were not joy but shock, grief and incredulity. Hours after Ayat Akhras blew herself up in a Jerusalem supermarket, residents from her neighbourhood were handing out sweets and firing guns in the air in celebration, while her distraught mother exclaimed, 'Why didn't she tell me she was going to die? I would have stopped her.' Other parents have expressed similar sentiments, even as they describe their children as heroes and martyrs. For many parents the idea that their child had died a glorious martyr's death was the only way of making sense out of an otherwise futile tragedy. According to one Palestinian psychiatrist who dealt with relatives of suicide bombers, the public affirmation of martyrdom obliged parents to play a role, which made it impossible for them to mourn their children and accept 'the legitimacy of grief'.[28] Though some families rationalised the loss of their children or relatives as part of the collective patriotic sacrifice demanded by the intifada, many Palestinians have become prisoners, rather than devotees, of a cult of martyrdom that is itself a product of violence and despair.

What kind of person volunteers to become a suicide bomber? The statistics show that nearly all Palestinian suicide bombers are under the age of thirty, and 64 per cent of them are aged between 18 and 23; 40 per cent of suicide bombers have an academic education and approximately 20 per cent have at least been to high school; 68 per cent of all bombers came from the Gaza Strip, one of the poorest and most densely populated areas in the world and an Islamist stronghold. In his field research in the Gaza Strip, the Palestinian psychiatrist Dr Eyad Sarraj has reported that 25 per cent of Palestinian children aspire to martyrdom, and that many refuse to go to school because they are afraid of coming back to find that their parents have been arrested or shot or their houses destroyed. Many others have witnessed their parents humiliated or beaten up by Israeli soldiers. In this claustrophobic atmosphere of violence and fear, Sarraj has argued, 'The amazing thing is not the occurrence of the suicide bombing but rather the rarity of them.'[29]

Some Israeli analysts have tended to focus on a standard 'profile' of suicide bombers as vulnerable young men, manipulated or brainwashed by Islamist propaganda. It was clearly in Israel's interests to highlight this kind of motivation rather than the background described by Sarraj. Though reliable psychological profiles of suicide bombers are difficult to obtain for obvious reasons, there is evidence to suggest that the propaganda image of the 'happy martyr' is often as remote from its human reality as the notion of sexually obsessed young men intent on gaining access to the virgins in paradise. The disparity is particularly striking in the case of the few female *istishaadi*. When Wafa Idris, a 28-year-old female member of the secular al-Aqsa Martyrs' Brigade, blew herself up on Jerusalem's Jaffa Road in January 2002, killing several passers by, she was celebrated across the Occupied

Territories and the Arab world. One Egyptian psychiatrist compared her to the Virgin Mary, while a Jordanian journalist saw Idris as a model of a new kind of femininity, who 'did not carry in her suitcase makeup, but rather, enough explosives to fill the enemies with horror'.

These eulogies concealed a less glorious trajectory. Idris worked as a paramedic in the West Bank, where she saw wounded demonstrators bleed to death because the Israeli army refused to allow them to hospital. According to her family, these experiences outraged her to the point when she volunteered to participate in a martyrdom operation. But Idris had also been married and suffered a miscarriage. When she was declared infertile, her husband divorced her and some commentators have theorised that she saw martyrdom as the only way out of a difficult and lonely future in a patriarchal society in which she faced humiliation and exclusion.

The biographies of other female Palestinian suggest a similar desire to escape from grim personal circumstances rather than patriotic or religious fervour.[30] But if some *istishaadi* saw martyrdom as a way out of personal crisis, others regarded it as an escape from the violence and futility of life under occupation. Some suicide bombers were motivated by anger as well as despair, often in response to particular clashes with the Israeli army. A few may certainly have been psychologically disturbed or vulnerable to manipulation, but many, perhaps the majority, appear to have been 'normal' people, for whom a glorious act of martyrdom offered a means of striking back at the enemies of their community and a means of escape from an unbearable existence.[31] In the claustrophobic atmosphere of violence and humiliation, Eyad Sarraj described it thus: 'Taking your own life, and even your death, literally into your own hands – along with the lives and deaths of perhaps two dozen others – is the ultimate power.'[32]

Was it this desire for power and control that prompted Muhammed Mahmoud Nassr, a 28-year-old Palestinian, to enter the crowded Wall Street Café in Haifa in 2001 with a belt of explosives strapped to his waist? Instead of detonating the device immediately, Nassr lifted his T-shirt to reveal the explosives to a waitress and asked her if she knew what it was. The waitress and customers screamed and ran outside, throwing chairs at their would-be assassin. Nassr waited until the café was empty then shouted 'Allahu akbar' and blew himself up. By allowing his victims time to escape, he had committed suicide without the compensation of martyrdom. For a few seconds he had struck terror into the enemy, but none of the witnesses reported that he was smiling.

Martyrs without God

In secular Western societies where the majority of the population aspires to live as long as possible, the suicide bomber has often appeared to be the ultimate manifestation of 'sacred terror', and 'Islamic' terror in particular. But the most devastating campaign of suicide bombings was carried out in Sri Lanka, by the Liberation Tigers of Tamil Eelam (LTTE), a secular nationalist organisation in pursuit of a separate Tamil state: Tamil Eelam. Even before they began to carry out suicide attacks, the willingness to die was an accepted part of the Tigers' military ideology and all its fighters wore a cyanide capsule around their necks to take when captured. In July 1987, however, a Tamil fighter identified only as 'Captain Miller' drove a truck loaded with explosives into a Sri Lankan army base on the Jaffna peninsula, killing an estimated seventy soldiers. Miller was a member of a new Tamil unit called the Black Tigers, whose members were recruited solely to carry out suicide operations on land and sea.

Over the next decade the Black Tigers carried out some 200 suicide attacks, killing an estimated 901 people including two heads of state, numerous Sri Lankan army officers and politicians. Other targets included the Central Bank in Colombo, one of Sri Lanka's most famous Buddhist shrines and the island's oil refineries. The Tigers were also the only organisation to use suicide bombings as a military weapon on the battlefield. In some cases Black Tigers primed with explosives crawled hundreds of yards into an enemy bunker or military base and blew themselves up like human artillery shells. Other attacks were carried out against the Sri Lankan navy, using boats primed with explosives. In 2001 thirteen Black Tigers attacked Colombo's international airport, destroying thirteen civil and military planes in a simulation of an artillery bombardment. The following year a ceasefire was signed, by which time 240 Black Tigers had died in a campaign that some analysts believe changed the course of the war.

How did a supposedly non-religious organisation manage to motivate so many people to carry out such attacks? Some analysts have cited the youth of many Tamil Tiger fighters as an explanation. From 1995 onwards approximately 60 per cent of Tamil fighters were aged between 10 and 16, many of them war orphans, steeped in the strict military discipline and the spirit of self-sacrifice that permeated the Tigers' training camps. Other commentators have pointed to the 'cult of personality' constructed around the figure of the Tigers' leader, Vellupai Prabhakaran, and the ferocity of a savage ethnic conflict in which some 70,000 people died. Both these factors feature in the Indian director Santosh Sivan's claustrophobic film *The Terrorist* (1999), in which a female Black Tiger volunteers to kill a visiting 'VIP' in an incident that was clearly modelled on the assassination of the Indian prime minister Rajiv Gandhi by a female Tiger named 'Dhanu'. The steely 19-year-old Mali is a woman forged by war, haunted by the atrocious violence she has seen and inflicted. After her ritual 'last supper' with the faceless Tigers leader, the 'thinking bomb' is sent to live undercover with a local farmer, while she waits for the VIP's arrival. The contact with the everyday human world proves fatal. When Mali discovers that she is pregnant, doubts begin to undermine her resolve. When the moment of the assassination arrives, Mali drapes a garland round the faceless VIP's neck but she cannot bring herself to press the button on her explosive device.

Gandhi's assassin, a young Tamil woman raped by Indian soldiers, did not make the same choice. As Robert Pape has argued, the idea that the survival of the Tamil people was at stake generated a spirit of extraordinary self-sacrifice and created a collective acceptance of martyrdom amongst the Tamil community as a whole.[33] This veneration of martyrdom was encouraged by the establishment of a 'martyrological calendar' on the Lebanese model, which included a 'Black Tigers day' in July, when garlands of flowers were hung round the photographs of the more than 200 martyrs whom Prabhakaran called 'the children of the flame'. Though the Tigers used the Sanskrit term *tiyaki* – one who abandons life – to describe their fallen fighters, the organisation did not conceive of martyrdom in an explicitly religious sense. The *tiyaki* did not live on in the afterlife, but became 'seeds' that would be 'planted' in the future independent Tamil state. Their place in posterity was commemorated in roadside monuments, shrines and the names of streets and disseminated through a professionalised propaganda apparatus consisting of films, CDs of martyr songs, postcards and posters.[34]

As in Lebanon and Palestine, individual Black Tigers became exemplary heroes, whose lives were celebrated in hagiographic biographies in Tamil newspapers, steeped in a sombre mixture of heroism and tragic sacrifice, such as the following obituary in *Erimalai* (Volcano) commemorating a female Black Sea Tiger, 'Major Santhana', who died during a multiple operation against the Sri Lankan navy, in which she and five of her colleagues 'settled into the sea permanently'. As always, the operation was preceded by a last visit home, in which the eager volunteer says goodbye to her parents and family:

> Major Santhana knew well that her long dream and the objective would be successful this time. With that in mind she visited her mother at home for the

last time. Her mother told her, 'Child, will you visit us frequently?' She replies, 'Shortly, Mother, very shortly.' Her mother, at that moment, didn't understand the meaning of her daughter ... She said farewell to her daughter, by hugging and kissing her, with tears. Then her mother was unaware that she would surely return home shortly; but, as a photograph![35]

Other Black Tiger biographies carry the same themes of home, mother, and the poignant last farewell. Unlike the Palestinians, the Black Tigers did not record valedictory farewell messages. Instead they were filmed in videos known as 'memory tapes' in which they appeared in boats or walking through soft grass, waving and smiling at the camera with a soundtrack of dubbed music. The Tigers also filmed their actual operations, which were afterwards edited and woven into a seamless narrative of self-sacrificial heroism. The apparently inexhaustible supply of available recruits was a clear demonstration of the success of these procedures. In this way the Tigers were able to compensate for their military weakness and demonstrate once again that suicide bombings owed more to the strategic requirements of 'asymmetrical warfare' than they did to religion or the sacred.

11

Waiting for Catastrophe

Almost everyone will agree that we live in a deeply troubled society
The 'Unabomber' Manifesto, 1995

It came from Nazi Germany,
A dangerous little chemical weapon,
   Sarin, sarin,
If you inhale the mysterious vapour,
You will fall with bloody vomit from your mouth,
Sarin, sarin, sarin,
The chemical weapon
'Song of Sarin the Magician', Aum Shinrikyo work song, circa 1995

In the last decade of the twentieth century the 'age of terrorism' entered a new and paradoxical phase. On the one hand there was an overall decline in the number of recorded terrorist incidents worldwide compared with the 1980s. At the same time there was an increasingly alarmist consensus amongst Western security analysts that terrorism was now more dangerous and unpredictable than it had ever been. With the end of the Cold War, some experts argued that terrorism had undergone a 'paradigm shift', character-ised by what a 1999 US government report on profiling terrorists called 'a different attitude toward violence – one that is extranormative and seeks to maximize violence against a perceived enemy'.[1] That same year the FBI's 'Project Meggido' warned that a 'volatile mix of apocalyptic religions and NWO [New World Order] conspiracy theories may produce violent acts aimed at precipitating the end of the world as prophesied in the Bible'. Not only were these 'new' post-modern terrorists supposedly less subject to moral constraints than their more ideological or 'political' predecessors, and therefore more disposed to inflict mass casualties, but they were now perceived as having greater potential ability to do so, using technical infor-mation found on the Internet or by gaining access to the nuclear arsenal of the former Soviet Union. Throughout the decade these fears generated a stream of catastrophic hypotheses, particularly in the United States, where politicians and security experts issued increasingly dire predictions of terrorist attacks using chemical and biological weapons or home-made nuclear 'dirty bombs' concealed in suitcases. Others warned of the possibility of a 'cyberspace Pearl Harbor' in which terrorist hackers shut down the US electricity grid or caused the international financial system to collapse.

These fears were reflected and to some extent encouraged by a spate of Hollywood blockbusters in which a succession of crazed foreigners carried out 'megaterrorist' attacks on the United States. Despite nearly half a century under threat of Mutually Assured Destruction, the world was now considered to be even more unstable and dangerous than it had been during the Cold War. 'Megaterrorism' was only one of various terrorist neologisms to emerge in the same period, along with cyberterrorism, narcoterrorism, ecoterrorism and even sexual terrorism, the last term coined by an American feminist academic to describe male violence against women. By this time 'terrorism' had acquired such dreadful potency that its semantic application appeared to be limitless, even if its actual meaning became increasingly difficult to determine. All these different manifestations of 'terrorism' flitted across the pre-millennial landscape as an increasingly nervous Western world looked to the new century with more trepidation than enthusiasm.

Terror in the heartland

These 'new terrorism' narratives reflected a new perception in the US foreign-policy establishment of the world's only superpower as a vulnerable colossus, facing an unpredictable array of threats, from terrorists and apocalyptic religious sects to fundamentalist terror groups working in tandem with 'rogue states'. With the collapse of the Soviet Union, a number of US foreign-policy analysts depicted Islamic fundamentalism as the primary threat to American security. In the early 1990s the conservative Middle East specialist Bernard Lewis and the Harvard political scientist Samuel Huntington predicted that Islamic fundamentalism would replace communism as an existential threat to the West and that the ideological confrontation of the previous hundred years would be superseded by a 'clash of civilisations'.

Within a few years of the end of the Cold War, the 'new' terrorism and the fundamentalist threat narratives appeared to converge, as the fallout from the Afghan jihad reached the United States itself. The first manifestation of this process occurred in November 1990, when the racist Jewish demagogue Rabbi Meir Kahane was assassinated in New York by an Egyptian-American named El Sayyid Nosair. Though Nosair was tried as a 'lone gunman' there was evidence that he was connected to a US-based cell, consisting of 'Arab Afghan' veterans, connected to the Egyptian cleric Sheikh Omar Abd al-Rahman. The 'Blind Sheikh' had been granted a tourist visa in May 1990 by a CIA officer at the US embassy in Sudan, even though his name was included in a State Department terrorist watch-list. On arrival in the United States Rahman established himself at the al-Kifah Refugee Center in Brooklyn's Atlantic Avenue, a long-established recruiting office for the Afghan jihad.

The reasons for the CIA's largesse towards a man who denounced Americans in his sermons as 'descendants of apes and pigs' are not known, though one FBI official later told the *Village Voice* reporter Robert Friedman that the Sheikh was in America 'under the banner of national security, the State Department, the NSA and the CIA.'[2] Though the Sheikh was not arrested for the Kahane assassination, the FBI nevertheless infiltrated an Egyptian informer into the Sheikh's circle, who warned his superiors of a forthcoming plot to blow up the World Trade Center. The informer even offered to switch the bomb for a harmless dummy, but these warnings were disbelieved. On 26 February 1993, however, a 1,200lb device containing cyanide, hydrogen gas and urea concealed in a rented Ryder van exploded in a garage underneath the World Trade Center. Astonishingly, even though it blasted a massive hole under the building three storeys deep, the explosion killed only six people, though it wounded more than a thousand. A communiqué sent to the *New York Times* from the 'fifth battalion in the Liberation Army' claimed responsibility and called on the United States to withdraw its support for Israel and to cease interference in 'the Middle East countries interior affairs'.[3] Within a few weeks a number of arrests had been made, which traced the bombing to the same group of 'Afghan Arabs' that had produced Kahane's assassin.

In the wake of the bombing the FBI launched a sting operation using the same agent, which led to the arrest of the Blind Sheikh and other members of his circle for involvement in a subsequent plot to blow up a series of landmarks in New York. In January 1996 Rahman was tried for his involvement in the 'landmark plot' and sentenced to life imprisonment. It was not until two years later that the man who had constructed the World Trade Center bomb went on trial and it emerged just how cataclysmic the attack might have been.

The most dangerous man in the world
To Western counter-terrorist investigators, the incarnation of the new terror-

ism 'paradigm shift' was the young man known by one of his many aliases as Ramzi Yousef. The son of a Kuwaiti mother and a father from Baluchistan, Yousef was a talented electronics student, who first became involved in jihadist circles in Afghanistan in the early 1990s, where he revealed a talent for bomb making and a taste for catastrophic terrorist spectaculars. The World Trade Center bombing was conceived by Yousef and his uncle, Khalid Sheikh Mohammed, a Baluchi businessman and veteran of the Afghan jihad. Yousef entered the United States in 1992 by pretending to seek political asylum and went on to construct the bomb. Yousef fled the US before his role was discovered and based himself in the Philippines, where he and his uncle continued to plot new terrorist outrages, including the so-called 'Bojinka plot', an astonishing operation which included the destruction of twelve US airliners in mid-air over the Pacific on a single day, using small bombs equipped with Yousef's trademark Casio digital watch timers. The plot was foiled when Yousef and an accomplice named Abdul Hakim Murad accidentally caused a fire while preparing a bomb. Though Murad was arrested, Yousef escaped again.

In February 1995 the man described by the Filipino police as 'the most dangerous man alive' was arrested in a guesthouse in Pakistan by a hastily assembled team of US agents. On the plane escorting him back to the US, Yousef admitted responsibility for the World Trade Center bombing and informed his escorts that his bomb had been intended to bring one tower crashing down into the other, in order to bring about an estimated 250,000 casualties and thereby demonstrate to the United States that it was 'at war'. Yousef did not fit the profile of the fundamentalist terrorist. Unlike Sheikh Rahman, he was neither pious nor devout and displayed an un-Islamic fondness for luxury hotels, strip clubs and karaoke bars. His primary motivation appears to have been a passionate identification with the Palestinian cause and an implacable loathing for Israel, a state that he regarded as 'void morally and legally', rather than the 'aggressive fanaticism of the believer' that Bernard Lewis saw as an innate characteristic of Islamic fundamentalism.

Though he escaped the death penalty on technical grounds, he was sentenced in February 1997 to 240 years in prison and his terms of imprisonment were subject to a number of exceptional restrictions, which the judge insisted were necessary to contain 'a virus which, if loosed, could cause plague and pestilence throughout the world'. In his statement to the court Yousef defined himself as 'a terrorist and proud of it' and denounced the US government and Israel as 'butchers, liars and hypocrites'. Yousef compared the World Trade Center bombing to Israel's policy of collective punishment in the Occupied Territories, arguing that since the United States was Israel's main source of military and economic aid then American citizens were 'logically and legally' responsible for the oppression of the Palestinians. He also listed examples of the way that the United States killed 'innocent people ... just to force countries to abandon their policies', from Hiroshima and the Vietnam war to the more recent sanctions against Iraq.[4]

If Yousef's willingness to inflict such massive casualties seemed to bear out the 'megaterrorist' thesis, the logic that he invoked to defend his actions was not entirely alien to the civilised consensus. In a May 1996 television interview on UN sanctions against Iraq, the UN ambassador Madeleine Albright was asked, 'We have heard that a half a million children have died. I mean, that's more children than died in Hiroshima. Is the price worth it?' Albright famously replied, 'I think this is a very hard choice, but the price – we think the price is worth it.' Yousef and his circle had clearly made their own calculations and the World Trade Center bombing was only the first act in a process that would culminate in the September 11 attacks. It was a process that Yousef himself would play no further part in. He was sent to serve his sentence in the high security 'Supermax' prison, where he was placed under 24-hour watch. Though some of the restrictive conditions were subsequently lifted, the terrorist career of the most dangerous man in the world was over.

The American terrorist

The spectre of a seditious foreign enemy is a recurring theme in American history, from the xenophobic public response to the Haymarket incident in Chicago to the obsession with communist 'sleeper cells' during the McCarthy era. In the wake of the World Trade Center bombing, various pundits warned of a looming terrorist onslaught from Islamic fundamentalists both inside and outside America. In a 1994 documentary entitled *Jihad in America*, journalist Steven Emerson portrayed a nation riddled with Islamic terrorist groups. In February 1996, the Nixon Center held a conference on 'megaterrorism' during which the academic Laurie Mylroie warned of future attacks from 'Muslim bombing brigades and sabotage units'. Not for the first time, the perception of the threat bore no relation to the scale of the violence itself. That same month the *Christian Science Monitor* quoted FBI statistics dating back to 1980 showing that 'only two of the 170 acts of terror on US soil by foreign nationals were committed by Islamists'.

The fact that the World Trade Center bombing was the work of a jihadist cell, many of whose members were veterans of CIA covert operations in

Afghanistan, rarely featured in the 'fundamentalists are coming' narratives. Where 1970s terrorologists had once accused the US intelligence establishment and the 'liberal media' of deliberately ignoring Soviet-backed terrorism, proponents of the Islamic terror thesis insisted that the intelligence services were blinded by 'political correctness' from recognising the threat. The preoccupation with 'Islamic' terrorism was also reflected in a number of Hollywood films of the nineties. In the Arnold Schwarzenegger vehicle *True Lies* (1994) a maniacal Palestinian terrorist group called 'Crimson Jihad' attempt to set off nuclear warheads in New York. In *Executive Decision* (1996), Palestinian terrorists attempt to wipe out the entire Eastern seaboard with nerve gas. In *The Siege* (1998), an Islamic terror cell kills 700 people in a wave of bombings and suicide attacks, leading to martial law and the internment of the Arab-American population of New York. Hollywood's fixation with fundamentalist terrorism culminated in *Rules of Engagement* (2000), in which a Marine colonel is court-martialled for ordering his men to open fire on anti-US protests in Yemen, killing eighty-three people. Though the victims initially appear to be civilians, the colonel is finally exonerated when evidence reveals that the entire crowd consists of armed terrorists, including the women and children.

The crazed 'Islamic' terrorists with garbled politics and homicidal agendas who appeared in these films were drawn from a tradition that could be traced back to the anarchist caricatures drawn by Thomas Nash and others in the era of the Haymarket bombing. If these stereotypes were monstrous and frightening, the presentation of 'terrorism' as the work of the cultural, racial or ideological 'Other' ignored more domestic sources of violence. Between 1991 and 1995 there were 4,456 pipe-bomb attacks across America, 900 incidents involving Molotov cocktails and grenades, and 200 arson attacks on churches.[5] As in Germany in the same period, the majority of these incidents were carried out by individuals or organisations connected to the far right. Throughout the decade Christian fundamentalists and neo-Nazis were responsible for bombings, murders and arson attacks, whose targets included abortion clinics, gay bars and synagogues.

These events failed to generate the kind of threat narratives that accrued to 'Islamic' terrorism. The spectre of fundamentalist terror surfaced once again on 19 April 1995, when a 7,000lb bomb destroyed the Alfred Murrah federal building in Oklahoma City, which housed the offices of the FBI and the Bureau of Alcohol, Tobacco and Firearms (ATF). The blast ripped open the glass-fronted building, collapsing nine storeys of offices and a day-care nursery on the second floor, killing 168 people, including nineteen children, and injuring another 500. Television cameras captured the harrowing after-math of the explosion as the injured and bleeding victims were carried from the ruins and a distraught fireman emerged from the building carrying a dead toddler in his arms.

Most viewers shared the shocked incomprehension of the Oklahoma fire chief, who told the cameras: 'This isn't supposed to happen in the heart-land'. Though no organisation claimed responsibility, there was no doubt in the minds of the usual media pundits who was responsible. Thus the academic Daniel Pipes, one of the most prominent Islamic threat polemi-cists, told *USA Today*: 'The fundamentalists are on the upsurge, and they make it very clear that they are targeting us. They are absolutely obsessed with us', while Steven Emerson told *CBS News* that the bombing was carried out 'with the intent to inflict as many casualties as possible. That is a Mid-Eastern trait.'[6]

Within a few days, however, it was announced that the FBI had arrested a 27-year-old American Gulf War veteran named Timothy McVeigh and charged him with the bombing. McVeigh's unremarkable blue-collar back-ground defied conventional explanations regarding the essential 'Otherness' of terrorism. Apart from a teenage preoccupation with guns and survival-ism, there was nothing in his personal life or behaviour to explain how the 18-year-old who wrote in his high-school yearbook of his plans to 'take life as it comes ... buy a Lamborghini ... California girls' evolved into a seditious mass murderer.

The decisive episode in the transformation of the 'boy next door' into an 'American terrorist' appears to have been his participation as a soldier in the first Gulf War. Though McVeigh was initially enthusiastic about his first experience of combat and received a commendation for bravery, he was shocked by the unequal nature of the war and came to feel that his govern-ment had misrepresented it. After leaving the army in the early 1990s he became involved in the heterogeneous collection of groups and organisa-tions that made up the right-wing 'anti-government' or 'Patriot' movement. These organisations covered a wide spectrum of beliefs, from racist Chris-tian Identity churches and survivalists who believed that America had been taken over by the Zionist Occupation Government (ZOG) on behalf of the New World Order, to anti-government activists who refused to recognise any authority above county level. But the core issues that united all the dif-ferent factions were a common hostility to 'big government' and an opposi-tion to any form of firearms legislation.

The belief that the US government was overstepping its powers was reinforced by a number of violent confrontations between law enforcement agents and right-wing militants that occurred during the early years of the Clinton administration, culminating in the disastrous assault on the Branch Dravidian religious sect at Waco in April 1993 by the FBI, in which dozens of Branch Dravidians were killed, many of them children. Though the siege was presented as an act of mass suicide, subsequent investigations revealed that the FBI themselves may have precipitated the fire. McVeigh visited Waco during the siege and, according to the official account, he and an army buddy named Terry Nichols were so enraged by its bloody denouement that they began their own unilateral preparations to blow up the Alfred Murrah building as an act of revenge.[7]

Though McVeigh's politics were right wing, his tactical conception of the bombing as a 'message' belonged to the nineteenth-century revolutionary terrorist tradition. His letters written in the months leading up to Oklahoma reveal the same narcissistic heroism, the same sense of overwhelming griev-ance and the willingness to sacrifice himself for the transcendental cause, that has prevailed in many different groups and organisations from the same lineage. A child of the television age, McVeigh later claimed that he chose the Alfred Murrah building because its glass-fronted façade presented a suitably telegenic target, with its wide, open car park where television cameras and photographers would be able to capture the most dramatic visual images afterwards. The result, according to James 'Bo' Gritz, a former Green Beret and the leader of a white supremacist survivalist group called Almost Heaven, was a 'Rembrandt – a masterpiece of science and art'.

The 'explanation' for the worst terrorist attack in American history was found in McVeigh's car at the time of his arrest, in a folio of documents which included quotations from American revolutionaries in the War of Independence and from John Locke and Winston Churchill together with a copy of the Declaration of Independence. McVeigh also included excerpts from the racist cult novel *The Turner Diaries*, which describes an armed rebel-lion by a Nazi group called 'The Organisation' against the US government, including a bomb attack on the FBI headquarters in Washington which was remarkably similar to the Oklahoma bombing.

The lone wolf

To much of the American public these 'clues' failed to explain why an American citizen could have carried out such an atrocity. Not only did the Oklahoma bombing reveal for the first time the existence of a seditious and entirely home-grown movement whose membership was estimated to be in the millions, but members of this same movement publicly approved of the bombing. Nor could the anti-government movement be dismissed as a lunatic expression of the political fringe. Its hyperbolic anti-government rhetoric was routinely espoused by fundamentalist televangelists such as Pat Robertson and right-wing radio talk show hosts who referred to law enforcement agents as 'goon squads' and 'jackbooted thugs'. A few observers pointed out McVeigh's ideological connections to the political mainstream, but in general the US media preferred to present him as a freakish aberration and an isolated misfit from a broken home.

Much of this was pure speculation and invention. Various character witnesses, including a prison psychiatrist, testified to McVeigh's lucidity and normality, and his 'normality' was frequently highlighted at his trial in June 1997, where his lawyers set out to depict him as a sincere but misguided patriot. The jury rejected these arguments and McVeigh was found guilty and sentenced to death. His lawyers then began a long drawn-out appeals process. In 1998, while awaiting execution in Terre Haute penitentiary, McVeigh entered into correspondence with the writer Gore Vidal, whose views on the authoritarian tendencies of the US government were not entirely removed from his own. Though some critics of the 'lone wolf' presentation of McVeigh have depicted him as a brainwashed right-wing patsy, his letters to Vidal are lucid and coherent in both his critique of the US government and his justification for the Oklahoma bombing. In his last letter, written in 2001, he compared the bombing of the Murrah building to the US bombing of Baghdad, and told Vidal how,

> borrowing a page from US foreign policy, I decided to send a message to a government that was becoming increasingly hostile, by bombing a government building and the government employees within that building who represent that government. Bombing the Murrah Federal Building was morally and strategically equivalent to the US hitting a government building in Serbia, Iraq, or other nations ... From this perspective what occurred in Oklahoma City was no different than what Americans rain on the heads of others all the time, and subsequently, my mindset was and is one of clinical detachment.[8]

This rationale was not that different from the logic espoused by Ramzi Yousef, one of McVeigh's fellow prisoners in the maximum security 'Supermax' prison, even if McVeigh invoked a more conventional 'military' defence of his actions. McVeigh always presented himself as a prisoner of war and even used the jargon he had acquired during the Gulf War to describe the bombing, referring to the children he had killed as 'an awful lot of collateral damage'. The former Gulf War veteran continued to demonstrate the same 'clinical detachment' for the remaining years of his life. In February 2001 the mother of one of the Oklahoma victims wrote McVeigh an anguished letter, in which she asked him:

> Have you thought about the people who died or were injured? Have you thought about their families and friends? Can you imagine what it must be like for those of us who have been left behind? Are you sad about their deaths? Can you see them as innocent victims, not as representatives of a government you believed was evil?[9]

It is not known if McVeigh replied, but there is no reason to think that he would have entered into a dialogue of this kind. In the spring that year, he abruptly cancelled the appeal process, even after his lawyers discovered new evidence suggesting that he had not acted alone, and announced his intention to commit 'state-assisted suicide'. On 11 June 2001 McVeigh was executed by lethal injection in the Terre Haute penitentiary, leaving many questions unanswered about the wider network that some observers believed had been involved in the bombing. In his death certificate, under 'usual occupation' the author of what was then the bloodiest terrorist attack in American history described himself as 'soldier'.

Towards Armageddon?

The Oklahoma bombing occurred less than a month after the Japanese religious cult Aum Shinrikyo carried out a nerve-gas attack on the Tokyo subway on 20 March 1995, and confirmed the impression that terrorism was forming new and unpredictable tributaries of madness and fanaticism. Founded by a half-mad confidence trickster and self-proclaimed spiritual master named Shoko Asahara, Aum Shinrikyo, Supreme Truth, appeared on the surface to be one of many 'new religions' which flourished in Japan at the end of the century, albeit one with some bizarre practices, such as the obligatory wearing of 'Perfect Salvation Initiative' headsets that supposedly transmitted Asahara's brainwaves to his disciples.

Asahara's teachings were an eclectic mixture of yoga, New Age philosophy, apocalyptic prophecy and anti-Semitism, fused by a paranoid millenarianism and a megalomaniac fascination with high-tech weaponry that borrowed from science fiction and Japanese manga comics.[10] Aum's fixation with Armageddon was shared by other apocalyptic groups in different parts of the world, but Asahara's organisation went much further than any other group had gone to actually prepare for this eventuality. In addition to its religious activities, the organisation functioned as a successful business corporation, with a portfolio of national and international investments valued at between $300 million to $1 billion. These legal business dealings concealed a range of criminal activities, from drug dealing and extortion to illegal property deals and murder. The profits from these various sidelines enabled Aum to develop a $30 million weapons programme involving more than 100 scientists, researchers and technicians, who worked on a range of projects from the manufacture of Russian AK-74 rifles to the production of biological pathogens, such as anthrax and botulism.

Asahara also explored the possibility of acquiring atomic weapons and material from the former Soviet Union, without success. Aum nevertheless managed to develop a range of chemical weapons, including phosgene, Zyklon B, VX gas and sarin and carried out various live experiments in Japanese cities, with mixed results. Incredibly, this activity remained undiscovered, despite one nerve-gas attack on the town of Matsumoto in June 1994 which killed seven people and seriously poisoned dozens more. On 20 March 1995, ten members of the organisation, operating in pairs, boarded different trains in the crowded Tokyo underground and punctured polythene bags filled with sarin with sharpened umbrellas. By the end of the day some 5,000 people had been affected, some of whom remained in a permanent vegetative state. In total twelve people died. Had the sarin been purer the casualties might have run into hundreds of thousands.

The reason for the attacks was never entirely clear, even to their perpetrators, but they appeared to be partly intended to head off an impending police investigation into Aum's activities. Instead, the resulting national panic finally forced the authorities to take action, as 2,500 police wearing protective clothing descended on Aum compounds around Mount Fuji and carried out hundreds of arrests. In May that year Asahara, the incarnation of Christ and Buddha, was found hiding in a cubicle in one of his Aum compounds in a puddle of his own urine, surrounded by piles of Japanese banknotes. By that time Aum Shinrikyo had already begun to shape perceptions of terrorism at the end of the new century

The uses of fear

On the surface, Aum Shinrikyo was a freakish millenarian sect that does not belong to the revolutionary terrorist tradition at all. Nevertheless, the incident had a decisive impact on the emerging 'megaterrorist' narratives in the United States, where the Senate Armed Services Committee carried out its own inquiry into the Tokyo incident. The committee considered various hypothetical 'megaterrorist' attacks on the United States, including one scenario in which a radio-guided drone might fly into the Capitol during the State of the Union address, wreaking what one senator described as 'tremendous death and destruction and havoc on the leadership of the American government'.

The fact that a scenario from a Tom Clancy novel should be cited in the US Senate as a genuine possibility was not uncommon in the elaboration of megaterrorist hypotheses. But the Tokyo attacks also occurred at a time when the American and British governments were seeking to ratchet up the pressure on Iraq to permit UNSCOM weapons inspections. In 1997 US government officials issued a series of dire predictions on the consequences of a chemical or biological attack on the United States, which reached a crescendo in November 1997, when defence secretary William Cohen appeared on the ABC's *This Week* with a five-pound bag of sugar and claimed that an equivalent amount of anthrax used in an attack on Washington 'would destroy at least half the population'.

In a syndicated newspaper column the defence secretary referred directly to the Tokyo gas attacks and warned 'the race is on between our perpetrators and those of our adversaries ... There is not a moment to lose.'[11] President Clinton also entered the fray, telling an audience in Sacramento on 15 November to examine the current crisis over Iraq 'in terms of the innocent Japanese people that died in the subway when the sarin gas was released'. In the same speech Clinton warned of the risk of an attack from biological or chemical weapons and insisted that it was more imperative than ever 'not to let irresponsible people develop the capacity to put them in warheads on missiles or put them in briefcases that could be exploded in small rooms. And I say this not to frighten you.'

Clinton was being disingenuous. Fear was precisely the point of his administration's bioterrorism doomsday hypotheses, and fear of Iraq in particular. The attempts to link Iraq and Aum Shinrikyo were partly motivated by political convenience, but the administration's bioterrorism fixation was also another example of the slippage between fact, fiction and paranoia that so often informs the perception of terrorism. That year Clinton read Richard Preston's thriller *The Cobra Event*, in which terrorists attack New York by infecting the subway system with smallpox. Clinton was so impressed by the book that he asked intelligence agents to evaluate its credibility. As a result Preston, a thriller writer and *New Yorker* journalist, appeared before various senatorial committees as an expert on the subject of bioterrorism in 1998.

That same year the Clinton administration requested $94 million funding to build up a civilian stockpile of medicines in the event of a chemical or biological attack. Despite the 'not if, but when' predictions emanating from the administration, not all analysts were convinced that biological and chemical attacks could have the apocalyptic effects attributed to them. Some experts pointed out that chemical and biological weapons demanded a level of expertise that even Aum Shinrikyo, with all its vast financial and technical resources, had not been able to achieve. Others noted that anthrax was extremely difficult to use as a weapon of mass destruction because of the technical difficulties in disseminating it over a wide area. While these difficulties did not preclude the possibility that solutions might be found, they did cast serious doubts on the administration's insistence that a chemical or biological terrorist attack was inevitable. Despite the availability on the Internet of do-it-yourself terrorist manuals such as *The Terrorist's Cookbook*, *The Poor Man's James Bond* and *The Mujahideen Poisons Handbook*, most of the information available in these manuals bore little relation to the catastrophic mass destruction that politicians such as Cohen and Senator Sam Nunn envisaged. According to Henry Sokolski, executive director of the Nonproliferation Policy Education Center in Washington, in the whole of the twentieth century there were only seventy-one known terrorist incidents using chemical or biological weapons worldwide, not including the use of such weapons in wartime. In the United States in the same period 784 non-fatal injuries were known to have occurred through the use of biowarfare, 751 of which were in 1985, when the Baghwan Rajneesh sect in Oregon deliberately infected a restaurant with salmonella bacteria in order to reduce the number of voters in local elections. Though Sokolski did not preclude the possibility that such attacks could take place, he nevertheless advised against 'focusing on the most horrific scenarios at the expense of preparing for the most likely ones'.[12]

A July 1999 article in the *Bulletin of Atomic Scientists* on chemical and biological terrorism entitled 'An Unlikely Threat' criticised the 'whiff of hysteria' in US government presentations of unconventional terrorist attacks, which the authors claimed derived in part from an 'obsessive fascination with catastrophic terrorism in Hollywood films, best-selling books and other mainstays of pop culture'. By this time more than forty US government agencies were competing for a share of the burgeoning chemical and biodefence budget and a new generation of 'megaterrorist' theoreticians imagined an ever-expanding range of possible terrorist attacks on the United States, involving nuclear bombs in suitcases, nerve gas, germs, plagues, pathogens from anthrax and ricin to typhoid and botulinum, cobra venom and shell-fish toxin. The most charitable explanation for these alarmist megaterrorist scenarios was an overzealous desire to protect the American public. But just as the 'old' terrorism of the 1970s had been used as an instrument of Cold War disinformation, so the 'new' terrorism was increasingly woven into a political agenda directed against America's current enemies.

In June 2001 a two-day simulation of a bioterrorist attack on America called 'Dark Winter' was staged at a US Air Force base near Washington. Fourteen participants and sixty observers explored a fictional scenario in which terrorists plant smallpox bacteria in Oklahoma and set off a nation-wide epidemic. The meeting was convened by James Woolsey, an ex-CIA director with close ties to Ahmed Chalabi's Iraqi National Congress, and its participants included Judith Miller, a *New York Times* journalist and author of *Germs*. In 2005 Miller was exposed as a conduit for disinformation on the Iraqi biological and chemical weapons programme and forced to leave the paper, after serving a prison sentence over her involvement in the 'Plameg-ate' scandal.[13] At the time, however, Miller was regarded as an authority on biological warfare and her presence added a further touch of gravitas to the proceedings. The simulation imagined a catastrophe, with some 6,000 Americans dying in the first month and millions of refugees trying to flee the infected areas before the army introduced martial law. Who was responsible for these events? A simulated satellite news channel, NCN, informed the participants 'that Iraq may have provided the technology behind the attacks to terrorist groups based in Afghanistan'.

Much of this was a variant on a terrorist disaster movie, given a semblance of authenticity by the presence of real 'experts'. But the simulation was filmed and videotapes sent to officials in the Bush administration, including Vice-President Dick Cheney, who subsequently proposed a national vaccination scheme against smallpox. Dark Winter also produced dozens of news stories and at least one television docudrama. Once again, more sober assessments of the possible consequences of a smallpox epidemic were available, but such information was less dramatic and less politically convenient than the official emphasis on terrorism, rogue states and weapons of mass destruc-tion. In this way the madness of Aum Shinrikyo continued to hover over the new millennium, a reference point for the worst possible future.

The rise of Osama bin Laden

On 22 February 1998 a group of Islamist militants at an armed camp in Afghanistan gave a press conference to announce the formation of the 'World Islamic Front for Jihad against the Jews and the Crusaders'. The centre of the group was a little-known Saudi Arabian veteran of the Afghan war named Osama bin Laden, flanked by the former Egyptian al-Jihad militant Ayman al-Zawahiri. Bin Laden calmly listed the 'crimes and calamities' inflicted on the Muslim nation by the 'Crusader–Zionist alliance', beginning with the American presence in the Arabian peninsula:

> For over seven years the United States has been occupying the lands of Islam in the holiest of places … plundering its riches, dictating to its rulers, humiliating its people, terrorising its neighbours, and turning its bases in the Peninsula into a spearhead through which to fight the neighbouring Muslim peoples.[14]

Since these and other 'Crusader' depredations amounted to 'an explicit dec-laration by the Americans of war on God, his messenger, and Muslims', Bin Laden declared that 'The ruling to kill and fight Americans and their allies, whether civilian or military, is an obligation for every Muslim who is able to do so in any country.' The declaration caused no immediate official reaction in the United States. On 7 August, however, a massive truck bomb exploded outside the American embassy in Nairobi, killing more than 200 people, the majority of them Africans. Nine minutes after the explosion another bomb exploded outside the American embassy in Dar-es-Salaam, killing eleven Tanzanians. President Clinton immediately accused bin Laden of respon-sibility and ordered simultaneous missile strikes against 'terrorist facilities and infrastructure' in Afghanistan and the al-Shifa pharmaceutical factory in Sudan that was part owned by bin Laden and alleged to be manufac-turing chemical weapons. The US retaliation turned into a public relations disaster when it emerged that the pharmaceutical plant was manufacturing not chemical weapons, but anti-malaria pills for the Sudanese population. If the world had not known about Osama bin Laden before, it did now, and there was no doubt who had won the first round in the emerging confronta-tion.

The terror master

In the pantheon of terrorist monsters, Osama bin Laden occupies a unique and unrivalled position. In the Western world he has been variously described as the Pied Piper of the modern jihad, a terrorist entrepreneur who speculates on the stock exchange yet seeks to take the world back into the seventh century, and a brilliant propagandist and military strategist, adept at the manipulation and exploitation of his opponents' weaknesses. In some parts of the Muslim world, bin Laden has assumed the status of a folk hero. His face appears on posters and match boxes and T-shirts, riding a white horse in imitation of the Prophet and Salah-al-Din. To his more fervent admirers he is a warrior/saint, a millionaire who abandoned a life of luxury to fight the jihad in the Afghan mountains out of his love of God and Muslims. He is a brave fighter who has fought against two superpowers, whom the newspaper *Al-Quds al-Arabi* interviewed in 1996 in a spartan Afghan cave, with a small library of religious books, its walls 'decorated with Kalashnikovs'.

Bin Laden's friends and associates are virtually unanimous in describing him as a humble, courteous man, utterly lacking in vanity or pretension. If he is fierce and uncompromising in war he is also generous, kind and charitable, visiting wounded Afghan and Arab veterans in Peshawar hospitals to dispense chocolates and nuts, compensating their families with generous cheques, building roads in Afghanistan. All these conflicting images have attached themselves to a man whose legendary status is already assured, yet whose exact role in the violent events of the last decade or so have yet to be fully clarified. He was born in 1957, the son of the founder of the Saudi Binladen Group, the largest construction company in Saudi Arabia. Bin Laden's transformation into an ardent Islamist warrior was a direct result of the anti-Soviet jihad in Afghanistan, which he joined in 1980. Bin Laden placed his family's personal wealth at the disposal of the jihad and fought courageously in various battles, gathering a coterie of dedicated fighters around him. In addition he established a close relationship with the Pakistani and Saudi Arabian intelligence services and collaborated closely with the charismatic jihad fundraiser Abdullah Azzam.

The CIA has always disclaimed any responsibility for bin Laden, claiming that its officials had no direct contact with him. These claims have been disputed by some critics of American policy in Afghanistan, but given the fact that the Pakistani and Saudi secret services acted as US surrogates, there was no need for such direct contact. What is certain is that as the Afghan war moved towards a conclusion, bin Laden and Azzam began to consider ways in which the spirit of the jihad might be mobilised beyond Afghanistan. In 1987 Azzam wrote in the Afghan Arab journal *al-Jihad*:

Every principle needs a vanguard to carry it forward and, while focusing its way into society, puts up with heavy tasks and enormous sacrifices. There is no ideology, neither earthly nor heavenly, that does not require such a vanguard that gives everything it possesses in order to achieve victory for this ideology. It carries the flag all along the sheer, endless and difficult path until it reaches its destination in the reality of life, since Allah has destined that it should make it and manifest itself.[15]

The name Azzam gave to this projected vanguard was *al-qaeda al-sulbah*, the 'base' or 'strong foundation' – the name that was subsequently attached to bin Laden's organisation. In the immediate aftermath of the anti-Soviet jihad it was not immediately obvious what this projected vanguard would do. In 1989 Azzam was blown up by a car bomb in Peshawar and the following year bin Laden returned to Saudi Arabia, where he fell out with the Saudi regime following the Iraqi invasion of Kuwait, when his offer to recruit an army of Afghan veterans to defend the kingdom was turned down. Bin Laden was infuriated by the Saudi royal family's decision to grant this task to the United States instead and regarded the presence of infidel troops in the 'Land of the Two Holy Places' as a blasphemous intrusion, even though US facilities were partly built by his father's company. Two years later bin Laden moved to Sudan, where he continued to add to his considerable fortune and began constructing the international network to which the name 'al-Qaeda' would subsequently be given.

It was in this period that bin Laden's group allegedly began to carry out attacks on American targets for the first time, including the 'Black Hawk down' ambush in Mogadishu in 1993 and the Khobar Towers bombing in Saudi Arabia in June 1996, in which nineteen US military personnel were killed. In August 1996 bin Laden issued a 'Declaration of Jihad Against the Americans Occupying the Land of the Two Holy Mosques' – a document that marks the formal beginning of his confrontation with the United States. That same year bin Laden was forced to leave Sudan, following strong US pressure. The Sudanese government later claimed that it offered to hand bin Laden over into US custody and that these offers were refused, a claim that the United States denies. Instead, bin Laden was allowed to return to Afghanistan, where he forged close links with the ultra-conservative Taliban regime, a creation of the Pakistani intelligence services, which seized power that same year.

For the next five years Afghanistan would remain bin Laden's base of operations, where he supposedly trained an army of international terrorists and planned the suicide bomb attack on the destroyer USS *Cole* in 2000, which killed seventeen US sailors. By that time bin Laden's notoriety was confirmed by a $5 million reward on his head and a number of US counter-terrorism investigators had confirmed him as America's most implacable and dangerous enemy. Yet even then bin Laden retained a surprising degree of international mobility. In October 1997 bin Laden attended an international conference of jihadist organisations in London, flying into Heathrow in his private jet, in one of several trips he made to the United Kingdom.

Officially, bin Laden had been persona non grata in Saudi Arabia since his expulsion to Sudan. But a number of US analysts and law-enforcement officials, such as the tenacious former FBI counter-terrorism investigator John O'Neill, have alleged that bin Laden never entirely severed his connections to the Saudi political and intelligence establishment and that his relationship with his former Saudi and Pakistani contacts from the anti-Soviet jihad continued to survive his public anathema.[16] Nor were Saudi Arabia and Pakistan the only countries whose intelligence services maintained links with bin Laden's network. In 2002 the Dutch government published the results of its official inquiry into the 1995 Srebrenica massacre in the former Yugoslavia, in which up to 7,000 Bosnian Muslims were killed by Bosnian Serb and Serbian forces. Among other findings, the inquiry revealed the existence of a secret alliance between the United States, Turkey, Iran and Afghan-Arabs to smuggle weapons and assistance to Bosnian Muslims.[17] And in 1996, if the dissident MI6 officer David Shayler and others are to be believed, MI6 attempted to recruit one of bin Laden's lieutenants in Libya in a plot to assassinate Colonel Qaddafi.[18]

Perhaps one of the strangest and most bizarre of bin Laden's linkages was the long relationship between the bin Laden family and the Bush dynasty, a connection that went back to 1978, when George W. Bush established his first business, an oil exploration partnership called Arbusto, with the help of a $50,000 loan from a Texan businessman and former air-force buddy named James Bath, who also acted as the US investment counsellor for the bin Laden family. One of Bath's associates was a Saudi businessman named Khalid bin Mahfouz, a major shareholder in the BCCI 'outlaw bank' and the head of the National Commercial Bank in Saudi Arabia. In the late 1980s a number of Arab investors with BCCI connections helped rescue Harken Energy, another of George W. Bush's failed business ventures, in a gesture believed by some commentators to have been a Saudi ploy to cultivate a special relationship with the son of the then US vice-president George Bush, Sr. One investor was a Saudi real estate magnate and an associate of bin Mahfouz, named Abdullah Taha Bakhsh, who in 1991 bought 17.6 per cent of Harken's stock at a time when the company was in financial difficulties.

The exact nature and purpose of the nebulous financial transactions between the presidential family, the BCCI and Saudi plutocrats is impossible to determine. What is certain, however, is that in 1999 a Saudi government audit revealed a $3 million deficit in bin Mahfouz's finances that had reportedly been diverted to Islamic charities acting as bin Laden fronts. That same year the US Treasury accused an Islamic charity named Blessed Relief, whose board included bin Mahfouz's son, of siphoning funds to al-Qaeda.[19] The involvement of a suspected terrorist financier with the Bush family's murky business practices was certainly a striking coincidence, and the Bush family has not surprisingly denied any connection with bin Mahfouz. The Bush–bin Laden connection also stemmed from a mutual interest in the Carlyle Group, a hugely successful private equity firm, which specialised in the strategic purchase of ailing defence companies which were later refloated at a profit. Though the bin Laden family's stake in the company was never disclosed, it would certainly have benefited financially from the expansion in the US defence industry, raising the intriguing prospect that the terrorist threat posed by bin Laden actually enhanced the profits of the family company as well as those of his supposed enemies.[20]

The new Terror International

If bin Laden is seen in the Western world as the archetypal terrorist godfather and the latest incarnation of Hassan-I-Sabbah's 'Old Man of the Mountains', al-Qaeda has often been presented as the most formidable of all terrorist organisations, an Islamic version of SPECTRE in Ian Fleming's James Bond novels, with clandestine cells and agents in more than eighty countries, all of whom ultimately owe allegiance to bin Laden himself. Its members are often depicted as consummate terrorist professionals, who seek to return the modern world to the age of the Prophet yet remain entirely at home in the twenty-first century, communicating with each other through encrypted emails, issuing fatwas written on Apple Macs, conducting complicated financial transactions across continents. To the terrorism writer Rohan Gunaratna, al-Qaeda is an 'enigma, a shadowy body' membership of which is a sought-after privilege reserved for the terrorist elite who fulfil 'the very strict selection criteria it imposes'.[21]

Of the thousands of jihadists who are believed to have 'graduated' from 'al-Qaeda training camps' between 1989 and 2001, Gunaratna estimates that only 3,000 of the 'most committed, most trustworthy and most capable operatives' were eventually selected by the organisation. The main evidence of the existence of al-Qaeda as a centrally directed terrorist organisation stems from the January 2001 trial *The United States* v. *Osama bin Laden*, which investigated bin Laden's responsibility for the US embassy bombings in Africa. The prosecution's principal witnesses were a former member of bin Laden's circle in Sudan called Jamal Ahmed al-Fadl, who had fled Sudan after embezzling $110,000 from one of his companies, and a former US special-forces solider named Ali Mohammed, who had at various times combined his role in the US military as trainer of jihadist fighters in Afghanistan and a CIA double agent, though it was never entirely clear on whose behalf he was acting.

Both men had a strong interest in telling the authorities what they wanted to hear, while the prosecution had an equally compelling interest in depicting al-Qaeda as a Mafia-style terror organisation that allowed bin Laden and his associates to be tried on conspiracy charges. This is not to suggest that al-Qaeda was a legalistic fantasy, but the evidence of an all-powerful terrorist multinational with a hierarchical chain of command is not conclusive. The *Observer* journalist Jason Burke and others have argued that al-Qaeda functioned more as a network or clearing house for the jihad than a central organisation, whose members shared a similar ideology and methodology without necessarily being under any central direction.

Nor is it clear that the bin Laden network consists of superbly skilled 'professional' terrorists trained to wreak havoc on an unsuspecting world. Graduates of the al-Qaeda 'terror camps' included men such as Richard Reid, the pathetic English 'shoe bomber' who was caught trying to blow up a plane using a bomb concealed in the heel of his shoe in 2002. Reid was a petty criminal with low intelligence and so painfully inept as a terrorist that he tried to detonate his bomb with matches in full view of the passengers. Reid might be dismissed as a 'useful idiot' were it not for the fact that other supposed al-Qaeda members have been made from similarly flawed alloy.

To some extent the Western perception of al-Qaeda was based on a misrepresentation of the jihad itself, which tended to regard all 'jihadis' as international terrorists intent on the destruction of Western Christendom. But not all visitors to the Afghan and Pakistani training camps attempted to blow up aeroplanes and kill Western civilians. Thousands of jihadists fought and died in Kashmir, with the tacit or direct approval of the Pakistani government. Others went on to fight in Bosnia, Chechnya and other conflicts in fulfilment of the jihadist pledge to defend Muslims or Muslim territory. The attitude of the reactionary Wahhabist Afghan-Arab volunteers towards the less conservative brand of Islam that they sometimes encountered was often disapproving and even openly hostile.

Nevertheless, there were differences between the members of this jihadist

'International Brigade' and the transnational network engaged in carrying out terrorist attacks in the United States and Europe.[22] Many participants in the transnational jihad did not visit the camps at all, but came to the jihad through the Internet, where a new generation of deculturised Muslims sought to create what the French Islamic scholar Olivier Roy called a 'virtual umma'. If the image of al-Qaeda propagated by many governments was frightening, it also provided a convenient 'explanation' for virtually any manifestation of violence involving Muslims, from Chechnya to bomb plots in Europe. At the same time the threat of al-Qaeda was magnified by its perceived interest in acquiring nuclear weapons of mass destruction and its possible links to 'rogue states' such as Iraq and Iran.

This possibility was frequently invoked by American politicians, regardless of whether there was any evidence to support it. In May 2001, for example, the US secretary of state, Donald Rumsfeld, announced that bin Laden already possessed chemical and bacteriological weapons and was in the process of assembling an atomic bomb and preparing to launch a satellite. These sensational declarations came and went without ever being substantiated. On the one hand, Rumsfeld's allegations borrowed from 'megaterrorism' narratives, in which the possibility that terrorists might acquire such weapons became a basis for supposing that they were actively trying to do so. On the other, such allegations were part of a deliberate attempt to frighten the American public, by an administration that was looking for ways to justify a projection of military power across the world. In this way al-Qaeda became a successor to Aum Shinrikyo and the latest terrorist organisation onto which the Western world could project its perennial fears of universal destruction.

Knights of the Prophet

What does bin Laden actually want? In the long term, his vision of a purified and regenerated Islamic nation combines the utopian Islamism of Sayyid Qutb and the Muslim Brotherhood with the arid and austere version of Islam known as Salafism. Bin Laden has cited the Taliban theocracy in Afghanistan as the nearest approximation to an ideal Islamic society, but like Sayyid Qutb himself, his ultimate social and political objectives are vague and imprecise compared with his bitter critique of the existing political regimes in the Islamic world. Despite the numerous commentators who have depicted al-Qaeda as the cutting edge of an Islamo-fascist offensive against Western 'values', bin Laden's confrontation with the United States has always been based primarily on American actions in the Islamic world, particularly its strategic alliances with the Saudi ruling family and Israel. To some extent, bin Laden articulates an older anti-imperialist agenda that was once at the heart of secular Arab nationalism, but his critique of foreign intervention is always couched in religious terms. Ali Shariati, one of the ideologues of the Islamic revolution in Iran, used the Koranic term the *mustadafin* – the humiliated – as a substitute for Franz Fanon's concept of 'the wretched of the earth' in order to suggest a broader Third World solidarity that was not exclusively Muslim.

The vision of bin Laden, the millionaire-turned-revolutionary, has always been much narrower. Both bin Laden and his lieutenant al-Zawahiri have consistently presented even the most atrocious acts of the jihad as *defensive* actions against a 'Zionist–Crusader' assault directed not just at 'Muslim territory and resources but at the very existence of Islam itself'. Bin Laden has always shown a keen awareness of the wider grievances in the Muslim world and his inflammatory and often paranoid rhetoric tends to depict any acts of violence against Muslims as evidence of the same sinister global conspiracy, from the Russian assault on Chechnya to sanctions against Iraq. In bin Laden's estimation, even UN support for East Timorese independence in 2000 represented another 'loss' of Muslim territory and another example of American attempts to dominate the world, despite the fact that the United States had supported the Indonesian invasion of Timor in the first place and provided the Indonesian army with military aid for years afterwards.

On the one hand bin Laden's provocative presentation of these events as a clash between Islam and the 'Crusader' West was intended to mobilise the Islamic world behind a broader religious revival. At the same time his vision of a strong unified Islamic world contained within it the unfulfilled aspirations of secular Arab nationalism. For this reason his message had a powerful appeal. To the mostly middle and lower-middle class professionals who made up al-Qaeda's transnational networks, this vision of endless jihad in defence of the faith was a noble and heroic endeavour. Not for nothing was Ayman al-Zawahiri's memoir entitled *Knights under the Prophet's Banner*. For al-Zawahiri and bin Laden, the war against the apostate regimes and their infidel sponsors was an epic struggle that recalled the Prophet's wars against the pagan tribes in pre-Islamic Arabia, in which the pure defenders of the faith would ultimately prevail against an evil and overwhelmingly powerful enemy.

The only way to prevent this inexorable Crusader advance, in al-Zawahiri's view, was through the establishment of 'a Muslim authority, established on a Muslim land, that raises the banner of jihad and rallies the Muslims behind it'. By the end of the century, however, this project had stalled. Throughout the Arab world the 'apostate' regimes remained intact and the jihad had failed to establish the territorial bases that al-Zawahiri believed were essential to advance the jihadist cause. The main reason for this failure, from al-Qaeda's point of view, was the support given to these regimes by the American 'far enemy'. In al-Zawahiri's estimation, it was necessary to force the United States to re-evaluate its commitment to its allies in the Arabian Gulf and Egypt or enter into a direct confrontation with the jihadist movement in the Muslim world itself. In order to bring about this transformation, it was necessary to take the battle directly to the 'far enemy' and carry out operations that would 'inflict the maximum casualties against the opponent, for this is the language understood by the West'.[23] And as the new century opened, these principles were put into practice in a way that even the most lurid 'ultimate terrorism' scenarios had not foreseen.

A Raid on the Path:
9/11 and the War on Terror

We're certain there are madmen in this world, and there's terror, and there's missiles, and I'm certain of this.

George W. Bush, campaign speech at Albuquerque, New Mexico, May 2000

Here is America struck by Allah in its most vulnerable point, destroying, thank Allah, its most prestigious buildings and we thank Allah for that. Here is America filled with terror from north to south and from east to west, and we thank Allah for that. Allah has guided the footsteps of a group of Muslims, a vanguard that has destroyed America and we implore Allah to elevate their rank and receive them in Paradise.

Osama bin Laden speaking on *Aljazeera* TV, November 2001

Ever since the nineteenth century, the fantasy of an airborne terrorist catastrophe has flitted in and out of fictional portrayals of terrorism, from E. Douglass Fawcett's anarchist Zeppelin attack on London in *Hartmann the Anarchist* to the Tom Clancy blockbuster *Debt of Honour* (1994), in which a Japanese kamikaze pilot flies an airliner into the Capitol building in Washington, wiping out most of the US government. The idea of using planes to enact a terrorist spectacle has also surfaced from time to time in history, such as Boris Savinkov's aborted plot to direct a 'flying machine' into St Petersburg's Winter Palace in 1909 and Wadi Haddad's experiments with a suicide pilot in Lebanon. At 8.46 on the morning of 11 September 2001, the terrorist equivalent of an aerial bombardment was finally achieved, when an Egyptian postgraduate student in Urban Planning named Mohammed Atta flew American Airlines Flight 11 into the North Tower of the World Trade Center in New York. The moment of impact was captured on an amateur video, in what later became one of the most widely transmitted sequences in history. Initially the malevolent purpose behind the collision was concealed by the belief that a horrendous accident had taken place. Not until seventeen minutes later, when Marwan al-Shehi, a student from the United Arab Emirates and a former flatmate of Atta's in Hamburg, flew United Airlines Flight 175 into the South Tower, did it become clear that New York was being subjected to an unprecedented terrorist assault.

In the era of satellite television and 24-hour rolling news millions of television viewers across the world became spectators of the unbelievable sequence of events that unfolded in real time. The initial footage was so improbable that various viewers actually believed they were watching a trailer for a Hollywood disaster film, but the horrific reality of what was taking place soon became clear, as trapped office workers waved for help from upstairs windows and then jumped to their deaths to avoid being burned alive even as firemen made their way up the stairs towards the fires.[1] At 9.59 the spectacle abandoned the last vestiges of plausibility when the South Tower collapsed in on itself, taking less than ten seconds for its 110 floors to reach the ground. Twenty-nine minutes later the North Tower collapsed, like a vaporised building from *Independence Day*, leaving a combined pile of rubble protruding from the underground car park that reached seven storeys high.

Around the fallen towers downtown New York became a scene of terror and devastation that had no parallel outside wartime, as terrified crowds ran for safety, many of them covered with the choking dust that blotted out the sky completely. There were two other hijackings that morning, which received less media attention. At 9.38 a third plane crashed into the west wing of the Pentagon and at approximately 10.03 United Airlines Flight 93 crashed in Pennsylvania on its way to Washington, apparently after passengers had stormed the cockpit in order to prevent another attack on the capital.

Though initial casualty estimates reached as high as 10,000, the eventual death toll was estimated at just over 3,000, of whom 2,823 died in the World Trade Center attacks. By the end of the day all commercial air traffic in the United States was grounded and the most powerful nation on earth had been brought to a complete standstill. The following morning photographs of the stricken North Tower appeared on the front page of almost every newspaper in the world. It was a bleak and awe-inspiring image, symbolising a confrontation whose parameters were not yet clear. But even then there was no doubt that the United States had been subjected to the most devastating terrorist strike in history, whose authors had combined human ingenuity, technology and the media to create a violent spectacle that was unlike anything the world had ever seen. After all the warnings and alarmist scenarios regarding the inevitability of chemical, biological and nuclear attacks, something like an act of megaterrorism had finally occurred, whose primary instruments were not suitcase bombs or plague viruses taken from Iraq or the former Soviet Union, but innocuous short-bladed cutting tools known as 'boxcutters'. In this sense reality had outstripped the wildest fictional scenarios regarding the potential means through which a terrorist attack might be delivered, even as it confirmed the apocalyptic and murderous intentions of terrorism itself. But if the attacks represented a 'new' threshold of terrorist achievement, they were nevertheless incorporated into an official narrative that was as banal as it was familiar.

The attack on America

On the evening of September 11 George Bush told the nation in a televised address that America had been attacked by 'the enemies of human freedom' because 'we are freedom's home and defender'. Over the coming weeks and months this explanation was endlessly repeated with varying degrees of intellectual sophistication by an array of politicians and media pundits on both sides of the Atlantic. If the idea that America had been attacked because of its virtues followed the established contours of official anti-terrorist discourse, there was also a consensus that the world faced what Bush called 'a new kind of evil'. In a speech to the UN General Assembly that same month, the US ambassador to the UN, John Negroponte, offered a similarly metaphysical interpretation:

> Men suicidally intoxicated with a vision of the void perverted the basic elements of civilised life and dared call their deeds the works of God. Some power possessed them but not a higher power ... some power that is the dark antithesis of the light we all want to see at the dawn of the new millennium.[2]

Even less theological interpreters saw September 11 as a clash of diametrically opposed and absolute opposites, between 'Islamo-fascism' and 'democracy', between a resentful and atavistic Islamic fundamentalism and a benevolent America. To human-rights academic and journalist (turned Liberal politician) Michael Ignatieff, the attacks were an act of 'apocalyptic nihilism' whose 'desire to give ultimate meaning to time and history' supposedly transcended any political goals.[3] This presentation ignored the fact that the targets had been carefully chosen as symbols of US financial, military and political power. Had the attacks been truly 'apocalyptic' in their intentions, there were other targets, from nuclear power stations to dams and oil refineries, which would have yielded even greater destruction.[4]

Few observers noted that the destruction of the World Trade Center was the completion of a project begun many years before by Ramzi Yousef's jihadist cell, whose underlying rationale was stated by Yousef at his trial, and reiterated in various statements from bin Laden, that American civilians would have to pay a price for the policies of their government in the Middle East, particularly regarding US support for Israel. Even if the attacks were 'unsigned', there was abundant evidence to demonstrate that they were inspired by specific political grievances, virtually all of which were related to US foreign policy decisions rather than American 'values'. All this was generally obscured in the collective outpouring of rage and wounded patriotism, as a chorus of indignant media commentators dismissed any attempt to contextualise the attacks as a spurious attempt at 'moral relativism' which 'blamed the victim' rather than the perpetrators. When the late essayist and novelist Susan Sontag, in a brief article in the *New Yorker*, denounced the 'sanctimonious, reality-concealing rhetoric spouted by American officials and media commentators' and insisted that the attacks were 'a consequence of specific American alliances and actions' she became a hate figure in the US right-wing media, where she was variously depicted as a 'moral idiot' and 'Osama bin Sontag'.[5]

Across the world governments denounced the attacks as an assault on civilisation and democracy and rushed to express their solidarity with America. The attacks were also condemned by a number of 'terrorist organisations' such as the IRA, Hezbollah and the Tamil Tigers. Despite television footage of demonstrators in the Occupied Territories apparently celebrating the attacks, almost every Palestinian political organisation, including Hamas, condemned them, while nearly a million Palestinian students observed five minutes' silence in memory of the victims. In other parts of the Muslim world there were flower-laying ceremonies outside American embassies. Even in Iran, America's arch-enemy, thousands attended a candlelit vigil on behalf of the victims.

Whatever the perspective, there was unanimous recognition that '9/11', as it was quickly dubbed, was an event that would shape the coming century. Some commentators predicted that the attacks would act as a watershed in the history of the modern world, marking the beginning of a new moral sobriety. The gratuitous slaughter of 3,000 civilians clearly belonged to the category of a crime against humanity. But the fact that these attacks were hailed as universal events by so many governments, while the killing of

7,000 Bosnian Muslims or the genocide of 1 million Tutsi were not, demonstrates once again the peculiar ability of 'terrorism' to generate levels of moral outrage that rarely accrue to crimes carried out in wartime or even genocide. This disparity was not merely due to the fact that the victims were Americans and therefore regarded in the Western world as more fully human than Bosnians, Rwandans or Chechens, nor even to the cataclysmic images of terror and panic that were endlessly broadcast across the world. What made the attacks so shocking was the fact that 3,000 people had been murdered in a society that was not at war, in a place where such events were not expected to happen. In shattering the aura of security that was so crucial to America's conception of itself, the attacks also shattered the inviolability of the Western world itself and provided a glimpse of the worst possible future, even as they ushered in a chain of violent events that has yet to be fully played out.

The cell

In the immediate aftermath, it was generally assumed by US counter-terrorism officials that an operation on such a scale could only have been carried out by a 'professional' terrorist organisation with the kind of global reach that al-Qaeda was deemed to possess. Within days, however, the FBI revealed that the attacks were carried out by nineteen hijackers, who one astonished CIA official later described as the equivalent of a 'pick-up basketball team'.[6] The core of the group consisted of three former students who had shared a flat in Hamburg before coming to the US, where they learned to fly at private flying schools in Florida. All three were middle-class Arab students with a technical or scientific background, products of what Professor Gilles Kepel, a French expert on Islam, has called 'an unlikely marriage between Wahhabism and Silicon Valley'.[7]

The leader of the group was identified by the FBI as an Egyptian student named Mohammed Atta, whose cruel features became the malignant mask of terror in a widely reproduced photograph. The details of Atta's life and personality are as contradictory as many other aspects of September 11. The son of a wealthy Cairo lawyer, Atta originally came to Germany to take a postgraduate thesis in urban planning in Hamburg in the mid-1990s. The glimpses of Atta's student life in Germany compiled by *Der Spiegel*'s reporters reveal a devout, repressed Muslim, unsuited to the Western world and so uncomfortable with women that he refused to shake their hands and spoke to them only in monosyllables. He was angered by the transformation of his native Cairo into 'McEgypt' and harboured a series of Islamist grievances, from the treatment of the Palestinians to the effects of sanctions in Iraq.

In 1999 Atta finished his thesis on urban development in the Syrian city of Aleppo, by which time he was believed to have visited 'bin Laden training camps' in Afghanistan and become involved in the September 11 plot. In June the following year, according to the FBI, he arrived in the United States to begin his flight training in Florida, together with his flatmates Marwan al-Shehi and Ziad al-Jarrah. On the surface, Atta's biography suggests the same tormented misogyny and sexual puritanism that resulted in Sayyid Qutb's moment of revulsion in the church hall in Colorado. But the depiction of the 9/11 hijackers as devout Salafist holy warriors has been contradicted by various eyewitnesses, who described Atta, al-Shehi and the other 'pilots' at bars, parties and lap-dancing clubs, flush with money and getting drunk and aggressive in public, looking like *Miami Vice* hoodlums in loud flashy clothes and gold jewellery. An American investigative journalist, Daniel Hopsicker, carried out his own investigations in Florida after the attacks. Hopsicker discovered that Atta had an American girlfriend, a stripper-cum-escort who worked for a company named Fantasies and Lingerie and remembered Atta's fondness for cocaine, strip joints and flashy clothes.

Such behaviour might have been an al-Qaeda ploy to throw potential surveillance teams off the scent, or it may have been that the hijackers felt able to immerse themselves in the forbidden pleasures of the infidel world, secure in the knowledge that their sins would be redeemed by their forthcoming act of martyrdom. But Hopsicker also discovered that Atta and his fellow pilots trained at the Huffman Flying School in Venice, Florida, a company linked to suspected CIA dummy airlines involved in some of the murkier covert operations of the 1980s and beyond. Not only did Hopsicker's research directly contradict the FBI chronology regarding the hijackers' movements in Florida, but it raised the possibility that Atta and the other 'pilots' had taken advantage of training networks initially established by the CIA during the anti-Soviet jihad and subsequently maintained for reasons that remain unclear. The suggestion that the hijackers had benefited from a covert operations 'pipeline' was supported to some extent by reports in the US press that virtually all the fifteen Saudi 'muscle hijackers' received their US visas from the same consulate used by the CIA in Jeddah to send Arab jihadists for training in the United States during the Afghan war. In addition, a number of these visas were granted despite numerous irregularities in their applications which had apparently been overlooked.[8]

Hopsicker's portrait of Mohammed Atta bore little relation to the glorious image of the devout holy warriors described by Ramzi Binalshibh, another member of the Hamburg cell, who told the Aljazeera reporter Yosri Fouda in

2002 that each of the hijackers who participated in the 'holy raids' had been given a *kunyah*, or 'hidden name', taken from one of the Prophet's companions. In Binalshibh's view the hijackers were heroic soldiers and martyrs who participated in 'a very large military battle, an unconventional battle against the most powerful force on earth.'[9]

A similar narrative is contained in the anonymous primer supposedly found in three different airports after the attacks, including one in Atta's travel bag, which outlined a series of spiritual exercises to be performed before what he called 'the deed' and 'the act'. The author depicts the hijackers as warriors in a timeless cosmic drama, in which the forthcoming operation is compared to the *ghazwah*, or raids carried out by the Prophet. Throughout the text the paraphernalia of the modern world, from taxi cabs and luggage, to aeroplanes and identification papers, form a backdrop to the mythic journey on which the hijackers are about to embark. There is also an element of religious ritual in the instructions to the hijackers to wash and shave excess hair and perfume their bodies on the night before the operation and to spend the night praying and reading the Koran. Following the take-off, which the document described as 'the hour of the encounter between the two camps' the author told his companions to

> clench your teeth, as did [your] predecessors, God rest their souls, before engaging in battle. Upon the confrontation, hit as you would hit heroes who desire not to return to the World, and loudly proclaim the name of God, that is because the name of God instils terror in the heart of the nonbelievers.[10]

According to the translation used by Kanan Makiyah and Hassan Mneimneh, the author chose the Arabic word *dhabala*, or 'slaughter', rather than *qatala*, 'to kill', with its suggestion of the slaughter of an animal by throat-cutting. But the word also had ritualistic overtones, exemplified by the text's instructions on how to deal with any resistance by the passengers or crew:

> If God grants any one of you a slaughter, you should perform it as an offering on behalf of your father and your mother, for they are owed to you.[11]

It will never be known to what extent the hijackers identified with this repellent document, but it certainly bears little relation to their behaviour before the attacks. On their last night on earth, according to *Der Spiegel*, al-Shehi's group appeared to have spent their time not in prayer or meditation, but by ringing round the Boston area in search of a prostitute willing to have sex with four men in their hotel. When the cost of $400 proved to be prohibitive, the raiders on God's path reportedly paid for a pornographic film in their hotel instead.

If these contradictory details of the hijackers suggest a more complex and confused motivation than religious zealotry, it is still not entirely clear that the nineteen individuals named by the FBI actually carried out the attacks at all. Since September 11 at least eight of the hijackers have actually been found alive and interviewed by mainstream newspapers, suggesting that their names were used by others. Who these individuals were has not yet been revealed. On 15 September 2001 *Newsweek* reported that five of the hijackers had received training at 'secure US military installations in the 1990s' and that three of the hijackers listed the Naval Air Station in Pensacola, Florida, on their driving licences. *Newsweek* did not ask what five fundamentalist terrorists supposedly planning suicide attacks on American targets were doing at US military bases. Other occasional snippets of information have emerged in the media which have raised more questions than they have been able to answer. In June 2005 five US intelligence officers revealed the existence of a Pentagon surveillance programme named 'Able Danger' which had recognised Atta and two other hijackers as members of al-Qaeda since mid-2000. These startling revelations raised the question of why no arrests had been made and suggested, once again, that the official version of the 9/11 attacks was at best incomplete.

The chronicle of a plot foretold?

Though the September 11 attacks appeared to the outside world as something previously unimaginable and inconceivable, they were not entirely without precedent or forewarning. According to the 2004 report by the National Commission on the Terrorist Attacks in the United States, known as the 9/11 Commission, the plan to carry out suicide attacks using planes was first proposed to Osama bin Laden by Khalid Sheikh Mohammed, Ramzi Yousef's uncle and co-conspirator in the Bojinka plot that followed the first World Trade Center bombing in 1993. Investigations carried out by the journalist Peter Lance suggests that the plot preceded bin Laden's involvement. According to Lance, interrogations of Yousef's accomplice, Abdul Hakim Murad, by the Philippine police in late 1994 revealed that Yousef and Sheikh Mohammed had already begun preparations for an alternative operation to the Bojinka plot, in which hijacked planes were to be crashed into various American targets, including the World Trade Center. Murad told his Filipino interrogator, Colonel Mendoza, that he had already attended US flight schools and that other pilots were being trained for the operation inside the United States. Though the Filipino police relayed this information to the FBI, it was never acted upon.[12]

This was only one of many astounding failures of the American intelligence community. Throughout 2001 both the CIA and the FBI and other US counter-terrorist agencies received multiple indications that al-Qaeda was planning major attacks against US targets, which reached a peak in August, when the CIA director George Tenet later admitted that 'the system was blinking red'. The US counter-terrorist community also received warnings from numerous foreign intelligence agencies that al-Qaeda was planning attacks against targets inside the United States. Even allowing for the retrospective logic of hindsight, the complacency with which the various US law enforcement and intelligence agencies responded to these general warnings is astounding and inexplicable. Not only did the agencies responsible fail to follow up lines of inquiry that might have unravelled the plot beforehand, but the actions of those responsible for defending the United States on the morning of the attacks were characterised by paralysis and confusion. The incompetence was epitomised by the president himself, who remained in a Florida classroom listening to children reading a story about a pet goat more than half an hour after he had been informed of the first attack, for reasons that have never been fully explained.

The new Pearl Harbor

A historic event of the scale of 9/11 was always likely to generate alternative explanations, but the combination of failure and incompetence has generated a profusion of hypothesis, theory and urban legend, much of which drifts into the category of 'parapolitics', with its emphasis on 'shadow governments' and clandestine conspiracies as the driving force behind contemporary political events. A number of critics of the official version have argued that the failures of the US intelligence and military establishment were not failures at all and that the attacks were carried out with the complicity of the Bush administration or rogue elements within the US military and intelligence services in order to justify a militaristic and interventionist foreign policy and enable the US government to impose more direct control over oil reserves in the Middle East and central Asia. Some '9/11 sceptics' have seen possible indications in the 'grand chessboard' geopolitical strategies articulated by former secretary of state Zbigniew Brzezinski calling for US military domination of 'Eurasia'. Others have pointed to the September 2000 document entitled 'Rebuilding America's Defenses' by the neo-conser-

vative think tank the Project for a New American Century (PNAC), which
called for a massive escalation in the US military budget and speculated that
such a transformation could not be achieved without 'some catastrophic and
catalysing event like a new Pearl Harbor'.[13]

The most extreme complicity thesis accuses elements within the US government of actually participating in or facilitating the attacks, using the
hijackers as unwitting instruments in a 'false flag' operation. Some critics
have seen possible precedents in the 1964 Tonkin Gulf incident that was
used to justify US military escalation in Vietnam and the revelations by the
US security expert James Bamford of a 1962 scheme devised by the US Joint
Chiefs of Staff entitled 'Operation Northwoods'. The documents obtained
by Bamford revealed a plan by top US generals to justify an attack on Cuba
by staging faked terrorist operations that would be blamed on the Castro
regime. The options considered included a bombing campaign in Florida
and the substitution of a passenger plane by a remote-controlled 'drone' that
would be blown up near Cuba and presented as a Cuban atrocity.[14]

This project was not acted on, but it has been seen by some sceptics as an
indication that sections within the US government have been prepared to
contemplate the use of 'black operations'. The mechanics of the alleged 9/11
conspiracy have become the subject of endless speculation and hypothesis.
Some have argued that key officials stood back and allowed the attacks to
happen and deliberately undermined any attempt to prevent them. Others
have suggested that the hijacked planes were flown by remote control, that
the Pentagon was attacked by a US missile rather than a plane, that the
twin towers were brought down by controlled demolitions, that US secret
service agents interjected false radar blips onto the air-traffic control system
in order to slow down the official response. One video entitled *In Plane Sight*
purports to show that the two planes that brought down the World Trade
Center had missiles attached to their fuselage, which were fired into the
building at the moment of impact.

The suggestion of US government complicity has tended to draw scandalised indignation from across the political spectrum, but such allegations
are not restricted to *X-Files* fantasists on the outer fringes of the Internet. An
opinion poll taken in August 2004 by the Zogby organisation found that 49.3
per cent of New York City residents believed that some US leaders 'knew
in advance that attacks were planned on or around September 11 2001, and
that they consciously failed to act'.[15] Academics, journalists, politicians and
relatives of the September 11 victims have also formed part of the '9/11
truth movement', while a number of tenacious amateur researchers, such

as Jared Israel and Paul Thompson, have drawn attention to aspects of 9/11 that the mainstream media has either ignored or tended to pass over.

The outrage that has often been directed towards such efforts ignores the fact that the official version of 9/11 contains numerous lacunae and anomalies that have yet to be fully explained, from the conflicting chronologies issued by the Federal Aviation Administration (FAA) and the US military regarding who knew what and when on the morning of the attacks to the failure to observe standard operating procedures regarding the deployment of fighter planes in the event of a suspected hijacking. In the wake of the attacks both the FAA and the North American Aerospace Defense Command (NORAD) have issued entirely different timetables regarding their actions that morning, the disparity of which has never been coherently explained.[16] Similar discrepancies surround other aspects of September 11, such as the presence of key officials during the morning's events. Thus General Richard Myers, the acting chairman of the Joint Chiefs of Staff, has consistently claimed that he was at a private meeting in Washington and that he was unaware of the unfolding attacks until the one on the Pentagon. Yet the White House counter-terrorism 'tsar', Richard Clarke, has described seeing Myers at a video conference at least half an hour before the Pentagon was hit.[17]

Both these statements cannot be true, yet no explanation has ever been given for this discrepancy. Whole swathes of 9/11 research have been dedicated to picking apart such minutiae and examining the many odd coincidences surrounding the events of that morning, such as the staging of multiple war games by the US air force that same day, some of which reportedly involved exercises involving hijacked aircraft. Another coincidence involves the presence of Lieutenant-General Mahmood Ahmad, the chief of the Pakistani intelligence service, the ISI, in Washington that week for meetings with his intelligence counterparts. On the morning of the attacks Ahmad was attending a meeting with representatives of the Senate and House Intelligence committees, where they reportedly discussed terrorism in Afghanistan. Yet following the attacks the *Times of India* reported that Ahmad had ordered a cheque to be sent to Mohammed Atta for $100,000 shortly before September 11.

The fact that a top Pakistani intelligence officer should have been meeting with US intelligence officials while attacks were taking place which he had apparently helped to facilitate was one of many striking anomalies and 'unanswered questions' surrounding September 11, which the subsequent behaviour of both the law enforcement agencies and the Bush administration have done little to clarify. There is hardly a single aspect of the official version of the attacks that has not been muddied by confused or contradictory statements, questionable assumptions or outright inventions.[18] Yet even though the Bush administration has continually cited the 'attack on America' as a transformative moment in world history, its officials have shown a marked reluctance to clarify the murkier areas surrounding the events themselves. From the outset the White House issued misleading and blatantly false explanations for the failure to prevent the attacks, claiming that no one in the US government or intelligence community had foreseen the possibility that planes could be used as weapons. Yet there had been numerous indications over the previous few years that al-Qaeda or other groups might carry out attacks using hijacked planes, to the point when Bush himself had been warned at the G8 summit in Genoa in July 2001 that al-Qaeda was planning to blow up the eight leaders using a plane filled with explosives. The suggestion of a US counter-terrorist community taken by surprise by the sheer evil of the terrorist imagination was matched by the administration's equally questionable insistence that it responded to the al-Qaeda threat warnings with sufficient urgency – claims that have been challenged by various counter-terrorist officials.

The fact that so many officials continued to make such manifestly false statements have further fuelled allegations of conspiracy and cover-up. Not only have key pieces of evidence and information been withheld or removed from public scrutiny, but the Bush administration has shown a marked reluctance to permit an independent investigation into the events surrounding September 11. In the immediate aftermath of the attacks the White House actively lobbied to prevent a congressional investigation, before finally allowing a limited inquiry by the Joint Intelligence Committees into the intelligence failures that preceded the attacks. The narrow remit of the inquiry was limited still further when censored on the grounds that its contents would be prejudicial to national security.

In 2003 the administration finally agreed to convene a full independent inquiry, following an energetic lobbying campaign spearheaded by the relatives of 9/11 victims known as the Jersey Girls. The result was the bipartisan National Commission on the Terrorist Attacks in the United States – the 9/11 Commission. Once again the White House seemed determined to limit the investigation in various ways, from the appointment of a pro-Bush academic named Philip Zelikow as Executive Director to withholding or restricting access to key documents. In the summer of 2004, the Commission published its final report in the midst of the presidential election campaign, amid great expectation that the mysteries and contradictions of 9/11 would finally be clarified. Despite its detailed research and first-hand interviews, the Commission accepted the official version of a 'failure of imagination' virtually in its entirety, insisting that 'no analytic work foresaw the lightning that could connect the thundercloud to the ground'.[19]

These conclusions flew in the face of allegations made by a number of intelligence and law enforcement officials that the Bush administration failed to take the terrorist threat seriously. They also ignored or distorted allegations from FBI whistleblowers such as Colleen Rowley, the Minneapolis agent who accused her superiors of 'deliberately sabotaging' her office's application for a warrant to search the computer of Zacarias Moussaoui, the so-called 'twentieth hijacker'. The Commission did not even interview or mention Robert Wright, another FBI agent who accused his superiors of blocking his investigations into Osama bin Laden's Saudi support network in the United States and accused the FBI of 'merely gathering intelligence so they would know who to arrest when a terrorist attack occurred', instead of trying to prevent such attacks in the first place.

Not only did the Commission exonerate the administration of any charge of negligence or complicity, but its tepid bureaucratic recommendations were matched by an uncritical endorsement of the Bush administration's subsequent efforts in the international arena against an enemy whose 'hostility toward us and our values is limitless'. Not surprisingly, the report was enthusiastically praised by the White House, but it failed to quell the allegations of an official cover-up.[20] Some of these criticisms emanated from within the US intelligence and law enforcement community. In September 2004 an open letter sent by twenty-five FBI and counter-terrorist officials to the US Congress accused the Commission of having deliberately ignored 'officials and civil servants who were, and still are, clearly negligent and/or derelict in their duties to the nation'. The authors also referred to 'intentional actions or inaction by individuals responsible for our national security ... dictated by motives other than the security of the United States'.[21]

These were serious allegations, which warrant further examination, but the mainstream media has generally remained reluctant to carry out such an undertaking. It is not necessary to believe in phantom planes and missile-carrying pods to recognise that there is a great deal about the events of 9/11 that has not been told and which the Bush administration is not anxious to reveal. Such reluctance may be motivated by a desire to conceal gross negligence rather than complicity. It may be that a secrecy-obsessed administration does not wish to shed light on the more sordid networks spawned by the anti-Soviet jihad and harm vital strategic and economic relationship with key US allies such as Pakistan and Saudi Arabia. Or it may be that the White House does not want any inconvenient facts to undermine its presentation of '9/11' as a terrorist 'Pearl Harbor' attack on an innocent America, an explanation which provided a range of previously unimaginable political opportunities.

The war on terror

One of the perennially morbid features of terrorism is its ability to bring the most repressive and authoritarian instincts of the state to the surface, whether intentionally or not. The 9/11 attacks were no exception and the scale of them made the authoritarian response proportionally greater. In the shocked aftermath of 9/11 the Bush administration introduced a tranche of drastic new anti-terrorist legislation, which effectively suspended habeas corpus and allowed the authorities to detain suspected terrorists indefinitely as 'unlawful combatants' without providing any evidence against them. Further legislation called for terrorists to be tried by Peruvian-style 'faceless tribunals' in which secret military courts were empowered to impose the death penalty. The headlong rush towards the construction of an anti-terrorist state took place against a background of continued threat. On 5 October 2001 a Defense Intelligence Agency report claimed that terrorists might be headed for New York with a 10-kiloton nuclear weapon from the former Soviet Union stockpile. That same month 'haz-mat' (hazardous material) teams in protective clothing were called out to analyse a suspicious green substance on a Chicago pavement which turned out to be guacamole, eliciting the memorable declaration from Mayor Richard Daley that 'Guacamole is not dangerous'.[22]

In October a number of congressmen were sent letters containing anthrax, together with garbled messages, apparently from an unidentified Islamic organisation; they killed five postal workers and clerical staff. Subsequent FBI investigations traced the anthrax used to the 'Ames' strain developed in US military laboratories, raising the possibility that the attacks originated from within the US military itself. Amid this 'atmosphere of edgy alarm', as the *New York Times* described it, the 'USA Patriot Act' was rushed through Congress with little debate, which granted unprecedented new powers of surveillance to the government, including the right to read personal email and impel public libraries to hand over records of borrowed books. The Patriot Act's broad definition of terrorism as an 'illegal' act intended to 'intimidate or coerce the government or civil population' allowed for a wide range of potential offences and the Act has subsequently been used to justify the eviction of homeless people from a New Jersey train station and to investigate drug dealers as well as numerous suspected 'terrorists'. Though liberal critics argued that the legislation undermined fundamental civil liberties, the parameters of the debate were established beforehand by the attorney-general, John Ashcroft, known as the 'Minister of Fear', who warned that any criticism might 'aid terrorists' and 'encourage people to remain silent in the face of evil'.

The new sense of vulnerability resulted in the creation of a new bureaucracy called the Department of Homeland Security, with over 180,000 employees and an annual budget of $50 billion. There were also unrealised projects, such as the national network of anti-terrorist informers called the Terrorism Information and Prevention System (TIPS) and the massive central database on all US citizens entitled Total Information Awareness (TIA) proposed by the former Contragate veteran Admiral John Poindexter. Some local and federal authorities contemplated the installation of biometric cameras to scan the faces of pedestrians and match them to a database of suspected terrorists. Other technological proposals included 'iris recognition' and 'gait recognition' and even 'odour recognition' that would make it possible to detect potential terrorists by their sweat or urine. One Harvard neurologist patented a technique known as 'brain fingerprinting' that claimed to be able to separate terrorists from 'innocent persons' by measuring their brainwaves in reaction to stimuli, such as photographs of terrorist training camps in Afghanistan.

Hollywood was also enlisted in the anti-terrorist campaign, as the Pentagon recruited a team of Hollywood scriptwriters, including the authors of *Die Hard* and *Being John Malkovich*, to 'brainstorm about terrorist targets and schemes in America and to offer solutions to these threats'. One of the zaniest proposals came from the Pentagon Defense Advanced Research Projects Agency (DARPA), which planned to create a futures market in which traders would buy and sell contracts based on their predictions of what might happen in the Middle East and elsewhere in the event of a terrorist attack. Critics of the scheme pointed out that it might actually encourage terrorist organisations to carry out attacks in order to profit from them and the market was eventually scrapped, shortly before its scheduled trading time was due to begin in October 2003.[23]

The enemy within
The fact that such a scheme should even have been considered was another

indication of the strange new country that America was becoming in the wake of 9/11, where colour-coded warnings were provided on a daily basis like meteorological reports to indicate the probability of a terrorist attack, where public officials advised citizens to use duct tape to seal their windows in the event of a chemical attack and the government and law enforcement agencies continually warned of horrendous plots and nebulous terrorist conspiracies which came and went without explanation. After failing to act on so many warnings before the attacks, the authorities now saw potential Islamic terrorists everywhere, arresting hundreds of Muslims often on the most ludicrous premises and holding press conferences to announce the discovery of alleged 'al-Qaeda sleeper cells' and thwarted terrorist conspiracies.

On 10 June 2002 Ashcroft gave a special news conference in Moscow in which he announced the arrest of Jose Padilla, a Puerto Rican Islamic convert who had visited Afghanistan. According to Ashcroft, Padilla was 'a known terrorist' who planned to explode a radioactive 'dirty bomb' in the United States. Various counter-terrorist officials contradicted Ashcroft's assertion that Padilla had been 'researching radiological dispersal devices', claiming that he was an ineffectual petty criminal whose 'research' had consisted mostly of surfing the Internet. Nevertheless, Padilla was declared an 'enemy combatant' and vanished into the new legal netherworld created by the administration.[24]

Other alleged plots have been similarly dubious. On 13 September that year six American Muslims of Yemeni descent were arrested in Lackawanna, New York, and charged with providing material support to terrorism. The charges were based on a brief visit the six had made to Afghanistan in the summer of 2001, where they stayed at a jihad training camp in order to 'learn about Islam'. Though the group admitted to having received weapons training, no weapons or explosives were found in their possession and there was no evidence to bear out FBI Director Robert Mueller's claim that they were 'poised' to carry out terrorist attacks, let alone the CIA's depiction of the group as 'the most dangerous terrorist cell in the country'.

Though the six pleaded guilty to attending an al-Qaeda camp, critics of the trial alleged that they had done so only in order to avoid being labelled 'unlawful combatants' and vanishing permanently. Instead they were given sentences averaging nine years and the government congratulated itself on having saved the nation from another al-Qaeda plot.[25] Not for the first time, the portrayal of a nation under siege by the fundamentalist enemy tended to overlook more domestic sources of violence, such as Joseph Konopka, a 26-year-old self-proclaimed 'anarchist-terrorist' who was arrested in a tunnel beneath the University of Illinois in Chicago in March 2002 in possession of a lethal collection of chemicals. In April 2003 federal agents in Texas searching the property of 62-year-old William Joseph Klar, a gunsmith and white supremacist, uncovered an arsenal of guns, pipe bombs and explosive devices, together with a home-made chemical weapon containing 800 grams of sodium cyanide and two vials of hydrochloric acid, which one analyst at Stanford University concluded was sufficient to kill more than 6,000 people under optimal conditions.[26]

These cases emanated from outside the fundamentalist/al-Qaeda siege narrative and were unaccompanied by the kind of celebratory press conferences that would certainly have greeted the discovery of similar quantities of chemical weapons in the hands of 'Islamic' terrorists. Again and again Bush administration officials insisted that further al-Qaeda attacks were inevitable and raised the possibility that such attacks would include weapons of mass destruction, a threat that Donald Rumsfeld once described as 'an energiser for the American people'. At the same time the manipulation of the terrorist threat was accompanied by an increasingly oppressive and hysterical political climate reminiscent of West Germany during the seventies. In November 2001 the American Council of Trustees and Alumnis published a report entitled 'Defending Civilisation: How Our Universities are Failing America and What Can Be Done About It', which accused American universities of having 'invoked tolerance and diversity as antidotes to evil'.

In March 2002 William Bennett, the author of *Why We Fight: Moral Clarity and the War on Terrorism*, launched an organisation called Americans for Victory over Terrorism to combat an 'internal threat' consisting of 'those who are attempting to use this opportunity to promulgate their agenda of "blame America first"'.[27] When the National Education Association produced an online teaching aid on the first anniversary of 9/11 which argued that Arab-Americans should not be held collectively responsible for the attacks, its authors were accused by Colonel Oliver North of 'terrorism in the classroom'. As in West Germany during the 1970s, a terrorist emergency was increasingly becoming a pretext to browbeat and discourage any form of political dissent or opposition and root out suspected 'internal enemies'. But in post-9/11 America the anti-terrorist anathema was made even more potent by the fact that the country had now entered what amounted to a state of permanent war.

The Bush crusade

In conversation with *New Yorker* journalist Nicolas Lehman shortly after the attacks, a senior US official described September 11 as 'a transformative moment', whose real significance was 'not so much that it revealed the existence of a threat of which officials had previously been unaware as that it drastically reduced the American public's usual reluctance to American military involvement overseas, at least for a while'.[28] Other Bush administration officials similarly referred to 9/11 as an unprecedented 'opportunity' to 'go massive', as Donald Rumsfeld recommended on the morning of the attacks. Such was the changed political context that it now seemed possible to fulfil a virtually limitless range of longstanding right-wing foreign-policy objectives that went far beyond the elimination of the groups responsible for the attacks themselves.

Like the Reagan administration a decade earlier, the White House presented the global projection of American military power as a moral enterprise against 'terror'. On 16 September Bush told reporters that the response to the September 11 attacks would take the form of a 'crusade'. Though his advisors subsequently apologised for the term when it was realised how badly it would play in the Islamic world, the notion of a holy war against evil was as integral to the Bush administration's presentation of its actions as it was to al-Qaeda itself. On 20 September 80 million Americans watched the president address a joint session of Congress in which he declared that America was now engaged in a 'War on Terror' whose goals went beyond al-Qaeda to the elimination of every single terrorist group in the world. In this war, Bush warned Americans to 'expect not one battle, but a lengthy campaign unlike any we have ever seen', which would include a range of methods from diplomacy, law enforcement and intelligence to 'dramatic strikes, visible on TV, and covert operations secret even in success'.

That same day forty prominent neo-conservatives published an open letter to the White House in which they outlined a list of possible 'terrorist' targets, from Iraq and Hezbollah to Syria and Iran. None of these targets had any proven connection to 9/11, but the cynicism and opportunism of the War on Terror was matched by officials within the Bush administration itself, such as the neo-con stalwart Paul Wolfowitz, who argued that the US should attack Iraq rather than Afghanistan, on the grounds that the former was more 'doable' and offered more bombing targets. Nevertheless, the opening offensive in the War on Terror was directed against al-Qaeda's bases in Afghanistan. When the Taliban regime refused to hand over bin Laden unless the US produced evidence against him, the American-led coalition began bombing raids on Afghan towns and cities, moving to a rapid victory that was always inevitable. It was nevertheless an inglorious beginning to the crusade, in which an estimated 5,000 Afghan civilians died and where victory owed as much to bribes and politicking amongst the assorted warlords of the Northern Alliance as it did to US-led air strikes.

The fall of Kabul and the major Afghan cities was followed by a phantasmal hunt for al-Qaeda and Osama bin Laden in the Tora Bora mountains by US special forces and their unreliable Afghan allies. Despite reports that al-Qaeda had been wiped out as a military organisation, few bodies were ever found and bin Laden and his followers were able to evade the various encirclements and escape into the lawless tribal areas in Pakistan. By January, most of Afghanistan was under the control of the American-led forces and their Northern Alliance allies and the Bush administration felt sufficiently emboldened to extend the war on terror to Iraq. For more than a year the US–British propaganda machine relentlessly linked al-Qaeda, 9/11 and Iraq in their invocation of the threat supposedly posed by Saddam Hussein's regime.

In January 2003, a supposed al-Qaeda plot was unearthed in Britain when a group of Muslims in London were arrested for manufacturing the poison ricin. During a police raid in Manchester, an Algerian suspect named Kamel Bourgass stabbed a policeman to death. The existence of a north London 'ricin factory' was mentioned by US secretary of state Colin Powell in a speech to the UN Security Council shortly afterwards, as further evidence of 'a sinister nexus between Iraq and the al-Qaeda terrorist network'. In April 2005, however, Bourgass and eight defendants were tried with 'conspiracy to cause a public nuisance by the use of poisons and/or explosives'. The conspiracy theory quickly unravelled as four defendants were acquitted and charges dropped against another. Only Bourgass was found guilty and sentenced to seventeen years on top of the life sentence he had already received for murder, after a leading toxins expert dismissed the plot as 'incredibly amateurish and unlikely to succeed'.

The 'ricin plot' was followed by other terrorist scares in the build-up to war. On 10 February 2003, in the midst of crucial debates in the United Nations on Iraq, 1,700 police and 450 troops in armoured vehicles surrounded Heathrow airport to deal with a threat that was never explained to the public. In the same period the Department of US Homeland Security warned of a 'code orange' terrorist alert in New York and armed special forces patrolled the streets, while anti-missile batteries were deployed in Washington in response to a 'perceived increase in terrorist threats' that went similarly unexplained. On 20 March 2003 Tony Blair even mentioned al-Qaeda in a speech to the British public announcing the first bombing raids on Baghdad.

Over the next few weeks the tabloid press in Britain and America thrilled to another dazzling display of 'shock and awe' bombardments and high-tech 'surgical strikes' in a video-game simulacrum of war, whose human consequences were generally concealed, in the Western world at least, by censored news reports and a diet of sanitised media images. As in Afghanistan, 'Operation Iraqi Freedom' achieved a rapid if not entirely seamless victory over a decrepit Third World dictatorship and its architects congratulated themselves on a 'clean' war that had defied predictions of a bloodier conflagration. Within months of the end of formal military operations, however, the occupation forces found themselves battling a vicious insurgency centred mostly among the Sunni Muslim population. By 2004 the insurgents were carrying out an average of seventy attacks a day on American troops and the nascent Iraqi security forces and Iraq had become one of the most violent countries on earth. International institutions and organisations connected with the occupation were also targets for assassinations, bombings and kidnappings, as were Iraqi and Western civilians. As the violence intensified, Salafist elements connected to a mysterious Jordanian militant named Abu-Mussab al-Zarqawi staged horrific assaults on Shia civilians, apparently with the aim of provoking civil war.

The relentless barbarism was marked by the new use of the Internet as a medium for broadcasting terrorist spectacles, as some of the insurgent groups took to broadcasting video and webcam footage of blindfolded Western hostages appealing to their respective governments to withdraw their troops, followed by filmed beheadings when these appeals were rejected. The more the initial reasons for the invasion of Iraq were revealed to be lies, fabrications and delusions, the more the politicians responsible fell back on terrorism narratives dating back to the anti-colonial era, in which the bloodthirstiness and barbarism of the terrorist enemy became a validation for the continued occupation. According to the new parameters, Iraq was now the 'crucible' in the War on Terror, where the civilised world would confront the forces of evil and defeat them.

All the familiar ingredients of the anti-terrorist malediction were invoked as the coalition attributed all acts of violence to former Ba'athists, foreign infiltrators and jihadist associates of al-Qaeda. In September 2005, however, the Washington-based Center for Strategic and International Studies (CSIS) reported that foreigners constituted less than 10 per cent of the Iraqi insurgents. The CSIS report also contradicted the presentation of Iraq as a 'crucible' in the War on Terror, claiming that 'The vast majority of Saudi militants who have entered Iraq were not terrorist sympathizers before the war; and were radicalized almost exclusively by the coalition invasion.'[29] Virtually all independent research pointed to the unpalatable conclusion that the great showcase of Western democracy in the Middle East was in fact bringing new recruits to the jihadist cause, for whom the invasion of 'the land of two rivers' appeared to bear out Osama bin Laden's thesis of a 'Crusader' assault. Nevertheless, the architects of the invasion continued to depict the insurgents as psychopathic killers, Islamo-fascists and former Ba'athists motivated by a pathological hatred of 'democracy'.[30] And the more Iraq was depicted as a battlefront between the forces of civilisation and a subhuman and barbaric enemy, the more the methods employed to fight him resembled those of previous counter-terrorist crusades, as US forces launched their own bloody operations against the insurgents, supported by a mercenary army of some 20,000 private 'security contractors' which included veterans of the Argentinian 'Dirty War' and former 'counter-terrorists' from apartheid-era South Africa.

Fighting Satan

The propaganda image of the universal terrorist has often provided a pretext for the abandonment of legality and morality by governments, and the War on Terror was no exception. In November 2001 Donald Rumsfeld announced that captured Taliban and al-Qaeda prisoners in Afghanistan would not be subject to the Geneva Convention. Hundreds of prisoners were shipped to detention centres in Afghanistan and in Guantanamo Bay in Cuba, where they were held as 'unlawful combatants' rather than prisoners of war. Among the prisoners depicted by the US military as 'the worst of the worst' was a 105-year-old man, who was eventually released from Guantanamo in October 2002 without having been charged with any crime. The innocence or guilt of such men was impossible to determine, since the US military did not explain why they had been arrested in the first place. Within this murky legal subworld prisoners could be detained indefinitely without trial, even as they were subjected to the new methods of interrogation that were becoming a routine instrument of the War on Terror.

In the aftermath of September 11 a number of CIA and FBI officials suggested that 'the rules had changed' and that interrogations of terrorist suspects might need to go 'beyond name, rank and serial number' in order to avoid a similar catastrophe. A Harvard law professor, Alan Dershowitz, argued that moral reservations about torture had to be balanced against the 'safety and the security of a nation's citizens' and proposed that interrogators apply for 'torture warrants' in cases where a terrorist suspect was believed to have vital information. These interrogators would be authorised to use an array of 'non-lethal' methods, which included 'a sterilised needle inserted under the fingernails to produce unbearable pain without any threat to health or life, or the method used in the film *Marathon Man*, a dental drill through an unanaesthetised tooth'.[31]

Dershowitz did not say what interrogators might do if these 'non-lethal' methods failed to extract the information required, nor did he say how it could be known that these prisoners possessed such information without torturing them in the first place. For Dershowitz, the use of torture was a 'tragic choice' facing 'democracies' confronted with the 'ticking-bomb terrorist'. The fantasy of the terrorist who knows the whereabouts of the 'ticking bomb' has been invoked as a justification for torture in previous counter-terrorist crusades, from Algeria to Argentina. The Algerian example had a particular influence on the War on Terror, so much so that the US Directorate for Special Operations and Low-Intensity Conflict at the Pentagon provided a special screening of *The Battle of Algiers* in August 2003, in order to provide what one Defense Department official called 'historical insight into the conduct of French operations in Algeria.'

Among other things Pontecorvo's film demonstrated how the French army's use of torture defeated the FLN militarily in Algiers, while simultaneously paving the way for a broader political defeat. But this message was conspicuously absent in conduct of the War on Terror, where the French use of sexual humiliation was seen as a useful instrument against Muslim 'terrorists'. In Afghanistan the US military introduced 'enhanced interrogation techniques' into its chain of camps, including beatings, stress positions, prolonged isolation and nakedness, the 'manipulation of phobias' and a technique called 'waterboarding', in which suspects were strapped to a board and dipped repeatedly into a tank of water. Other detainees were beaten or hung upside down from chains. Some of these interrogations were carried out by private contractors. Others were carried out by the US military itself or 'rendered' for interrogation to US allies such as Saudi Arabia, Morocco, Egypt and even Syria, whose methods were not subject to democratic scrutiny.[32]

In May 2004 the world was presented with shocking evidence that the new dispensation had reached Iraq, with the publication of photographs from Iraq's Abu Ghraib prison showing naked prisoners chained up like dogs, forced to simulate sex with each other, and hooded prisoners wired with electricity. One of the architects of the regime at Abu Ghraib was General William 'Jerry' Boykin, the deputy-undersecretary of defence for intelligence at the Pentagon and a fervent evangelical Christian, who went on a speaking tour of America in the summer of 2003 in which he told one church meeting in Boring, Oregon, that 'Satan wants to destroy this nation, he wants to destroy us as a nation, and he wants to destroy us as a Christian army.' Boykin was the man chosen by the Pentagon to find out why the methods used at Camp X-Ray in Guantanamo, known as GTMO or 'Gitmo' to the US military, were yielding better intelligence results than those used in Iraq against the insurgency. As a result of Boykin's investigations, the Abu Ghraib prison was 'Gitmoised' and the Guantanamo methods were taken to new extremes.[33]

The photographs represented a political and PR disaster for the US occupiers, confirming virtually every Islamist cliché concerning the moral depravity of America. Even in his most wildly optimistic moments, bin Laden could not have predicted that American soldiers would one day be forcing Muslim prisoners to renounce their faith, sodomising them with truncheons and allowing themselves to be photographed cheerfully holding naked prisoners on leads like dogs. Faced with such graphic evidence of the reality of the American civilising mission, supporters of the Iraq invasion were reduced to arguing that the methods used at Abu Ghraib were not as bad as the tortures carried out under Saddam Hussein's regime or the webcammed executions of Western hostages. These arguments evaded the crucial point that societies that claim to be civilised and democratic are usually judged by a different set of standards than those of dictatorships. And the fact that the world's foremost liberal democracy should be engaging in such practices was another indication of the inexorable downward spiral that the War on Terror had unleashed, not only in Iraq, but across the world.

Planet Terror
Like its predecessor in the Reagan era, the global War on Terror, or GWOT, as it was known to its protagonists, provided a pretext for an escalation of violence in the name of counter-terrorism, as various governments across the world adapted the logic and the rhetoric of the Bush crusade to their own conflicts. In Israel Ariel Sharon declared himself an ally of the United States in the war between 'good and evil and humanity and the bloodthirsty' and stepped up military operations in the Occupied Territories in an attempt to crush the Palestinian intifada through brute force. In the spring

of 2002 the Israeli army reoccupied large areas of the West Bank in response to a suicide bombing in the town of Netanya. The incursion wrecked much of the infrastructure of Palestinian society and culminated in the destruction of large swathes of the town of Jenin. Russia also took advantage of the GWOT in its military operations against Chechen insurgents. In 1999, the Putin government had used the bombings of Russian apartments as a pretext for a second and even bloodier intervention in Chechnya, despite evidence that the bombings had been carried out by the Russian intelligence services themselves.

Before 9/11 the Russian assault on Chechnya drew some muted criticism from the international community. Within weeks of the attacks, however, Bush declared that 'Arab terrorists' linked to al-Qaeda were operating on Chechen territory as a quid pro quo for Russian support in the War on Terror and acquiescence to the new American military presence in Georgia and the central Asian republics. As a result Vladimir Putin, the sinister ex-secret policeman now leading Russia, was able to intensify Russian operations in the 'reconquered areas' and 'zone of anti-terrorist operations' of Chechnya to such effect that by June 2003 some 70,000 civilians had been killed and much of Chechnya had been reduced to a lawless wasteland.

Other regimes also took advantage of the opportunities presented by the GWOT or set out to create their own. In July 2003 army officers in the Philippines took over a Manila shopping mall, which they then mined with explosives in a protest against government corruption. Among other things, the officers accused their superiors of carrying out a series of bombings in March and April the previous year, which had been blamed on Muslim separatists, in an attempt to obtain more US military aid. The War on Terror also brought an end to US restrictions on arms sales to the Algerian military, after William Burns, assistant secretary of state for Near Eastern affairs, announced in 2002 that 'Washington has much to learn from Algeria on ways to fight terrorism'. The return of Algeria to the ranks of civilised nations was boosted by the regime's assurances that al-Qaeda was attempting to establish a base of operations in the Maghreb. In the spring of 2003, more than two dozen European tourists were kidnapped by supposed Islamists led by a renegade former special services officer nick-named 'El Para', whom the Algerian regime described as an associate of Osama bin Laden. Other journalists reported that he was in fact an agent of the Algerian secret services, the Department of Intelligence and Security (DRS), and that the kidnappings were staged in order to facilitate Algeria's rehabilitation.[34]

Indonesia was another former pariah state that benefited from the War on Terror, where the US and Britain renewed military aid to the Indonesian army, which had been cut off in response to atrocities in East Timor. Galvanised by this support, in May 2003 the Indonesian military went on the offensive against separatist Muslim insurgents belonging to the Free Aceh Movement (GAM) in the oil-rich Aceh province in Sumatra. The offensive brought to an end nearly three years of protracted negotiations to a conflict in which some 12,000 people had been killed in nearly three decades. In a pattern repeated across the world, the Indonesian government took advantage of the global climate of fear to introduce emergency anti-terrorist legislation on the US model, which it used to arrest and detain GAM negotiators en route for a meeting in Japan. The 2003 report by the literary and human-rights organisation International PEN, titled *Anti-Terrorism and Freedom of Expression*, listed thirty-five countries which had experienced 'an increasingly hostile climate towards freedom of expression' since September 11, from China, Liberia and Zimbabwe to the authoritarian regime of former communist Islam Karimov in Uzbekistan.

Democratic governments also used the new post-9/11 climate of fear to rush through emergency anti-terrorist legislation. In Britain the Anti-Terrorism, Crime and Security Act of December 2001 allowed suspected terrorists to be detained indefinitely, without trial and without any evidence, on the orders of the home secretary. The British government also set a new national legal precedent, by permitting evidence obtained through torture in other countries to be used in anti-terrorist trials in the United Kingdom.[35] Like their American counterparts, government ministers made increasingly stark warnings to the effect that longstanding civil liberties might have to be 'sacrificed' in a post-9/11 world in which the 'rules of the game had changed'.

Though critics argued that the official response to terrorism represented a greater risk to Britain's democratic freedoms than the bombs of Osama bin Laden, the government insisted that the exceptionally lethal nature of post-9/11 terrorism required extraordinary measures to protect national security. These arguments appeared to be confirmed in July 2005, when simultaneous bombings on London underground trains and a double-decker bus killed fifty-two people and wounded hundreds more. Within hours, Tony Blair was invoking the familiar clichés and claiming that the bombings were an attack on 'our values' and 'way of life'. With characteristic sleight of hand, Blair even suggested that the bombings were 'particularly barbaric' because they had taken place on the day when the G8 summit had been about to announce an increase in aid to Africa and measures to combat climate change.

The idea that the attacks had been directed against the philanthropic world leaders at the G8 summit was mendacious and self-serving nonsense, but few questioned Blair's posturing as politicians and media pundits united in presenting the London bombings as an insane and evil expression of fundamentalist barbarism. As always, the ritualistic official response denied any political context or logic to the events themselves. Initial police investigation revealed that the bombings had been suicide attacks carried out by four British citizens of Pakistani descent living in Leeds, only one of whom was believed to have any previous involvement with al-Qaeda. Though government ministers immediately denied any connection between the bombers and the Iraq war, the bombings followed a clear pattern of attacks directed against the countries that had participated in the invasion, and reflected a growing radicalisation and disaffection amongst young Muslims which had to some extent been predicted in a Joint Intelligence Committee report produced before the invasion of Iraq.[36]

In October 2005 the government responded to the London bombings with an even more draconian package of new anti-terrorist measures, which allowed terrorist suspects to be held for up to three months without trial and made 'condoning or glorifying terrorism' a criminal offence. As in the United States, politicians invoked the magnitude of the terrorist threat in order to suppress public debate over these measures, to the point when government ministers even warned the judiciary not to raise objections to the new legislation.

These arguments did not go unchallenged. In October 2005 one senior judge compared the government's attitude towards the judiciary to the Nazis, while Anthony Scrivener QC warned that 'Britain would be a significant step closer to a police state' if the government's proposed anti-terrorist legislation went unamended'.[37] While some critics accused the new legislation of undermining habeas corpus, others pointed out that the vagueness and imprecision of the concept of 'glorifying terrorism' made it legally unworkable. Though these criticisms were dismissed by the government, they were nevertheless taken seriously in Parliament, which voted against the proposed legislation in November, forcing the government to limit the detention period to twenty-eight days.[38]

Coming only months after the London suicide bombings, this unexpected overturning of the Labour government's previously unassailable majority represented a rare challenge to the notion of the authoritarian anti-terrorist state and the 'changed world' arguments used to support it. At the same time this breach of the anti-terrorist consensus was tentative and subject to populist accusations, in the event of another terrorist attack, that the MPs and not the government had placed the public at risk. That same month an organisation calling itself 'al-Qaeda in Iraq' claimed responsibility for three suicide bombings in hotels in Jordan, suggesting that the Iraq insurgency was spilling beyond its borders. On the one hand such attacks provided graphic evidence that the GWOT had failed in its declared objective of eradicating 'terror'. But by this time the GWOT had created its own morbid dynamic, in which each new bombing and atrocity provided its architects with a justification to extend the 'war' to new fronts.

The Fourth World War

It is one of the paradoxes of the War on Terror that few of the individuals believed to be responsible for the September 11 attacks have been arrested. Even the arrest of the plot's alleged mastermind, Khalid Sheikh Mohammed, in 2003 has not resulted in a trial, while Osama bin Laden and his lieutenant Ayman al-Zawahiri have remained at large. Though the US military claimed that the war in Afghanistan had disrupted al-Qaeda's 'command structures' and destroyed its base of operations, there was no evidence that the War on Terror had brought about any reduction in the kind of violence it was supposedly intended to suppress. On the contrary, the invasion of Iraq and its aftermath coincided with a series of spectacular atrocities in Morocco, Turkey, Indonesia and elsewhere. In October 2002 a bomb in a Bali nightclub killed 202 people, the majority of whom were Western tourists. That same month Chechen fighters took the entire audience of a Moscow theatre hostage and threatened to blow themselves up unless Russian troops withdrew from Chechnya. The crisis was eventually resolved when the Russian security forces poured an unknown gas into the theatre, killing the kidnappers and many of their hostages. Many of these deaths occurred afterwards, when the Russian security forces refused to tell doctors which gas had been used and so intoxicated victims could not be given appropriate treatment. In March 2004 a series of bombs planted on Madrid trains killed nearly 200 commuters and wounded hundreds more. In the space of a single week in August and September 2004 Chechen ' Black Widows' blew themselves up in two passenger planes, killing everyone on board, while another bomb exploded in the Moscow subway. The bloody sequence of events culminated in the horrendous siege at the Russian town of Beslan, when armed Chechen guerrillas took more than 1,000 schoolchildren and their parents hostage on the first day of term and threatened to blow themselves up unless Russian troops withdrew from Chechnya. The siege ended in a chaotic and bloody gun battle, in which some 330 hostages were killed, the majority of them children.

These events were not necessarily connected to al-Qaeda or the transnational jihad, but they nevertheless appeared to bear out the narrative of a civilised world besieged by psychotic assassins and mass-murderers. Even official statistics pointed to an exponential increase in acts of unofficial terrorist violence across the world. In April 2005 the recently created National Counterterrorism Center in the United States reported 624 'significant' terrorist attacks in 2004, compared with 175 the previous year. Even excluding the ongoing mayhem in Iraq, these figures were higher than at any time since 1985. That same year the US secretary of state, Condoleeza Rice, ordered the 'sanitation' of the State Department's 19-year-old *Patterns of Global Terrorism* report, on the grounds that its 'methodology' was at fault.[39] Despite the evidence to the contrary, American and British politicians continued to insist that the war in Iraq had made the world safer with the same grotesque confidence with which they had once denounced the threat of Saddam Hussein's imaginary arsenals.

By this time even hawkish members of the US counter-terrorist establishment, such as the CIA Afghanistan specialist Michael Scheuer, had begun to criticise the conduct of the War on Terror, claiming that the occupation of Iraq was a distraction from the international effort against al-Qaeda. These criticisms ignored the fact that the elimination of al-Qaeda had always been a pretext for the GWOT, rather than its principal objective. The suggestion that al-Qaeda represented an existential threat to the United States comparable to Nazism or the former Soviet Union was partly a paranoid fantasy, but it was also a manufactured deception, which made it possible for politicians on both sides of the Atlantic to engage in Churchillian posturing and dismiss opponents of the GWOT as Munich-style 'appeasers' while engaging in a limitless war against anyone considered to be an enemy of the United States. In October 2001 the neo-conservative house journal *The Weekly Standard* predicted that the war in Afghanistan 'is going to spread and engulf a number of countries in conflicts of varying intensity . . . It is going to resemble the clash of civilizations that everyone has hoped to avoid.'[40]

To its neo-conservative ideologues, the Fourth World War would not be restricted to bin Laden or al-Qaeda. In October 2001 the neo-con covert operations conspirator, Michael Ledeen, told the American Enterprise Institute, 'We are fighting a lot of enemies ... If we just let our vision of the world go forth ... and we don't try to piece together clever diplomacy, but just wage a total war ... our children will sing great songs about us years from now.'[41] The main object of this war was the Middle East, which was increasingly presented in US foreign policy circles not just as a collection of 'failed states' but as a failed civilisation that had abandoned the train of modernity and progress and given itself over completely to jihad, dictatorship and fanaticism. This depiction was matched by an equally fanatical conviction that the only antidote to this diseased 'civilisation' was US military intervention, in a region described by David Frum and Richard Perle, two of the most strident advocates of such action, as a 'fetid swamp'.[42] If the neo-conservative vision of a Pax Americana in the Middle East constitutes the 'idealist' component of the War on Terror, the 'realist' component is represented by counter-terrorist exterminators such as Lieutenant-Colonel Ralph Peters, a former US intelligence officer and an implacable proponent of a bloody war of attrition against what he calls 'the psychotic progeny of a neurotic civilisation'. For Peters, the only solution to the terrorist 'devils' is 'to kill them and keep on killing them' until America's enemies finally abandon the field.[43]

This philosophy has also been evoked by the terrorist 'devils' themselves. In a communiqué claiming responsibility for what it called the 'death train operations' in Madrid the 'Abu Hafs al-Masri Brigades al-Qaeda' made this clear when it promised 'endless, bloody war' and expressed their hope that 'Bush does not lose the upcoming elections' on the grounds that his 'idiocy and religious fanaticism' helped awaken the Muslim nation.[44] The symmetry is not coincidental. Both al-Qaeda and their neo-conservative counterparts share the same belief in the 'moral clarity' of violence and the same contempt for those on their own side who refuse to join the great battle against evil. There has always been an element of symbiosis in the confrontation between bin Laden and America, in which each side uses the other to fulfil an agenda that goes beyond the immediate confrontation itself.

The danger is that these phantasmal 'wars' will exacerbate racial and religious fault lines and suck the world into a vortex of violence, in which each side uses the atrocities and lawless actions of its opponents to justify its own, while simultaneously constructing a vision of the 'Other' as an absolute evil worthy only of annihilation. Even the Nobel Prize-winning writer V. S. Naipaul has used similar language, arguing that countries such as Iran and Saudi Arabia which 'foment' terrorism should be 'destroyed'.[45] For some GWOT ideologues the threat is not from 'radical Muslims' or 'Islamic extremism' but Islam itself, which the Reverend Franklin Graham, the son of the evangelist Billy Graham, has described as 'a very evil and wicked religion'. A host of right-wing intellectuals in the United States, such as

Robert Spencer, Daniel Pipes and the Italian journalist Oriana Fallaci, have depicted 'radical Islam' as a global movement whose ultimate goal is the destruction and submission of Western civilisation. In a virulently Islamo-phobic diatribe entitled *The Rage and the Pride*, Fallaci described a credulous Europe and America blinded by political correctness to the presence of the 'various bin Ladens, SS and Black Shirts on their soil' and the existence of an enemy whose members could be counted in 'millions and millions'.

Such depictions owe more to bigotry than they do to objective analysis. For all the popularity that Osama bin Laden has attained in parts of the Islamic world, both the strategies and objectives of al-Qaeda and its off-shoots represent only a tiny proportion of the world's Muslim population. Nor does such popularity equate with the notion of a pan-Islamic desire to impose a Taliban-style theocracy on the Western world. On the contrary, the popularity of bin Laden owes more to the perception that he has 'stood up' to two superpowers than it does to a desire to subject the whole world to sharia law. To conservative Western pundits such as Pipes and Mark Steyn, however, any violence involving Muslims anywhere in the world is a manifestation of the same aggressive anti-Christian or anti-Jewish jihad, just as any leftist revolutionary violence was once seen as the product of an international communist plot. Even the revolt in the French *banlieues* in November 2005 was depicted by Steyn as an 'early skirmish in the Eurabian civil war',[46] while Pipes saw the riots as further evidence of a 'permeating Islamist ideology ... to dominate the country and replace its civilisation with Islam's'.[47]

Other pundits similarly described the French riots as an 'intifada' and a 'jihad'. The idea that the French riots were motivated by 'Islam' flew in the face of consistent evidence of socio-economic causes that had nothing to do with religion, while simultaneously ignoring the large participation of African youths who were neither Muslims nor immigrants of Arab descent. Such distortions were routine elements in GWOT discourse, in which any act of violence involving Muslims anywhere in the world could be inte-grated into the overarching narrative of an 'Islamo-fascist' offensive aimed at the final overthrowing of Western civilisation.

The consequences of this confrontation are potentially catastrophic, in terms of its impact not only on the relationship between Muslims and the surrounding population in the West, but between the West and the Muslim world as a whole. In some Christian fundamentalist circles, the Fourth World War is regarded as the fulfilment of Biblical prophecy and the beginning of the final conflagration predicted in the Book of Revelation in which four angels 'bound in the great river Euphrates' will be unleashed to 'slay the third part of men'. Apocalyptic fantasies are also on the ascendant in parts of the Middle East, where the war in 'the land of two rivers' has similarly been interpreted by some clerics as the onset of a wider cosmic conflagration. At present these fantasies belong to the margins of the unfolding confrontation, but the longer it continues the more likely it is that each side will finally get the kind of enemy and the 'clash of civilisations' they both want.

In a Time of Terror

We have come a long way since Sergei Kravchinsky's terrorist titan first stepped on to the world stage. Today the brutal dynamic of terrorism and counter-terrorism has come to cast a chill shadow over the politics of the new century, in ways that the 'reluctant assassins' of Alexander II could never have imagined and would almost certainly have condemned. In the wake of the September 11 attacks the world has been dragged along by a tide of violence and cruelty that shows no sign of abating, where a constant stream of media-driven violent spectacles compete for the limited attention span of a global audience that has become accustomed to horror. It is a world in which webcammed executions of helpless hostages in Iraq are lauded by their perpetrators as acts of divine justice and posted on the Internet as political 'messages' aimed at undermining the will to support the occupation. In this marriage of terror and technology it is possible to bypass the conventional media and watch unexpurgated footage of the *Wall Street Journal* reporter Daniel Pearl having his throat cut or digital photographs of Iraqi prisoners being humiliated and beaten in the Abu Ghraib prison. In the United States a pornographic website allows US soldiers free access in exchange for posting photographs of mutilated and dead Iraqis. The pornographic celebration of violence and atrocity is only one element in the wider obscenity generated by an atrocious pseudo-war, in which helicopter gunships and artillery 'flush out' cities harbouring the terrorist 'Satan' while suicide bombers calling themselves 'soldiers' kill Shia worshippers, London underground commuters or customers at a Casablanca café in the name of God.

It is a world where the most powerful democracy fights a war on behalf of freedom by using a private airline to fly terrorist prisoners to the torture chambers of Syria, Egypt, Jordan or Algeria and where thousands of 'ghost detainees' have vanished into a chain of prison camps across the world without being charged with any crime. It is a world in which British police may shoot an innocent Brazilian commuter eight times in the head on the mere suspicion that he might have been a suicide bomber. It is a world in which Khalid el-Masri, a German-Lebanese Muslim, went on holiday to

Macedonia on New Year's Eve in 2003 only to be kidnapped by Macedonian special forces as a terrorist suspect and flown to Afghanistan. Five months later el-Masri was dumped in Albania after being beaten, drugged and interrogated by US forces. Such events are part of the phantasmal world of the GWOT. It is a world that lives in fearful expectation of catastrophic attacks from terrorists using an ever-widening array of ingeniously lethal means. In January 2005, on the eve of the US presidential inauguration, *Time* magazine warned of a new potential danger from 'limousine terror' in which al-Qaeda terrorists might use 'vehicle-borne improvised explosive devices', or VBIEDS, to transport flammable and toxic gases and attack the capital. In May 2005 the president was evacuated from the White House in flight from a 'dense incoming cloud' that turned out to be nothing more than a dense incoming cloud. In this world tormented by the fantasy of absolute terror and fixated by a futile search for absolute security, where intelligence satellites seek to monitor billions of phone conversations and emails in search of 'word clusters' that might indicate a possible terrorist plot, such as 'anthrax' and 'bomb', we are moving ever closer to the future predicted by French sociologist Denis Duclos, in which 'Surveillance is the religion of a well-oiled mechanised society.'[1] It is a world in which some 600 demonstrators and protestors, including an 85-year-old man, can be detained by police at the September 2005 Labour Party conference under new anti-terrorist legislation, with barely a comment or a murmur of protest.[2]

All this is part of the post-9/11 nightmare – a nightmare which owes as much to the War on Terror as it does to the events that supposedly provoked it. None of this was inevitable. The decision to respond to the September 11 attacks through a global 'war' was a political and strategic choice. There were, and are, other means through which the world might have responded to the attacks, which did not require torture, clandestine prison camps, curtailments on civil liberties, the creation of a permanent state of emergency and an apparently limitless series of fraudulent and dishonest wars.[3] Though the GWOT has been portrayed as a response to an unprecedented threat, its rhetoric, its assumptions and many of its methods have been borrowed from previous counter-terrorist crusades. Once again, the anti-terrorist anathema has presented an image of a civilised and benevolent world threatened by a uniquely evil enemy, whose bloodthirsty deeds are beyond comprehension. Once again, the official depiction of 'terrorism' has become a propaganda smokescreen, which denies any responsibility for the violence it depicts in favour of an absurd fantasy of a benign Western world threatened by monsters who hate its essential goodness.

Such manipulation does not have to go unquestioned. The Madrid train bombings occurred on the eve of elections which the ruling Partido Popular was widely predicted to win, despite the huge unpopularity of the war in Iraq. Within hours of the explosions the government was suggesting that the bombings were the work of Basque separatists, even after evidence was already beginning to emerge of an Islamist connection. The Spanish government mobilised all its resources nationally and internationally to reinforce the ETA thesis, even suggesting that ETA had collaborated with al-Qaeda to carry out the bombings. Within forty-eight hours the government faced a popular democratic revolt, mobilised through emails, text messages and word of mouth, in which Spaniards across the country demonstrated against the disinformation they were receiving from their government.

As a result of this popular upsurge, the unfavoured Socialist Party won the elections, largely on the basis of its commitment to withdraw Spanish troops from Iraq. In Britain and the United States, proponents of 'moral clarity' predictably accused the Spanish population of 'surrendering' to terrorism. There is no doubt that the bombings were intended to bring about this outcome. In their immediate aftermath, however, the horrendous bombings provoked an expression of national solidarity that might easily have worked in the government's favour, had it not been for the Partido Popular's blatant attempts to mislead the public. For the bombers themselves there was only universal anger and disgust.

Rather than an act of moral surrender, the Spanish civic revolt represented a rare episode in the War on Terror in which ordinary citizens responded to a terrorist atrocity as active participants rather than frightened and passive spectators. Such interventions have been conspicuous by their absence in a post-9/11 world dominated by the kind of rhetoric invoked by David Frum and Richard Perle in *An End to Evil: How to Win the War on Terror*:

> For us, terrorism remains the great evil of our time, and the war against this evil, this generation's great cause. We do not believe that Americans are fighting this evil to minimize it or to manage it. We believe they are fighting to win to end this evil before it kills again, and on a genocidal scale. There is no middle way for Americans: it is victory or holocaust.[4]

If the world is to escape from the Manichean fantasy world of the GWOT, it is important to recognise such discourse for the hollow propaganda that it is. Since 9/11 thousands more civilians have been killed in the name of counter-terrorism than have died in terrorist 'holocausts'. A civilisation that aspires to be worthy of the name cannot accept atrocities such as the Madrid and Bali bombings or the taking of child hostages at Beslan as legitimate acts. But societies that reserve their condemnation for such actions and ignore the carnage wrought by 'military' violence in Fallujah, Jenin or Grozny are not only living in a false moral universe, they are inviting further attacks.

Rage

In Greek mythology, Jason's spurned wife Medea kills both her own children and his new wife in order to take revenge for her husband's betrayal. In Euripides' version, the wiser elder Creon and the chorus advise her to flee the country and start a new life with her children, but Medea's sense of wronged indignation is so powerful that she is prepared to destroy even her own children to hurt her husband. Stripped of its political and strategic objectives, unofficial terrorist violence is often motivated by the same all-consuming rage. In an article in the *New York Review of Books* on the Iraqi insurgency, the veteran war correspondent Chris Hedges noted 'the red-hot rage, the utter humiliation and indignation that have pushed Iraqis to turn their country into an inferno'.[5] A week after the London bombings the *New York Times* interviewed friends of the suicide bomber Shehzad Tanweer, one of whom told the reporter how Tanweer '... was sick of it all, all the injustice and the way the world is going about it'. From Emile Henry to Timothy McVeigh and Osama bin Laden, the history of modern terrorism is filled with groups and individuals who believed themselves to be acting in response to intolerable wrongs, real or imagined, committed against them or others. The more the world is perceived to be indifferent to such injustices, the more will organisations and individuals claim the right to make the tragedy mutual. These actions are not necessarily 'proportional' or morally justifiable in themselves. Even as she prepares to kill her children Medea recognises

> The evil that I do, I understand full well.
> But a passion drives me greater than my will.

Many so-called terrorists might make the same observation, were they disposed to examine their own motives. But even the bloodiest acts of unofficial terrorism are invariably seen by their perpetrators as a legitimate *response* to the actions of their enemies. Such legitimacy may appear spurious or opportunist to outsiders, but without it, the shallow aura of heroism which has so often surrounded the most horrendous acts of unofficial terrorist violence could not exist. For this reason alone, societies that seriously wish to eliminate or reduce such violence need to address the wider causes and grievances that inspire it and accept their share of responsibility for even the most ostensibly 'evil' terrorist acts. The architects of the War on Terror have sometimes paid lip service to this objective, more often than not as part of a propaganda marketing exercise. The problem is that the language, assumptions and stereotypes of the War on Terror are themselves a denial of any mutual responsibility. Once again, as in so many other terrorist episodes, the monstrous figure of the terrorist makes violent counter-terrorism appear to be the only logical response. Yet once again there is a disparity between the anti-terrorist discourse issued by governments for public consumption and the more nuanced perspectives of intelligence and military officials. Even in Iraq, where so many commentators have portrayed the Iraqi insurgents as fascists, bloodthirsty psychopaths and insane 'jihadis' motivated by hatred of democracy, the *Sunday Times* announced in June 2005 that the US military had engaged in secret negotiations with insurgent leaders.[6] The results of these negotiations are not known, but the fact that they occurred at all suggests a recognition on the part of the US military that there were at least areas for discussion – a recognition that is rarely reflected in the public insistence by the US government that there can be no negotiation or compromise with 'terror'.

To point out this disparity does not mean that all 'terrorist' violence can be resolved through negotiation, let alone that events such as the bombings in Madrid, Bali or London can be regarded as legitimate means of expressing political grievances or objectives. There is no easy solution to the complex international phenomenon of Islamist violence that has emerged in recent years, whose ranks include disaffected French-Moroccan Muslim converts such as Zacarias Moussaoui, intelligence agents of ambiguous loyalties such as the US covert operative Ali Mohammed and religious zealots dreaming of the lost Caliphate. But such violence cannot be resolved through reheated imperialist adventures dressed up as moral crusades against 'evil', let alone the bloody, dishonest and incompetent attempt to create a Western client state in Iraq as a supposed antidote to Islamo-fascism. In 1998 a Pakistani activist scholar, Eqbal Ahmad, observed of US support for the anti-Soviet jihad that, 'A superpower cannot promote terror in one place and reasonably expect to discourage terrorism in another place. It won't work in this shrunken world.'[7] The current 'war on terror' is likely to repeat the same pattern of covert operations and secret alliances which did so much to spawn the modern jihadist networks in the first place. In January 2005 a former high-level intelligence official told the journalist Seymour Hersh that future Pentagon tactics in the War on Terror might include the use of special forces 'action teams' modelled on the death squads in El Salvador to 'find and eliminate terrorist organisations'. According to the same official, other forthcoming projects involved the recruitment of local citizens in various countries to penetrate terrorist groups, whose activities 'could potentially involve organising and carrying out combat operations, or even terrorist activities'.[8]

With US covert operations already under way in more than eighty countries, the interplay of terrorism and counter-terrorism looks set to form new tributaries, whose consequences may make themselves felt in unexpected ways. If the coming century is not to become a permanent state of emergency, in which frightened and manipulated populations are herded into anti-terrorist corrals, it may be necessary to develop a more mature and honest attitude towards violent conflicts. Such a transformation would require a renunciation of the terrorist malediction. It would require an end to the self-serving moralistic rhetoric that has so often prevailed in previous terrorist emergencies, and a recognition that even the most violent terrorist organisations might stem from political conflicts and causes that are not addressed in the infantilising official representations of 'terrorism'. It would require a more honest approach to nuclear weapons proliferation, which does not use the supposed link between terrorism and rogue states as a selective excuse to attack or dominate countries considered to be enemies of the West. It would require a recognition that the present eruption of Islamist violence is perhaps a symptom of an imbalance of power and the consequence of decades of manipulation, deceit and hypocrisy in Western foreign policy towards the Arab world.

In the current climate, such a transformation remains hypothetical and even utopian, but it may be necessary if the world is ever to emerge from the macabre shadow that 'terrorism' has cast over our era. The 'technique' of terrorism is available to any group or individual who wishes to use it, and the current eruption of Islamist violence may one day be superseded by other terrorist threats and emergencies. Nevertheless, the threat of unofficial terrorism needs to be kept in perspective. Between 2001 and 2003, according to the US State Department's *Patterns of Global Terrorism*, approximately 4,645 people were killed in acts of international terrorism, nearly 3,000 of whom died in the September 11 attacks. In the same period some 3.3 million people died in civil wars in the former Congo with barely a murmur from the Western media. In 2003, a year in which 625 people were reported to have died in worldwide terrorist attacks, 549 people were murdered in the city of Chicago alone in acts of 'ordinary' criminal violence. The death toll caused by a locust infestation that destroyed harvests in many African countries in 2004 may already have outstripped all the casualties of international terrorism since records began.

In 2005, despite billions of dollars spent on 'homeland security' in the United States, Hurricane Katrina revealed the same chaos, passivity and bureaucratic confusion that had preceded the September 11 attacks. The disaster in New Orleans is one more sign that the human race may well be facing far greater threats to its security than Osama bin Laden.

'We should not have allowed nineteen murderers to change our world,' wrote Robert Fisk in an article commemorating the third anniversary of 9/11.[9] Fisk was absolutely correct that this transformation was 'allowed' to happen. It might be time to reclaim the world we have lost. The alternative is a dystopian future of permanent war against an invisible enemy, in which the fear of terrorism becomes the raison d'être not only of individual governments but of the entire international order. If that happens, the world will finally have surrendered to 'terrorism' and to those who would protect us from it.

Notes

Prologue: The Bomb in the Baby Carriage

1. 'Terrorist's brain to be returned', *New York Times*, 15 November 2002.
2. Alix Kates Shulman (ed.), *Red Emma Speaks: Selected Writings and Speeches by Emma Goldman*, Vintage, 1972, p. 33.
3. *La Vida Barcelonesa a Traves de la Vanguardia* (1900–1917). Author's translation.
4. For a comprehensive list of definitions see John Richard Thackrah, *Encyclopedia of Terrorism and Political Violence*, Routledge & Kegan, 1987, pp. 58–63.
5. Benjamin Netanyahu (ed.), *Terrorism: How the West Can Win*, Farrar, Straus & Giroux, 1986, p. 9.
6. Edmund Leach, *Custom, Law, and Terrorist Violence*, Edinburgh University Press, 1977, p. 36.
7. Netanyahu, *Terrorism*, p. 202.

Chapter 1: The Hero Takes the Stage

1. Though the People's Will saw terrorism as an offensive tactic, they also regarded it as a means of protecting an incipient revolutionary movement from its counter-revolutionary enemies. In this sense their use of terror was entirely in accordance with the principles espoused by Robespierre in 1794 that, 'If the sphere of popular government in peacetime is virtue, in revolution it is at one and the same time virtue and terror; virtue, without which terror is quite deadly; and terror, without which virtue is powerless. Terror is nothing more than rapid, severe, and inflexible justice; it is therefore something that emanates from virtue.' Quoted in Albert Soboul, *The French Revolution, 1787–1799: from the Storming of the Bastille to Napoleon*, NLB, 1974, p. 370.
2. Sergei Kravchinsky, *Underground Russia*, Charles Scribner's Sons, 1888, p. 88.
3. Quoted in Walter Laqueur, *The Terrorism Reader*, New American Library, 1978, p. 82.
4. Kravchinsky, *Underground Russia*, p. 257.
5. Quoted in Franco Venturi, *Roots of Revolution*, Grosset & Dunlap, 1960, p. 364.

6. Quoted in Laqueur, *The Terrorism Reader*, p. 68.

7. Ibid., p. 69.

8. Quoted in Venturi, *Roots of Revolution*, p. 563.

9. Vera Figner, *Memoirs of a Revolutionist*, Northern Illinois University Press, 1991, p. 33.

10. Ibid., p. 50.

11. Zasulich later became a member of the Russian Social Democratic Party and renounced her terrorist past, describing terrorism as a 'very sombre form of struggle'. Other prominent members of the People's Will gravitated towards the extreme right and became fervent pro-tsarists before and during World War I.

12. Kravchinsky, *Underground Russia*, p. 39.

13. Figner, *Memoirs of a Revolutionist*, p. 116.

14. Ibid., p. 99.

15. Naivety was on occasion accompanied by opportunism of the most misplaced kind, such as the support given by some members of the Executive Committee to the anti-Semitic pogroms in the Ukraine that followed Alexander's assassination. Though these pogroms were fuelled by the belief among the peasantry that the 'Jews were responsible' for the assassination, the People's Will journal in October 1882 called them acts of 'popular retribution' and recommended that the revolutionary movement should 'seize leadership of those forces and endorse their point of view'. See Adam Ulam, *Prophets and Conspirators in Prerevolutionary Russia*, Transaction Publishers, 1998, pp. 368–72.

16. Kravchinsky, *Underground Russia*, p. 41.

17. Ibid., p. 39.

18. Edward Lawrence Levy, 'Russian Nihilism', paper presented to the Alliance Literary and Debating Society, 1880, p. 9.

19. Karl Marx and Friedrich Engels, Reviews from the *Neue Rheinische Zeitung Politisch-Okonomische Revue*, 4 (1850), quoted in *Marx and Engels Collected Works*, vol. 10, *1849–51*, Lawrence & Wishart, 1985, pp. 311–25.

20. Victor Serge, *Memoirs of a Revolutionary, 1901–1941*, Oxford University Press, 1963, p. 2.

21. Quoted in Lionel Kochan, *Russia in Revolution, 1890–1918*, Weidenfeld and Nicolson, 1966, p. 58.

22. Boris Savinkov, *Memoirs of a Terrorist*, Albert & Charles Boni, 1931, p. 108.

23. Ibid., p. 42.

24. V. Ropshin (pseud. Boris Savinkov), *The Pale Horse*, Maunsell and Co., 1917, p. 88.

25. Leon Trotsky, 'The Collapse of Terrorism', May 1909; quoted in Laqueur, *The Terrorism Reader*, p. 218.

26. For a fuller account of the spread of the 'Russian method' see Steven G. Marks, 'Organizing Revolution: the Russian Terrorists', in S. G. Marks, *How Russia Shaped the Modern World*, Princeton University Press, 2003, pp. 7–38.

27. For a detailed and sympathetic account of the IMRO see Stoyan Christowe, *Heroes and Assassins*, Victor Gollancz, 1935.

28. Maurice Paléologue, *An Ambassador's Memoirs*, vol. III, George H. Doran Co., 1925, entry for Saturday, 17 April 1917.

29. Ibid.

Chapter 2: Anarchists and Dynamitards

1. Ernest Vizetelly, *The Anarchists: Their Faith and their Record*, Bodley Head, 1911, p. 163.

2. R. H. Savage, *The Anarchist: a Story of Today*, Routledge, 1894, p. 242.

3. Statistics quoted from 'Latter Day Witches', in Bob James, *Anarchism and State Violence in Sydney and Melbourne, 1886–1896*, Annares Books, 1986; available at www.takver.com/history.

4. Quoted in Felix Dubois, *The Anarchist Peril*, T. Fisher Unwin, 1894, p. 154.

5. *The Alarm*, 2 May 1885. Document available at The Haymarket Affair Digital Collection and The Dramas of Haymarket at: www. chicagohistory.org/dramas.

6. Andrieux later described *La Révolution Sociale* as 'a telephone line between the conspiratorial centre and the office of the Chief of Police'. See George Woodcock, *Anarchism*, World Publishing Co., 1962, p. 298.

7. The bomb was believed to be destined 'for Russia'. *The Times* nevertheless celebrated the sentences on more general grounds, claiming that the prisoners' real offence was 'the most dastardly and wicked which it is possible to conceive. Like treason it is aimed at the very heart of the State, but it is not designed to destroy the existing Government alone. It strikes at all Governments, and behind all Governments it strikes at those eternal, social rights for which all forms and methods of civil rules exist' (*The Times*, 5 April 1892). For a detailed account of the Walsall anarchists' trial and evidence of police

collusion, see John Quail, *The Slow Burning Fuse: the Lost History of the British Anarchists*, Flamingo, 1978, ch. 6.

8. Some of the worst abuses took place in Spain, where the authorities habitually carried out indiscriminate arrests of suspected anarchists in response to both real bombings and imagined conspiracies. Confessions were frequently extracted through torture, in the absence of evidence, and became the basis for executions and draconian prison sentences. Similar anarchist round-ups took place elsewhere in Europe, though not on the same scale or level of brutality, in an attempt to uncover anarchist conspiracies. Not all of them were successful. In France in 1894, French authorities attempted once more to conjure up a conspiracy linking some of the country's leading libertarian intellectuals to the activities of a gang of anarcho-burglars, in what became known as the 'Trial of the Thirty'. The trial collapsed after a week, and only the gang members were convicted.

9. The Chicago Historical Society has assembled a fine array of online documents and materials pertaining to the Haymarket incident. See The Haymarket Affair Digital Collection and The Dramas of Haymarket at www.chicagohistory.org/dramas.

10. Quoted in Sender Garlin, *Three American Radicals: John Swinton, Crusading Editor; Charles. P. Steinmetz, Scientist and Socialist; William Dean Howells and the Haymarket Era*, Westview Press, 1991, p. 117.

11. From original documents in The Haymarket Affair Digital Collection (see n. 8).

12. Serge, *Memoirs of a Revolutionary*, p. 218.

13. *The Times*, 29 March 1892.

14. Quoted in J. C. Longoni, *Four Patients of Dr. Deibler*, Lawrence & Wishart, 1970, p. 173.

15. Cesare Lombroso, 'Illustrative Studies in Criminal Anthropology', *The Monist*, 1 (1881), pp. 336–43.

16. The conference nevertheless found its way into Conrad's *The Secret Agent*, where it forms the background for the plot by anarchists and foreign agents provocateurs to blow up the Greenwich Observatory.

17. The Bonnot Gang was strongly influenced by the ultra-individualistic anarchism propagated by the German philosopher Max Stirner and their activities consisted almost entirely of bank robberies, some of which were carried out, for the first time, using motorcars. They nevertheless generated a mood of public hysteria that recalled the 'anarchist terror' and the gang became the object of a massive

manhunt. Defiant to the last, the majority of the *bandits tragiques* died in shootouts and sieges rather than allow themselves to be arrested. In one incident in the town of Choisy-Le-Roi, police and soldiers used machine-guns and dynamite to destroy the hideout of the gang's leader, Jules Bonnot, and a companion. See Richard Parry, *The Bonnot Gang*, Rebel Press, 1987.

18. Quoted in Longoni, *Four Patients of Dr. Deibler*, p. 172.
19. Luigi Fabbri, *Bourgeois Influences On Anarchism*, trans. Chaz Bufe, Sharp Press, 2001, p. 17.
20. Ibid., p. 12.
21. The 1894 Bourdin incident made a particularly strong impression on Joseph Conrad, and a fictionalised version of it became the fulcrum of *The Secret Agent*. For a fuller account of the impact of the Bourdin bombing on Conrad and his contemporaries see David Mulry, 'Popular Accounts of the Greenwich Bombing and Conrad's *The Secret Agent*', in *Rocky Mountain Review of Language and Literature*, 54 (2) (2000), pp. 43–64.
22. Quoted in Walter Laqueur, *The Age of Terrorism*, Little, Brown and Co., 1987, p. 313.
23. Karl Marx, letter to Friedrich Engels, 14 December 1867, quoted in *Marx and Engels Collected Works*, vol. 21, *Letters, 1864–68*, International Publishers, 1988, p. 501.
24. Quoted in Roland Quinault, 'Underground Attacks', *History Today*, 55 (9) (2005), pp. 18–19. Quinault also makes some interesting comparisons between this episode and the response to the July 2005 suicide bomb attacks in London.
25. For a detailed account of the British attempts to link Parnell to Fenian terrorism through the 'Jubilee Plot' to assassinate Queen Victoria, see Christy Campbell's groundbreaking *Fenian Fire*, HarperCollins, 2002.
26. Quoted in Bernard Potter, 'Terrorism and the Victorians', *History Today*, 36 (12) (1986), pp. 6–7.

Chapter 3: Terror and Resistance

1. Quoted in Lord Russell of Liverpool, *The Scourge of the Swastika*, Cassell, 1954, p. 86.
2. Quoted in Ulrick O'Connor, *A Terrible Beauty Is Born*, Granada, 1975, p. 173.
3. Quoted ibid., p. 129.

4. Quoted in James Mackay, *Michael Collins: a Life*, Mainstream Publishing, 1997, p. 151.
5. Quoted in O'Connor, *A Terrible Beauty Is Born*, p. 137.
6. Quoted in Robert B. Asprey, *War in the Shadows: the Guerrilla in History* (2 vols), vol. I, Doubleday, 1975, p. 410.
7. Quoted ibid.
8. These tactics placed SOE and the resistance organisations in a difficult moral dilemma, in which they were obliged to choose between carrying out attacks in the knowledge that hostages would be shot or abandoning the underground struggle altogether. In general the imperatives of the resistance came first. For Richard Pinder, an SOE operative in Czechoslovakia, the assassination of Heydrich 'was an act of justice that lightened our darkness and gave us hope', in spite of the terrible punishment visited on Czech civilians afterwards. If the wartime resistance accepted such reprisals as an unavoidable consequence of war, the 'intensification of calamities' was also seen in some quarters as a means of radicalising the population, in ways that Nechaev would have understood. As Bill Stevenson, the Canadian head of the British Security Coordination which directed the secret war in Europe, later observed, 'There was only one way to mobilise popular support for the secret armies, and that was to stage more dramatic acts of resistance and counter-terrorism'; William Stevenson, *A Man Called Intrepid*, Book Club Associates, 1976, p. 359.
9. Quoted in Magnus Linklater, Isabel Hilton and Neal Ascherson, *Klaus Barbie: the Fourth Reich and the Neo-fascist Connection*, Hodder & Stoughton, 1984, p. 132.
10. Julie Frederikse, *None but Ourselves*, Ravan Press, 1982, p. 158.
11. Doris Katz, *The Lady Was a Terrorist*, Shiloni, 1953, p, 190.
12. Quoted in Asprey, *War In the Shadows*, vol. I, p. 901.
13. Michael Walzer, *Just and Unjust Wars*, Pelican, 1980, p. 229.
14. Menachem Begin, *The Revolt*, W. H. Allen, 1983, p. 52.
15. Ibid., p. 55.
16. Yasser Arafat. 'Address to the UN General Assembly (November 13, 1974)', in Walter Laqueur and Barry Rubin (eds), *The Israel–Arab Reader*, Pelican, 1984, p. 510.

Chapter 4: Savages

1. Margery Perham, Introduction to J. M. Kariuki, *'Mau Mau' Detainee*, Oxford University Press, 1963 , p. xiii.

2. Lawrence Durrell, *Bitter Lemons*, Faber and Faber, 1957, p. 246.

3. Jules Roy, *The War in Algeria*, Grove Press, 1961, p. 65.

4. Noel Barber, *The War of the Running Dogs*, Bantam, 1987, p. 72.

5. F. Spencer Chapman, *The Jungle Is Neutral*, Transworld, 1957, p. 134. See also John Newsinger, 'The Military Memoir in British Imperial Culture: the Case of Malaya', *Race and Class*, 35 (3) (1994), pp. 47–63.

6. Alan Hoe and Eric Morris, *Re-enter the SAS: the Special Air Services and the Malayan Emergency*, Lee Cooper, 1994, p. 31.

7. Oliver Crawford, *The Door Marked Malaya*, Rupert Hart-Davis, 1958, p. 211.

8. Arthur Campbell, *Jungle Green*, George Allen & Unwin, 1953, p. 210.

9. Victor Purcell, *Malaya: Communist or Free?*, Victor Gollancz, 1954 , p. 9.

10. Robert Asprey, *War in the Shadows: the Guerrilla in History* (2 vols), Doubleday, 1975, vol. II.

11. C. T. Stoneham, *Mau Mau*, Museum Press, 1953, p. 29.

12. Quoted in David Anderson, *Histories of the Hanged: Britain's Dirty War in Kenya and the End of Empire*, Weidenfeld & Nicolson, 2005, p. 281.

13. Kariuki, *'Mau Mau' Detainee*, p. 33.

14. Quoted in Frank Furedi, *Colonial Wars and the Politics of Third World Nationalism*, I. B. Tauris, 1994, p. 215.

15. See David Maughan-Brown, *Land, Freedom and Fiction*, Zed Books, 1985, pp. 38–41.

16. Anderson, *Histories of the Hanged*, pp. 119–180.

17. Frank Kitson, *Bunch of Five*, Faber and Faber, 1977, p. 27.

18. Donald L. Barnett and Karari Njama, *Mau Mau from within*, MacGibbon & Kee, 1972, p. 146.

19. Kariuki, *'Mau Mau' Detainee*, p. 35.

20. Waruhiu Itote, *Mau Mau in Action*, TransAfrica Book, 1985, p. 5.

21. Koigi wa Wamwere, *I Refuse to Die*, Seven Stories Press, 2002, p. 132.

22. Asprey, *War in the Shadows*, vol. II, p. 886.

23. Anderson, *Histories of the Hanged*, p. 4.

24. One of the most prominent advocates of a public recognition of *wiyathi* was J. M. Kariuki himself, who served as Kenyatta's secretary following independence. Kariuki later became disillusioned with the corruption and inequality of post-colonial Kenyan society and bitterly criticised his former mentor. In 1975 he was found murdered, his body half-eaten, a killing that was widely believed to have been carried out on Kenyatta's orders.

25. The official version may not prevail indefinitely. In 2005 Kenyan survivors from the Mau Mau era sued the British government for abuses carried out by the colonial regime during the period. The case has yet to be resolved.

26. Franz Fanon, *Studies in a Dying Colonialism*, Earthscan, 1989, p. 58. For a fictional exploration of the female 'fire carriers' of the Algerian revolution see Assia Djebar, *Women of Algiers in Their Apartment*, University Press of Virginia, 1992.

27. Quoted in Alistair Horne, *A Savage War of Peace: Algeria: 1954–1962*, Penguin, 1979, p. 185.

28. Edward Behr, *The Algerian Problem*, Penguin, 1961, p. 112.

29. Quoted in Horne, *A Savage War of Peace*, p. 186.

30. For a fictional evocation of the atmosphere in Algiers during this period see Mohammed Dib's haunting short story 'The Savage Night', in *The Savage Night*, University of Nebraska Press, 2001.

31. Quoted in Asprey, *War in the Shadows*, vol. II, p. 919.

32. Paul Aussaresses, *The Battle of the Casbah: Terrorism and Counter-Terrorism in Algeria, 1955–1957*, Enigma, 2002, p. 128.

33. Massu subsequently underwent a change of heart about torture. In the spring of 2001 he publicly regretted the use of torture during the Algerian war in a letter to *Le Monde*. Massu was criticised by Aussaresses himself, who insisted that torture had been not only justified but effective. Though successive amnesties make it impossible for French soldiers to be tried for actions carried out in the Algerian 'events', the unrepentant Aussaresses was stripped of his Legion of Honour and tried for 'justifying war crimes'. Had it not been for the amnesties, Aussaresses's boastful account of his previously unknown involvement in the murders of FLN prisoners, including Larbi ben M'hidi, might have resulted in a prison sentence. Instead he was eventually fined a token sum after a trial that attracted widespread international attention. See Adam Shatz, 'The Torture of Algiers', *New York Review of Books*, 49 (18), 21 November 2002. Also Richard Viner, 'Electric Koran', *London Review of Books*, 23 (11), 7 June 2001.

34. Henri Alleg, *The Question*, John Calder, 1958, p. 83.

35. Albert Camus, 'Preface to Algerian Reports', in *Resistance, Rebellion, and Death*, Alfred A. Knopf, 1960, p. 84.

36. Germaine Tillion, *France and Algeria: Complementary Enemies*, Alfred A. Knopf, 1961, p. 35.

37. Franz Fanon, *The Wretched of the Earth*, Penguin, 1967, p. 74.

38. Ibid., p. 19.
39. Quoted in James D. Le Sueur, *Uncivil War: Intellectuals and Identity Politics During the Decolonization of Algeria*, University of Pennsylvania Press, 2001, p. 111.
40. Herbert Lottman, *Albert Camus: a Biography*, Picador, 1981, p. 593.
41. Camus, *Resistance, Rebellion, and Death*, pp. 81–93.
42. Mouloud Feraoun, *Journal, 1955–1962: Reflections on the French–Algerian War*, University of Nebraska Press, 2000, p. 85.
43. PierNico Solinas (ed.), *Gillo Pontecorvo's 'The Battle of Algiers'*, Charles Scribner's Sons, 1972, p, 195.

Chapter 5: The Romance of the Urban Guerrilla

1. Quoted in Julio Cortázar, *A Manual for Manuel*, Pantheon, 1978, p. 323.
2. Quoted in Martin Oppenheimer, *The Urban Guerrilla*, Quadrangle, 1969, p. 103.
3. Donald Hodges (ed.), *Philosophy of the Urban Guerrilla: the Revolutionary Writings of Abraham Guillén*, William Morrow, 1973, p. 132.
4. Ibid., p. 241.
5. The future dissident CIA official Philip Agee arrived in Montevideo as station officer in 1965. His diaries contain vivid first-hand descriptions of the political turbulence in Uruguay in this period, where public-sector strikes and violent clashes between demonstrators and police alternated with rumours of impending coups. See Philip Agee, *Inside the Company: CIA Diary*, Penguin, 1975.
6. The presentation of Mitrione as an innocent victim of terrorist barbarity has continued to surface amongst other terrorism writers. For a detailed and more objective account of this incident, see A. J. Languth, *Hidden Terrors*, Pantheon, 1978.
7. Costa Gavras and Franco Solinas, *State of Siege*, Ballantine Books, 1973, p. 157.
8. Geoffrey Jackson, *People's Prison*, Readers Union, 1973, p. 179.
9. Carlos Martínez Moreno, *El Infierno*, trans. Ann Wright, Readers International, 1988.
10. V. S. Naipaul, *The Return of Eva Perón*, André Deutsch, 1980, p. 139.
11. Régis Debray, *The Revolution on Trial: a Critique of Arms*, vol. II, Penguin, 1978, p. 264.
12. For a moving and harrowing account of the treatment meted out to Uruguayan 'terrorists' and political prisoners alike, see Mauricio Rosencof , 'On Suffering and White Horses', in Louise B. Popkin (ed.),

Repression, Exile and Democracy: Uruguayan Culture, Duke University Press, 1993.

13. Like many events that took place during those years, this killing was not as clear cut as it seemed and there has been speculation that it was facilitated by army officers who feared Aramburu's political ambitions. See Martin Erwin Andersen, *Dossier Secreto: Argentina's Desaparecidos and the Myth of the 'Dirty War'*, Westview Press, 1994, pp. 65–7.

14. The exact figures are difficult to determine, since the armed forces always exaggerated them for their own political purposes. Though one Argentine general claimed in 1975 that the guerrillas numbered 30,000 combatants, María José Moyano estimates a peak membership of 5,000 from all the different armed organisations in the same year. Other estimates are considerably lower. See María José Moyano, *Argentina's Lost Patrol: Armed Struggle 1969–1979*, Yale University Press, 1995, pp. 102–105.

15. Quoted in Richard Gillespie, *Soldiers of Perón: Argentina's Montoneros*, Oxford University Press, 1982, p. 118.

16. Andrew Graham-Yooll, *A Matter of Fear*, Lawrence Hill & Co., 1981, p. 62.

17. Horacio Verbitsky, *The Flight*, The New Press, 1996, p. 30.

18. Quoted in Margherita Feitlowitz, *A Lexicon of Terror: Argentina and the Legacies of Torture*, Oxford University Press, 1998, p. 26.

19. Quoted in Michael McGaughan, *True Crimes: Rodolfo Walsh*, Latin America Bureau, 2002, p. 265.

20. Quoted in Verbitsky, *The Flight*, p. 94.

Chapter 6: The Revolutionary Festival

1. Quoted in Tom Vague, *Televisionaries*, AK Press, 1994, p. 21.

2. Ibid., pp. 26–9.

3. See Beau Grosscup, *The Newest Explosions of Terrorism*, New Horizon Press, 1998, p. 218.

4. The difference can certainly not be explained in terms of the actual level of violence. Between 1970 and 1979 31 deaths, 25 bombings and approximately 100 injuries were attributed to various left-wing groups. In 1992, the year of German unification, some 2,000 violent attacks were carried out by neo-Nazi and extreme right-wing groups, resulting in 17 deaths and more than 2,000 injuries. Yet in November 1991, in the midst of a ferocious wave of anti-Semitic and anti-foreigner violence, Attorney General Alexander von Stahl declared that 'Right-wing

terrorism is no visible danger.' See Warren Hinckle, 'The Ascendancy of the Fourth Reich', *Argonaut*, 138 (1993), pp. 73–85.

5. Felix Guattari, 'Like the Echo of a Collective Melancholia', in Sylvere Lotringer (ed.), *Semiotexte*, 4 (2), 'The German Issue', 1982, p. 110.

6. Hans-Joachim Klein, 'Slaughter Politics', in Sylvere Lotringer (ed.), *Semiotexte*, 4 (2), 'The German Issue', 1982, p. 89.

7. '1998 Statement officially disbanding the RAF', available at www. baader-meinhof. com.

8. Markus Wolf, *Memoirs of a Spymaster*, Pimlico, 1988, p. 279.

9. Jillian Becker, *Hitler's Children*, Granada, 1978, p. 216.

10. Quoted in Maxwell Taylor and Ethel Quayle, *Terrorist Lives*, Brassey's, 1994, p. 133.

11. Michael 'Bommi' Baumann, *Terror or Love? Bommi Baumann's own Story of His Life as a West German Urban Guerrilla*, Grove Press, 1979, p. 105.

12. Quoted in Robert C. Meade, Jr, *Red Brigades: the Story of Italian Terrorism*, Macmillan, 1990, p. 37.

13. Quoted in Raimondo Catanzano (ed.), *The Red Brigades and Left-Wing Terrorism in Italy*, Pinter, 1991, p. 184.

14. Quoted ibid., p. 146.

15. Umberto Eco, *Travels in Hyper-reality*, Picador, 1985, p. 121.

16. A friend of Ulrike Meinhof and her husband before Meinhof joined the RAF, the jet-setting Feltrinelli was so impressed by the wartime resistance that he named his own urban guerrilla group the Partisan Action Groups (GAP) – the same name given to the anti-fascist partisans. Feltrinelli's career as an urban guerrilla ended abruptly on 15 March 1972, when he blew himself up while planting explosives at an electricity pylon.

17. Quoted in Meade, *Red Brigades*, p. 235.

18. Quoted in Daniele Ganser, *NATO's Secret Armies: Operation Gladio and Terrorism in Western Europe*, Frank Cass, 2005, p. 7. The involvement of NATO itself in these activities has never been fully clarified, but a 2000 report by the Italian Senate into the 'strategy of tension' concluded: 'Those massacres, those bombs, those military actions had been organized or promoted or supported by men inside Italian state institutions and . . . by men linked to the structures of United States intelligence' (ibid., p. 14).

19. For the most detailed account of the manipulation thesis, see Philip Willan, *Puppetmasters: the Political Uses of Terrorism in Italy*, Constable, 1991.

20. Alberto Franceschini has even claimed that the Israeli secret service Mossad offered to sell weapons to the Red Brigades in order to destabilise Italy and so preserve its own status as a key American ally in the Mediterranean. See Meade, *Red Brigades*, p. 222.

21. Quoted in Ganser, *NATO's Secret Armies*, p. 80.

22. Quoted in Richard Drake, *The Revolutionary Mystique and Terrorism in Contemporary Italy*, Indiana University Press, 1989, p. 147.

23. Tom Vague, *Anarchy in the UK: the Angry Brigade*, AK Press, 1997, p. 51.

24. Quoted in John George and Laird Wilcox, *American Extremists*, Prometheus, 1996, p. 136.

25. Robin Morgan, *The Demon Lover: the Sexuality of Terrorism*, Mandarin, 1990, p. 232.

26. Bill Ayers, *Fugitive Days*, Penguin, 2003.

Chapter 7: Patriots

1. In David Hirst, *The Gun and the Olive Branch*, Faber and Faber, 1997, p. 274. *Our Palestine* is the journal of the Palestinian organisation al-Fatah.

2. Quoted in Bill Rolston and David Miller (eds), *War and Words: the Northern Ireland Media Reader*, Beyond the Pale Publications, 1996, p. 423.

3. David McKittrick, Seamus Kellers, Brian Feeney and Chris Thornton, *Lost Lives: the Stories of the Men, Women and Children who Died as a Result of the Northern Ireland Troubles*, Mainstream Publishing, 1999, pp. 1473–93.

4. Quoted in David Miller, 'The Northern Ireland Information Service and the Media: Arms, Strategy, Tactics', in Rolston and Miller, *War and Words*, p. 228.

5. Quoted in Liz Curtis, *Ireland: the Propaganda War*, Pluto Press, 1984, p. 119.

6. Quoted in Jeffrey A. Sluka (ed.), *Death Squad: the Anthropology of State Terror*, University of Pennsylvania Press, 2000, p. 135.

7. Quoted in Kevin J. Kelley, *The Longest War: Northern Ireland and the IRA*, Zed Books, 1982, p. 295.

8. For a detailed insider account of how the hunger strikes contributed to secret negotiations with the British government and the eventual peace process, see Ed Moloney, *A Secret History of the IRA*, Penguin, 2002.

9. David Miller and Greg McGlaughlin, 'Reporting the Peace in Ireland', in Rolston and Miller, *War and Words*, p. 423.

10. Ron Hutchinson, *Rat in the Skull*, Methuen, 1995.

11. Martin Dillon, *Twenty-five Years of Terror*, Bantam, 1994, p. 378.

12. Eamon Collins with Mick McGovern, *Killing Rage*, Granta, 1997, p. 37.

13. Ibid., p. 190.

14. McKittrick et al. *Lost Lives*, p. 1466. For a detailed account of the background to Collins's murder, see Kevin Toolis, 'Death Foretold', *Guardian*, 3 July 1999.

15. Quoted in Dan Georgakas and Lenny Rubenstein, *Art, Politics, Cinema: the Cineaste Interviews*, Pluto Press, 1984, p. 309.

16. Quoted in Peter Taylor, *States of Terror*, Penguin, 1983, p. 159.

17. Elixabete Garmendia Lasa et al., *Yoyes Desde su Ventana*, Garrasi, 1987, p. 167. Author's translation.

18. Ibid., p. 162. Author's translation.

19. Quoted in Taylor, *States of Terror*, p. 177.

20. Quoted in Joseba Zulaika, *Basque Violence: Metaphor and Sacrament*, University of Nevada Press, 1988, p. 265.

21. Ibid., p. 266.

22. Quoted in: Philip Schlesinger, George Murdock and Philip Elliott, *Televising 'Terrorism': Political Violence in Popular Culture*, Comedia, 1983, p. 30.

23. Quoted in Meade, *Red Brigades*, p. 173.

24. Zulaika, *Basque Violence*, p. 70.

25. Quoted in Jeffrey A. Sluka, 'From Graves to Nations: Political Martyrdom and Irish Nationalism', in Joyce Pettigrew (ed.), *Martyrdom and Political Resistance*, VU University Press, 1997, p. 46.

26. Quoted in Jeremy MacClancy, 'To Die In the Basque Land', in Pettigrew (ed.), *Martyrdom and Political Resistance*, p. 123.

27. Quoted in Yezid Sayigh, *Armed Struggle and the Search for State: the Palestinian National Movement, 1949–1993*, Oxford University Press, 1997, p. 212.

28. Quoted in Livia Rokach, *Israel's Sacred Terrorism*, Association of Arab-American University Graduates, 1980, p. 21.

29. Ibid., p. 40.

30. Ibid., p. 37.

31. Quoted in Edward Herman and Gerry O'Sullivan, *The 'Terrorism' Industry*, Pantheon, 1989, p. 30.

32. Ibid., p. 35.

Chapter 8: The Dawn of International Terrorism

1. Bassam Abu-Sharif and Uzi Mahnaimi, *Tried by Fire*, Little, Brown and Co., 1995, p. 60.
2. Unidentified PFLP member quoted in Leila Khaled, *My People Shall Live*, Hodder & Stoughton, 1973, p. 126.
3. Quoted in Hirst, *The Gun and the Olive Branch*, p. 439.
4. The debates in the General Assembly failed to agree on a common definition of terrorism and the eventual ad hoc committee's recommendations were so nuanced and watered down as to be virtually ineffectual as a policy document.
5. For a fuller investigation of this thesis and a detailed account of Abu Nidal's activities, see Patrick Seale, *Abu Nidal: a Gun for Hire*, Random House, 1992.
6. Noam Chomsky, *Pirates and Emperors, Old and New*, Pluto Press, 2001, p. 140.
7. Paul Wilkinson, *Terrorism and the Liberal State* (2nd edn), Macmillan, 1986, p. 181.
8. Quoted in Grant Wardlow, *Political Terrorism: Theory, Tactics and Counter-Measures*, Cambridge University Press, 1989, p. 50.
9. Quoted in Herman and O'Sullivan, *The 'Terrorism' Industry*, p. 57.
10. The concepts of 'subversion' and 'counter-terrorism' for these companies often covered a wide spectrum of activities. In the 1960s the Wackenhut Corporation compiled the largest private database on 'subversive' American citizens in the United States. It has also been accused of arms trafficking, the development of private weapons programmes and involvement with right-wing paramilitary groups in Latin America. See ibid., pp. 129–31.
11. The apartheid regime also extended 'anti-terrorist' training to schoolchildren, who were trained in the use of firearms against the communist hordes at 'veldt camps', modelled on the Scouting movement.
12. The criminologist Ronald Crelinsten has analysed the indexes of two newspapers and two periodicals for the period 1966–85 in an attempt to trace the changing amount of media coverage given to terrorism. Crelinsten's research found that, before the early 1970s, actions that were subsequently included under terrorism were generally listed under different headings, such as 'Bombs and Bomb Plots', 'Kidnapping' or 'Guerrillas'. What Crelinsten's research suggested was that it was not the actions that had changed, but the way these actions

were understood and conceptualised, so that previously disparate acts of violence could all be included under the general category of 'Terrorism'. See Crelinsten, 'Images of Terrorism in the Media: 1966–1985', *Terrorism*, 12 (1989), pp. 167–98.

13. Brian Crozier, *Free Agent: the Unseen War, 1941–1991*, HarperCollins, 1994, p. 124.
14. The author of a book on Machiavelli and an admirer of Mussolini, Ledeen was a Cold War conspirator in the Crozier mould and a covert operations fetishist, with close ties to both the Israeli and Italian secret services. In the early 1980s Ledeen worked as a terrorism consultant to the Reagan administration and became a minor player in the Iran-Contra scandal. Under the current Bush administration he has emerged as a fervent neo-conservative ideologue of the 'War on Terror.'
15. Wilkinson, *Terrorism and the Liberal State*, p. 53.
16. Jillian Becker, Foreword to Robert Goren, *The Soviet Union and International Terrorism*, George Allen & Unwin, 1984, p. x.
17. Christopher Dobson and Ronald Payne, *The Carlos Complex: a Pattern of Violence*, Book Club Associates, 1977, p. 7.
18. Becker in Goren, *The Soviet Union and International Terrorism*, p. xi.
19. Richard Nixon, *The Real War*, Sidgwick & Jackson, 1980, p. 41.
20. Dobson and Payne, *The Carlos Complex*, p. 1.
21. See David Yallop, *To the Ends of the Earth*, Corgi, 1994.
22. Wolf, *Memoirs of a Spymaster*, p. 274.
23. Klein, 'Slaughter Politics', p. 86.
24. Claire Sterling, *The Terror Network: the Secret War of International Terrorism*, Berkeley Books, 1981, p. 6.
25. In 1989 Bosch applied for political asylum in the United States. His application was rejected by the US Department of Justice, on the grounds that 'For 30 years Bosch has been resolute and unwavering in his advocacy of terrorist violence'. See 'Exclusion Proceeding for Orlando Bosch Avila', US Department of Justice, Office of the Attorney General, available at http://cuban-exile.com. In July 1990 Bosch was pardoned by the former director of the CIA, President George Bush, who also granted him residency. Posada participated in the Contra war against Nicaragua and continued to carry out bomb attacks on Cuban targets before successfully re-applying for political asylum in the United States. In October 2005 a US judge rejected an application from the Venezuelan government for Posada to be extradited to stand

trial for the 1976 airline bombing, on the grounds that he might be 'tortured'. Posada's status remains unresolved and the presence in the United States of a man described by the FBI as an international terrorist has continued to pose problems for an administration supposedly at war with terrorists and states that harbour them.

26. Quoted in Stuart Christie, *Stefano delle Chaie: Portrait of a Black Terrorist*, Anarchy Magazine/Refract Publications, 1984, p. 28.

27. See Ganser, *NATO's Secret Armies*, pp. 115–21.

Chapter 9: The First War on Terror

1. For a more detailed account of these debates see Bob Woodward, *Veil: the Secret Wars of the CIA, 1981–1987*, Simon & Schuster, 1987, pp. 89–130.

2. Quoted in Jonathan Marshall, Peter Dale Scott and Jane Hunter, *The Iran–Contra Connection: Secret Teams and Covert Operations in the Reagan Era*, South End Press, 1987, p, 208.

3. The Teheran hostage crisis was a decisive episode in the unfolding confrontation between the United States and Iran, which did much to establish the phenomenon of 'Islamic terrorism' as a major threat to the West. The crisis began on 4 November 1979, when militant Iranian students and Revolutionary Guards took sixty-three Americans captive in the US embassy in Teheran, in retaliation for the entry of the deposed Shah into the United States. For more than a year the United States government was powerless to intervene, and the damage to US prestige was intensified by a botched rescue attempt by the Carter administration. The standoff was not resolved until January 1981, when the last hostages were released.

4. Quoted in Avi Shlaim, *The Iron Wall*, Penguin, 2000, p. 442.

5. 'Police chief: Lockerbie evidence was faked', *Scotland on Sunday*, 28 August 2005.

6. These tactics generated levels of terror and trauma in rural Mozambique that bear no comparison with the 'messages' transmitted by 'international terrorists' of the Abu Nidal type, even though such violence received little attention from the outside world. For a graphic account of the impact of Renamo see Carolyn Nordstrum 'The Backyard Front', in Carolyn Nordstrom and JoAnn Martin (eds), *The Paths to Domination, Resistance and Terror*, University of California Press, 1992. See also Lina Magaia, *Dumba Nengue: Run For Your Life. Peasant Tales of Tragedy in Mozambique*, Africa World Press, 1988.

7. Quoted in Joseph Hanlon, 'The New Missionaries', *New Internationalist*, February 1989.

8. Crozier, *Free Agent*, p. 282.

9. US Department of Defense, *Terrorist Group Profiles*, 1988. Quoted in Herman and O'Sullivan, *The 'Terrorism' Industry*, p. xii.

10. Celerino Castillo III and Dave Harmon, *Powderburns: Cocaine, Contras and the Drug War*, Mosaic Press, 1994, pp. 151–4.

11. Susan Ornstein, 'El Salvador: a Mercenary's View,' *Fort Myers' News Press* 23 October 1983; quoted in Alexander George, 'The Discipline of Terrorology', in Alexander George (ed.), *Western State Terrorism*, Polity Press, 1991, p. 78.

12. Neil Livingstone, 'Death Squad', *Journal of World Affairs*, 4 (3) (1986), pp. 239–48.

13. Sam C. Sarkesian, 'Low-Intensity Conflict: Conflicts, Principles, and Policy Guidelines,' *Air University Review*; January–February 1985; quoted in Michael Klare and Peter Kornbluh (eds), *Low-Intensity Warfare: Counterinsurgency, Proinsurgency and Antiterrorism in the Eighties*, Pantheon, 1988, p. 78.

14. William J. Casey, 'The International Linkages: What Do We Know?' in Ari Ra'anan et al., *Hydra of Carnage: International Linkages to Terrorism – the Witnesses Speak*, Lexington Books, 1986, p. 5.

15. Quoted in Leslie Cockburn, *Out of Control: the Story of the Reagan Administration's Secret War on Nicaragua, the Illegal Arms Pipeline, and the Contra-Drug Connection*, Bloomsbury, 1988, p. 9.

Chapter 10: The Armies of God

1. See Bruce Hoffman, *Inside Terrorism*, Victor Gollancz, 1998, p. 93.

2. Quoted in: John Calvert. '"The World is an Undutiful Boy!": Sayyid Qutb's American Experience', *Islam and Christian–Muslim Relations*, 11 (1) (2000), pp. 87–103.

3. The ability of both Ibn Taymiyya and Qutb to adapt the concept of jihad to suit radically different political agendas was itself a demonstration of the way in which jihad is subject to pragmatic interpretation, rather than an inflexible and unchanging notion of 'holy war' that has remained constant since the era of the Prophet. For a nuanced overview of the differing interpretations of jihad within Islamic tradition, see Rudolph Peters, *Jihad in Classical and Modern Islam*, Markus Wiener, 1996.

4. A key figure in jihadist circles, the devout Rahman was acquitted on charges of conspiracy in the Sadat assassination. Like many Egyptian Islamists, the 'Blind Sheikh' subsequently went to Afghanistan, where he played an inspirational role in recruiting foreign volunteers for the anti-Soviet jihad. For an overview of Rahman's influential trajectory in the modern jihad, see Mary Ann Weaver, *A Portrait of Egypt*, Farrar, Straus & Giroux, 2000.

5. Tal'at Fu'ad Qasim quoted in Hisham Mubarak, 'What Does the Gama'a Islamiyya Want?', in Joel Benin and Joe Stork (eds), *Political Islam: Essays from Middle East Report*, University of California Press, 1997, p. 320.

6. Geneive Abdo, *No God but God: Egypt and the Triumph of Islam*, Oxford University Press, 2000, p. 195.

7. Abdo, *No God but God*, is an excellent account of the phenomenon of 'Islamism from below'.

8. For an analysis of 'femicide' in Algeria see Ron Skilbeck, 'The Shroud over Algeria', *Journal of Arabic, Islamic and Middle Eastern Studies*, 2 (2) (1995), pp. 43–54.

9. For a comprehensive analysis of the economic basis of the jihad see Luis Martinez, *The Algerian Civil War, 1990–1998*, trans. Jonathan Derrick, Hurst & Co., 2000.

10. Amnesty International, *Amnesty International Report, 1998*, Amnesty International Publications, 1998.

11. See John Sweeney and Leonard Doyle, 'We Accuse 80,000 Times', *Observer*, 16 November 1997. Also John Sweeney, 'Police Role in Algeria Killings Exposed', *Observer*, 11 January 1998.

12. Adam Shatz, 'Algeria's Failed Revolution', *New York Review of Books* 50 (11), 3 July, 2003.

13. 'The ABC's of Jihad in Afghanistan', *Washington Post*, 23 March, 2002.

14. George Crile, *My Enemy's Enemy*, Atlantic Books, 2003, p. 149.

15. Mohammad Yousaf and Mark Adkin, *Afghanistan the Bear Trap: the Defeat of a Superpower*, Leo Cooper, 1992, p. 146.

16. For further details on the BCCI's Byzantine criminal linkages and their connection to the sponsors of the Afghan jihad, see Jonathan Beaty and S. C. Gwynne, *The Outlaw Bank: a Wild Ride into the Secret Heart of BCCI*, Random House, 1993, pp. 279–319. See also Senators John Kerry and Hank Brown, 'The BCCI's Criminality', chapter 4 of *The BCCI Affair: a Report to the Committee on Foreign Affairs, United States Senate*, 1993, available at www.fas.org/irp/congress/1992_rpt/bcci/.

17. Interview with Brzezinski in *Le Nouvel Observateur* (Paris), 15–21 January 1998, quoted in John K. Cooley, *Unholy Wars: Afghanistan, America and International Terrorism*, Pluto Press, 1999, p. 20.

18. See Chalmers Johnson, *Blowback: the Costs and Consequences of American Empire*, Time Warner, 2002.

19. Quoted in Jeffrey Goldberg, 'In the Party of God', *The New Yorker*, 14 October 2002. Goldberg's reportage is strongly pro-Israeli and dependent on Israeli sources. For a more objective journalistic account of Hezbollah see Adam Shatz, 'In Search of Hezbollah', *New York Review of Books*, 51 (7), 29 April 2004, and 'In Search of Hezbollah II', ibid., 51 (8), 13 May, 2004.

20. One of the pilgrims 'inspired' by Goldstein's act was Yigal Amir, the assassin of the Israeli prime minister Yitshak Rabin in 1995, who regarded Goldstein as a 'saint'. See Michael Karpin and Ina Friedman, *Murder in the Name of God: the Plot to Kill Yitshak Rabin*, Granta, 1998.

21. Amal Saad-Ghorayeb, *Hizbu'llah: Politics and Religion*, Pluto Press, 2002, p. 131.

22. Quoted in Hala Jaber, *Hezbollah: Born with a Vengeance*, Fourth Estate, 1999, p. 84.

23. Ibid., p. 91.

24. Statistics from Robert A. Pape, *Dying to Win: the Strategic Logic of Suicide Terrorism*, Random House, 2005, p. 15.

25. Mark Harrison, 'The Immediate Effects of Suicide Attacks: Israel, 2000–2003', available at www2.warwick.ac.uk.

26. Quoted in Human Rights Watch, 'Erased in a Moment: Suicide Bombing Attacks against Israeli Civilians', Human Rights Watch, 2002, available at www.hrw/reports/2002.

27. Pape, *Dying to Win*. Pape's detailed and sober analysis of suicide bombing campaigns in various countries is refreshingly devoid of terrorological clichés.

28. For a fuller account of the complex and often contradictory Palestinian responses to these events see Joyce M. Davis, *Martyrs: Innocence, Vengeance and Despair in the Middle East*, Macmillan, 2003, and Christoph Reuter, *My Life Is a Weapon: a Modern History of Suicide Bombing*, Princeton University Press, 2002.

29. Quoted in Davis, *Martyrs*, p. 105.

30. For detailed biographies of female suicide bombers, see Barbara Victor, *Army of Roses: Inside the World of Palestinian Women Suicide Bombers*, Constable & Robinson, 2000.

31. The economist Mark Harrison has described the relationship between suicide bombers and the organizations that recruit them as a kind of 'transaction'. In Harrison's analysis the would-be suicide bomber exchanges the intractable problems of life under military occupation for a glorious new identity as a martyr, which the organisation pledges itself to create for him or her. In this 'transaction' the organisation gains political prestige for itself by claiming credit for the operation. See Harrison 'An Economist Looks at Suicide Terrorism', available at www2.warwick.ac.uk.

32. Quoted in Reuter, *My Life Is a Weapon*, p. 110.

33. Pape, *Dying To Win*. In Pape's estimation, suicide bombing is a variant on the sociologist Emile Durkheim's concept of 'altruistic suicide' on behalf of the wider community, rather than an expression of religious fervour. According to Pape, suicide bombing is more likely to be motivated by 'altruistic' motives in cases where the existential survival of a particular community is considered to be under threat, as it was perceived to be in the case of the Tamils.

34. For a detailed analysis of the Tamil Tigers 'martyrological calendar' see Peter Schalk, 'The Revival of Martyr Cults among Llavar', *Tememos* 33 (1997), pp. 151–91, and 'Resistance and Martyrdom in the Process of State Formation in Tamil Eelam', in Joyce Pettigrew (ed.), *Martyrdom and Political Resistance*, VU University Press, 1997, pp. 61–83.

35. Quoted in Sachi Sri Kantha, 'Vignettes on Three Black Tigers in the Battlefield', 17 August 2004, available at www.tamilnation.org.

Chapter 11: Waiting for Catastrophe

1. Rex Hudson, *Who Becomes a Terrorist and Why: the 1999 Government Report on Profiling Terrorists*, The Lyons Press, 1999, p. 6.

2. Robert. I. Friedman, *Sheikh Abdel Rahman, the World Trade Center Bombing and the CIA*, Open Magazine Pamphlet Series, 1993, p. 3.

3. Simon Reeve, *The New Jackals: Ramzi Yousef, Osama bin Laden and the Future of Terrorism*, André Deutsch, 1999, p. 278.

4. Quoted in Reeve, *The New Jackals*, p. 130.

5. Joel Dyer, *Harvest of Rage: Why Oklahoma City Is only the Beginning*, Westview Press, 1998, p. 244.

6. Quoted in John Trumpbour, 'The Clash of Civilizations', in Emran Qureshi and Michael A. Sells (eds), *The New Crusades: Constructing the Muslim Enemy*, Columbia University Press, 2003, p. 95.

7. Like many aspects of the official version of the Oklahoma bombing, this detail may not be accurate. Not only is there evidence that others may have been involved in the bombing, but Kerry Noble, a reformed member of the racist Christian Identity paramilitary commune Covenant, Sword, and Arm of the Lord (CSA), has claimed that the Alfred Murrah building was first considered as a target as far back as the early 1980s. See Kerry Noble, *Tabernacle of Hate: Why They Bombed Oklahoma City*, Voyageur, 1998.

8. Gore Vidal, *Perpetual War for Perpetual Peace*, Clairview Books, 2002, p. 109.

9. The letter and other prison documents can be found at www.thesmokinggun.com.

10. For a brilliant and comprehensive analysis of Asahara's doctrines and their historical and cultural context, see Robert Jay Lifton, *Destroying the World in Order to Save It: Aum Shinrikyo, Apocalyptic Violence, and the New Global Terrorism*, Henry Holt, 2000.

11. William S. Cohen, 'In the Age of Terror Weapons', *Washington Post*, 26 November 1997.

12. Henry Sokolski, 'Rethinking Bio-Chemical Dangers', *Orbis*, Spring 2000, pp, 207–19.

13. Valerie Plame was a CIA agent whose diplomat husband, Joseph Wilson, rejected the Bush administration's claims that Iraq had attempted to buy uranium from Niger and accused the government of having 'manipulated' and 'twisted' intelligence findings to justify war. Plame's identity as a CIA operative was subsequently made public, in a breach of national security that many commentators believed was an act of political revenge by the administration. One of the conduits through which the leak became public was Judith Miller, who went to jail for refusing to reveal her source within the administration.

14. Quoted in Daniel Benjamin and Steve Simon, *The Age of Sacred Terror*, Random House, 2003, p. 149.

15. Quoted in Jason Burke, *Al-Qaeda: the True Story of Radical Islam*, Penguin, 2004, p. 8.

16. O'Neill believed that his investigations were being blocked by the US government in order to protect its strategic relationship with Saudi Arabia. In 2001 he resigned from the FBI and became head of security at the World Trade Center. He was killed in the September 11 attacks. See Lawrence Wright, 'The Counter-Terrorist', *The New Yorker*, 1 June 2002. O'Neill was not the only FBI official to make these allegations.

See Greg Palast and David Pallister, 'FBI and US Spy Agents Say Bush Spiked bin Laden Probes Before September 11', *The Guardian*, 7 November 2001.

17. For a detailed analysis of US involvement in the covert arms 'pipeline' to Bosnia, see Cees Wiebes, *Intelligence and the War in Bosnia, 1992–1995*, James Bennett, 2003, pp. 157–213. According to Wiebes's painstaking research, a number of proscribed international 'terrorist' organisations also supplied volunteers to fight alongside the Bosnian army as 'shock troops', including Hamas, Hezbollah and the Algerian FIS. Whether the Pentagon officials who provided assistance to the Bosnian Muslims sanctioned or assisted such participation is not clear. But such apparently improbable alliances were not uncommon in the twilight world of covert operations, which were generally informed by a logic and set of ethical standards very different from those proclaimed in the official anti-terrorist anathema, even if the Western public was not aware of the discrepancy.

18. See Martin Bright, 'MI6 "halted bid to arrest bin Laden"', *Observer*, 10 November 2002. See also Nafeez Mosaddeq Ahmed, *The War on Truth: 9/11, Disinformation and the Anatomy of Terrorism*, Olive Branch Press, 2005, pp. 113–19.

19. The most comprehensive examination of the Saudi–Bush family relationship is contained in Craig Unger, *House of Bush, House of Saud*, Gibson Square, 2004. For a wider analysis of bin Mahfouz's relevance to oil politics, the jihad and al-Qaeda, see Michael Griffin, *Reaping the Whirlwind: Afghanistan, Al Qa'ida and the Holy War*, Pluto Press, 2003, and Cooley, *Unholy Wars*.

20. On 5 March 2001 the public interest law firm Judicial Watch called George Bush, Sr's relationship with the Carlyle Group 'a conflict of interest [which] could cause problems for America's foreign policy in Middle East and Asia', and called on Bush to resign. Following the September 11 attacks, Judicial Watch declared that 'the conflict of interest has now turned into a scandal', following revelations that the bin Laden family bank records had been subpoenaed by the FBI. 'Bush Sr. in Business with bin Laden family through Carlyle Group', *Wall Street Journal*, 30 September 2001.

21. Rohan Gunaratna, *Inside al-Qaeda*, Hurst & Co., 2002, p. 8.

22. This distinction was sometimes recognised by the participants even if it was not obvious to external observers, who regarded all jihadists as terrorists. One graduate of the Afghan training camps was an

American Muslim named Aukai Collins, who lost a leg fighting in Chechnya. Collins's disgust with al-Qaeda led him to offer his services as a spy for the CIA. This offer was refused and Collins went on to write a compelling blood-and-guts account of his experiences in *My Jihad*, Pocket Star Books, 2002.

23. Extracts from *Knights under the Prophet's Banner* published by the London-based Arab newspaper *Asharq al-Awsat* in December 2001 and available at www.liberalsagainstterrorism.com.

Chapter 12: A Raid on the Path: 9/11 and the War on Terror

1. For a brilliant exploration of the 'fictional' qualities in the September 11 attacks, see Mike Davis, 'The Flames of New York', in his *Dead Cities: and Other Tales*, The New Press, 2004.

2. John Negroponte, Address to the General Assembly's Plenary Session on Terrorism, 1 October 2001, available at www.un.org. As former ambassador to Honduras in the 1980s, Negroponte played a pivotal role in the Contra wars against Nicaragua. A number of critics have accused the US embassy in this period of deliberately playing down allegations of human rights abuses by the Honduran army, including hundreds of murders and disappearances of leftists and trade unionists carried out by a covert unit called Battalion 316. Negroponte was one of various Reagan-era functionaries whose careers were resurrected by the 'War on Terror', serving first as US ambassador in post-Saddam Iraq before taking up the Bush-created post of Director of National Intelligence in 2005. For a critical analysis of Negroponte's tenure in Honduras see Stephen Kinzer, 'Our Man in Honduras', *New York Review of Books*, 48 (20), 20 September 2001.

3. Michael Ignatieff in the *Guardian*, 1 October 2001.

4. At 8.39 a.m. on September 11 the hijacked Flight 11 flew over the Indian Point nuclear power station but continued on its path. In an interview with the Aljazeera journalist Yosri Fouda, the plot's alleged organiser, Khalid Sheikh Mohammed, said that al-Qaeda originally considered 'striking at a couple of nuclear facilities' but rejected this possibility on the grounds that such an attack 'would go out of control.' See Yosri Fouda and Nick Fielding, *Masterminds of Terror*, Mainstream Publishing, 2003.

5. Susan Sontag in *The New Yorker*, 24 September 2001.

6. Seymour Hersh, 'What Went Wrong?' *The New Yorker*, 8 October 2001.

7. See Gilles Kepel, *Islam and the West: the War for Muslim Minds*, Belknap Press, 1985.

8. In November 2001 the former US consul in Jeddah, Michael Springman, told the BBC current affairs programme *Newsnight* that he had protested to his superiors during the Afghan war that numerous US visas were being granted to unqualified applicants. According to Springman, the facilitation of these visas was part of 'an effort to bring recruits, rounded up by Osama bin Laden, to the US for terrorist training by the CIA', after which they would be returned to Afghanistan to fight the Soviets. See transcript Greg Palast, 'Has Someone Been Sitting on the FBI?', *Newsnight*, 6 November 2001, at http://news.bbc.co.uk/1/hi/events/newsnight/1645527.stm.

9. Fouda and Fielding, *Masterminds of Terror*, p. 142.

10. Hassan Mneimneh and Kanan Makiyah, 'Manual for a "Raid"', *New York Review of Books*, 49 (1), 17 January 2002.

11. Ibid.

12. For a detailed examination of the links between the September 11 attacks and Ramzi Yousef's foiled 'Bojinka plot' see Peter Lance, *Cover-up: What the Government is still Hiding about the War on Terror*, HarperCollins, 2004.

13. 'Rebuilding America's Defenses', Project for the New American Century, September 2000, available at www.newamericancentury.org.

14. For more details on Operation Northwoods see James Bamford, *Body of Secrets*, Arrow, 2002, pp. 82–91. The Tonkin Gulf incident took place in August 1964, when two alleged attacks by North Vietnamese torpedo boats on US destroyers were used by the Johnson administration to elicit congressional approval for more direct US involvement in Vietnam. Subsequent investigations have cast doubt on the veracity of the allegations.

15. Poll details available at www.zogby.com/news/.

16. For a meticulous analysis of these conflicting chronologies, see David Ray Griffin, *The New Pearl Harbor*, Arris, 2004, and Paul Thompson, *The Terror Timeline*, HarperCollins, 2004.

17. Richard Clarke, *Against all Enemies: Inside America's War on Terror*, Simon & Schuster, 2004, p. 5.

18. There are numerous websites and books dedicated to these 'unanswered questions', the most comprehensive of which is Thompson, *The Terror Timeline*.

19. National Commission on Terrorist Attacks upon the United States, *The 9/11 Commission Report* (final report), W. W. Norton, 2004, p. 277.

20. For a comprehensive analysis of the 9/11 Commission's failings see David Ray Griffin, *The 9/11 Commission: Omissions and Distortions*, Arris, 2005, and Lance, *Cover-up*. Also Benjamin DeMott, 'Whitewash as Public Service', *Harper's Magazine*, 13 November 2004.

21. Quoted in James Ridgeway, 'Ex-Feds Blast 9-11 Panel and Bush', *Village Voice*, 13 September 2004.

22. Julian Borger, 'Guacamole Is not Dangerous', *Guardian*, 30 October 2001.

23. 'Bets Off on Terror Futures Index', Associated Press release, 29 July 2003.

24. In November 2005, after three and a half years in military custody, Padilla's case was handed over to a civilian court, where he was indicted on charges linking him to what the US attorney-general, Alberto R. Gonzales, called 'an alleged North American terrorist support cell'. Though Padilla was charged with providing 'material support to terrorists', there was no mention of dirty bombs or any other home-made weapons of mass destruction.

25. For an examination of the Padilla case and other alleged post-9/11 plots see James Bovard, *Terrorism and Tyranny: Trampling Freedom, Justice and Peace to Rid the World of Evil*, Macmillan, 2003.

26. Michael Reynolds, 'Homegrown Terror', *Bulletin of the Atomic Scientists*, 60 (6), 2004, pp. 48–57.

27. Quoted in Sheldon Rampton and John Stauber, *Weapons of Mass Deception*, Constable & Robinson, 2003, p. 150.

28. Nicholas Lehman, 'The Next World Order', *The New Yorker*, 1 March 2002.

29. See 'Report Attacks "Myth" of Foreign Fighters', *Guardian*, 23 September 2005. Also 'The "Myth" of Iraq's Foreign Fighters', *Christian Science Monitor*, 23 September 2005.

30. There was certainly no shortage of 'hatred' amongst the disparate groups that made up the Iraqi insurgency. Nevertheless, research carried out by the Iraqi Body Count/Oxford Research Group has found that only 9 per cent of the estimated 24,000 civilians killed between 2003 and 2005 had been inflicted by the insurgents. Though the willingness of some Iraqi insurgent groups to kill civilians has often been cited as evidence of terrorist barbarity, these figures were well below the 37 per cent of the total attributed to the coalition forces

that represent the civilised world. See 'A Dossier of Civilian Casualties in Iraq, 2003–2005', at www.iraqbodycount.net.

31. Alan Dershowitz, *Why Terrorism Works*, Yale University Press, 2002, p. 144.

32. Sometimes the difference between 'private contractor' and US military operative was not clear, such as the former Green Beret Jonathan K. Idema, known as 'Kabul's Colonel Kurtz', who fought alongside US forces in Afghanistan. The model for George Clooney's special forces officer in *The Peacemaker*, Idema left the military and became a 'bounty hunter'. In July 2004 he was arrested by Afghan security forces for running a 'private torture chamber' in the basement of a Kabul house. It was not clear on whose behalf he was carrying out such interrogations, but they fitted squarely within the pattern. See Nick Meo, 'Kabul's Colonel Kurtz', *Sunday Herald*, 11 July, 2004.

33. See Seymour Hersh, *Chain of Command: the Road from 9/11 to Abu Ghraib*, Allen Lane, 2004. Also Sidney Blumenthal, 'The Religious Warrior of Abu Ghraib', *Guardian*, 20 May 2004.

34. See Salima Mellah and Jean-Baptiste Rivoire, 'El Para – the Maghreb's bin Laden', *Le Monde Diplomatique* (English edition), February 2005.

35. On 8 December 2005 this precedent was reversed when the House of Lords ruled that evidence that may have been obtained through the use of torture could not be used in British courts against terrorist suspects. The government accepted the ruling, while claiming that it had never approved of the use of torture in the first place.

36. 'Leaked No. 10 Dossier Reveals al-Qaeda's British Recruits', *Sunday Times*, 10 July 2005.

37. 'Judges Liken Terror Laws to Nazi Germany', *Independent*, 16 October 2005.

38. As a result of these debates, the government amended its original proposals. Nevertheless the April 2006 Terrorism Act included the twenty-eight day detention period. The Act also criminalised activity which 'glorifies the commission and preparation' of terrorist actions, or 'directly or indirectly' encouraged such actions.

39. The Bush administration's decision to disregard the State Department's own data followed a political embarrassment in June the previous year, in the midst of the US presidential campaign, when the State Department revised its own figures for the number of worldwide terrorist incidents in 2003. The April 2004 *Patterns of Global Terrorism* report for 2003 listed 190 terrorist attacks with 307 deaths. However,

the State Department then published new figures in June 2004, counting 208 attacks with 625 dead in 2003, leading to accusations that the original count had been deliberately lowered to make it seem that the War on Terror was working.

40. Robert Kagan and William Kristol. 'The Gathering Storm', *The Weekly Standard*, 29 October 2001.

41. Michael Leeden, 'The Battle for Ideas in the US War on Terrorism', 29 October 2001, conference transcript available at www.aei.org/events.

42. Advocates of US military intervention in the Middle East, and Iraq in particular, drew much comfort from the 2002 UN *Arab and Human Development Report*, which identified a range of serious economic, social and political problems in the Arab world, including a 'democracy deficit' which included the position of women. Though the problems were real, there was a difference between the report's call for 'holistic development' and the militarist solutions advocated by Richard Perle and others. For a critique of the report, and a more nuanced and positive view of the Middle East in general, see Mark LeVine's remarkable *Why They Don't Hate Us: Lifting the Veil on the Axis of Evil*, Oneworld, 2005.

43. Ralph Peters, 'In Praise of Attrition', *Parameters*, Summer 2004, pp. 24–32. See also Ralph Peters, 'When Devils Walked the Earth: the Mentality and Roots of Terrorism and How to Respond', available at www.au.af.mil.au/awc/awcgate/usmc/ceto/when_devils_walk_the_earth.pdf.

44. Quoted in Lawrence Wright. 'The Terror Web', *The New Yorker*, 2 August 2004.

45. Quoted in 'A Home for Mr Naipaul', *Observer*, 12 September 2005.

46. Writing in the *Daily Telegraph*, 8 November 2005.

47. Daniel Pipes, 'Reflections on the Revolution in France', *New York Sun*, 8 November 2005.

Epilogue: In a Time of Terror

1. Denis Duclos, 'Watching Them Watching Us', *Le Monde Diplomatique* (English edition), September 2004.

2. 'Over 600 Held under Terror Act at Labour Conference', *The Scotsman*, 3 October 2005.

3. For an intelligent and non-terrorological discussion of alternative responses to the September 11 attacks, see the Club de Madrid Series

on Democracy and Terrorism, June 2005, available at: www.english.
safe-democracy.org.

4. David Frum and Richard Perle, *An End to Evil: How to Win the War on Terror*, Ballantine, 2004, p. 9.

5. Chris Hedges, 'On War', *New York Review of Books*, 51 (20), 16 December 2004.

6. Hala Jaber, 'US "in Talks with Iraq rebels"', *Sunday Times*, 26 June 2005.

7. Eqbal Ahmad, *Terrorism: Theirs and Ours*, Seven Stories Press, 2001, p. 24.

8. Seymour Hersh, 'The Coming Wars: What the Pentagon Can Now Do in Secret', *The New Yorker*, 24 January 2005.

9. Robert Fisk, 'We Should not Have Allowed 19 Murderers to Change our World', *Independent*, 11 September 2004.

Selected Bibliography

Non-fiction

Abdo, Geneive, *No God but God: Egypt and the Triumph of Islam*. Oxford University Press, 2000

Abu-Sharif, Bassam and Uzi Mahnaimi, *Tried by Fire*. Little, Brown and Co., 1995

Achcar, Gilbert, *The Clash of Barbarisms: September 11 and the Making of the New World Disorder*. Monthly Review Press, 2002

Ackroyd, Carol, Karen Margolis, Jonathan Rosenhead and Tim Shallice, *The Technology of Political Control*. Pluto Press, 1980

Adams, Gerry, *The Politics of Irish Freedom*. Brandon, 1986

Agee, Philip, *Inside the Company: CIA Diary*. Penguin, 1975

Ahmad, Eqbal, *Terrorism: Theirs and Ours*. Seven Stories Press, 2001

Ahmed, Nafeez Mosaddeq, *The War on Freedom: How and Why America Was Attacked, September 11, 2001*. Tree of Life Publications, 2002

— *Behind the War on Terror: Western Secret Strategy and the Struggle for Iraq*. Clairview Books, 2003

— *The War on Freedom: 9/11, Disinformation and the Anatomy of Terrorism*. Olive Branch Press, 2005

Akbar, M. J., *India: the Siege within*. Penguin, 1985

— *In the Shade of Swords*. Routledge, 2002

Alcedo Moneo, Miren, *Militar en ETA*. Haranburu, 1996

Aldrich, Richard, *The Hidden Hand: Britain, America and Cold War Secret Intelligence*. John Murray, 2000

Alleg, Henri, *The Question*. John Calder, 1958

Alpert, Jane, *Growing Up Underground*. William Morrow, 1981

Al-Zayyat, Montasser, *The Road to Al-Qaeda: Bin Laden's Right-Hand Man*. Pluto Press, 2004

Amin, Mohamed and Malcolm Caldwell, *Malaya: the Making of a Neo-colony*. Spokesman Books, 1977

Amnesty International, *Report on Torture*. Duckworth, 1975

— *Political Killings by Governments*. Amnesty International Publications, 1983

— *Amnesty International Report, 1998*, Amnesty International Publications, 1998

Andersen, Martin Erwin, *Dossier Secreto: Argentina's Desaparecidos and the Myth of the 'Dirty War'*. Westview Press, 1994

Anderson, David, *Histories of the Hanged: Britain's Dirty War in Kenya and the End of Empire*. Weidenfeld & Nicolson, 2005

Andrew, Herbert, *Who Won the Malayan Emergency?* Graham Brash, 1995

Anonymous, *Imperial Hubris: Why the World Is Losing the War on Terror*. Brassey's, 2004

Armony, Ariel C., *Argentina, the United States and the Anti-Communist Crusade in Central America 1977–1984*. Ohio University Press, 1997

Arquilla, John and David Ronfeldt, *Networks and Netwars*. Rand, 2001

Asprey, Robert, *War in the Shadows: the Guerrilla in History* (2 vols). Doubleday, 1975

Aussaresses, Paul, *The Battle of the Casbah: Terrorism and Counter-Terrorism in Algeria, 1955–1957*. Enigma, 2002

Aust, Stefan, *The Baader-Meinhof Group: the Inside Story of a Phenomenon*. Bodley Head, 1985

— (ed.), *Inside 9-11: What Really Happened*. St. Martin's Press, 2002

Avrich, Paul, *Anarchist Portraits*. Princeton University Press, 1998

Ayers, Bill, *Fugitive Days*. Penguin, 2003

Baer, Robert, *See No Evil: the True Story of a Ground Soldier in the CIA's War on Terrorism*. Crown, 2002

Bamford, James, *Body of Secrets*. Arrow, 2002

— *A Pretext For War: 9/11, Iraq and the Abuse of America's Intelligence Agencies*. Anchor Books, 2005

Barber, Noel, *The War of the Running Dogs*. Bantam, 1987

Barnaby, Frank, *Instruments of Terror*. Vision Paperbacks, 1996

Barnet, Richard J., *Intervention and Revolution*. Paladin, 1972

Barnett, Donald L. and Karari Njama, *Mau Mau from within*. MacGibbon & Kee, 1966

Baudrillard, Jean, *The Spirit of Terrorism*. Verso, 2002

Baumann, Michael 'Bommi', *Terror or Love? Bommi Baumann's own Story of His Life as a West German Urban Guerrilla*, Grove Press, 1979

Bearden, Milton and James Risen,*The Main Enemy: the CIA's Battle with the Soviet Union*. Century, 2000

Beaty, Jonathan and S. C. Gwynne, *The Outlaw Bank: a Wild Ride into the Secret Heart of BCCI*. Random House, 1993

Beck, Chris Aronson, Reggie Emilia, Lee Morris and Ollie Paterson, *'Strike One to Educate One Hundred': the Rise of the Red Brigades in Italy in the 1960s–1970s*. Seeds Beneath the Snow, 1986

Becker, Jillian, *Hitler's Children*. Granada, 1978

Begin, Menachem, *The Revolt*. W. H. Allen, 1983

Behr, Edward, *The Algerian Problem*. Penguin, 1961

Benin, Joel and Joe Stork (eds), *Political Islam: Essays from Middle East Report*. University of California Press, 1997

Benjamin, Daniel and Steve Simon, *The Age of Sacred Terror*. Random House, 2003

Bennett, Richard, *The Black and Tans*. E. Hulton & Co., 1959

— *Elite Forces: the World's Most Formidable Secret Armies*. Virgin, 2003

Beresford, David, *Ten Men Dead*. Grafton, 1987

Bergen, Peter, *Holy War, Inc.: Inside the Secret World of Osama bin Laden*. Orion, 2002

Berkman, Alexander, *Prison Memoirs of an Anarchist*. Schocken, 1970

Berman, Bruce and John Lonsdale, *Unhappy Valley: Conflict in Kenya and Africa. Violence and Ethnicity, Bk 2*. James Currey, 1992

Black, Crispin, *7-7: the London Bombs. What Went Wrong?* Gibson Square, 2005

Bougereau, Jean Marcel and Hans-Joachim Klein, *The German Guerrilla: Terror, Reaction and Resistance*. Cienfuegos Press, 1978

Bovard, James, *Terrorism and Tyranny: Trampling Freedom, Justice and Peace to Rid the World of Evil*. Macmillan, 2003

Bowyer Bell, J., *The Secret Army: a history of the IRA, 1916–1970*. Sphere, 1970

— *IRA Tactics & Targets*. Poolbeg Press, 1990

Brée, Germaine, *Camus and Sartre*. Calder & Boyars, 1974

Brenan, Gerald, *The Spanish Labyrinth*. Cambridge University Press, 1960

Britain, Victoria, *Hidden Lives, Hidden Deaths: South Africa's Crippling of a Continent*. Faber and Faber, 1988

Broido, Vera, *Apostles into Terrorists*. Maurice Temple Smith, 1978

Burke, Jason, *Al-Qaeda: the True Story of Radical Islam*. Penguin, 2004

Calvert, John. '"The World is an Undutiful Boy!": Sayyid Qutb's American Experience'. *Islam and Christian–Muslim Relations*, 11 (1) (2000), pp. 87–103

Campbell, Arthur, *Jungle Green*. George Allen & Unwin, 1953

Campbell, Christy, *Fenian Fire*. HarperCollins, 2002

Campbell, Douglas S., *Free Press V. Fair Trial: Supreme Court Decisions since 1807*. Praeger, 1994

Camus, Albert, *Resistance, Rebellion, and Death*. Alfred A. Knopf, 1960

Carr, E. H., *The Romantic Exiles*. Penguin, 1949

Carr, Reg, *Anarchism in France: the case of Octave Mirbeau*. Manchester University Press, 1977

Castillo, Celerino III and Dave Harman, *Powderburns: Cocaine, Contras and the Drug War*. Mosaic Press, 1994

Catanzano, Raimondo (ed.), *The Red Brigades and Left-Wing Terrorism in Italy*. Pinter, 1991

Caute, David, *The Year of the Barricades: a Journey Through 1968*. HarperCollins, 1988

Cawthra, Gavin, *Brutal Force: the Apartheid War Machine*. International Defence & Aid Fund, 1986

Chaliand, Gerard, *The Palestinian Resistance*. Penguin, 1972

— *Terrorism: from Popular Struggle to Media Spectacle*. Saqi, 1987

Chomsky, Noam, *The Culture of Terrorism*. Pluto Press, 1989

— *Pirates and Emperors, Old and New*. Pluto Press, 2001

Christie, Stuart, *Stefano delle Chialle: Portrait of a Black Terrorist*. Anarchy Magazine/Refract Publications, 1984

Christowe, Stoyan, *Heroes and Assassins*. Victor Gollancz, 1935

Clarke, Richard, *Against all Enemies: Inside America's War on Terror*. Simon & Schuster, 2004

Clarke, Thurston, *By Blood & Fire: the Attack on the King David Hotel*. G. P. Putnam's Sons, 1981

Cleaver, Eldridge, *Soul on Ice*, McGraw-Hill , 1967

— *Post-Prison Writings and Speeches*. Panther, 1971

Cline, Ray and Alexander Yonah, *Terrorism: the Soviet Connection*. New York, Crane, Russak, 1984

Clutterbuck, Richard, *The Long, Long War: Counterinsurgency in Malaya and Vietnam*, Praeger, 1966

— *Protest and the Urban Guerrilla*. Abelard-Schuman, 1974

Cockburn, Leslie, *Out of Control: the Story of the Reagan Administration's Secret War in Nicaragua, the Illegal Arms Pipeline, and the Contra Drug Connection*. Bloomsbury, 1988

Cohen, Susan and Daniel Cohen, *PanAm 103*. Signet, 2001

Cohen-Solal, Annie, *Sartre: a Life*. Minerva, 1991

Coll, Steve, *Ghost Wars: the Secret History of the CIA, Afghanistan, and Bin Laden, from the Soviet Invasion to September 10, 2001*. Penguin, 2005

Collins, Aukai, *My Jihad*. Pocket Star Books, 2002

Collins, Eamon with Mick McGovern, *Killing Rage*. Granta, 1997

Confino, Michael (ed.), *Daughter of a Revolutionary*. Alcove Press, 1974

Coogan, Tim Pat, *The I.R.A.* Pall Mall Press, 1980

Cooley, John. K., *Unholy Wars: Afghanistan, America and International Terrorism*. Pluto Press, 1999

Costa Gavras, Constantine and Franco Solinas, *State of Siege*. Ballantine, 1973

Costantini, Flavio, *The Art of Anarchy*. Cienfuegos Press, 1986

Craig, Gordon, *The Germans*. Penguin, 1991

Crawford, Oliver, *The Door Marked Malaya*. Rupert Hart-Davis, 1958

Crawley, Eduardo, *A House Divided: Argentina, 1880–1980*. Hurst & Co., 1984

Crelinsten, Ronald, 'Terrorism and the Media: Problems, Solutions, and Counterproblems'. *Political Communication and Persuasion*, 6 (1989), pp. 311–39

— 'Images of Terrorism in the Media: 1966–1985'. *Terrorism*, 12 (1989), pp.167–98

Crenshaw, Martha, *Revolutionary Terrorism: the FLN in Algeria, 1954–1962*. University of Virginia Press, 1973

— (ed.), *Terrorism, Legitimacy and Power*. Wesleyan University Press, 1983

Crile, George, *My Enemy's Enemy*. Atlantic, 2003

Cross, Colin, *The Fall of the British Empire*. Hodder & Stoughton, 1968

Crozier, Brian, *The Rebels: a Study of Post-War Insurrections*. Beacon Press, 1960

— *Free Agent: the Unseen War, 1941–1991*. HarperCollins, 1994

Curtis, Liz, *Ireland: the Propaganda War*. Pluto Press, 1984

Curtis, Mark, *Web of Deceit*. Vintage, 2003

Danner, Mark, *The Massacre at El Mozote: a Parable of the Cold War*. Vintage, 1994

— *Torture and Truth: Abu Ghraib and America in Iraq*. Granta, 2005

Davies, Nicholas, *Ten-Thirty-Three: the Inside Story of Britain's Secret Killing Machine in Northern Ireland*. Mainstream Publishing, 1999

Davis, Joyce M., *Martyrs: Innocence, Vengeance and Despair in the Middle East*. Macmillan, 2003

Davis, Mike, *Dead Cities: And Other Tales*. The New Press, 2004

Dawisha, Adeed, *The Arab Radicals*. Council on Foreign Relations, 1986

De Baroid, Ciaran, *Ballymurphy and the Irish War*. Pluto Press, 1999

De Becker, Gavin, *Fear Less: Real Truth about Risk, Safety and Security in a Time of Terrorism*. Little, Brown and Co., 2002

de Villemarest, Pierre F., *The Strategies of Fear*. Editions Voxmundi, 1981

Deacon, Richard, *A History of the Russian Secret Service*. Frederick Muller, 1972

— *The Israeli Secret Service*. Hamish Hamilton, 1977

Debray, Régis, *The Revolution on Trial: a Critique of Arms*, vol. II. Penguin, 1978

Dershowitz, Alan, *Why Terrorism Works*. Yale University Press, 2002

Didion, Joan, *Fixed Ideas. America since 9.11*. New York Review of Books, 2003

Dillon, Martin, *The Dirty War*. Arrow, 1990

— *Twenty-five Years of Terror*. Bantam, 1994

— *The Trigger Men*. Mainstream Publishing, 2003

Dine, Philip, *Images of the Algerian War*. Clarendon Press, 1994

Dinges, John, *The Condor Years*. The New Press, 2004

Djebar, Assia, *Algerian White*. Seven Stories Press, 2000

Dobson, Christopher and Ronald Payne, *The Carlos Complex: a Pattern of Violence*. Book Club Associates, 1977

— *The Weapons of Terror: International Terrorism at Work*. Macmillan, 1979

Drake, Richard, *The Revolutionary Mystique and Terrorism in Contemporary Italy*. Indiana University Press, 1989

Dreyfuss, Robert, *Devil's Game: How the United States Helped Unleash Fundamentalist Islam*. Metropolitan Books, 2005

Dubois, Felix, *The Anarchist Peril*. T. Fisher Unwin, 1894

Dyer, Gwynne, *Future: Tense*. McClelland & Stewart, 2004

Dyer, Joel, *Harvest of Rage: Why Oklahoma City Is only the Beginning*. Westview Press, 1998

Eco, Umberto, *Travels in Hyper-reality*. Picador, 1985

Elkins, Caroline, *Britain's Gulag: The Brutal End of Empire in Kenya*. Cape, 2005

Elliott, Paul, *Brotherhoods of Fear: a History of Violent Organizations*. Blandford, 1998

El-Rayyas, Riad N. and Dunia Natas, *Guerrillas For Palestine*. An-Nahar Arab Report, 1974

Engel, Barbara Alpern and Clifford N. Rosenthal, *Five Sisters: Women against the Tsar*. Weidenfeld and Nicolson, 1975

English, Richard, *Armed Struggle: a History of the IRA*. Macmillan, 2003

Esposito, John. L, *Unholy War: Terror in the Name of Islam*. Oxford University Press/Faber and Faber, 2002

Fabbri, Luigi, *Bourgeois Influences on Anarchism*, trans. Chaz Bufe. Sharp Press, 2001

Fairteather, Eilleen, Roisin McDonagh and Melanie McFadyean, *Only the Rivers Run Free*. Pluto Press, 1984

Falk, Richard, *Revolutionaries and Functionaries*. E. P. Dutton, 1988

Fallaci, Oriana, *The Rage and the Pride*. Rizzoli International, 2002

Fanon, Franz, *The Wretched of the Earth*. Penguin, 1967

— *Studies in a Dying Colonialism*. Earthscan, 1989

Faraj, Mohammed 'Abdus Salam, *The Absent Obligation*. Maktabah Al-Ansaar, 2000

Farrell, William. R., *Blood and Rage: the Story of the Japanese Red Army*. Lexington Books, 1990

Feitlowitz, Margherita, *A Lexicon of Terror: Argentina and the Legacies of Torture*. Oxford University Press, 1998

Feraoun, Mouloud, *Journal, 1955–1962: Reflections on the French–Algerian War*. University of Nebraska Press, 2000

Ferriter, Diarmand, *The Transformation of Ireland, 1900–2000*. Profile, 2004

Figes, Orlando, *A People's Tragedy*. Pimlico, 1997

Figner, Eva, *Memoirs of a Revolutionist*. Northern Illinois University Press, 1991

Follain, John, *Jackal: the Secret Wars of Carlos the Jackal*. Orion, 1999

Foot, M. R. D., *Resistance*. Paladin, 1978

Fouda, Yosri and Nick Fielding, *Masterminds of Terror*. Mainstream Publishing, 2003

France, Miranda, *Bad Times in Buenos Aires*. Weidenfeld & Nicolson, 1998

Frederikse, Julie, *None but Ourselves*. Ravan Press, 1982

— *South Africa: a Different Kind of War*. Ravan Press, 1986

Freeborn, Richard, *The Russian Revolutionary Novel: Turgenev to Pasternak*. Cambridge University Press, 1982

Friedman, Robert I., *Sheikh Abdel Rahman, the World Trade Center Bombing and the CIA*. Open Magazine Pamphlet Series, 1993

Frum, David and Richard Perle, *An End to Evil: How to Win the War on Terror*. Ballantine, 2004

Furedi, Frank, *The Mau Mau War in Perspective*. James Currey, 1989

— *Colonial Wars and the Politics of Third World Nationalism*. I. B. Tauris, 1994

Galeano, Eduardo, *Dias y Noches De Amor y De Guerra*. Editorial Laia/Barcelona, 1978

Gallagher, Ailleen, *The Japanese Red Army*. Rosen, 2003

Ganser, Daniele, *NATO's Secret Armies: Operation Gladio and Terrorism in Western Europe*. Frank Cass, 2005

Garlin, Sender, *Three American Radicals: John Swinton, Crusading Editor; Charles P. Steinmetz, Scientist and Socialist; William Dean Howells and the Haymarket Era*. Westview Press, 1991

Garmendia Lasa, Elixabete, Glori González Katarain, Ana González
    Katarain, Juli Garmendia Lasa and Juanjo Dorronsoro, *Yoyes Desde su
    Ventana*. Garrasi, 1987
Gavaghan, Terence, *Of Lions and Dung Beetles*. Arthur H. Stockwell, 1999
Geifman, Anna, *Thou Shalt Kill: Revolutionary Terrorism in Russia, 1894–
    1917*. Princeton University Press, 1993
George, Alexander (ed.), *Western State Terrorism*. Polity Press, 1991
George, John and Laird Wilcox, *American Extremists*. Prometheus, 1996
Georgakas, Dan and Rubenstein, Lenny, *Art, Politics, Cinema: the Cineaste
    Interviews*. Pluto Press, 1984
Geraghty, Tony, *The Irish War*. HarperCollins, 1998
Gerassi, John, *The Great Fear in Latin America*. Collier, 1963
Gildea, R., *Barricades and Borders: Europe, 1800–1914*. Oxford University
    Press, 1987
Gilio, Maria Esther, *The Tupamaro Guerrillas*. Ballantine, 1970
Gillespie, Richard, *Soldiers of Perón: Argentina's Montoneros*. Oxford
    University Press, 1982
— 'The Urban Guerrilla in Latin America', in Noel O'Sullivan (ed.),
    Terrorism, Ideology and Revolution: the Origins of Political Violence.
    Westview Press, 1986
Ginsburg, Paul, *A History of Contemporary Italy*. Penguin, 1990
Glenny, Misha, *The Balkans, 1804–1999*. Granta, 2000
Goldberg, Jeffrey, 'In the Party of God'. *The New Yorker*, 14 October 2002
Goldman, Emma, *Living My Life*. Dover, 1970
Goren, Robert, *The Soviet Union and International Terrorism*. George Allen &
    Unwin, 1984
Gott, Richard, *Guerrilla Movements in Latin America*. Thomas Nelson &
    Sons, 1970
Graham-Yooll, Andrew, *A Matter of Fear*. Lawrence Hill & Co., 1981
Gratwohl, Larry, *Bringing Down America: an FBI Informer with the
    Weathermen*. Arlington House, 1976
Graziano, Frank, *Divine Violence: Spectacle, Psychosexuality and Radical
    Christianity in the Argentine 'Dirty War'*. Westview Press, 1992
Greene, Graham, *Ways of Escape*. Penguin, 1982
Greer, Herb, *A Scattering of Dust*. Hutchinson, 1962
Griffin, David Ray, *The New Pearl Harbor*. Arris, 2004
— *The 9/11 Commission: Omissions and Distortions*. Arris, 2005
Griffin, Michael, *Reaping the Whirlwind: Afghanistan, Al Qa'ida and the Holy
    War*. Pluto Press, 2003

Griset, Pamela. L. and Sue Mahan (eds), *Terrorism in Perspective*. Sage, 2003

Grosscup, Beau, *The Newest Explosions of Terrorism*. New Horizon Press, 1998

Guattari, Felix, 'Like the Echo of a Collective Melancholia', in Sylvere Lotringer (ed.), *Semiotexte*, 4 (2), 'The German Issue', 1982, pp. 102–110

Guillén, Abraham and Donald Hodges, *Philosophy of the Urban Guerrilla*. William Morrow, 1973

Gunaratna, Rohan, *Inside al-Qaeda*. Hurst & Co., 2002

Hall, Sam, *Counter-Terrorist*. Warner, 1987

Halperin, Ernst, *Terrorism in Latin America*. The Center for Strategic and International Studies, Georgetown University, 1976

Hammil, Desmond, *Pig in the Middle: the Army in Northern Ireland, 1969–1975*. Methuen, 1985

Harclerode, Peter, *Secret Soldiers: Special Forces in the War against Terrorism*. Cassell Military Paperbacks, 2000

Harman, Chris, *The Fire Last Time: 1968 and after*. Bookmarks, 1988

Harnden, Toby, *'Bandit Country': the IRA & South Armagh*. Hodder & Stoughton, 1999

Harrison, Mark, 'The Immediate Effects of Suicide Attacks: Israel, 2000–2003', available at www2.warwick.ac.uk

— 'An Economist Looks at Suicide Terrorism', available at www2.warwick.ac.uk

Hawes, Stephen and Ralph White, *Resistance in Europe, 1939–45*. Penguin, 1976

Hearst, Patricia Campbell, *Every Secret Thing*. Arrow, 1983

Hedges, Chris, 'On War'. *New York Review of Books*, 51 (20), 16 December 2004

Henshall, Ian and Rowland Morgan, *9/11 Revealed: Challenging the Facts behind the War on Terror*. Constable & Robinson, 2005

Henissart, Paul, *Wolves in the City*. Paladin, 1973

Herman, Edward. S., *The Real Terror Network*. South End Press, 1982

Herman, Edward. S. and Gerry O'Sullivan, *The 'Terrorism' Industry*. Pantheon, 1989

Hersh, Seymour, *Chain of Command: the Road from 9/11 to Abu Ghraib*. Allen Lane, 2004

Hinckle, Warren, 'The Ascendancy of the Fourth Reich'. *Argonaut*, 138 (1993), pp. 73–85

Hinckle, Warren and William Turner, *Deadly Secrets: the CIA–Mafia War against Castro and the Assassination of J.F.K.* Thunder's Mouth Press, 1992

Hirst, David, *The Gun and the Olive Branch*. Faber and Faber, 1997

Hobsbawm, Eric. J., *Primitive Rebels*. W. W. Norton, 1965

Hodges, Donald (ed.), *NLF: National Liberation Fronts*. William Morrow, 1972

— *Philosophy of the Urban Guerrilla: the Revolutionary Writings of Abraham Guillén*. William Morrow, 1973

— *Argentina, 1943–1976: the National Revolution and Resistance*. University of New Mexico Press, 1976

Hoe, Alan and Eric Morris, *Re-enter the SAS: the Special Air Services and the Malayan Emergency*. Lee Cooper, 1994

Hoffman, Bruce, *Inside Terrorism*. Victor Gollancz, 1998

Hoffman, David, *The Oklahoma Bombing and the Politics of Terror*. Feral House, 1998

Holland, Jack, *The American Connection: US Guns, Money and Influence in Northern Ireland*. Penguin, 1989

Holman, Dennis, *Bwana Drum: the Unknown Story of the Secret War against the Mau Mau*. W. H. Allen, 1964

Hopkinson, Michael, *The Irish War of Independence*. Gill & MacMillan, 2002

Hopsicker, Daniel, *Welcome to Terrorland: Mohamed Atta and the 9/11 Cover-Up in Florida*. MadCow Press, 2004

Horne, Alistair, *A Savage War of Peace: Algeria, 1954–1962*. Penguin, 1979

Huband, Mark, *Warriors of the Prophet: the Struggle for Islam*. Westview Press, 1999

Hudson, Rex, *Who Becomes a Terrorist and Why: the 1999 Government Report on Profiling Terrorists*. The Lyons Press, 1999

Human Rights Watch, 'Erased in a Moment: Suicide Attacks against Israeli Civilians'. Human Rights Watch, 2002; available at www. hrw/reports/2002

— 'Opportunism in the Face of Tragedy: Repression in the Name of Anti-Terrorism'. Human Rights Watch, 2002; available at: www.hrw. org/campaigns/september11

Huntington, Samuel, *The Clash of Civilizations and the Remaking of World Order*. Simon & Schuster, 1998

Hyams, Edward, *Terrorists and Terrorism*. J. M. Dent & Sons, 1975

Ingram, Martin and Greg Harkin, *Stakeknife: Britain's Secret Agents in Ireland*, 2004

Itote, Waruhiu, *Mau Mau in Action*. TransAfrica Book Distributors, 1985

Jaber, Hala, *Hezbollah: Born with a Vengeance*. Fourth Estate, 1999

Jackson, Geoffrey, *People's Prison*. Readers Union, 1973

James, Bob, *Anarchism and State Violence in Sydney and Melbourne, 1886–
    1896*, Annares Books, 1986; available at: www.takver.com/history

Jhally, Sut and Earp, Jeremy, *Hijacking Catastrophe: 9/11, Fear and the Selling
    of American Empire*. Arris, 2004

Johnson, Chalmers, *Blowback: the Costs and Consequences of American Empire*.
    Time Warner, 2002

Joll, James, *The Anarchists*. Grosset & Dunlap, 1966

Jones, Adam (ed.), *Genocide, War Crimes and the West*. Zed Books, 2004

Juergensmeyer, Mark, *Terror in the Mind of God: the Global Rise of Religious
    Violence*. University of California Press, 2001

Kaplan, David E. and Andrew Marshall, *The Cult at the End of the World: the
    Incredible Story of Aum*. Huchinson, 1996

Kaplan, Temma, *Red City, Blue Period: Social Movements in Picasso's
    Barcelona*. University of California Press, 1992

Karim, Karim. H., *Islamic Peril: Media and Global Violence*. Black Rose Books,
    2003

Kariuki, J. M., *'Mau Mau' Detainee*. Oxford University Press, 1963

Karpin, Michael and Ina Friedman, *Murder in the Name of God: the Plot to
    Kill Yitshak Rabin*. Granta, 1998

Katz, Doris, *The Lady Was a Terrorist*. Shiloni, 1953

Katz, Robert, *Days of Wrath: the Public Agony of Aldo Moro*. Granada, 1980

Kelley, Kevin J., *The Longest War: Northern Ireland and the IRA*. Zed Books,
    1982

Kellner, Douglas, *Media Spectacle and the Crisis of Democracy: Terrorism, War
    and Election Battles*. Paradigm, 2005

Kemp, Anthony, *The SAS: Savage Wars of Peace*. Signet, 1995

Kepel, Gilles, *The Prophet and Pharoah*. Al-Saqi Books, 1985

— *Jihad: the Trail of Political Islam*. I. B. Tauris, 2002

— *Islam and the West: the War for Muslim Minds*. Belknap Press, 2004

Kerry, John and Hank Brown, 'The BCCI's Criminality', chapter 4 of *The
    BCCI Affair: a Report to the Committee on Foreign Affairs, United States
    Senate*, 1993, available at www.fas.org/irp/congress/1992_rpt/bcci/

Kershaw, Alister, *A History of the Guillotine*. Tandem, 1965

Kershaw, Greet, *Mau Mau from Below*. James Curney, 1997

Khaled, Leila, *My People Shall Live*. Hodder & Stoughton, 1973

Kiernan, Victor. G., *European Empires from Conquest to Collapse, 1815–1960*.
    Fontana, 1982

Kitson, Frank, *Bunch of Five*. Faber and Faber, 1977

— *Low Intensity Operations*. Faber and Faber, 1991

Klare, Michael and Peter Kornbluh (eds), *Low-Intensity Warfare: Counterinsurgency, Proinsurgency and Antiterrorism in the Eighties.* Pantheon, 1988

Klein, Hans-Joachim, 'Slaughter Politics', in Sylvere Lotringer (ed.), *Semiotexte*, 4 (2), 'The German Issue', 1982, pp. 80–98

Kochan, Lionel, *Russia in Revolution, 1890–1918.* Weidenfeld and Nicolson, 1966

Koonings, Kees and Dirk Krujit, *Societies of Fear: the Legacy of Civil War, Violence and Terror in Latin America.* Zed Books, 1999

Kraft, Joseph, *The Struggle for Algeria.* Doubleday, 1961

Kravchinsky, Sergei, *Underground Russia.* Charles Scribner's Sons, 1888

Kropotkin, Peter, *Memoirs of a Revolutionist.* Dover, 1971

Kurlansky, Mark, *The Basque History of the World.* Vintage, 2000

Kurzman, Dan, *Subversion of the Innocents: Patterns of Communist Penetration in Africa, the Middle East, and Asia.* Random House, 1963

Labévière, Richard, *Dollars for Terror: the United States and Islam.* Algora, 2000

Labrouosse, Alain, *The Tupamaros.* Penguin, 1973

Laffin, John, *The PLO Connections.* Corgi, 1982

Lance, Peter, *Cover-up: What the Government Is still Hiding about the War on Terror.* HarperCollins, 2004

Langguth, A. J., *Hidden Terrors.* Pantheon, 1978

Lapham, Lewis, *Waiting For the Barbarians.* Verso, 1997

— *Theater of War.* The New Press, 2002

Laqueur, Walter, *The Terrorism Reader.* New American Library, 1978

— *The Age of Terrorism.* Little, Brown and Co., 1987

— *The New Terrorism.* Phoenix Press, 2001

Laqueur Walter, and Barry Rubin (eds), *The Israel–Arab Reader.* Pelican, 1984

Lawrence, Bruce. B., *Shattering the Myth: Islam beyond Violence.* Princeton University Press, 1998

— (ed), *Messages to The World: the Statements of Osama bin Laden.* Verso, 2005

Le Sueur, James D., *Uncivil War: Intellectuals and Identity Politics During the Decolonization of Algeria.* University of Pennsylvania Press, 2001

Leach, Edmund, *Custom, Law and Terrorist Violence.* Edinburgh University Press, 1977

Leakey. L. S. B., *Mau Mau and the Kikuyu.* Methuen, 1952

Leppard, David, *Fire and Blood: the True Story of David Koresh and the Waco Siege.* Fourth Estate, 1993

LeVine, Mark, *Why They Don't Hate Us: Lifting the Veil on the Axis of Evil.* Oneworld, 2005

Levy, Edward Laurence, 'Russian Nihilism'. Paper presented to and published by the Alliance Literary and Debating Society, 1880

Lewis, Bernard, *The Assassins: a Radical Sect in Islam.* Orion, 2003

— *The Crisis of Islam: Holy War and Unholy Terror.* Phoenix, 2004

Lifton, Robert Jay, *Destroying the World in Order to Save It: Aum Shinrikyo, Apocalyptic Violence, and the New Global Terrorism.* Henry Holt, 2000

Linklater, Markus, Isabel Hilton and Neal Ascherson, *Klaus Barbie: the Fourth Reich and the Neo-fascist Connecton.* Hodder & Stoughton, 1984

Livingstone, Neil, 'Death Squad'. *Journal of World Affairs*, 4 (3) (1986), pp. 239–48

Lodge, Juliet (ed.), *Terrorism: a Challenge to the State.* Martin Robertson, 1981

Lombroso, Cesare, 'Illustrative Studies in Criminal Anthropology'. *The Monist*, 1 (1881), pp. 336–43

Longoni, J. C., *Four Patients of Dr. Deibler.* Lawrence & Wishart, 1970

Lord Russell of Liverpool, *The Scourge of the Swastika.* Cassell, 1954

Lottman, Herbert, *Albert Camus: a Biography.* Picador, 1981

Lotringer, Sylvere (ed.), *Semiotext(e)* 4 (2), 'The German Issue', 1982

Lotringer, Sylvere and Christian Marazzi (eds), *Semiotext(e)* 3 (3), 'Italy: Autonomia. Post-Political Politics', 1980

MacCarthy, Fiona, *William Morris: a Life for Our Time.* Faber and Faber, 1994

MacClancy, Jeremy, 'To Die in the Basque Land', in Joyce Pettigrew (ed.), *Martyrdom and Political Resistance*, VU University Press, 1997

MacDonald, Eileen, *Shoot the Women First.* Fourth Estate, 1991

Macey, David, *Franz Fanon: a Life.* Granta, 2000

Mackay, James, *Michael Collins: a Life.* Mainstream Publishing, 1997

Mackay, John Henry, *The Anarchists: a Portrait of Civilization at the Close of the Nineteenth Century.* Revisionist Press, 1972

Magaia, Lina, *Dumba Nengue: Run for Your Life. Peasant Tales of Tragedy in Mozambique.* Africa World Press, 1988

Magee, Patrick, *Gangsters or Guerrillas?* BTP Publications, 2001

Mahajan, Rahul, *Full Spectrum Dominance: US Power in Iraq and Beyond.* Seven Stories Press, 2003

Majdalany, Fred, *Defeating Mau Mau.* Methuen, 1954

— *State of Emergency: the Full Story of Mau Mau.* Houghton Mifflin, 1963

Malik, Aftab Ahmad, *The Empire and the Crescent: Global Implications for a New American Century.* Amal Press, 2003

Mandela, Nelson, *Long Walk to Freedom.* Little, Brown and Co., 1994

Manguel, Alberto, *Into the Looking Glass Wood*. Bloomsbury, 2000

Marchak, Patricia, *God's Assassins: State Terrorism in Argentina in the 1970s*. McGill-Queens University Press, 1999

Marighela, Carlos, *For the Liberation of Brazil*. Penguin, 1971

Marks, Steven G., *How Russia Shaped the Modern World*. Princeton University Press, 2003

Marshall, Jonathan, Peter Dale Scott and Jane Hunter, *The Iran-Contra Connection: Secret Teams and Covert Operations in the Reagan Era*. South End Press, 1987

Marshall, Paul, *Demanding the Impossible: a History of Anarchism*. HarperCollins, 1992

Martin, David and John Walcott, *Best Laid Plans: the Inside Story of America's War against Terrorism*. Harper & Row, 1988

Martinez, Luis, *The Algerian Civil War, 1990–1998*, trans. Jonathan Derrick. Hurst & Co., 2000

Maugham-Brown, David, *Land, Freedom and Fiction*. Zed Books, 1985

McCann, Eamon, *War and an Irish Town*. Pluto Press, 1993

McClintock, Michael, *Instruments of Statecraft: US Guerrilla Warfare, Counterinsurgency and Counterterrorism, 1940–1990*. Pantheon, 1992

McConnell, Brian, *Assassination*. Leslie Frewin, 1969

McDermott, Terry, *Perfect Soldiers. The Hijackers: Who They Were, Why They Did It*. HarperCollins, 2005

McGaughan, Michael, *True Crimes: Rodolfo Walsh*. Latin America Bureau, 2002

McKittrick, David, Seamus Kellers, Brian Feeney and Chris Thornton, *Lost Lives: the Stories of the Men, Women and Children who Died as a Result of the Northern Ireland Troubles*. Mainstream Publishing, 1999

McKnight, Gerald, *The Mind of the Terrorist*. Michael Joseph, 1974

Meade, Robert C., Jr, *Red Brigades: the Story of Italian Terrorism*. Macmillan, 1990

Meeropol, Rachel (ed.), *America's Disappeared: Detainees, Secret Imprisonment and the 'War On Terror'*. Seven Stories Press, 2005

Meyssan, Thierry, *9/11: the Big Lie*. Carnot Publishing, 2002

Michel, Lou and Dan Herbeck, *American Terrorist: Timothy McVeigh and the Oklahoma Bombing*. HarperCollins, 2001

Miller, Harry, *Menace in Malaya*. Harrap, 1954

Miller, John, Michael Stone and Chris Mitchell, *The Cell*. Hyperion, 2002

Miller, Judith, *God Has Ninety-Nine Names*. Touchstone, 1996

Mneimneh, Hassan and Kanan Makiyah, 'Manual for a "Raid"', *New York Review of Books*, 49 (1), 17 January 2002

Moloney, Ed, *A Secret History of the IRA*. Penguin, 2002

Morgan, Robin, *The Demon Lover: the Sexuality of Terrorism*. Mandarin, 1990

Moss, David, *The Politics of Left-Wing Violence in Italy, 1969–85*. Macmillan, 1989

Moss, Robert, *Urban Guerrillas*. Alister Taylor, 1972

Moss, Walter, *Russia in the Age of Alexander II, Tolstoy and Dostoevsky*. Anthem Press, 2002

Moussaoui, Abd Samad, *Zacarias Moussaoui: the Making of a Terrorist*. Serpent's Tail, 2003

Moyano, María José, *Argentina's Lost Patrol: Armed Struggle, 1969–1979*. Yale University Press, 1995

Mulry, David, 'Popular Accounts of the Greenwich Bombing and Conrad's *The Secret Agent*'. *Rocky Mountain Review of Language and Literature*, 54 (2) (2000), pp. 43–64

Murakami, Haruki, *Underground*. Harvill, 2000

Naipaul, V. S., *The Return of Eva Perón*. André Deutsch, 1980

Napoleoni, Loretta, *Modern Jihad: Tracing the Dollars Behind the Terror Networks*. Pluto Press, 2003

Narayan Swamy, M. R., *Tigers of Lanka*. Konark, 1994

National Commission on Terrorist Attacks upon the United States, *The 9/11 Commission Report* (final report). W. W. Norton, 2004

Neff, Donald, *Warrior against Israel*. Amona Books, 1988

Neillands, Robin, *A Fighting Retreat: the British Empire, 1947–97*. Hodder & Stoughton, 1996

Netanyahu. Benjamin (ed.), *Terrorism: How the West Can Win*. Farrar, Straus & Giroux, 1986

Newsinger, John, *Fenianism in Mid-Victorian Britain*. Pluto Press, 1994

— 'The Military Memoir in British Imperial Culture: the Case of Malaya'. *Race and Class*, 35 (3) (1994), pp. 47–63

Nixon, Richard, *The Real War*, Sidgwick & Jackson, 1980

Noble, Kerry, *Tabernacle of Hate: Why They Bombed Oklahoma City*. Voyageur, 1998

Nordstrom, Carolyn and JoAnn Martin (eds), *The Paths to Domination, Resistance and Terror*. University of California Press, 1992

Nouzeilles, Gabriella (ed.), *The Argentina Reader: History, Culture, Politics*. Duke University Press, 2003

O'Connor, Ulrick, *A Terrible Beauty Is Born*. Granada, 1975

— *Michael Collins and the Troubles: the Struggle for Irish Freedom, 1912–1922*. Mainstream Publishing, 2001

O'Sullivan, Noel (ed.), *Terrorism, Ideology and Revolution*. Harvester, 1986

Oppenheimer, Martin, *The Urban Guerrilla*. Quadrangle, 1969

Osborne, Milton, *Region of Revolt*. Penguin, 1971

Paléologue, Maurice, *An Ambassador's Memoirs*, vol. III, *19 August 1916–17 May 1917: Last French Ambassador to the Russian Court*, trans. F. A. Holt. George H. Doran, 1925

Pallmeyer, Jack, *School of Assassins*. Orbis, 2001

Pape, Robert A., *Dying to Win: the Strategic Logic of Suicide Terrorism*. Random House, 2005

Parker, John, *The Gurkhas*. Headline, 1999

— *Death of a Hero: Captain Robert Nairac GC and the Undercover War in Northern Ireland*. Metro Publishing, 1999

Parry, Richard, *The Bonnot Gang*. Rebel Press, 1987

Pernicone, Nunzio, *Italian Anarchism, 1864–1892*. Princeton University Press, 1993

Peters, Edward, *Torture*. Basil Blackwell, 1985

Peters, Ralph, 'In Praise of Attrition'. *Parameters*, Summer 2004, pp. 24–32

Peters, Rudolph, *Jihad in Classical and Modern Islam*. Markus Wiener, 1996

Pettiford, Lloyd and David Harding, *Terrorism: the New World War*. Arctuturus Publishing, 2003

Pettigrew, Joyce (ed.), *Martyrdom and Political Resistance*. VU University Press, 1997

Phillips, David, *Skyjack: the Story of Air Piracy*. George Harrap, 1973

Pipes, Richard, *Russia under the Old Regime*. Weidenfeld and Nicolson, 1974

Politkovskaya, Anna, *Putin's Russia*. Harvill, 2004

Porter, Cathy, *Fathers and Daughters: Russian Women in Revolution*. Virago, 1976

Potter, Bernard, 'Terrorism and the Victorians'. *History Today*, 36 (12) (1986), pp. 6–7

Powers, Thomas, *Intelligence Wars: American Secret History from Hitler to Al-Qaeda*. New York Review of Books, 2004

Purcell, Victor, *Malaya: Communist or Free?* Victor Gollancz, 1954

Quail, John, *The Slow Burning Fuse: the Lost History of the British Anarchists*. Flamingo, 1978

Quinault, Roland, 'Underground Attacks'. *History Today*, 55 (9) (2005), pp. 18–19

Quinlivan, Patrick and Paul Rose, *The Fenians in England, 1865–1872*. John Calder, 1982

Qureshi, Emran and Michael A. Sells (eds), *The New Crusades: Constructing the Muslim Enemy*. Columbia University Press, 2003

Qutb, Sayyid, *Milestones on the Road to Islam*. Islamic Book Service, 2002

Ra'anan, Ari, Robert L. Pfaltzgraff, Jr, Richard H. Shultz, Ernst Halperin and Igor Lukes, *Hydra of Carnage: International Linkages to Terrorism – the Witnesses Speak*. Lexington Books, 1986

Ramakrishna, Kumar, *Emergency Propaganda*. Curzon Press, 2002

Rampton, Sheldon and John Stauber, *Weapons of Mass Deception*. Constable & Robinson, 2003

Rapoport, David, 'Fear and Trembling: Terrorism in Three Religious Traditions', in Pamela. L. Griset and Sue Mahan (eds), *Terrorism in Perspective*. Sage, 2003

Ray, Ellen and William J. Schaap (eds), *Covert Action: the Roots of Terrorism*. Ocean Press, 2003

Rees, Phil, *Dining with Terrorists*. Macmillan, 2004

Reeva, Simon.S., *The Middle East in Crime Fiction*. Lilian Barber, 1989

Reeve, Simon, *The New Jackals: Ramzi Yousef, Osama bin Laden and the Future of Terrorism*. André Deutsch, 1999

Reich, Walter (ed.), *Origins of Terrorism: Psychologies, Ideologies, Theologies, States of Mind*. Cambridge University Press, 1996

Retort (Iain Boll, T. J. Clark, Joseph Matthews and Michael Watts), *Afflicted Powers: Capital and Spectacle in a New Age of War*. Verso, 2005

Reuter, Christoph, *My Life Is a Weapon: a Modern History of Suicide Bombing*. Princeton University Press, 2002

Rey, Benoist, *The Throatcutters*. John Calder, 1961

Reynolds, Michael, 'Homegrown Terror'. *Bulletin of the Atomic Scientists*, 60 (6), 2004, pp. 48–57

Richie, Alexandra, *Faust's Metropolis: a History of Berlin*. HarperCollins, 1999

Ridgeway, James, *Blood in the Face*. Thunder's Mouth Press, 1995

Rivers, Gayle, *The Specialist*. Sidgwick & Jackson, 1985

Roberts, Hugh, *The Battlefield: Algeria, 1988–2002*. Verso, 2003

Rokach, Livia, *Israel's Sacred Terrorism*. Association of Arab-American University Graduates, 1980

Roll, Astrid, *Baader-Meinhof: Pictures on the Run, 67–77*. Scalo, 1998

Rolston, Bill and David Miller (eds), *War of Words: the Northern Ireland Media Reader*. Beyond the Pale Publications, 1996

Romero Maura, J., 'Terrorism in Barcelona and its Impact on Spanish Politics, 1904–1909'. *Past & Present*, 41 (1968), pp. 130–84

Rosen, Jeffrey, *The Naked Crowd: Reclaiming Security and Freedom in an Anxious Age*. Random House, 2004

Rosencof, Mauricio, 'On Suffering and White Horses', in Louise B. Popkin (ed.), *Repression, Exile and Democracy: Uruguayan Culture*. Duke University Press, 1993

Rosie, George, *The Directory of International Terrorism*. Mainstream Publishing, 1986

Roy, Jules, *The War in Algeria*. Grove Press, 1961

Roy, Olivier, *The Failure of Political Islam*. I. B. Tauris, 1994

Roy, Olivier and Mariam Abou Zahab, *Islamist Networks: the Afghan–Pakistan Connection*. Columbia University Press, 2004

Rubenstein, Richard, *Alchemists of Revolution*. I. B. Tauris, 1987

Rudorff, Raymond, *Belle Epoque: Paris in the Nineties*. Hamish Hamilton, 1977

Ruppert, Michael, *Crossing the Rubicon*. New Society, 2004

Ruthven, Malise, *Torture: the Grand Conspiracy*. Weidenfeld & Nicolson, 1978

— *A Fury for God*. Granta, 2002

Ryan, Mark, *War and Peace in Ireland: Britain and the IRA in the New World Order*. Pluto Press, 1994

Saad-Ghorayeb, Amal, *Hizbu'llah: Politics and Religion*. Pluto Press, 2002

Said, Edward, *Covering Islam*. Vintage, 1997

Said, Edward and Christopher Hitchens, *Blaming the Victims: Spurious Scholarship and the Palestinian Question*. Verso, 1988

Sardar, Ziauddin and Merryl Wyn Davies, *Why Do People Hate America?* Icon Books, 2002

— *American Dream: Global Nightmare*. Icon Books, 2004

Savinkov, Boris, *Memoirs of a Terrorist*. Albert & Charles Boni, 1931

Sayigh, Yezid, *Armed Struggle and the Search for State: the Palestinian National Movement, 1949–1993*. Oxford University Press, 1997

Scarry, Elaine, *The Body in Pain: the Making and Unmaking of the World*. Oxford University Press, 1985

Schalk, Peter, 'The Revival of Martyr Cults among Llavar'. *Temenos*, 33 (1997), pp. 151–91

— 'Resistance and Martyrdom in the Process of State Formation in Tamil Eelam', in Joyce Pettigrew (ed.), *Martyrdom and Political Resistance*. VU University Press, 1997

Schlaim, Avi, *The Iron Wall*. Penguin, 2000

Schlesinger, Philip, George Murdock and Philip Elliott, *Televising 'Terrorism': Political Violence in Popular Culture*. Comedia, 1983

Sciascia, Leonardo, *The Moro Affair*. Carcanet Press, 1987

Seale, Patrick, *Abu Nidal: a Gun for Hire*. Random House, 1992

Segaller, Steven, *Invisible Armies: Terrorism into the 1990s*. Michael Joseph, 1986

Seoane, María, *Todo o Nada: la historia secreta y la historia pública del jefe guerrillero Mario Roberto Santucho*. Editorial Planeta, 1991

Serge, Victor, *Memoirs of a Revolutionary, 1901–1941*. Oxford University Press, 1963

Serrano, Richard A., *One of Ours: Timothy McVeigh and the Oklahoma City Bombing*. W. W Norton, 1998

Seth, Ronald, *The Russian Terrorists*. Barrie & Rockliff, 1966

Shatz, Adam, 'The Torture of Algiers'. *New York Review of Books*, 49 (18), 21 November 2002

— 'Algeria's Failed Revolution'. *New York Review of Books*, 50 (11), 3 July 2003

— 'In Search of Hezbollah.' *New York Review of Books*, 51 (7), 29 April 2004

— 'In Search of Hezbollah II'. *New York Review of Books*, 51 (8), 13 May 2004

Sheehan, Thomas, 'Italy: behind the Ski Mask'. *New York Review of Books*, 26 (13), 16 August 1979

— 'Italy: Terror on the Right'. *New York Review of Books*, 27 (21), 22 January 1981

Sheridan, Michael, *Romans: Their Lives and Times*. Orion, 1985

Short, Anthony, *In Pursuit of Mountain Rats*. Cultured Lotus, 2000

Shulman, Alix Kates (ed.), *Red Emma Speaks: Selected Writings and Speeches by Emma Goldman*. Vintage, 1972

Sick, Gary, *All Fall Down: America's Tragic Encounter with Iran*. Random House, 1985

Sifoui, Mohamed, *Inside Al-Qaeda: How I Infiltrated the World's Deadliest Terrorist Organization*. Granta, 2003

Skilbeck, Ron, 'The Shroud over Algeria'. *Journal of Arabic, Islamic and Middle Eastern Studies*, 2 (2) (1995), pp. 43–54

Sluka, Jeffrey A., 'From Graves to Nations: Political Martyrdom and Irish Nationalism', in Joyce Pettigrew (ed.), *Martyrdom and Political Resistance*. VU University Press, 1997

Sluka, Jeffrey A. (ed.), *Death Squad: the Anthropology of State Terror*. University of Pennsylvania Press, 2000

Smucker, Philip, *Al-Qaeda's Great Escape: the Military and the Media on Terror's Tail*. Brassey's, 2004

Soboul, Albert, *The French Revolution, 1787–1799: from the Storming of the Bastille to Napoleon*. NLB, 1974

Sokolski, Henry, 'Rethinking Bio-Chemical Dangers'. *Orbis*, Spring 2000, pp, 207–19

Solinas, PierNico (ed.), *Gillo Pontecorvo's 'The Battle of Algiers'*. Charles Scribner's Sons, 1973

Special Operations Research Office, *Human Factors Considerations of Undergrounds in Insurgencies*. University Press of the Pacific, 2001

Spencer, Robert, *Onward Muslim Soldiers: How Jihad Still Threatens America and the West*. Regnery Publishing, 2003

Spencer Chapman, F., *The Jungle Is Neutral*. Transworld, 1957

Sri Kantha, Sachi, 'Vignettes on Three Black Tigers in the Battlefield', 17 August 2004, available at www.tamilnation.org

Sterling, Claire, *The Terror Network: the Secret War of International Terrorism*. Berkley Books, 1981

Stern, Jessica, *The Ultimate Terrorists*. Harvard University Press, 2000

— *Terror in the Name of God: Why Religious Militants Kill*. HarperCollins, 2004

Stevenson, William, *A Man Called Intrepid*. Book Club Associates, 1976

Stohl, Michael (ed.), *The Politics of Terrorism*. Marcel Dekker, 1979

Stoneham, C. T., *Mau Mau*. Museum Press, 1953

Storr, Robert, *Gerhard Richter October 18, 1977*. Museum of Modern Art, New York, 2000

Sykes, Christopher, *Crossroads to Israel*. Collins, 1965

Talbott, John, *The War without a Name: France in Algeria, 1954–1962*. Faber and Faber, 1981

Taylor, Maxwell and Ethel Quayle, *Terrorist Lives*. Brassey's, 1994

Taylor, Peter, *Beating the Terrorists?* Penguin, 1980

— *States of Terror*. Penguin, 1983

Thackrah, John Richard, *Encyclopedia of Terrorism and Political Violence*. Routledge & Keegan, 1987

Thompson, Paul, *The Terror Timeline*. HarperCollins, 2004

Thompson, Robert (ed.), *War in Peace: an Analysis of Warfare since 1945*. Orbis, 1981

Tillion, Germaine, *France and Algeria: Complementary Enemies*. Alfred A. Knopf, 1961

Timmerman, Jacobo, *Prisoner without a Name, Cell without a Number*.
    Vintage, 1982
Toolis, Kevin, *Rebel Hearts*. Picador, 1995
Troyat, Henri, *Tolstoy*. Penguin, 1970
John Trumpbour, 'The Clash of Civilizations', in Emran Qureshi and
    Michael A. Sells (eds), *The New Crusades: Constructing the Muslim Enemy*.
    Columbia University Press, 2003
Tuchman, Barbara, *The Proud Tower: a Portrait of the World before War,
    1890–1914*. Bantam Books, 1978
Ulam, Adam, *Prophets and Conspirators in Prerevolutionary Russia*.
    Transaction Publishers, 1998
Unger, Craig, *House of Bush, House of Saud*. Gibson Square, 2004
Urban, Mark, *Big Boys' Rules: the Secret Struggle against the IRA*. Book Club
    Associates, 1992
Usher, Graham, *Dispatches from Palestine*. Pluto Press, 1999
Vague, Tom, *Televisionaries*. AK Press, 1994
— *Anarchy in the UK: the Angry Brigade*. AK Press, 1997
Varis, Tapio, 'The Media in Postmodern War and Terrorism', in Ilkka
    Taipale (ed.), *War or Health? A Reader*. Zed Books, 2002
Venturi, Franco, *Roots of Revolution*. Grosset & Dunlap, 1960
Verbitsky, Horacio, *The Flight*. The New Press, 1996
Victor, Barbara, *Army of Roses: Inside the World of Palestinian Women Suicide
    Bombers*. Constable & Robinson, 2000
Vidal, Gore, *Perpetual War for Perpetual Peace*. Clairview Books, 2002
Vidal-Naquet, Pierre, *Torture: Cancer of Democracy*. Penguin, 1963
Viner, Richard, 'Electric Koran'. *London Review of Books*, 23 (11), 7 June 2001
Vines, Alex, *Renamo Terrorism in Mozambique*. Centre for Southern African
    Studies, 1991
Vizetelly, Ernst, *The Anarchists: Their Faith and Their Record*. Bodley Head,
    1911
wa Wamwere, Koigi, *I Refuse to Die*. Seven Stories Press, 2002
Wagner-Pacifici, Robin Erica, *The Moro Morality Play*. University of Chicago
    Press, 1986
Walker, Tony and Andrew Gower, *Arafat: the Biography*. Virgin Books, 2003
Walzer, Michael, *Just and Unjust Wars*. Pelican, 1980
Wardlow, Grant, *Political Terrorism: Theory, Tactics, and Counter-Measures*.
    Cambridge University Press, 1989
Wasiolek, Edward, *Dostoevsky: the Major Fiction*. MIT Press, 1964
Weaver, Mary Ann, *A Portrait of Egypt*. Farrar, Straus & Giroux, 2000

Weir, Jean (ed.), *The Angry Brigade: Documents and Chronology, 1967–1984*. Elephant Editions, 1985

West, Rebecca, *Black Lamb and Grey Falcon*. Canongate, 1993

Wheatcroft, Andrew, *Infidels: a History of the Conflict between Christianity and Islam*. Penguin, 2003

Wiebes, Cees, *Intelligence and the War in Bosnia, 1992–1995*. James Bennett, 2003

Wieviorka, Michel, *The Making of Terrorism*. University of Chicago Press, 1993

Wilkinson, Paul, *Terrorism and the Liberal State* (2nd edn). Macmillan, 1986

Willan, Philip, *Puppetmasters: the Political Uses of Terrorism in Italy*. Constable, 1991

Wolf, Markus, *Memoirs of a Spymaster*. Pimlico, 1988

Woodcock, George, *Anarchism*. World Publishing Co., 1962

Woodward, Bob, *Veil: the Secret Wars of the CIA, 1981–1987*. Simon & Schuster, 1987

— *Bush At War*. Simon & Schuster, 2002

Woodworth, Paddy, *Dirty War, Clean Hands: ETA, the GAL and Spanish Democracy*. Yale University Press, 2002

Wright, Joanne, *Terrorist Propaganda: the Red Army Faction and the Provisional IRA, 1968–86*. Macmillan, 1991

Wright, Robin, *Sacred Rage: the Wrath of Militant Islam*. Touchstone, 1985

Wright, Thomas C., *Latin America in the Era of the Cuban Revolution*. Praeger, 2001

Wynia, Gary W. (ed.), *Argentina: Illusions and Realities*. Holmes & Meier, 1992

Yaari, Ehud, *Strike Terror: the Story of Fatah*. Sabra Books, 1970

Yallop, David, *To the Ends of the Earth*. Corgi, 1994

Younger, Carlton, *Ireland's Civil War*. Fontana, 1970

— *A State of Disunion*. Fontana, 1970

Yousaf, Mohammad and Mark Adkin, *Afghanistan the Bear Trap: the Defeat of a Superpower*. Leo Cooper, 1992

Zulaika, Joseba, *Basque Violence: Metaphor and Sacrament*. University of Nevada Press, 1988

Zulaika, Joseba and William A. Douglass, *Terror and Taboo: the Follies, Fables and Faces of Terrorism*. Routledge, 1996

Novels, stories, plays and poetry

Abish, Walter, *How German Is It?* Faber and Faber, 1982

Andreyev, Leonid, *The Seven that Were Hanged and Other Stories*. Random House, 1958

Biely, André, *St Petersburg*. Grove Press, 1959

Boll, Heinrich, *The Safety Net*. Sphere, 1981

— *The Lost Honour of Katerina Blum*. Minerva, 1993

Burgess, Anthony, *The Long Day Wanes: a Malayan Trilogy*. Penguin, 1981

Camus, Albert, *The Rebel*. Alfred A. Knopf, 1956

— 'The Just', in *Collected Plays*. Hamish Hamilton, 1965

Chesterton, G. K., *The Man Who Was Thursday*. Dover, 1986

Collins, Larry and Dominique LaPierre, *The Fifth Horseman*. Book Club Associates, 1981

Conrad, Joseph, *Under Western Eyes*. Pan, 1975

— *The Informer and Other Stories*. Pickering, 1991

— *The Secret Agent*. Penguin, 1994

Cortázar, Julio, *A Manual for Manuel*. Pantheon, 1978

Deane, Seamus, *Reading in the Dark*. Vintage, 1997

De Borchgrave, Arnaud and Robert Moss, *The Spike*. Weidenfeld & Nicolson, 1980

DeLillo, Don, *Mao II*. Vintage, 1991

Dib, Mohammed, *The Savage Night*. University of Nebraska Press, 2001

Djaout, Tahar, *The Last Summer of Reason*. Ruminator Books, 2001

Djebar, Assia, *Women of Algiers in Their Apartment*. University Press of Virginia, 1992

Dostoevsky, Feodor, *The Devils*. Penguin, 1972

Durrell, Lawrence, *Bitter Lemons*. Faber and Faber, 1957

Greene, Graham, *The Quiet American*. Penguin, 1977

Hampton, Christopher, *Savages*. Faber and Faber, 1974

Harris, Frank, *The Bomb*. Feral House, 1996

Hutchinson, Ron, *Rat in the Skull*. Methuen, 1995

Ignatius, David, *Agents Of Innocence*. W. H. Allen, 1989

James, Henry, *The Princess Casamassima*. Penguin, 1987

Khadra, Yasmina (pseud. Mohammed Moulessehoul), *Morituri*. Toby Press, 2002

— *Wolf Dreams*. Toby Press, 2003

Larteguy, Jean, *The Centurions*. Hutchinson, 1961

Le Carré, John, *The Little Drummer Girl*. Bantam, 1983

Lessing, Doris, *The Good Terrorist*. Grafton, 1986

MacDonald, Andrew, *The Turner Diaries*. Barricade Books, 1978

Malraux, André, *Man's Fate*. Random House, 1968

Martínez Moreno, Carlos, *El Infierno*, trans. Ann Wright. Readers International, 1988

McNamee, Eoin, *Resurrection Man*. Faber and Faber, 2004

Meredith, Isabel (pseud. Helen and Olivia Rosetti), *A Girl amongst the Anarchists*. University of Nebraska Press, 1992

Moravia, Alberto, *Time of Desecration*. Granada, 1982

O'Flaherty, Liam, *The Informer*. Harcourt, 1980

Piercy, Marge, *Vida*. Penguin, 1986

Reid, V. S., *The Leopard*. Heinemann Educational, 1958

Ropshin, V. (pseud. Boris Savinkov), *The Pale Horse*. Maunsell and Co., 1917

Ruark, Robert, *Something of Value*. Hamish Hamilton, 1955

Sartre, Jean-Paul, 'Dirty Hands', in *No Exit and Three Other Plays*. Vintage, 1955

Saizarbitoria, Ramon, *Cien Metros*. Editorial Nuestra Cultura, 1979

Savage, R. H., *The Anarchist: a Story of Today*. Routledge, 1894

Sillitoe, Alan, *Key to the Door*. Paladin, 1981

Soriano, Osvaldo, *A Funny, Dirty Little War*. Readers International, 1986

Suyin, Han, *And the Rain My Drink*. Mayflower, 1970

Thomas, Leslie, *The Virgin Soldiers*. Arrow, 2005

'Trevanian' (?pseud Rodney William Whitaker), *Shibumi*. Granada, 1980

wa Thiong'o, Ngugi, *Petals of Blood*. Penguin, 1977

— *A Grain of Wheat*. Penguin, 2002

Zola, Emile, *Paris*. Chatto & Windus, 1898

— *Germinal*. Penguin Classics, 2004

Films

4 Days in September (1997), dir. Luis Baretto

The Assignment (1997), dir. Christian Duguay

The Basque Ball – the Skin against the Stone (2003), dir. Julio Medem

The Battle of Algiers (1966), dir. Gillo Pontecorvo

Executive Decision (1997), dir. Stuart Baird

Germany in Autumn (1978). Various directors

Good Morning, Night (2003), dir. Marco Bellochio

The Hour of the Furnaces (1968), dir. Fernando Solanas

Journeys from Berlin/1971 (1986), dir. Yvonne Rainer

Lost Command (1966), dir. Mark Robson

Marianne and Julianne (1981), dir. Margaretha von Trotta

The Moro Affair (1986), dir. Giuseppe Ferrara

Nighthawks (1981), dir. Bruce Malmuth
One Day in September (1999), dir. Kevin Macdonald
Operation Ogro (1979), dir. Gillo Pontecorvo
Patriot Games (1992), dir. Philip Noyce
The Peacemaker (1997), dir. Mimi Leder
Rules of Engagement (2000), dir. William Friedkin
The Second Time (1996), dir. Mimo Calopresti
The Siege (1998), dir. Edward Zwick
State of Siege (1973), dir. Costa Gavras
The Sum of All Fears (2002), dir. Philip Alden Robinson
The Terrorist (1999), dir. Santosh Sivan
The Third Generation (1979), dir. Rainer Werner Fassbinder
True Lies (1999), dir. James Cameron

Acknowledgments

It has taken nearly three years of my life to research and write this book, and various people have had an impact on the finished product in different ways. I wish to thank my editor, Daniel Crewe, for his astute and painstaking reading and re-reading of the manuscript. His comments and suggestions have greatly improved the final text. Trevor Horwood submitted the manuscript to a meticulous copy-editing inspection, and I have nothing but admiration and gratitude for his sharp-eyed vigilance. Any remaining errors are, of course, my responsibility alone.

I owe a particular debt of gratitude to my agent Judith Murray, who nurtured the book throughout its long and often tortuous gestation, and remained supportive and optimistic throughout the process. It can be said without exaggeration that this book would not have occurred without her and no writer could ask for a more supportive advocate and a more alert and careful reader.

I would like to thank the staff at my local library in Matlock, who hunted down endless dusty tomes on terrorism, war and violence for me from libraries across the country. Their patience and helpfulness are a tribute to the library system as a public service.

Thanks to Sachi Sri Kantha for permission to quote from his translations of Tamil Tiger obituaries. Ronald Crelinsten generously sent me copies of his valuable articles, which would otherwise have been difficult to access. Professor Mark Harrison at Warwick University was also extremely kind in facilitating his research papers on Palestinian suicide bombers. The Han Suyin quotation that opens Chapter 4 is reproduced with kind permission of the Ed Victor agency.

I would like to thank Jo Cannon and Peter Borchers for their support and encouragement throughout this project.

I owe, as always, more than I can say to Jane, my companion for so many years, who was always there to offer advice and her indispensable presence, even when the bleakness of the material sometimes ground me down.

My daughter Lara endured an endless torrent of alarming books that flowed relentlessly through our household during the period this book was written, showing a sangfroid beyond her years. She provided a constant and necessary respite from the dark labyrinth of terror in which I sometimes lost myself. I would like to hope that she and her generation may live to see a world in which the barbaric events that this book describes seem like relics from a bygone era.

Index